Whoopi Goldberg on
Stage and Screen

Whoopi Goldberg on Stage and Screen

LISA PERTILLAR BREVARD

McFarland & Company, Inc., Publishers
Jefferson, North Carolina, and London

LIBRARY OF CONGRESS CATALOGUING-IN-PUBLICATION DATA

Brevard, Lisa Pertillar.
  Whoopi Goldberg on stage and screen / Lisa Pertillar Brevard.
      p.   cm.
  Includes bibliographical references and index.

  ISBN 978-0-7864-6887-4
  softcover : acid free paper ∞

  1. Goldberg, Whoopi, 1950-   2. Comedians — United States — Biography.   3. African American comedians — Biography.   4. African American motion picture actors and actresses — Biography.   5. Motion picture actors and actresses — United States — Biography.   I. Title.
  PN2287.G578B74   2013
  791.43'028'092—dc23
  [B]   2012049111

BRITISH LIBRARY CATALOGUING DATA ARE AVAILABLE

© 2013 Lisa A. Pertillar-Brevard. All rights reserved

No part of this book may be reproduced or transmitted in any form or by any means, electronic or mechanical, including photocopying or recording, or by any information storage and retrieval system, without permission in writing from the publisher.

On the cover: Whoopi Goldberg in *Boys on the Side*, 1995 (Warner Bros./Photofest)

Manufactured in the United States of America

McFarland & Company, Inc., Publishers
  Box 611, Jefferson, North Carolina 28640
  www.mcfarlandpub.com

For my husband, Frank

Table of Contents

Preface   1

1. *Made in America*   3
2. The Influence of Jackie "Moms" Mabley and George Carlin   20
3. An American Artist in Hollywood   36
4. Black and Blue(s): Celie as Blueswoman in *The Color Purple*   57
5. The Impact of Richard Pryor and Bert Williams   79
6. Sister Rhythm and Blues: *Sister Act* Success   100
7. A Shoulder to Cry On/A Woman to Stand Strong   125
8. Crossing the Lines: Acting and Activism   166
9. Playing the Part: The Actor as Sidekick and Supporter   185
10. Returning to Her Roots: *Back to Broadway* and Beyond   213

Works Cited   233
Index   251

Preface

Whoopi Goldberg on Stage and Screen began as a series of musings on Goldberg's quirky, multifaceted, successful career — notes that I penned in New Orleans, Louisiana, pre–Hurricane Katrina. When the hurricane came, it drowned our home, our places of work and nearly all of our belongings, including the original makings of this manuscript (save scant portions, which I fortunately, casually, and almost absent-mindedly, had e-mailed to myself). As my husband, Frank, and I transitioned into a new life in a new place, my sister Tammy gave me a book of quotations attributed to famous American women known especially for their humor. In presenting the book to me, Tammy told me, pointedly, "You need to laugh." Whoopi Goldberg is one of the women whose humorous wit, speaking out of that book, buoyed my spirits and encouraged me to begin writing this book all over again.

This book is not a biography. While it certainly includes biographical details, I really intend it as contributing to and enlarging the American studies and women's studies genres, given its emphasis upon American identity and Whoopi Goldberg as an American woman working (Goldberg "on stage and screen"). Having published several academic biographies, I classify biography as a literary work that strictly adheres to a linear timeline, tracing the subject's life from birth to death (or the current time, if the subject is still living). In the present work, the timeline is purposefully and decidedly broken. Each chapter deals not with a specific time in Goldberg's life; but, rather, an aspect of her work on stage (theater or the larger world) and screen (television or film).

Take, for example, Chapter 5: The Impact of Richard Pryor and Bert Williams, which makes connections between Goldberg's work, and the legacies of Richard Pryor, a community-based performer who helped a nation (re)define and find different ways to discuss race; and Bert Williams, multi-talented star of the vaudeville stage and musical theater innovator, who died decades before Goldberg was born. In a similar vein, Chapter 2: The Influence of Jackie "Moms" Mabley and George Carlin, highlights comedic contributions of Mabley (who used her stage show to wryly champion elder rights, civil rights and women's rights, and whose lengthy performing career was winding down when Goldberg's was just beginning); and Carlin, who openly encouraged Americans to question authority and (re)claim their Constitutional right to freedom of expression. Studying the creativity of Mabley and Carlin helps us better understand Goldberg's artistry and related philosophies.

Other chapters also decidedly employ thematic approaches. Chapter 1: *Made in America*, presents the United States as the backdrop against which Goldberg makes her presence known as artist and American citizen. Chapter 3: An American Artist in Hollywood, describes the actor's work ethic and wide-ranging skills, as well as her rapid rise in becoming one of Hollywood's busiest and best-paid actors. Chapter 4: Black and Blue(s): Celie as Blueswoman in *The Color Purple*, defines and discusses the concept of the blueswoman as relates to Whoopi Goldberg, the actor, and Celie, the fictional character that Goldberg portrays in the major motion picture adaptation of Alice Walker's novel, *The Color Purple*. Chapter 6: Sister Rhythm and Blues: *Sister Act* Success, describes Goldberg's work as the fictional Delores Van Cartier/Sister Mary Clarence, in the Disney films *Sister Act* and *Sister Act 2: Back in the Habit*; and how such successes led not only to other opportunities with Disney, but also meaningful connections with the life and legacy of Célia Cruz, the Queen of Salsa. Chapter 7: A Shoulder to Cry On/A Woman to Stand Strong, describes Goldberg's overall believability as a strong, dependable woman, as evidenced by her roles in such major motion pictures as *Corinna, Corinna, Girl, Interrupted, Ghost*, and *The Associate*, among others; and two television series: *Bagdad Café* and *Star Trek: The Next Generation*. Chapter 8: Crossing the Lines: Acting and Activism, describes Goldberg's work as actor and activist. Chapter 9: Playing the Part: The Actor as Sidekick and Supporter, provides an overview of some of her best acting roles as best friend, in such vehicles as the independent Rodrigue film, *The Blue Dog*, as well as such major motion pictures as *Homer and Eddie, Boys on the Side* and *How Stella Got Her Groove Back*, among others. Chapter 10:Returning to Her Roots: *Back to Broadway* and Beyond, discusses the politics and cultural impact of Goldberg's personal decision to wear dreadlocks and also describes the actor's return to starring in a new, one-woman Broadway show, some 20 years after the success of her original one-woman Broadway show.

A Note on Web Sources. The website addresses provided in these references may have changed, because of the intrinsically volatile nature of the World Wide Web. However, all sites were active at the time of their consultation in the preparation of this book (2010–2012). Please be aware that many "retired" web sites are still accessible via the Internet Archive, also known as the "Wayback Machine": http://www.archive.org/web/web.php.

1

Made in America

> I am not an African American. I'm not from Africa. I'm from New York.
> —Whoopi Goldberg (Goldberg, *Book* 106)

A native New Yorker, Whoopi Goldberg absorbs and radiates the energies and possibilities of the fabled city she calls home. Reared in Chelsea, Manhattan, home of Tin Pan Alley, the place where such great American songwriters as Irving Berlin and George and Ira Gershwin composed popular American music; where Berlin wrote, "God Bless America," and George M. Cohan wrote, "Give My Regards to Broadway" and where the classic song "Take Me Out to the Ballgame" took form (WCBS-TV), Goldberg expresses American identity through connections with the neighborhood and city of her birth; former membership among a diverse group of neighborhood children; pride in her heritage as a descendant of former slaves-turned-homesteaders; revival of and participation in American public debate; and regular, deliberate questioning and breaking of stereotypes regarding race, gender and beauty. These traits and more illustrate and underscore Goldberg's determined understanding, pursuit and application of the American Dream.

The phrase "The American Dream" first appears in James Truslow Adams's *The Epic of America* (1931): "The American Dream is that dream of a land in which life should be better and richer and fuller for everyone, with opportunity for each according to ability or achievement" (Adams). A living example of the American Dream, Goldberg learned early that she had to dream, and dream big—for herself; that American society was not designed to encourage or inspire the descendants of African slaves, beyond the narrow socioeconomic space allowed. Despite the realities of race and gender, however, Goldberg rose to place herself among preeminent thinkers and doers, using acting as her medium. She is one of only a handful of artists awarded the Tony, the Emmy, the Grammy and the Oscar, an achievement atypical of Americans, generally speaking, and of blacks and women, particularly. Yet her American Dream of reaching her own potential through her own efforts and on her own terms, all the while exercising and defending her rights as citizen, were obvious to her, if to no one else. Goldberg's stance echoes the philosophy of Thomas Jefferson: "We hold these truths to be self-evident, that all men are created equal; that they are endowed by their Creator with inherent and inalienable rights; that among these, are life, liberty, and the pursuit of happiness" (Ford). Jefferson's words provide an important foundation for the exploration of Whoopi Goldberg, artist and activist.

Goldberg's career is a meaningful patchwork of applied liberties in the pursuit of happiness and a more just society, tied together with threads of dignity and common sense. Such is rooted in her childhood view of American identity. In *Book* (1997), Goldberg describes the Chelsea neighborhood of her youth, and the function of Hollywood film in articulating and uniting American identity among diverse children: neighborhood children were seen simply as children; the prevailing factor was the degree to which one was considered an "asshole": "There were big assholes and little assholes" (Goldberg 42). While the larger society defined Goldberg and her cohorts in terms of race and gender, Goldberg's growing sense of self included being part of the neighborhood and fabric of New York City.

In fact, New York City may be considered Goldberg's muse. In a 2002 interview with Dick Cavett, Goldberg explains that city's significance, mentioning the influence of such groups as the Young Lords, a Puerto Rican theatre ensemble "talking about life in America," and the Black Panthers, a Black Power Movement entity, talking politics in Central Park during the late 1960s and early 1970s (Cavett). Such experiences formed the basis of her growing sense of the world as a classroom. Noting the limitations of formal studies, Goldberg's philosophy reflects a kind of "school without walls" motif; instead of limiting her learning to formal studies, she reached up and out and beyond the traditional classroom to mine the community's rich resources, attending ballets, musical performances, museum and gallery exhibits, and the like; and taking in street performance art as it was realized. In speaking with fellow New Yorker Joy Behar, Goldberg muses, "As a kid I had access to anything I wanted.... I could go to museums.... If I wanted to know about the sky, I could go to the planetarium.... There were so many things I could go see." Whoopi credits her mother for encouraging her to make the most of all educational opportunities the City of New York had to offer (*The Joy Behar Show*). Not surprisingly, as an adult, she retuned the favor by narrating "Journey to the Stars," a groundbreaking planetarium exhibit at the American Museum of Natural History, which reviewer Dennis Overbye describes as "easily the most beautiful planetarium show I have ever seen and the most vertiginous" (Overbye). Overbye also praises Goldberg's even-handed narration style.

Goldberg's natural, informative vocal delivery style balances the deep expanse of space, creating a kind of "school without walls."

The concept of the "School Without Walls" dates to the early 1970s — the very period during which the former Caryn Elaine Johnson heard the siren call of the stage. A major characteristic of Schools Without Walls is using the city itself as both source and resource for furthering one's studies and sense of self in relation to community (SWW). Goldberg seems to radiate the same reflective, multicultural, community-centered ethos, as American citizen, artist and humanist. Having never finished formal high school studies — Goldberg unknowingly suffered from dyslexia, a reading disorder, which was not diagnosed until she reached adulthood; according to Goldberg, during her years of formal schooling, some administrators mistakenly, and painfully, labeled her "retarded," so she eventually left high school at the age of 17, to chart her own path (Randolph 111). Goldberg placed her intellect and skills within the larger, more dynamic structure of the city. In effect, the city itself became Goldberg's high school, college and graduate school. Her early work as a New York City performer included self-directed studies regarding the life and work of Jackie "Moms" Mabley; such came in conjunction with a process by which she recast and renamed herself.

The process of renaming and recasting the self has a long tradition in African and black American culture. In the West African tradition, the primary African cultural fount of black American peoples, for example, the process of names and naming provides a kind of declaration of freedom, all the while "locating" a person within the universe. Abolitionist Sojourner Truth (c. 1797–1883) was formerly known by the slave names Baumfree and later Isabella Van Wagenen. She gained her full freedom from slavery in part by escaping, and then by renaming herself as a human on a quest to find and reveal her truth and the truth of God's word. In 1843, as evidence of her acceptance of Christ as her lord and savior, and, she says, on God's very instruction, she adopted the name Sojourner Truth, befitting her new status as an evangelist. "In the late 1840s she connected with the abolitionist movement, becoming a popular speaker. In 1850, she also began speaking on woman suffrage. Her most famous speech, 'Ain't I a Woman?,' was given in 1851 at a women's rights convention in Ohio" (Lewis).

Truth's most famous speech was extemporaneous, forceful and forced by circumstance; as a former chattel slave, she had no rights as a human being, let alone an American citizen or woman; so she was not allowed to formally participate in the women's rights convention program. Nevertheless, she claimed her right to speak, in the public forum, and, by so doing, cut to the heart of the paradox of racism and sexism in the Christian New World.

In "Ain't I a Woman?" (1851) Sojourner Truth proclaimed, "Nobody ever helps me into carriages, or over mud-puddles, or gives me any best place!... I have ploughed and planted, and gathered into barns, and no man could head me!... I could work as much and eat as much as a man — when I could get it — and bear the lash as well!... I have borne thirteen children, and seen most all sold off to slavery, and when I cried out with my mother's grief, none but Jesus heard me! And ain't I a woman?" (Truth). Truth also questions how the concept of intellect (of which, according to popular lore, chattel slaves, like cattle, have none) has anything to do with human rights; and that white men's use of Christianity to bar women from their inalienable rights as citizens, on the grounds that Christ was a man, is unchristian, because Christ was born solely "from God and a woman" (Truth). Concluding her remarks to the surprised, promiscuous audience (during her times, a "promiscuous" audience consisted of men, women and children; traditionally, women were supposed to speak to only children and the elderly, in the sanctity of private homes), Truth references the story of Eve eating the forbidden fruit. She says that if the first woman "turn[ed] the world upside down" during Biblical times, then, surely, modern women have the capacity to "turn it back, and get it right-side up again" (Truth).

Truth's insistence that she have a say in declaring herself a woman and a human being belied her legal status as "non-entity." Instead of cowering and accepting the limited roles that society allowed her, she claimed American citizenship rights, using her personal experiences, the First Amendment right to free speech and the Bible as her philosophical platforms. "The First Amendment provides that '*Congress shall make no law respecting an establishment of religion, or prohibiting the exercise thereof;* or abridging the freedom of speech or of the press; or the right of people peaceably to assemble, and to petition the government for a redress of grievances'" (AHA 404–405). Truth also shrewdly recast herself, beginning with adopting a new name, which gave her the latitude to interface with, and eventually become, one of the key figures in the growing American Women's Movement.

Likewise, names and naming play a profound role in black American literature. For example, in Alex Haley's *Roots*, infant Kunta Kinte participates in a traditional West African naming ceremony. After being cared for in seclusion, long enough for the family to assure his strength to carry forth life outside his mother's womb, the infant Kunta Kinte is brought outside the family's hut, under the cloak of night, his father whispering his name into his tiny ear, and raising his naked body with two strong hands toward the moonlight, declaring, "Behold: The only thing greater than yourself" (Haley 4). Such declaration was to assure Kunta that he would always know himself, and that God would always know him. Hence, the tension becomes palpable, when a teenage Kunta is later captured as a chattel slave and forced to be called by the slave name "Toby." In actively refusing the name "Toby" and declaring his identity as Kunta in the New World, he makes great sacrifice by allowing his foot to be severed from his body, rather than being castrated, as was the typical form of punishment. The story of Kunta Kinte reminds readers of the West African proverb, "It's not what you call me; it's what I answer to"—in other words, people may cast aspersions; but as long as one has a strong sense of self, little else matters.

The former Caryn Elaine Johnson's determination to rename and recast herself was part of the era in which she came of age as a young artist during the 1970s. The Black Arts Movement, for example, embraced the concept of renaming and recasting, in favor of black empowerment. Such a process was rooted in the legacy of activist Malcolm X and cemented by the popularity of Haley's novel and the related television miniseries. Yet Johnson's determination seems to be greater than simply casting off an old name, or even embracing black empowerment; like Sojourner Truth, she also wanted to embrace new possibilities. Hence, Johnson renamed herself Whoopi, after whoopee cushion, and Goldberg, after a distant relative: "Her first name derived from whoopee-cushion jokes and her last was suggested by her mother to honor Jewish ancestors" (Sheff). Whoopi Goldberg's new name decidedly embraced and embodied the unexpected.

Goldberg's willingness to stake her claim in the world of acting and beyond should come as no surprise. She comes from a long line of achievers, including ancestor slaves-turned-homesteaders, who eschewed General Sherman's empty promise of "40 acres of tillable land" to former chattel slaves (*African American Lives*), in favor of independently staking their claim to unincorporated Florida land. As American homesteaders, William (b. November 1837) and Elsa (née Tucker, b. December 1845) Washington became legal owners of 104.5 acres of Alachua County, Florida, land during 1878. Such did not come without significant hardship and sacrifice, however. The Homestead Act of 1866, designed to clear and populate 46 million acres in Florida, Arkansas, Mississippi, Alabama and Louisiana, required homesteaders to locate an open 80-acre lot; pay a $5 filing fee; build upon and enclose the lot; plow, plant and prove their claim (*African American Lives*). In addition, homesteaders also were required to pay property taxes, while trying to hold on to the land and stave off debt. For the Washingtons, such risks were compounded by the fact that white supremacist "Regulators" (former slave-catchers), American Indian nations and all manner of wild flora and fauna were among very real threats to their determination to succeed (Ford 43). Moreover, while the Freedmen's Bureau created schools to advance education among freed slaves, the Washingtons had no such access to higher education, instead fighting for the right and title to their land as illiterate American citizens. As Henry Louis Gates, Jr., explains in the PBS television series, *African American Lives* (2006), "Of 3,000 African Americans who filed homestead claims in Florida, only 1 in 10 was able to withstand these pressures."

African American Lives shows Whoopi Goldberg proudly holding a copy of her ancestors' Homestead Proof. Speaking to series host Henry Louis Gates, Jr., she says that the copy of the Homestead Proof "cements" her intuition that her ancestors had decidedly made claim to this country. She laughs, in all seriousness, "Let somebody tell me to 'go back to where I come from' now!" (*African American Lives*).

The significance of the document in substantiating Goldberg's genuine American pride cannot be overestimated. Also during interviews for *African American Lives*, Goldberg laments the general lack of black American family history, in sharp contrast to those of her white American colleagues. As part of that television series, participants, including Oprah Winfrey and Bishop T.D. Jakes, among others, are given glimpses into their family histories; they are also administered DNA tests to determine approximate percentage of inherited African, American Indian and/or Caucasian traits. According to the series, Goldberg's family history can be traced to 1875, as her original, common family name of Johnson cannot be traced back any further. Goldberg quips that the lack of further information is the "dark period"; Gates agrees, calling the period "blackness," as in void.

Continuing, Goldberg says, "So, whole stories are gone; whole lives are gone, whole histories are gone ... there is no emotional compensation for that, you know" (*African American Lives*). She contrasts the common black American experience of not being sure of one's ancestral heritage against that of white Americans, many of whom can relatively easily trace their ancestry. When Gates asks her whether her parents discussed Africa as a point of origin, she emphatically says, "No!" explaining that they were, and saw themselves, as native New Yorkers. DNA tests reveal that Goldberg is 0 percent Native American and 92 percent Sub-Saharan African, with African roots connecting to the West African nation of Guinea-Bisseau. Upon hearing the news, Goldberg responds positively and also affirms that the United States is *hers*, quoting the verse from "My Country, 'Tis of Thee" (*African American Lives*).

Cementing and illustrating American identity, fittingly, The National Park Service now honors Goldberg's homesteader ancestors among initial builders of the city of Alachua. Billing itself as "The Good Life Community," Alachua County, Florida, was incorporated in 1905 (cityofalachua.com), 27 years after the Washingtons gained the deed to their property. Citing the contributions of both the Washingtons and Whoopi Goldberg, The Homestead National Monument of America honors "Whoopi Goldberg: Comedian, Actress, Winner of Grammy, Tony, Emmy and Academy Awards, Great-great-Granddaughter of Homesteaders, 1955 — Alachua County, Florida" (National Park Service).

As the National Park Service placard shows, in addition to acknowledging her ties to the states of Florida and New York, Goldberg also has garnered the highest awards in American recording, theater, television and film. In 1991, she received the Oscar for her groundbreaking role as Oda Mae Brown, the eccentric soothsayer in *Ghost*, opposite Patrick Swayze and Demi Moore. In 1995, she received a star on the Hollywood Walk of Fame, and, bucking tradition, firmly pressed one of her trademark dreadlocks, rather than handprints, into the cement sidewalk.

Goldberg's American identity is also tied to her appreciation of the contributions of generations of African and American chattel slaves, whose efforts helped to build American society and infrastructure. As the narrator of the HBO series *Unchained Memories: Readings from the Slave Narratives* (2002), Goldberg's matter-of-fact vocal delivery and distinct New York accent provide necessary counterbalance for the emotional depictions of the trials, tribulations and triumphs of the last generations of American slaves. The accompanying book of the same title presents "a riveting compilation of more than 40 narratives drawn from the Slave Narrative Collection in the Library of Congress" (Bullfinch Press).

At the start of *Unchained Memories*, Goldberg narrates against the backdrop of the African American spiritual "I'll Never Turn Back No More,"

> Although these ex-slaves did not speak in one voice, they were the last African Americans able to give a first-hand account of what it was like to be a slave in the years before the Civil War [*Unchained Memories*, Ch. 1].

Goldberg's calm delivery balances and underscores the emotional and physical turmoil which former slaves describe. One such former slave was Laura Clark, an 87-year-old former Alabama slave, portrayed by Oprah Winfrey: "Mammy said to Ol' Julie: 'Take care of my baby child (that was me). And if I never see her no more, raise her for God.' Mammy fell off the truck and sobbed" (*Unchained Memories*, Ch. 6). Don Cheadle dramatizes the life narrative of Robert Falls, a former Tennessee slave: "I would die fightin' rather than be a slave again. I want no man's yoke on my shoulders no more" (*Unchained Memories*, Ch. 6).

Goldberg's narration counterbalances the sounds of slave music, brought to the audience courtesy of contemporary recordings made by The McIntosh County Shouters (McIntosh County, Georgia): "Run, Mary, Run (You Got a Right to the Tree of Life)" and "Adam In The Garden"; the African American spirituals, "Fix Me, Lord," "Wade in the Water" and "One Mornin' Soon," performed by the Howard University Choir; and African American military fife and drum songs, dating at least to the American Civil War. As narrator, Goldberg contextualizes and gives voice to the general circumstances facing some "100,000 former slaves still alive" by the late 1930s. (*Unchained Memories*, Ch. 1) Such former slaves had lived a good portion of their lives in bondage, only to later suffer the poverty of the Great Depression as freedpersons. Scholars of black American slave narratives will find some of the stories familiar, as some previously were published via such edited volumes as Blassingame's *Slave Testimony: Two Centuries of Letters, Speeches, Interviews and Autobiographies* (1977) and Mellon's *Bullwhip Days: The Slaves Remember* (1990). In particular, *Unchained Memories* represents well the lives of former Virginia slaves, due in part to the efforts of the University of Virginia. Goldberg's willingness to narrate the series shows her pride in her heritage and determination to ensure recognition of the slaves' contributions to building America.

Another manifestation of Goldberg's American identity is her active, visible and purposeful revival of and participation in public debate. While many narrowly define her as a comedienne, the term "satirist" perhaps best befits Goldberg's role as humorist and public debater. Merriam-Webster defines satire as signifying fullness and saturation. Satire literally means, "1 : a literary work holding up human vices and follies to ridicule or scorn. 2 : trenchant wit, irony, or sarcasm used to expose and discredit vice or folly **synonyms** see **wit** ('Satire')" (Merriam-Webster). Fullness, ripeness, sharpness and wittiness are major characteristics of Whoopi Goldberg. In "Poem for a Lady Whose Voice I Like" (1970), the narrator describes a singer who is ridiculed by a man for, among other things, being self-absorbed. Unswayed by the man's ridicule, the singer offers the acute observation that one who does not recognize herself is perpetually lacking (Giovanni). The singer's statement bespeaks confidence, adaptability and self-reliance, all characteristics of Whoopi Goldberg. As an American, artist and humanist, Goldberg, like Giovanni's singer, is filled to overflowing, wanting for nothing. With respect to humor and satire, Goldberg's primary influences are American comedians Jackie "Moms" Mabley, Richard Pryor and George Carlin.

Jackie "Moms" Mabley (1897–1975) is perhaps Goldberg's earliest acknowledged professional influence. Born Loretta May Aiken, near Brevard, North Carolina, Aiken later married a Mabley and changed her stage name to "Moms," to befit a public persona free enough to critique the status of women, the behavior of men, and American society at large. Reportedly, Mabley's stage persona was a variation of her own grandmother "but with a distinctly cantankerous and sassy edge. She was known for her folksy humor and ribald jokes and affectionately referred to her audience as her 'children'" (African American Registry). A major aspect of her public persona was the manner in which she presented her character; for stage performances, she removed her dentures; wore oversized shoes and house dresses; and wore wigs covered with large hats. "Moms" Mabley's characterization served as a blueprint for what later became Carol Burnett's signature cleaning lady character on *The Carol Burnett Show* (1967–1978). Along the way, Mabley also influenced Phyllis Diller, whose wild getups and self-effacing housewife humor poked fun at herself and married life; Richard Pryor (especially his fictional character, Mudbone); and, of course, Whoopi Goldberg, particularly her live stage performances portraying Mabley; and her fictional Jamaican character in *Whoopi Goldberg: Direct from Broadway* (1985). Through her characters and deft use of words, Jackie "Moms" Mabley subtly dealt with the politics of gender and race; yet Goldberg, while influenced by Mabley, deliberately took the discussion of politics to the next level. With respect to the overtly political aspects of Goldberg's stage performance, we need look no further than George Carlin as a major influence.

In 2008, for the first time in its 11 years, the Kennedy Center Mark Twain Prize was posthumously awarded; the recipient was the late George Carlin, who learned of his having been chosen to receive the prize "just days before he died of heart failure" (NPR). "The Mark Twain Prize was the only comedy award Carlin believed was a legitimate comedy prize" (NPR). As is also true of Goldberg, Carlin, a fellow New Yorker, was reared Catholic and produced several one-person shows for HBO. Carlin's American-ness and Irish ancestry became the subject of several "Carlinisms," preserved especially via HBO specials featuring his stand-up work.

In particular, his views regarding his American-ness echo those of Goldberg. In his one-man show, *It's Bad for Ya* (2008), Carlin asserts that he is not Irish-American; nor is he "proud" of his Irish ancestry. Quips Carlin, "I could never understand ethnic or national pride. Because, to me, pride should be reserved for something you achieve or attain on your own; not something that happens by accident of birth" (Ch. 24). He openly questions why anyone would be "proud" to be a member of any racial or ethnic group. He makes a distinction between being "happy" about one's race and/or ethnicity, versus being "proud" of it; quoting the Biblical Book of Proverbs, he reminds the audience that "pride goeth before a fall" (Ch. 24). Taken at face value, it may appear as though Carlin is ashamed of his Irish heritage; when examined more closely, however, it is clear that Carlin acknowledges his Irish ancestry, but refuses to be defined by it, instead highlighting his American-ness, including fully embracing his Constitutional right to free speech. Carlin's declaration reminds us of Goldberg's insistence that, while she is of African ancestry, she is not African American; she is American, and, as an American, she wants recognition not for her racial or gender designations, but rather for the quality and consistency of her work.

Carlin's view of art as ever-evolving and reflecting an ever-changing society is also reminiscent of Goldberg's applied philosophies regarding art. Carlin explains that stand-up comedy is one of the performing arts; as a performing artist, he is "supposed to grow and evolve over time"—hence, his writing and perspectives have developed (Carlin). Similarly, Whoopi Goldberg, while not a stand-up comedienne but a performance artist, continues to evolve, trying new roles both on- and off-stage. Goldberg first came to national prominence with her one-woman show in San Francisco, honoring veteran comedienne Jackie "Moms" Mabley; on the heels of that show, Goldberg was invited to take her one-woman act to Broadway, which she did, creating her first HBO special, *Whoopi Goldberg: Direct from Broadway* (1985). *Direct from Broadway* showed the multifaceted nature of Goldberg's skill and repertoire, manifesting characters that have become contemporary classics, including Fontaine, the junkie with a Ph.D.; the crippled girl, who teaches humanness and creativity; and the little girl with the long, blonde hair. In 2005, with the HBO special *Whoopi Goldberg: Back to Broadway*, Goldberg revisits the aforementioned three characters. This 20th-anniversary HBO special reunites Goldberg with her original audiences and introduces her to a new generation. Her classic characters (Fontaine, and the crippled girl) now respond to contemporary issues; as times have changed, and America has become more accepting of a wider variety of female beauty (including Goldberg's brown skin and trademark dreadlocks); however, the girl with the long blond hair is not revisited. Instead, Goldberg experiments with a new character, Lurleen, a Southern belle in the making. Off-stage, Goldberg has lent her talents to charity fundraisers such as Comic Relief, with Billy Crystal and Robin Williams, and to such causes as abortion rights. As American artists who assert their rights to free speech, while reflecting contemporary concerns, Carlin and Goldberg are kindred spirits, philosophically speaking.

Not surprisingly, the Kennedy Center honored both Carlin, in 2008, and Goldberg, in 2001, with the Mark Twain Prize for American Humor. The list of Mark Twain Prize recipients is impressive: Richard Pryor (1998), Carl Reiner (1999), Jonathan Winters (2000), Bob Newhart (2002), Lily Tomlin (2003), Lorne Michaels (2004), Steve Martin (2005), Neil Simon (2006), Billy Crystal (2007), and Bill Cosby (2009). Like Mark Twain, all are American humorists whose "take" on American society deliberately and creatively forces audiences to re-evaluate themselves and society at large. As her career shows, the regular, deliberate questioning and breaking of stereotypes regarding race, gender and beauty are hallmarks of Goldberg's satirical humor. She is also willing to poke fun at herself, in the midst of "keeping it real." For example, in *Searching for Debra Winger* (2002), Goldberg explains to Rosanna Arquette, regarding the dearth of worthwhile acting roles for middle-aged women in Hollywood, "The reality is most people look like me" (Ch. 2). Here, Goldberg mentions the fact that most people do not resemble Hollywood's ideal of the tall, blonde and blue-eyed person; that audiences want to see actors who look like them in feature films; and that

1. Made in America   13

actors seeking work can find or create it, as long as they are willing to capitalize on the larger number of available roles for run-of-the-mill characters. Goldberg's dreadlocked hairstyle is an extension of the concept of "keeping it real," serving, at times, as a deliberate stab against Hollywood norms.

Goldberg's humor and unique "take" on American society made her a prime candidate for the position of moderator for ABC's *The View*; her determination to revive the spirit of American debate was a major reason why she took the job. As she explained to ABC's Robin Roberts on *Good Morning, America* (August 5, 2008), "[The process of debate] was what America was predicated on." She goes on to explain that the "deep discussions" that she and her co-hosts have mirror those which either are or should be happening in America. Moreover, she says, debate does not necessarily signal acrimony or fear. Via *The View*, Whoopi Goldberg intends to energize healthy American debate, while acknowledging peoples' right to dissent. Speaking to the audience, she explains that "ugly letters" from viewers "cannot stop debate in this country" (Roberts and Goldberg).

Goldberg understands that the American right to free speech also includes dissenting viewpoints. Since undertaking the important role of moderator on *The View* during the fall of 2007, she has engaged in passionate debates on many topics, including use of the "N" word and the right of artists to demand and protect their space. On July 17, 2008, Goldberg, debating with *The View* cohost Elizabeth Hasselbeck, declared that only black Americans have the right to use the "N" word; while Hasselbeck said that the word creates barriers between people and, therefore, should not be used. Inevitably, the women's passionate views re-opened national discussion on the use of the "N" word. The debate on *The View* was mistakenly perceived as Goldberg deliberately forcing Hasselbeck to tears. However, on July 21, 2008, Goldberg and Hasselbeck, joined by Barbara Walters, Sherri Shepherd and Joy Behar, described how heated debates, such as that between Goldberg and Hasselbeck, are "nothing personal"; Walters explained that she received e-mails from viewers upset that she did not step in (ostensibly to protect Hasselbeck from Goldberg)—and that such action was not necessary, because there was no "catfight." Goldberg expressed her disappointment that the American mass media "mis-characterized" her; she bluntly says that she was not attacking Hasselbeck, and that their debate was possible because the forum of *The View* allowed people with very different views to have a lively discussion, all the while respecting each other (ABC News Video) The "N-Word Debate" was not the first time Goldberg's views on *The View* caused a stir.

Responding to Christian Bale's now-famous on-set tirade targeting Director of Photography Shane Hurlbut during the filming of *Terminator: Salvation*, Goldberg stated, "We don't know if this [incident happened] at the end of the day, we don't know how many hours [he had] been working. It's tough. I know it sounds ridiculous, but I too have gone off on people, because if you're a professional, you know what you're not supposed to do" (Yahoo! OMG!). Goldberg's defense seems not so much for Bale's behavior as for the intensity of the craft of acting. Goldberg's determination to stimulate and participate in healthy debate is an extension of her self-identification as American and "human."

Goldberg declares, "So now I celebrate everything. I consider myself a humanist" (Goldberg 87). Accordingly, a black-and-white photo of Goldberg and members of her immediate family serves as the cover of *Generations of Women: In Their Own Words* (1998), featuring photographs by Mariana Cook and an introduction by Jamaica Kincaid. *Generations of Women* chronicles American women, broadly speaking, emphasizing the mothers and daughters of mothers. Kincaid writes, "Where did my mother's mother come from? Who was her mother?" (Cook 10). Cook's photo of Goldberg's immediate family of women, and related self-descriptions, contextualize them as creative human beings: "Emma Johnson, Great-grandmother; world traveler"; "Whoopi Goldberg: Grandmother; human"; "Alex Martin-Dean, Mother; singer" (Cook 42). Whoopi says that the most important lessons that her mother taught her were diligence and perseverance and to "*always* keep it real" (Cook 42).

Goldberg keeps it real and funny as Sarah Mathews, a proud "urban bushwoman" opposite hokey car salesman Hal Jackson (played by Ted Danson); Zora Mathews (portrayed by Nia Long); and Zora's boyfriend Tea Cake Walters (played by Will Smith), in the motion picture *Made in America* (1993). The plot is thin but tasty. Sarah Mathews, a widow, mother of Zora and proud owner of an Oakland, California, Afro-centric bookstore, learns that she had been artificially inseminated not with anonymous Black American sperm, but rather, with that emanating from a white man. Such is, initially, a surprising and curious matter for Sarah, but such does not become socially fatal, until she learns that Zora's birth father is none other than Hal Jackson, the local car salesman who regularly advertises his wares by staging television commercials starring himself and various circus animals. The plot thickens as Zora begins to accept Hal as her father, and Sarah begins to accept Hal's over-the-top antics, both on and off the small screen, falling in love with the man whom she initially detests.

Through such names as Zora and Tea Cake, the film alludes to author Zora Neale Hurston and a lead male character in her novel *Their Eyes Were Watching God* (1937). Brenner mentions *Made in America*'s intentional, tacit reference to the classic Sidney Poitier film *Guess Who's Coming to Dinner?* (1967), in which Poitier, playing a medical doctor by the name of Prentice, courts a wealthy white college woman, whose disapproving parents (played by Spencer Tracy and Katharine Hepburn) quiz the doctor at every turn. The overall thrust of *Guess Who's Coming to Dinner?* is that Dr. Prentice has all the qualities the parents want in a suitor for their daughter, except that, of course, Prentice is black. In *Made in America*, however, race is the very least of Sarah Mathews's concerns; initially, it is clear that Hal Jackson would never suit Sarah as a father for Zora, even if he were black.

Chapter 6 of *Made in America* is aptly called, "What Do You Mean, He's White?" In that scene, daughter Zora carefully approaches her mother, Sarah, to explain that her birth father is not only a white man, but *the* Hal Jackson. Incredulous, Sarah calls Jackson a "schmuck" who appears on television alongside circus animals. The film then abruptly cuts to a scene featuring Ted Danson as urban cowboy Hal Jackson, "hamming it up" with a monkey at the car dealership, filming one of several hokey television commercials.

Set in sunny Oakland and Berkeley, California, and poking fun at scenes featuring the Wicked Witch of the West riding her broom in *The Wizard of Oz* (1939), the opening scene of *Made in America* features Goldberg, as Sarah, riding against traffic. She is seated upon a Schwinn three-speed bicycle, repeatedly ringing the bicycle's bell; she is waving at friends, her African necklace and bracelets jangling; her mixed traditional African garb billowing in the breeze. Meanwhile, the film's soundtrack pumps Miami Sound Machine's salsa-influenced song, "Go Away." Sarah is a no-nonsense urban bush woman on the move, en route to her independent African-consciousness bookstore, ironically named "African Queen" (ostensibly after the 1951 Hollywood film of the same name, starring Humphrey Bogart and Katharine Hepburn).

A hilarious scene takes place when two elderly white women (played by Phyllis Avery and Frances Bergen, respectively) enter Sarah's bookstore, seeking mainstream wedding-related literature. When they learn that Sarah's bookstore carries titles featuring traditional African weddings, they browse about the bookstore seeking a suitable title, while Sarah desperately tries to get information from the sperm bank via landline telephone. Frustrated at continually being interrupted by the little old ladies, Sarah curtly directs them to find the African wedding books near the voodoo doll display. Meanwhile, as Sarah continues to query the sperm bank concerning their illegal mixup, the little old ladies find Urban Bush Woman T-shirts intriguing. Upon asking Sarah whether the T-shirts come in their size, they also quiz Sarah regarding the meaning of "Urban Bush Woman," to which Sarah, clearly exasperated, yells, "Me! Me!" Frustrated, Sarah locks the two women in the store and rushes off on her bike to confront "cowboy" Hal Jackson.

Dismounting from her bike, Sarah bursts through the double doors of the car dealership, like an outlaw confronting a nemesis at a saloon. For good measure, the scene is also underscored by a variation of the famous theme song, "Buono il Brutto il Cattivo (Titoli)," by Ennio Morricone, featured in Clint Eastwood's spaghetti western, *The Good, the Bad, and the Ugly* (1966). As the conflict between Sarah and Hal heats up, the scene, aptly called,

"Drinks in Hal's Office," Tea Cake arrives to take a car for a test drive, while Zora returns to the dealership to find and remove her mother, who nearly becomes too inebriated to bicycle home.

The crux of the story takes place when Zora, an excellent high school student, wins a prestigious Westinghouse Scholarship for college studies. At this point, she discovers that her biological father is not Hal at all, but rather an unnamed university science major. The story nevertheless ends on a high note as Hal takes pride in a daughter and only child, whom he otherwise never would have had. Sarah unexpectedly grows to love Hal; Zora accepts Hal as her "real" father; and Zora and Tea Cake remain best friends. The final scene shows an upbeat high school graduation, with Tea Cake awarding Zora the Westinghouse prize; Zora dedicating it to her mother, Sarah; and Hal publicly assuming the roles of husband to Sarah and father to Zora. Goldberg's portrayal of an initially pro-black urban bush woman-turned-humanist echoes her own concerns about being true to one's culture, while also acknowledging the diversity of the world at large.

Goldberg's New York pride shines through her portrayal of limo driver Edwina Franklin in Walt Disney's *Eddie* (1996). A fictional New York City limo driver, Eddie uses the company CB radio, becoming a self-appointed, self-styled commentator for the New York Knicks, with an audience consisting of fellow members of the cab company. She even leaves basketball trivia questions on her home answering machine. She can afford only season tickets for Madison Square Garden's nosebleed seats, however; and the Knicks seem to have lost their way; yet nothing dampens her enthusiasm for the Knicks or the game. During one Knicks home game, Eddie, wearing Earl "The Pearl" Monroe's #15 jersey, wins a chance to make a free-throw basket, with the hopes of becoming honorary coach. Sinking the ball into the basket, Eddie scores the coveted position.

Tensions rise when Eddie is viewed not even as a "woman coach," but rather as prize-winner and possession. The Knicks pay little regard to Eddie, considering her just a contest-winning broad; and the team's owner, the eccentric Texan called Wild Bill (played by Frank Langella), sees her as a commodity for which he has paid, to spark much-needed publicity for the flagging team. Nevertheless, Eddie's newfound fame gives her even more home-court advantage in her tough neighborhood.

On her own time, Eddie coaches neighborhood children on the neighborhood court. At one point, the mother of a neighborhood child accosts her, blaming Eddie for benching her child during games. Eddie tells the child's errant mother that she has no right to usurp her (Eddie's) authority in the presence of tough neighborhood children; she also tells the mother that she should be more concerned with her son's education than basketball. Eddie explains that, if the mother does not encourage her son's formal studies, then she is likely to see him "*in* court, instead of *on the court*. Okay?" Surprisingly schooled, the mother acquiesces to Eddie's wisdom.

The central plot of *Eddie*—that of restoring a beloved basketball team to its former glory—is reminiscent of another Disney production, *Celtic Pride* (1996), starring Daniel Stern, Dan Aykroyd and Damon Wayans. *Celtic Pride* centers around two Boston Celtics fanatics, so superstitious that they believe that sequestering the opposing team's top player, Louis Scott of the Utah Jazz, will lead to a Celtics victory in the Finals. Unbeknownst to Celtics fans, Mike O'Hara, a local grade school gym teacher, and Jimmy Flaherty, a home heating specialist and plumber known as "The Septic Tank King," is the fact that such sequestering constitutes kidnapping, according to Massachusetts state law. While Louis is strapped to a chair in Jimmy's basement (which is clogged with Celtics and other sports memorabilia), Mike and Jimmy try to convince Louis that his arrogance cheats fans and teammates out of the true spirit of basketball. Meanwhile, Louis shows his off-court analytical skills by showing his captors that their lives are meaningless, that Mike is a failure, not only for *not* making it to the NBA but also for coaching children's basketball in lieu of paying attention to his loving wife and son. Louis goes on to explain that Jimmy has no chance of *ever* getting a life, as long as he is more obsessed with the Celtics than anything else (scenes show that Susie, the hot dog vendor at the Boston Garden, clearly is smitten with Jimmy, but Jimmy is far more interested in pursuing the hot dogs and the game than she). In the meantime, Louis bargains with his captors, obtaining his release, with the understanding that he will tell the authorities of his kidnapping if the stalwart Celtics fans do not openly root for him and the Jazz, during the basketball finals, to be held at the soon-to-be-demolished Boston Garden. Adding realism to the pandemonium, Boston Celtics legend Larry Bird and football/baseball great Deion Sanders cameo in the film. Despite such realism, however, the film's over-the-top intentions are made clear, with a soundtrack playing off-the-wall jazz music when the Utah Jazz take the court; a Nike television commercial parody, in which Louis, à la Charles Barkley, declares, "I am not a role model"; and Mike's and Jimmy's descent into madness, when they jointly decide that, while they face prison, kidnapping Louis is worthwhile because they will help make Celtics history by virtually guaranteeing the team a win.

Unlike the fanatics of *Celtic Pride*, however, the movie *Eddie*'s Edwina Franklin becomes a model of maturity and restraint, utilizing her pride of basketball, New York City and the Knicks to encourage the players to get back to basics and focus on the game. For example, she requires Ivan, a Russian player with few skills other than sinking shots, to improve his English-speaking skills; she penalizes Jamal, who is more interested in star photography sessions than in required practice sessions; and she forces Stacy Patton to return to hard play instead of focusing upon endorsements. By the end of the film,

Eddie becomes an icon for the Knicks and their fans, with vendors outside the stadium selling $25 statuettes of Lady Liberty with dreadlocks, raising a basketball in lieu of the fabled torch.

The ultimate face-off takes place between Eddie and Wild Bill, when Eddie learns that Wild Bill has bought the Knicks only to serve his selfish greed to sell the team to St. Louis-based investors. At a pivotal moment toward the end of the film, during a Madison Square Garden game, Eddie takes center court and proclaims over the loudspeaker that people, especially the fans, are not commodities (*Eddie* Ch. 12). Eddie proves her skills as a coach, leading the team to the playoffs and cementing their New York address. Members of the team, as well as the assistant coach, support her declaration. Goldberg convincingly plays a role likely originally designed for a man, largely because she focuses upon Edwina Frank's sincere love of basketball, community and New York City.

During an interview on NBC's *The Today Show*, which originally aired January 13, 1986, Goldberg stated that she did not wish to be called an actress, but an actor: "An actress can only play a woman. I'm an actor; I can play anything" (Infoplease). Moreover, as Paul Chutkow observes in "Whoopi's Revenge: For Years Hollywood Executives Considered Her a Talented Pain in the Neck. Now Whoopi Goldberg's Making Them Pay,"

> Whoopi Goldberg is one very complicated lady; she defies easy labels, classifications or pigeonholing. There is a part of her that seems to be a pure Hollywood creature: hip, flip, party all night and never miss a celebrity gathering. This is the public Whoopi. The private Whoopi is very different. She keeps close to her mother, her brother and her daughter, who now has a daughter of her own, making Whoopi a grandmother before she hit 40 [Chutkow].

Goldberg's refusal of the terms "African American" and "actress" is not a denial of race or gender, but rather a determination to move beyond such in favor of (pro)claiming full American and human inheritance. Goldberg cites the significance of approaching new ideas and possibilities without preconceived notions, thus, "anything can happen," including her playing a role on Broadway theretofore always played by a man (Goldberg 232). While she does not name the particular Broadway show in which she played roles originally designated for men, given the publication date of *Book*, it is likely that she is referring to her roles of Prologus and Pseudolus in *A Funny Thing Happened on the Way to the Forum*. That Broadway play is set "two hundred years before the Christian era, a day in spring. A street in Rome in front of the houses of Erronius, Senex and Lycus" (IBDb). Categorized as "Musical, Comedy, Farce, Revival, Broadway" (IBDb) and mounted at the St. James Theatre, the Broadway revival of *A Funny Thing ...* extended from April 18, 1996 to January 4, 1998, with Nathan Lane, a white, gay actor, cast as the first incarnations of Prologus and Pseudolus, respectively. For his work in *A Funny*

Thing..., Lane was awarded the 1996 Tony Award and the 1996 Drama Desk Award, for "Outstanding Actor in a Musical" (IBDb). Following Lane's success, Goldberg played Prologus and Pseudolus; upon her departure, David Alan Grier, a black actor and Yale School of Drama alumnus, undertook both roles.

Goldberg's portrayal of traditionally male, classical stage roles highlights the flip side of the early Shakespearean tradition. During Shakespeare's time, and well into the 18th century, boys and/or men had portrayed the vast majority of stage roles. Adaptations of Shakespeare's works by such writers as John Dryden and William Davenant, however, paved the way for women to act upon the formal stage, in "Davenant's adaptation of *Macbeth*" in 1664, as well as such adaptations as *The Tempest; or, The Enchanted Island*, in 1667. Moreover, the Shakespeare Ladies' Club (1735–1738, formally organized in 1736) deliberately pushed to expand the variety of Shakespearean plays performed, thus resulting in more opportunities for women thespians (Kemp 120). Goldberg's ability and willingness to flip the script to showcase and expand her talents is in keeping with her status and work.

In his essay *The Negro Artist and the Racial Mountain* (1926), Langston Hughes describes the steep climb which some black American artists face when trying to articulate themselves as American artists, while deliberately ignoring their heritage as black people. Hughes muses, "This is the mountain standing in the way of any true Negro art in America ... to be as little Negro and as much American as possible" (Hughes 1311). Hughes considers black American artists' plumbing the depths of black experience as a stepping stone to greater success and respectability within and beyond the world of the arts. Continues Hughes, "We younger Negro artists ... intend to express our individual dark-skinned selves without fear or shame. If white people are pleased, we are glad. If they are not, it doesn't matter" (Hughes 1314). Similarly, he says that black artists should not be overtly concerned with whether black audiences like the art (Hughes 1314). While Hughes was specifically dealing with the aspect of racial identity and its expression during the era of Jim Crow racial segregation, his concluding statement, that black artists "stand on top of the mountain, free within ourselves" (Hughes 1314) alludes to the kind of stance which Goldberg makes, as an American artist during the post–Civil Rights era. Having reached the pinnacle of her profession, Goldberg openly acknowledges race, yet she never lets it define her; instead, as her career shows, she continually redefines and broadens the craft of acting itself. She declares, "Art is long and life is short" (Goldberg 225). If this is true, then her work will be with us for a very long time.

2

The Influence of Jackie "Moms" Mabley and George Carlin

> I am a spy for my government. I love my government. I'm an American. I don't know 'bout Nobody else, but I was born here. I'm an American. I'm from the United States. I don't know 'bout nothing *over there*."
>
> — Jackie "Moms" Mabley (Williams 3)

> I used to be Irish Catholic. Now I'm an American. You know — you GROW.
>
> — George Carlin (Carlin, *Last Words* 158)

A comedienne and descendant of chattel slaves, Jackie Mabley, portraying her world-famous alter-ego, "Moms," proclaims her American pride and heritage, saying that she knows absolutely nothing of the African continent; in fact, so deep is her patriotism, she says, that she works as a covert operative on behalf of the United States government. Her statement tacitly references Harriet Tubman (c. 1820–1913), former slave and "conductor of the Underground Railroad," who served as a "nurse, scout, spy and commando leader" (Bennett 148) for Union troops during the Civil War. It also smartly and subtly takes a jab at *Gone With the Wind* (1939), the classic American novel and film in which Prissy cries, "I don't know nothin' 'bout birthin' babies!" (*Gone With the Wind*, Ch. 21). The laughable nature of Moms's statement is obvious, when one takes into account her overall lack of status: Black, female, elderly, poor, informally educated. Moms's statement provides a significant entry into the Black American masking tradition and related blues philosophy, as well as the early work and philosophies of Whoopi Goldberg.

When Goldberg first hit Hollywood during the mid–1980s, she hit it in stride, striking a decidedly different chord with casting directors and audiences. When viewed at a glance, her approach seems simply offbeat; yet careful review of her work shows that hers is a carefully crafted, syncopated part of a much larger rhythmic pattern. Goldberg reached to and through the philosophies and examples of Mabley and George Carlin to artfully articulate her own style of humor.

While Mabley declares that Africa has no direct connection to her life and work, a scholarly examination of Black American humor reveals two primary founts: traditional West African culture and American slave plantation culture. Discerning and disentangling the African contribution requires some digging; like the spirituals and the blues, Black American humor offers a unique point of view, home-grown on American soil. In *The Humor of Jackie Moms Mabley: An African American Comedic Tradition* (1995), Elsie Williams says that Black American humor is an "inversion of experience of a dislocated and stolen people," an act of resistance. Such resistance survived and was transformed by the Trans-Atlantic slave trade and is akin to a form of escape, which included such acts as running away, or "committing suicide by drowning, refusing food or medicine, and mutinying and killing their captors as the slave ship unmooringly headed for the New World" (Williams 3–4). Williams mentions the use of the "laughing barrel" to contain the laughter of slaves fettered by both circumstances and chains (5).

The significance of the laughing barrel cannot be overstated. Slaves were forced to stand, while placing their hands along the sides of a wooden barrel, their heads in the mouth of the barrel, to drown out the sound of laughter, or muffle the sounds of prayers. Former slave John Little explains the survival of humor in the midst of degradation: "Happy men we must have been! We did it to keep from being completely broken: that is as true as the gospel! Just look at it — must not we have been very happy? Yet I have done it myself — I have cut capers in chains" (Williams 5).

The tradition of "laughing to keep from crying" (a Black American adage) is an example of the kind of cultural "inversion" that Williams mentions; such abounds in the music and poetry of Black Americans. In Black American music, the tone and force of singing often indicates the depth of sorrow; likewise, the kind and force of laughter shows the degree of discontent. As Frederick Douglass reminds us in his *Narrative of the Life of Frederick Douglass, an American Slave, Written by Himself* (1845), "Slaves sing most when they are most unhappy. The songs of the slave represent the sorrows of his heart; and he is relieved of them, only as a heart is relieved of its tears" (Douglass 26). Similarly, laughter represents catharsis and temporary transformation (humanity) for black slaves and their descendants rendered subhuman by law and social custom.

We see this concept explored in black diasporan poetry traditions. Langston Hughes explores it in his first autobiography, *The Big Sea* (1940). In that poem, via rhyming couplets characteristic of the Black American blues music form, the narrator expresses how he uses the mask of laughter to hide his tears (Hughes 185).

Hughes mentions a common verse from blues music traditions (offshoots of the spirituals, by way of the slave experience) to indicate the narrator's underlying humanity. Yet Black indebtedness to West African traditions does not explain the whole experience; alienation from the land of one's African ancestors, combined with alienation from the land of one's birth (the United States) creates a schism and irony that sets Black American humor apart.

Countee Cullen explores this aspect in his poem, *Heritage*, in which the narrator muses on the abstraction of Africa. As is true of most Black Americans, the narrator of the poem has no direct knowledge of Africa; rather, he has only the vaguest perception of the continent, gleaned from his exotic imaginings of Africa's topography, fruit and foliage (Cullen 1347).

The narrator's open questioning of Africa, by making reference to the passage of time, panoramic views that he or she will never see, and exotic spices that he or she likely will never taste, illustrate the growing distance between heritage and harsh realities. The narrator has inherited only the dark skin of Africa, and related discontents in the New World, not the beauty of even a memory of the actual place or people. The irony of such an experience is memorialized in yet another Cullen poem, "Yet Do I Marvel," in which the narrator wonders aloud how Black people could be so despised for their Africanness, and yet compelled and uniquely called upon to develop and share poignant musical artistry emerging out of such cultural traits (Cullen 1341).

The uniqueness of Black American humor is undeniable. "There is nothing like Negro humor. It is loud, profane, juicy, wondrous, scabrous, willful, tricky, and sometimes delivered in coded language. It is steeped, as well, in American history, in blackface and Jim Crow laws and segregation. And also in the stuttering integration we all still participate in. And it is funny as hell" (Haygood 31). The "juicy" aspects of Black American comedy indicate its tendency toward satire, the Greek word of ancient origins, meaning saturated, full and ripe. What Black Americans lack in the areas of civil rights and/or socioeconomic advancement, they compensate for through the expression of sadness and its polar opposite, humor.

Elsie Williams describes four types of Black American humorists as "the plantation survivalist, accommodationist, in-group social satirist, and integrationist of the sixties and seventies as the precursor of the contemporary comedian of the eighties and nineties" (Williams 7). While Williams defines such specifically in relation to Black American culture, one may also apply aspects of the latter examples to describe American humor, generally. Jackie "Moms" Mabley's humor clearly fits the "in-group social satirist" model; George Carlin's humor fits the "integrationist of the sixties and seventies" model; and Whoopi Goldberg's humor fits the mode of the "contemporary comedian of the eighties and nineties." While not a comedian, Goldberg certainly uses elements of American stand-up comedy to articulate her art.

As an in-group social satirist, Moms is the embodiment of "motherwit," the Black American folk term for the kind of wisdom with which one, ideally, is born. According to folklore, one is either born with common sense or one is not; common sense is not a birthright, but rather a gift that a mother bequeaths to a child during the birthing process. One cannot buy, trade or reason for common sense; one cannot acquire common sense, except that it is passed to a child through his or her mother. Jackie "Moms" Mabley, an on-purpose heritage reminder, is common sense in the flesh.

The universality of Mabley's stage persona is rooted in her deliberate use of the down-home, pared-down mother image. As "Moms," Mabley always addresses her audience as "children," purposefully de-emphasizing the physical aspects of sexuality, she removes her dentures, combs her hair forward and dons a rumpled fishing hat, a raggedy house dress, old stockings and oversized clodhoppers. "Clad in a flowered smock, checkered dress, knee-length wool stockings and house shoes several times too large for her size eight feet, she looks like somebody's toothless old grandmother. As a matter of fact, she is a grandmother ... [and] the clown princess of comedy" (JPC, *Behind the Laughter* 89). Through Moms, Mabley creates a set of audience expectations of an out-of-touch, harmless old woman, which are completely dashed by the end of her performance. The product of ripe satire, Mabley's full words cut in ways that her bare gums cannot. Moms's frank discussions of sex and politics belie her scrappy, fragile appearance.

Moms tells her "children" about having sexual relations with her husband while fantasizing about young men:

> Moms been accused of liking young men, and I'm guilty. [*Soundbite of laughter*] Tain't no old man do nothing for me [*Soundbite of laughter and applause*], but bring me a message from a young man, that's all he can do.... [*Soundbite of laughter*] [Smiley]. Let me tell you girls, something! George took me home last night and kissed me [*laughter*]. My big toe shot up in the air just like!" [Williams 80].

Moms's virility is evident by the erection that she claims to have had in her "big toe." She also claims that she enjoys sex as much as any man, this being a humorous extension of Sojourner Truth's speech, "Ain't I a Woman?" (1851), in which Truth mentions equality of the sexes and says that she can work as hard as a man and eat as much as a man, when sufficient vittles are made available to her (Truth 247); here, Moms tells her "children" that women appreciate sex as much as any man; and that age does not necessarily diminish sexual desire.

Moms also debunks the myth of inexhaustible male social and sexual prowess by describing an "old, puny, moldy man" who, at the age of 91, attended his sister's funeral. The minister, upon seeing the old man, recommended that he not even bother to go home, as death was imminent. So old was the old man, Moms says, "Santa Claus looked like his son.... His shadow weighed more than he did! He got out of breath threading a needle!" (Williams 81). Moms's mentioning of the old man's inability to thread a needle is her subtle way of showing the man's lack of virility.

Mabley fully mastered the art of double-entendre, making especial use of her character's lack of teeth and implied age-related hearing problems. In a performance at the Greek Theater in Los Angeles, Moms relates the experience of fear of flying, and her lack of ability to fully comprehend the stewardess's advice to help alleviate inner-ear pressure. (It is understood that the stewardess is white.) When the stewardess tells Moms to chew gum, Moms says,

> Oh, my head kept on turnin' round when we flew over them Great Rockies! My head was hurtin'. I say, "Honey, do somethin' for me, I feel like I'm dyin'." She say, "Moms, drop your jaws!" And I misunderstood her, you know? (*laughter*) ... I caught a terrible cold, I did [Williams 94].

Mabley plays with words and meaning; instead of lowering her jaws, as instructed, she lowers her *drawers* (bloomers or panties), exposing her genitals and posterior; as a result, she develops a cold, while she, in effect, tells the white woman (who symbolically represents the establishment) to kiss her behind. Later, at Sing Sing Prison, Mabley reprises the experience in another skit, whereby Moms calls for a medical doctor to visit her:

> I got that flu! Honey, I was sick! Oh, the doctor come to see me; I said, "Do somethin' for me, Honey, I'm dyin'." I said, "I cain't hear nothin'." He said, "Moms, just drop your jaws." And I misunderstood him [Williams 95].

Moms gets an old-fashioned house call from a medical doctor (it is understood that the medical doctor is white). While the doctor is clearly there to help her overcome her stated illness (the flu), Moms takes advantage of the situation, interpreting the doctor's house call as a booty call; dropping her *drawers* (underwear) instead of her "jaws," and once again willfully exposing her genitals and hind parts to the establishment. Mabley's bold, ribald humor implies that sexual relations can cure virtually any illness, no matter how severe, and no matter the age of the sufferer, especially if the sufferer is a woman.

Moms's take on the politics of relationships and everyday life also show motherwit at work. For example, in one skit, she calls out to a young man and asks him if he knows the location of his father, to which the young man replies, "He's in Chicago." Moms asserts, "Boy, your father is in Pittsburgh," which the young man vehemently denies. Moms proves her point, however, when she elaborates, "The man your mother married is in Chicago, but your father is in Pittsburgh," to which the audience responds with hearty laughter (Smiley). Moms shows the power of women in determining and/or acknowledging paternity, as well as the wisdom of skepticism; of not taking "facts" at face value. In another comedy sketch, Moms discusses the difficulty of Blacks finding decent housing in Harlem, New York, by way of describing a conversation between two men. A man approaches an apartment on Amsterdam Avenue, inquiring as to its availability, to which the current occupant replies that the visitor cannot have the apartment as its official resident has been drowned in the Harlem River. The visitor replies, "I know. I'm the one who pushed him in the river." The audience laughs in response (Smiley). Moms' motherwit illustrates that racism is not the only impediment for Black Americans; in-group competitiveness and selfishness are also factors. "This inside humor is welcomed because these comedians are laughing at everybody including Negroes, and often because it is daring.... Listening to a comedian pick his way through the constantly changing nuances of sanctioned attitudes ... can be exhausting as well as exhilarating" (Stearns). In *Frontiers of Humor: American Vernacular Dance*, Marshall and Stearns consider Jackie "Moms" Mabley a member of the "new humor" generation, which also includes such Black American luminaries as Slappy White, Redd Foxx, Nipsey Russell, Dick Gregory, Godfrey Cambridge and Flip Wilson, among others (Stearns).

Mabley's in-group satirist approach is reminiscent of that of Dewey "Pigmeat" Markham (1904–1981), a native of Durham, North Carolina, and a Black American comedy pioneer, with whom Moms often performed on the Chitlin' Circuit — a loosely connected chain of independent theaters located primarily in the American South. (The term "chitlin'" refers to pig intestines, the scraps given to American chattel slaves, which the slaves learned to clean and prepare as food, using spices to make such entrails more palatable; the rough conditions of the Chitlin' Circuit led Black American performers to liken themselves to feces being forced through a pig's colon, laughing to keep from crying.) Says Markham in his book, *Here Come the Judge* (1969),

> My act is not history, it's comedy. It's not white-man's comedy, it's Negro-born and Negro-bred and Negro-popular. It's not aimed at ridiculing anyone. The characters I have created (like the judge) are no more a slur on the Negro than Jackie Gleason's hot-headed bus driver or Art Carney's sewer cleaner or Dean's drunk or Red Skelton's fool or Jack Benny's stinginess are a slur on the white man [Markham Ch. 3].

Markham clearly sees his work in relation to that of a range of other (mainstream) American comedians, whose characters represent aspects of the human condition, rather than pigeonholing or stereotyping any particular person or group of people. Like Mabley, Markham sees himself as an American comedian, addressing American concerns. The fact that he is Black does not limit his perspective on his work, nor should it limit the audience's appreciation for the fullness of his approach.

His colleague, Jackie "Moms" Mabley, was born, in Brevard, North Carolina, where "her father was a respected businessman" (JCP 89). "Although

Moms spent her professional life making people laugh, her personal life had more than its share of grief.... She was raped at the age of 11 by an older black man, and raped again two years later by the white town sheriff. Both rapes resulted in pregnancies; both babies were given away" (Bennetts). By the age of 14, she was a married mother of three daughters, and her experiences with "school plays and vaudeville shows" helped her decide upon a career in comedy (JCP 88–89). She eventually became a grandmother of six (JCP 88). In sharp contrast to her disheveled, homely "Moms" persona, and illustrating her use of the masking tradition, Mabley was actually a deeply spiritual and "striking figure in tailored slacks, matching sports shirt, Italian shoes, horn-rimmed glasses — and teeth" (JCP 89). In her later years, she also lived as a lesbian (Bennetts), a fact which has become increasingly well known since her death in 1975.

During her early years as a performer, Whoopi Goldberg performed Mabley's character, Moms, as an homage (Noel 28). According to Goldberg, "Moms was able to do a lot of what she did because the people [in charge] recognized that she was telling the truth — they let her do certain things they wouldn't let other comedians do, because they understood Moms was reaching out to everyone" (Maslon and Kantor 330). Goldberg's open admiration for Mabley's pioneering work perhaps sparked people to mistakenly assume that she is gay; her portrayal of Celie in the major motion picture *The Color Purple* (1985), in which Celie has a homosexual experience with another character, blueswoman Shug Avery, portrayed by Margaret Avery, perhaps extended and cemented this erroneous belief. However, Goldberg, while using elements of stand-up comedy, is an actor; as such, she can play any role — playing a lesbian on stage and/or screen does not necessarily reflect her real life. We must include, but also look beyond, Goldberg's live stage skits to find Jackie "Moms" Mabley's influence. Just as Moms blasts the stereotype of the "asexual," powerless elder woman, Goldberg blasts through typical social divides with carefully rendered characters that challenge age, race, and gender assumptions.

A member of the next generation of performers, Goldberg uses many different talents to articulate her craft; a consummate actor, she believes that she can embody a wide range of quality characters. She says, "I'm fighting the label of 'Black' actress, simply because it's very limiting in people's eyes, especially people who are making movies. I don't want them to say, 'Oh, she's a black actor, we can't use her.' I want them to say, 'Here's a great role. Call Meryl Streep. Call Diane Keaton. Call Whoopi Goldberg'" (Noel 34). Hollywood called upon Goldberg to replace Bruce Willis as the lead in the feature film, *Burglar* (1986) (*A&E* Ch. 4). In that film, she plays Bernice "Bernie" Rhodenbarr, a professional thief and ex-con blackmailed into performing one last heist on behalf of a crooked former San Francisco police chief. The opening scene shows Goldberg adopting a variation of Moms as her character

Bernie's "cover," as Bernie robs an upscale private home. Instead of physically downplaying sexuality, as Mabley does with the character and alter-ego Moms, Goldberg hypersexualizes the role, wearing oversized prosthetic hips and breasts, scratching her behind and bending at the waist to present herself to the viewer (the camera angle deliberately mimics that of the San Francisco police). "Kiss my ass," Bernie seems to tell the police and the audience.

In an act reminiscent of Mabley's "drop your jaws" and "moldy old man" themes, Goldberg riffs on her characters, "Old Raisin," a dried-up old man who can barely "raise" himself, sexually speaking or otherwise; and an unnamed Jamaican woman, who runs a "curio stand," selling trinkets to tourists, in *Whoopi Goldberg: Direct from Broadway* (1985). In Goldberg's shtick, Old Raisin asks the Jamaican woman to come to the United States to work as his maid and also provide him with "a little nookie" (sex) of which she claims complete ignorance; she says that she decided to "improvise" (Ch. 6)—a comment which delights the audience. The Jamaican woman declares that Old Raisin is senile, for, she says, he confuses memories of his life with that of the setting of *Gone With the Wind*. As she comes to learn, however, Old Raisin is so infatuated with that Hollywood film that he has commissioned an architect to reproduce Tara as his private dwelling. Despite the enormous house and work involved in cleaning it, the Jamaican woman is happy to see indoor bathrooms; in her hometown of Kingston, she says, she lives in a section of town where she must use an outhouse and wrestle with spiders and skunks, and, she jokes that "sometimes you don't win" (Ch. 6). The ludicrousness of the Jamaican woman's situation piques audience interest, sparking laughter.

In Old Raisin's Tara, Goldberg's Jamaican woman becomes addicted to soap operas and says that the hypersexuality of such shows is unrealistic; for if men had as much sex as they do in the television show, then their penises would either "fall off" or shrink to minuscule size. Nevertheless, she says, she dutifully never misses an episode (Ch. 6)—a comment which draws howls of laughter from the audience.

The Jamaican woman tries to fight off Old Raisin's sly sexual advances, which he attributes to the effect of television commercials encouraging American tourists to "Come to Jamaica." She soon comes to learn that Old Raisin finds such tourism commercials, showing scantily clad black women and men peddling fresh fruit, an aphrodisiac—the audience laughs in response to Goldberg's sly use of double-entendre. The timeliness of Goldberg's shtick cannot be overstated, for Whoopi's characterization of Old Raisin took place during the time of the popularity of the California Raisins ad campaign, whereby Ray Charles and the Raelettes, portrayed as claymation raisins, performed a soulful version of "I Heard It Through the Grapevine" to television audiences worldwide. In contrast to Moms's toothlessness, the Jamaican woman has all her teeth, but Old Raisin does not — at one point, he removes his dentures, and they "click, click, click" and dance about, frightening the Jamaican (Ch. 6).

Despite his toothlessness, Old Raisin still sexually pursues his Jamaican maid, gifting her with "easy-access lingerie," courtesy of Frederick's of Hollywood. The woman responds by banning him from her room; nevertheless, he presents himself naked and hopelessly wrinkled, at which point she wishes only to press him with an iron — a statement prompting chuckles from the audience. One plus, according to the Jamaican woman, is that old men are sexually experienced. During one such occasion, Old Raisin dies while having sex with her. Through double-entendre, Goldberg implies that Old Raisin dies satisfied, conveniently and prematurely leaving his Jamaican maid before she reaches orgasm. The Jamaican woman declares of old men: "They come, and they go" (Ch. 6) — the audience howls. Goldberg, a consummate storyteller, skillfully brings the Jamaican woman's situation to a satisfying end. After Old Raisin's death, the maid is confronted by his family, whom she dubs "the Raisinettes," cleverly making a nod to both the popular American candy, the California Raisins television commercials, and Ray Charles back-up singers, the Raelettes. The Kingston woman gets the upper hand, however, when she learns that Old Raisin has willed her his entire fortune. Thus, the formerly exploitive situation is resolved to the satisfaction of both the woman and her sympathetic audience.

Like Moms, Goldberg riffs on fear of flying, explaining, through her character Fontaine, the "Junkie with a Ph.D.," that airports are notoriously uncomfortable, with clerks and flight attendants unnecessarily indifferent, especially toward people perceived as being different. Fontaine openly questions why airlines deliberately oversell flights; why people are overcharged for plane tickets, which do not guarantee seats, let alone safe and/or comfortable flights — a statement which draws laughter and sympathy from the audience. She continues: upon being forced to pay nearly one thousand dollars for a plane ticket, Fontaine finds airline food barely palatable, and the bathroom experience frightening (s/he fears falling from the plane, into the abyss, via the "flap" in the toilet).

Such a story line is reminiscent of that of Mabley's comedy; yet it also helps audiences to understand Goldberg's real-life avoidance of airplanes. Goldberg is not alone; she and the "Queen of Soul" Aretha Franklin both have suffered from aviophobia (JPC, 1999, 46). She regularly travels by private bus: "I have a bus that I take from Los Angeles to New York. It's great.... There's no fax on it [*laughs*].... I'm in complete command of my life. it's the calmest time I ever spend" (Cavett). Goldberg even made aviophobia a characteristic of her fictional character Mavis in her NBC sitcom, *Whoopi*. In real life, however, she confronted her fear of flying, on an April 1, 2009 episode of ABC's *The View*, for which she serves as moderator. In that episode, Dr. Roger Callahan outfits Goldberg and her co-hosts Sherri Shepherd, Joy Behar and Elizabeth Hasselbeck with goggles and all take a virtual "flight," using Callahan's Thought Field Therapy (TFT) "courtesy of Sir Richard Branson and Virgin Atlantic's Flying Without Fear program ... a drug-free, non-invasive procedure that can be self-applied" (TFT). Taking flight and echoing Mabley's lead, while charting her own path in the process, Goldberg also shows her comedic ties to the performance style and themes of George Carlin.

Through his lengthy career as a stand-up comedian, George Carlin's public image has ranged from that of upstart hippie to s(t)age philosopher to bitter, angry old man. Carlin's upstart hippie persona reveals itself to great effect during his January 25, 1969 visit to *The Jackie Gleason Show*; his status as s(t)age philosopher makes itself known in his book, *Brain Droppings* (1997), in which Carlin clarifies his stance. Pointedly criticizing the herd mentality of the average contemporary American, he has no interest in joining the herd; says the comedian, in all seriousness, "I love and treasure individuals as I meet them, I loathe and despise the groups they identify with and belong to" (xii). Moreover, he says, "I enjoy describing how things are, I have no interest in how they 'ought to be.' And I certainly have no interest in fixing them" (xii). One may consider such a matter-of-fact statement an example of bitterness, for Carlin expressly and pointedly counters any concept of "hope" with cold, hard examples and no realistic solutions. In fact, Carlin's shtick is that one cannot find or create solutions, unless one acknowledges and analyzes such pervasive social problems as "child worship" and "ethnic pride" (*It's Bad for Ya*, Chs. 24; 9). Nevertheless, Carlin counters, "I am a personal optimist but a skeptic about all else" (Carlin, *Brain Droppings* xii). One example is his proposed "solution" to global preoccupation with war: the advent of "twenty-four-hour, nonstop, worldwide folk dancing, once a year"—such an act, he says, would bring war to a halt during the actual dancing; thereafter, and in preparation for the next annual folkdance, people would be so preoccupied with talking about folk dancing that they would forget about war (183).

Carlin's determination to point out problems, without identifying realistic solutions (or solutions at all) is apparent in his take on American racial categories. To his way of thinking, the black/white racial divide is a political ploy, which deliberately and permanently separates people, by polarizing opposites. Says Carlin, "Black and white can never come together. Pink and brown, on the other hand, might just stand a chance of being blended.... Can't have that! Doesn't fit the plan" (Carlin, *Brain Droppings* 164). He also sharply criticizes dual heritage names, like African American, as they do not specify a particular African country of origin, and describes just about any American of African descent, including descendants of American slaves and recent immigrants from South Africa and Jamaica (164–165). Carlin concludes, "Labels divide people. We need fewer labels, not more" (165). He does not tell readers how to reduce the number of labels; rather he simply points out the necessity of doing so. Nor is pointing out solutions part of Carlin's self-described responsibility: "Getting laughs all the time *wasn't my only responsibility*. My responsibility was to engage the audience's mind for ninety minutes" (Carlin, *Last Words* 246).

Carlin does just that, with his last HBO special, *It's Bad for Ya* (2008), which shows him at his satirical best. That television special includes such topics as "Goin' Through My Address Book," in which he describes how he deletes the names of the deceased from his physical and digital address books (and the differences between the two processes); "He's Smiling Down," in which he discusses Christian preoccupation with God's omnipresence; "No One Questions Things"; and "Proud to Be an American." In "No One Questions Things," Carlin gives a laundry list of topics that he considers examples of American blind faith, such as "The American Dream," "Justice is blind," "The press is free," "Your vote counts," "Business is honest," "Your standard of living will never decline," and "Everything is going to be just fine" (Ch. 23). In "Proud to Be an American," he says that one should reserve pride for "something that you achieve or attain on your own," and that one should mention that one is "happy" with one's racial and/or ethnic group, rather than that one is "proud" of it (Ch. 24). He further goes on to talk about American appeals to God, in the name of morality, mentioning the popular "What Would Jesus Do?" (WWJD) campaign. He explains that WWJD adherents "don't want to know, so *they* can do it — they want to know, so they can *tell someone else* to do it" (Ch. 24). Carlin concludes that much of American rhetoric is just that; that Americans actually have no rights at all, but rather "a bill of temporary privileges," which can be revoked at any time (Ch. 28). He offers the Japanese internment as a case in point and reminds the audience that there is no right to "food every day" or a "roof over your head" (Ch. 28). The deep, comic irony of Carlin's pointed words is that they poke holes in what he considers the myth of American rights to freedom, while simultaneously exemplifying his Constitutional right to freedom of expression.

In an interview, "Too Hip for the Room," Carlin explains his coming-of-age as a philosopher, writer and performer. Initially patterning himself after Danny Kaye, he assumed that his career would follow the trajectory of "Disc jockey — Comedian — Actor," and mirror typical American middle-class aspirations ("Too Hip"). He realized, however, that he was a "rebel," as evidenced by his having been ejected from several schools, as well as such organizations as the U.S. Air Force, the church choir, the altar boys, summer camp and the Boy Scouts ("Too Hip"). He says that, while he was a "good student," he simply "didn't care" about the subject matter being taught in school, so he dropped out of school at the age of nine and "became a pot-smoker at thirteen" ("Too Hip"). He really came to terms with his rebellion during the summer of 1967, when he realized that, at the age of 30, he was sandwiched between his mainstream American audience and their children; thus, he decided to identify with his audience's children, the hippies ("Too Hip"). He classifies his initial work as having been largely autobiographical, with his coming-of-age material branching out to discuss universal, trivial topics, such as "detention," a word with which all Americans are familiar, in one form or another; and then finally maturing into a form in which he sees and works as a writer who performs his own material ("Too Hip").

Word processing was instrumental to Carlin's development as a writer; prior to reorganizing and recasting his words, using a word processor (and thereby deepening and broadening his communication skills), he considered himself a "comedian who wrote his own material" ("Too Hip"). Carlin considers his mature work a series of essays, punctuated by jokes for emphasis: "I think I can claim to have my essays.... The jokes are great ... but the jokes are there to decorate the ideas. The ideas ... are about what I'm disenchanted by.... I'm a writer" ("Too Hip"). Such disenchantment includes the Catholic Church, of which he is an open critic, much to the chagrin of his mother, who, while proud of his success and ability to reach audiences, still worried about his salvation, wishing him to once again partake of Holy Communion: he explained to his mother, "I'm a moral person. That's all the Church wants me to be." His mother's inability to understand his choice to practice morality, outside of the Church, he says, "was her sorrow" ("Too Hip").

With his career spanning more than five decades, including four Gold albums for comedy, Carlin is most famous for having written and performed a record 14 HBO comedy specials. He claims that HBO, an American cable television broadcast vehicle, revived and extended his career and allowed him to experiment with form and language and philosophies in ways that commercial television simply could not ("Too Hip"). Well aware of his legacy in American comedy, he knows that no one writing a history of late–20th century American comedy can ignore him. He mentions his ideal epitaph: "He was 'Too Hip' for the room" ("Too Hip").

Carlin was not "Too Hip," however, for the film, *Dogma* (1999), in which he plays Cardinal Glick — a double irony for viewers recognizing his very public questioning of the efficacy of the Catholic belief system. Not surprisingly, for his efforts as a writer and performer, in 2009, the Kennedy Center posthumously awarded him the Mark Twain Prize for American Humor — the very same prize which Goldberg received in 2001, and which Richard Pryor, the award's first recipient, received in 1998. Both Carlin and Goldberg capitalize on their New York moorings.

Carlin makes no excuse for, or pretense of, being a New Yorker. In fact, his New York mindset gives his humor especial bite and perspective. In his book, *Last Words* (2009), he mentions the appeal of Broadway, and its status as a major proving ground for comedians: "When you grow up in New York ... you know where all the stage doors are. Broadway is the center, the mecca, true magnetic north. Though I didn't aspire to be a Broadway actor, Broadway was the symbolic pinnacle of what I wanted to be and belong to." In reflecting upon his lengthy career, he says, "I've been writing a Broadway show all along. I've had this dream for a while now and I'd often worry that being on the road would never leave me time to fulfill it.... My characters will write their own words, when the time comes" (293–294). He also says that, unlike stand-up comedy, which is fully scripted "commentary, lists, observation," his Broadway characters will deliver their messages in narrative form, as theatrical performance demands (293–294). Carlin never did reach his goal of performing on Broadway; Goldberg, a member of the next generation of stage performers, did, however, and Carlin's influence certainly can be seen in select philosophies and approaches included in her HBO specials *Whoopi Goldberg: Direct from Broadway* (1985) and *Whoopi Goldberg: Back to Broadway (20th Anniversary)* (2005).

Comparisons between Carlin and Goldberg, both native New Yorkers reared in the Catholic faith, are considerable. Like Carlin, Goldberg also dropped out of school, as she found that it did not meet her needs (Randolph 111). Like Carlin, Goldberg also left the formal Church in favor of practicing and teaching morality in everyday life. Like Carlin, Goldberg exhibits traits of the upstart hippie and s(t)age philosopher. Her fictional character Fontaine, in *Whoopi: Direct from Broadway* (1985), explains that she has a Ph.D. in literature, from Columbia University—a degree that gives her no especial status in society or in the workplace; hence, Fontaine is a drug addict. Fontaine further explains: "I'm a junkie; I'm not stupid" (Ch. 2); moreover, despite her advanced academic degrees, Fontaine's wisdom comes largely from life, not textbooks. Like Carlin, Goldberg also mentions days when drug use became problematic: "Junkies never know that they have to stop and I don't know ... how I did" (Randolph 111); unlike Carlin, Goldberg does not elaborate on her past drug use; rather, she elaborates on the necessity of avoiding drugs: "There ain't no joy in a high—none.... You think there's a joy in a high, because it feels good temporarily.... It ain't your friend" (Randolph 111). Having struggled with addiction, Goldberg tried multiple times before stopping, crediting drug addicts (now deceased) for helping her quit her addiction: "I'm the living legacy of this group of talented, wonderful dope fiends who cleaned me up and made a lasting impression" (Randolph 111). She tells young people considering drugs to "save their money," because drug addiction is akin to slow suicide (Randolph 111). Goldberg's character

Fontaine is, perhaps, her attempt to humanize drug addicts, who, while marginalized, nevertheless have much to teach the world. Like Carlin, she uses every opportunity to call attention to social problems; unlike Carlin, however, she makes it a point to encourage audience members to be part of the change that they hope to see in the world, as her HBO specials illustrate. Goldberg's HBO specials, *Whoopi Goldberg: Direct from Broadway* (1985) and *Whoopi Goldberg: Back to Broadway (20th Anniversary)* (2005) discuss themes similar to those which George Carlin explored, especially with respect to race and ethnicity.

In *Direct from Broadway*, Goldberg tackles such topics as race and ethnicity, largely from the perspective of a native New Yorker, and encourages audiences to be the change that they wish to see in the world. Two of her most important characters in this regard are Fontaine and the Crippled Girl. Fontaine, the androgynous "Junkie with a Ph.D." and veritable fountain of worldly and otherworldly wisdom, riffs on her experience of flying to Amsterdam (ostensibly to do drugs), but nevertheless becoming transfixed and transformed by a visit to the Anne Frank House. Fontaine learns of Anne Frank's deathly fear of being discovered by Nazis, and Frank's general belief that good can be found in, and can prevail in, most people. Fontaine may be "high" on drugs, but, as a marginalized figure, s/he is also "high" above the pettiness of politics and "high" on the possibilities of achieving positive social change. Fontaine declares that "live and learn" should be a constant, a mantra, a mode of living, and that, while s/he is "jaded" by experience, s/he will "never get over" (Ch. 3) the experience of living and learning from the preserved and projected voice of the deceased Anne Frank, a young girl who sought the best in everyone. Later, she transforms herself into an unnamed young woman, who learns and teaches that, despite her palsy, atypical physical appearance, and related social marginalization, she is still human and still loves the sun, sand, and surf. (Her unnamed character later became known as the "Crippled Girl.") Goldberg's human(izing) characterizations of Fontaine and the Crippled Girl teach the audience sympathy and compassion, not only for the crippling circumstances of such characters, but also for people facing real-life challenges where choices are few, chances are many, and people — even total strangers — can "think globally and act locally," taking positive steps to improve the world.

Like a prodigal daughter, Goldberg returns to the scene 20 years later, with *Back to Broadway*, reprising some of the characters from her original show, introducing some new ones, and extending her message to inspire audiences to change themselves and the world for the better. In *Back to Broadway*, she talks about race and ethnicity in decidedly global terms. Speaking as Fontaine, the actor shares views on race and ethnicity, decrying censorship of such television shows as *Spongebob Squarepants* (which, according to critics, slyly allude to such adult topics as alcoholism, nudity and sadomasochistic sex) (Breimeier); and *Teletubbies* (which, critics say, purportedly show gay characters) (BBC News) and explaining that the United States is supposed to uphold citizens' rights to "believe whatever they want," and make up their own minds. Declares Fontaine, echoing George Carlin's related viewpoint, "People are concerned about morals: yours" (Ch. 4).

She also gives a no-nonsense, straightforward, native New Yorker perspective on Secretary of State Condoleezza Rice, facetiously saying that Rice is "the most powerful woman in the world," much to the chagrin of media mogul Oprah Winfrey. The audience heartily laughs in response. Fontaine then calls for an episode of *Celebrity Death Match*, in which Rice and Winfrey fight tooth and nail for cultural dominance.

The irony of the statement is twofold: in effect, Fontaine is saying that the American mass media has only one slot available, at any one time, to showcase a powerful black woman; and that Winfrey's vast media empire actually directly reaches more Americans than Rice's shrewd international diplomacy — where popularity is concerned, to the contemporary American mind, television trumps scholarship. Fontaine concludes her review of American rights and rhetoric by reminding the audience that such rights as "free speech," "religious preference," and "sexual preference" (Ch. 5) are eroding, and that Anne Frank's very real fear of being discovered and punished for being different is no different than the threats to freedom of expression in America today. Fontaine reminds us, though, that watchfulness goes both ways; just like there is American government surveillance of its citizens, so American citizens should be watchful and wary of the American government's erosion of Constitutional rights.

The conclusions that Goldberg reaches are the exact opposite of Carlin's. The bitterness and cynicism characterizing Carlin's later performances reflect his personal view ("I give up on my countrymen") ("Too Hip"), but are antithetical to Goldberg's philosophy and public persona. Carlin tells American audiences, whom, he says, have "been bought off silently by toys and gizmos," to "question authority" (*It's Bad for Ya*, Ch. 23). Yet Goldberg ends her 20th anniversary return to the Broadway stage singing the haunting chorus from the song, "Every Breath You Take," made famous by The Police, admonishing Americans about Big Brother and censorship (especially mounting threats to free speech and religious and sexual preferences) and reminding them that "Americans are more aware than the government thinks" (*WG: Back to Broadway*, Ch. 5). While Carlin seeks to arouse critical thinking among his audience, Goldberg actively prompts the audience to not only think, but also act; in this case, she charges the American audience with the responsibility of reawakening the dormant spirit of American democracy.

In all jest, Jackie "Moms" Mabley may have been a "spy" for the American government and George Carlin may have "given up on his countrymen." But Goldberg, frank and forthright native New Yorker, boldly steps forward, carrying the mantle of Moms and the concerns of Carlin to the next level, stepping outward and upward, paving as she steps, encouraging American audiences to reclaim and proclaim democracy and act accordingly.

3

An American Artist in Hollywood

> It's a mistake to try to rewrite things for me. Only I can take the material that's already there and have some fun with it.
>
> —Whoopi Goldberg (Rensin 58)

Whoopi Goldberg's journey to Hollywood was experimental, charting no straight path, but diligence, perseverance and a bit of luck led to her commercial success. Eventually becoming the highest-paid black woman Hollywood actor (Chutkow), one would think that Goldberg would have had her choice of choice parts to play. Actually, while she was highly paid and highly sought after, she was also highly misunderstood, especially where casting agents and movie reviewers were concerned. During the 1980s and into the early 1990s, as she forged her own voice among the din of poorly conceived story plots and tenuous lead roles in motion pictures—some of which were specifically designed for white men, and few of which specifically called for a black woman—she carved a unique place and profile for herself. In general, many of the scripts that she received were far beneath her level of talent; but her dedication to craft, creativity and determination made her characters "work." While many of the films are uneven, and generally received mixed reviews, today's careful viewers see Goldberg using her improvisatory and formal skills to take lumps of coal and transform them into diamonds.

During the 1980s, Goldberg starred in several major motion pictures, including: *The Color Purple* (1985), *Jumpin' Jack Flash* (1986), *Burglar* (1987), *Fatal Beauty* (1987), *The Telephone* (1988), *Clara's Heart* (1988) and *Homer and Eddie* (1989). She also starred in two made-for-television movies: *Whoopi Goldberg: Fontaine ... Why Am I Straight?* (1988), and *Kiss Shot* (1989). Thus began Goldberg's hectic entrée into the Hollywood acting scene and mainstream American audiences' appreciation for her work. Eventually, she also starred in *Ghost* (1990), for which she received an Academy Award for Best

3. An American Artist in Hollywood 37

Supporting Actress, and appeared in small, but pivotal, roles in *Soap Dish* (1991) and *The Player* (1992). Of her years of non-stop film work, Goldberg quips, "There should be a Whoopi Channel, because every time I turn the TV on, one of my movies or some movie that I don't even remember making is on" (JPC). Given its singular status with respect to literature and music, race, class and gender themes, and audience expectations, *The Color Purple* will be the sole focus of the next chapter. With the exception of *The Color Purple*, then, this chapter concerns all of Goldberg's theatrical motion picture and made-for-television film projects in which she starred, from 1985 to 1992; these form an eclectic collection of stepping stones, constituting the early part of Goldberg's path toward greater Hollywood success and world acclaim.

Watching Goldberg's upbeat, effervescent performance, no one would suspect that she had an "awful" (Rensin 57) time filming *Jumpin' Jack Flash*. While she mentions difficulties with respect to its filming and production, it remains one of Whoopi Goldberg's greatest creative triumphs. Originally designed to serve as a star vehicle for Shelley Long, in Goldberg's able hands, the lead character Teresa "Terry" Dolittle leaps off the screen. Part of the behind-the-scenes tension concerned the impact of fellow actor Eddie Murphy, also a New Yorker, who had similarly moved from live stage performances to feature films during the 1980s. According to Goldberg, casting agents and film directors expected her to be a female version of Murphy (Rensin 58), who began his career as a stand-up comedian, became a legendary *Saturday Night Live* cast member, and coasted to even greater fortune and fame, starring in *Beverly Hills Cop* (1984) and its sequels. Asserting her originality, Goldberg insists that she is "not the black female answer to anybody," and that the studio brought in a succession of writers to help rework and revise the story of Terry Dolittle, to no avail. Goldberg says, "Very little of what you see on the screen was on paper. It was me" (Rensin 58).

Critics offered negative reviews of *Jumpin' Jack Flash*. One of the most scathing came from Donald Bogle, leading scholar of Black Americans on film and television, who describes Goldberg's character Terry Dolittle as "cultural[ly] rootless" and "romantically stranded." Moreover, he says that Goldberg "pops her eyes and screams like mad" and that this "is not too different from the comically fearful Butterfly McQueen [as Prissy] screaming that the Yankees is coming [in *Gone With the Wind*]" (Bogle 297). Bogle's views aside, perhaps the growing appeal of cable television also had an impact upon American tastes in film; what viewers could not necessarily fully appreciate on the big screen became not only acceptable, but expected, and even enjoyed, via the small screen. America's steadily growing interest in cable television created a new audience for Goldberg's performances. Viewed from a small-screen perspective, Goldberg's craft in *Jumpin' Jack Flash* makes contemporary television viewers jump to attention.

Goldberg breathes life into lead character Teresa "Terry" Dolittle. In direct contrast to her character's name, however, her ingenious reworking of the script does a lot to charm the viewer. As a data-entry clerk and self-styled tech support person, Dolittle may "do little" on the company's time and dime, but after hours (and largely using such wide-ranging equipment as a Sperry computer, an audio cassette deck and a cast-iron frying pan) she cracks an international espionage case and courts romance. Dolittle's work presages and parallels that of today's popular internet communications forms. Viewed from this perspective, *Jumpin' Jack Flash*, and Goldberg's character, are even more relevant today.

Three of the most important scenes showcasing Goldberg's acting abilities include the scene in which Terry cracks the code; the scene in which she fights off a corporate paper shredder; and the scene in which she uses a cast-iron skillet as both communications device and weapon. After intercepting a text message from a spy with the handle "Jumpin Jack Flash," she returns to her small, garish and cozy New York apartment, and places a Rolling Stones cassette into her stereo, blaring the song, "Jumpin' Jack Flash" to learn the lyrics, in the hopes of discovering the "key" to the case. Terry, wearing wild dreadlocks, a large yellow sweater and long scarf, blue jeans and large, fuzzy canary-yellow slippers, rewinds and replays the Stones' song again and again, dancing and singing loudly (and incorrectly) at points, and taking notes on the lyrics. When Mick Jagger sings about the narrator's upbringing, Terry misunderstands and exclaims, "What? I was raised by two lesbians?!" In frustration, she again rewinds and replays the tape, eventually abandoning the oral tradition and basic dictation in favor of obtaining commercially available sheet music. The sheet music reveals the "key" of the song — a building-block of Black American blues music tradition (a cornerstone of rock 'n' roll): the key of E-Flat. When Terry hits the right "key," the Sperry Computer sings along and scrolls information across the screen. Audiences sense Goldberg's genuine appreciation of rock 'n' roll, and are encouraged to sing along with Mick, Terry and the Sperry Computer.

Later in the film, Terry fights off a corporate paper shredder à la Tina Turner. By this point, the viewer has already seen Terry openly confront sexism, not only from her boss, who ignores her programming talents and sees her only as another pair of hands to input data, but also from Jack himself. As it turns out, Jack originally thought that the name Terry denoted a male; upon learning out that Terry is a woman, he e-mails her, telling her that she must stop following up on the case, as the work is "too dangerous." Terry quickly switches from joy to anger. The seriousness of Terry's response in this scene, wherein she refuses to be ignored because she is a woman, offsets her later, over-the-top, stereotypical images of women, in particular the glamour queen/wildwoman images.

3. An American Artist in Hollywood

In another scene, having previously been denied access to the gathering of dignitaries while wearing dreadlocks, neon yellow Reeboks and a man's black overcoat, she returns in new garb, declaring herself "the entertainment." Terry saunters into the British consulate, playing a tape of the Supremes on a Sony Walkman and lip-synching "You Can't Hurry Love." She extemporaneously grabs a woman's white husband as her "date" and passport for the evening.

Later, exiting the gala by way of a staircase, the slit in her royal blue strapless glitter gown showing all of one leg, her high heels tripping up the stairs, Terry, slyly tiptoes into a corporate office to retrieve an important printout from a dot-matrix printer. While she collects the printout, the hem of her gown gets caught in an industrial shredder, threatening to devour not only the clothes, but also the woman wearing them. Terry struggles to maintain her balance, her dignity and her clothing, her blonde, bouffant 'do quickly becoming a wild mane à la Tina Turner. The shredder's groans consume Terry's screams; the beast eats nearly all of the bottom of her gown, pulling it down into its eager jaws, nearly exposing her breasts and narrowly missing her crotch. "Not the crotch!" Terry, extemporaneously exclaims, pulling the gown so that she keeps her breasts covered. During this scene, viewers see Goldberg transform from Terry Dolittle-as-Diana Ross, to Terry Dolittle as Tina Turner, complete with torn-hem minidress and wildwoman wig.

In another scene, Goldberg skillfully subverts the mammy/Aunt Jemima image, using a cast-iron skillet as both communications device and weapon. Typically, in American popular television and film, the cast-iron skillet symbolizes home and hearth, and Mammy's willingness to comfort white families by making griddle cakes and other foods to order. In the capable hands of Goldberg, viewers find Terry Dolittle the very antithesis of the Mammy/Aunt Jemima; for while she flashes her wide eyes and grins (stereotypically conciliatory mannerisms), she does so with a determination and fierceness, instead illustrating the character's cleverness.

Using her self-styled super-sleuthing skills, Terry discovers Jack's New York digs. After entering his apartment and searching about, she locates a cast-iron skillet, and, using a steel-wool scrubbing pad, scratches the rust from its underside to reveal hidden clues to the case. Fending off menacing intruders, Terry deftly takes the frying pan and clunks the intruder on the head and flees the premises.

Throughout much of the film, Terry is seen working at a computer. Such scenes are taken for granted today, but we must remember that in 1986 this form of communication was relegated only to select, highly trained technicians and scientists. Breaking new ground, *Jumpin' Jack Flash* predated the phenomenon of Microsoft operating systems and America Online, as well as such films as *The Net* (1995) and *You've Got Mail* (1998). *The Net*, starring Sandra

Bullock, is an action film, in which a computer erases the lead character's identity. *You've Got Mail*, starring Tom Hanks and Meg Ryan, is a contemporary comedy in which e-mail communications foster an unlikely romance between two rival bookstore owners, one corporate and the other independent; through the computer, the corporate executive and independent bookstore owner see each other as human beings, and not solely as business competition. Goldberg's role in *Jumpin' Jack Flash* piqued common American interest in computer-based communications technology.

In *Burglar* (1987), Goldberg plays a role originally designed for a male actor: Hollywood action star Bruce Willis. As Bernice ("Bernie") Rhodenbarr, a former thief blackmailed by a crooked former police chief, into performing one last heist, she uses her improvisation skills to great effect, despite the film's odd and inconsistent direction. Vincent Canby, of the *New York Times*, called *Burglar* "a wasteland for everyone in it," including Goldberg and her co-star Bobcat Goldthwait, who plays a dog-groomer/Bernie's best friend, and Lesley Ann Warren, who makes a cameo appearance as a dense dentist. In particular, Canby harbors resentment toward the oddly layered story line, the "demands" of which "keep interfering so Miss Goldberg never gets a chance to establish any identity whatsoever" (Canby). The critic's dissatisfaction with the film stems from the fact that its structure and premise are far beneath Goldberg's talent. In fact, Canby begins his overview of *Burglar* by mentioning her tour-de-force performance as lead character in the Alice Walker/Steven Spielberg film adaptation of *The Color Purple*; he also later mentions Goldberg's general "tonal elegance" and "character riffs" included in her successful one-woman Broadway show, *Whoopi: Direct from Broadway*. Moreover, he writes, *Burglar* unnecessarily and unsuccessfully makes direct parallels with Eddie Murphy's wildly successful films *Trading Places* and *Beverly Hills Cop*.

The slapstick, over-the-top nature of the film, even in the face of its unevenness, carries well when viewed on the small screen; in that medium, Goldberg's talent shines. It is not so much that she does not develop the character of Bernie (as Canby asserts); instead, the television audience readily identifies with the lead character, a woman placed in odd circumstances and surviving one ridiculous caper after another. On the small screen, Bernie comes alive, especially when playing opposite her former boss, the crooked San Francisco police chief Ray. In Scene 4, "Squeezed by Ray," we see Bernie's sensible side, opposite Ray's senseless insistence. In that scene, Ray is determined to collect $20,000 from Bernie, as the original buyer of the jewels which Bernie had stolen is dead. Ray gives Bernie a mere seven days to find a buyer for the hot rocks. In a matter-of-fact voice, Bernie makes it clear that she will not lose her cool or kill anyone unnecessarily just to make good on a trumped-up promise. Instead, she hawks the jewels with a pawn broker, who gives her information even more valuable: the identity and whereabouts of a female dentist willing to pay $10,000 cash to anyone willing to steal back the dentist's jewelry from her ex-husband.

One of the funniest scenes in *Burglar* takes place when Bernie, stealing back the dentist's jewels, inadvertently witnesses a murder. In that scene, Goldberg's wide-eyed shock and disbelief are a welcome, sharp contrast to her cucumber-cool stance as professional thief. While confined to a closet (with plantation shutter-style doors, to let in air and just enough light for viewers to see her), the actor makes it clear that, while Bernie has theft all figured out, murder is quite another issue.

Regardless of their initial reviews and box-office performances, the vast majority of Goldberg's Hollywood films have found new life on the small screen, especially given the growing popularity of cable television. Thus, the kinds of artistic, aesthetic, financial and social demands which a typical American viewer might naturally impose upon a theatrical release fall away; in the small-screen world of home-popped popcorn, potato chips, soda and the family sofa, films like *Burglar* are right at home. However unevenly conceived and initially received, *Burglar* was far from career ending.

Fatal Beauty, also released in 1987, reflects a similar fate. Goldberg plays detective Rita Rizzoli, opposite Sam Elliott, tracking down a public menace in the form of an illicit drug of the same name. *Fatal Beauty* received mixed reviews, such as that written by Janet Maslin, who declares that the shortcomings of the film are "not Miss Goldberg's fault, because Miss Goldberg is funny whenever she's given half a chance" (Maslin). According to Maslin, the many faults of the film include its rapid-fire succession of "guns and moronic thugs ... in a plot that seems intended to keep the audience awake," as well as its overall, unoriginal timbre and stance, à la Eddie Murphy in *Beverly Hills Cop*.

One example of the wit woven throughout *Fatal Beauty* is found in the opening scene, "Undercover Cop." In that scene, Detective Rita Rizzoli poses as a hooker, outfitted in a big, auburn-colored wig, a banana-yellow stretch tank minidress, red glitter pumps, a black and white polka-dot/silver swing coat, and oversized white-framed cat glasses, and carrying a huge, hobo-style shoulder bag. Despite this get-up, the viewer soon comes to learn that Rizzoli is the real deal. Working as part of an elaborate stakeout, attempting to penetrate the inner workings of Delgado, Fatal Beauty's chief distributor, she is wired, with several police officers listening in on the deal from a remote van. When the situation turns rough, Rizzoli gets tough: when one of the men curses her and tells her to go back to Africa, she shoots him, point-blank, and tells him, "And don't call me bitch." As Rizzoli, Goldberg intentionally strikes a necessary balance between farce and fierceness.

Goldberg's work as Vashti Blue in *The Telephone* (1988), a little-known film, is also noteworthy for its intense drama in the midst of ridiculousness. Unfortunately mis-marketed as a slapstick comedy, *The Telephone* is best understood as a dark comedy-drama, slowly revealing its lead character's descent into madness. Actually, *The Telephone* is, by far, the most misunderstood and underrated Whoopi Goldberg film. Directed by Rip Torn, *The Telephone* explores the far reaches of a mind encased in stark realities of poverty, urban decay and death. In the film, an actual telephone connects a woman to everyday life and everyday realities, while also ironically disconnecting her from such. At its start, we see Goldberg's character, Vashti Blue, walking about the city; stepping sprightly, she banters and bounds down the street, quickly addressing shop-keeps and even a rooftop owl. Wearing an Oxford shirt, dark pants, blue skullcap, purple crew-neck sweater and dreadlocks, she loans money to help an actor friend who needs the funds for a costume fitting. The viewer gets the impression that Blue is late for an appointment; she must make haste, lest she miss it. As viewers soon come to learn, however, Blue's "appointment" is not with an actual person, but rather, the telephone. The majority of the action and crux of the story take place in Vashti's darkened apartment, where the telephone takes center stage.

Vashti, a name derived from the Sanskrit which appears in the Biblical book of Esther, means "beautiful, the queen of Ahasuerus, who was deposed from her royal dignity because she refused to obey the king when he desired her to appear in the banqueting hall of Shushan the palace (Esther 1:10–12)" ("Vashti"). "Vashti comes from the Hebrew word *shtei*, meaning two" (Pessi). Moreover, "Vashti understood feminism thousands of years before it was given a name. Realizing the sexism of the fact that Ahasuerus made a party for only the men of Persia, she decided to level the playing field and make an equal party for the women.... [She was] an extremely proud, headstrong woman; there was no way that she would debase herself by dancing for Ahasuerus' drunken friends. She didn't refuse because she suddenly developed a skin ailment, but because she was a self-respecting woman" (Pessi). During ancient times, Vashti's refusal made her a pariah; it also marked her as a woman seen through two different lenses: through one lens, despised (for refusing to adopt a subservient role); through another, revered, for making her own decisions. In the film, Vashti's surname, "Blue," connotes the celestial sphere; wide oceans/sea change and a general, melancholy state of being. The fictional character Vashti Blue is, then, an embodiment of contradictions — and Goldberg successfully conveys them all.

The playful side of Vashti Blue is seen when she interacts with her lively pet goldfish, Moby (ostensibly named for Moby-Dick) and stern pet owl, Bert (the same owl that she greets during the film's opening scene). In one scene, she scoops Moby out of his fishbowl and introduces him to her bathtub (located in the living area of the tiny apartment). Promptly disrobing to bathe,

3. An American Artist in Hollywood

she admonishes Moby not to suck her toes. While she bathes, the audience hears the voice of a bill collector loudly demanding payment for the phone bill, to which Vashti responds with, "Up yours, crohn!" Disturbed and distracted, Vashti pulls the plug on the tub, and Moby goes down the drain. Vashti quickly uses a plunger to rescue her scaly golden friend, and reintroduces him to his fishbowl, where Moby regains his vitality. The water and fish going down the drain serve as foreshadowing — a metaphor for Vashti's deteriorating mental state.

Observant viewers find that Vashti Blue, like her Biblical namesake, also embodies duality: one, regret that critics ignored the acting talents of her lover, Larry, a fellow actor; and that Vashti's own career stalled because of her steadfast refusal to sleep with film producers and her determination to be treated as an artist in her own right. As Vashti speaks of this to her friend Jen, via the zebra-striped, plastic telephone, the fish and owl become Vashti's cheering squad, echoing her declaration of wanting all the world "now" (14.00). Slowly but surely, the audience is encouraged to cheer for Vashti, too.

Despite her willingness to give money to a struggling fellow actor, Vashti is broke. When she looks into the bare refrigerator, she accuses the owl and goldfish of "raiding the fridge" and smoking her Marlboro cigarettes. Improvising, Goldberg, as Vashti, announces that she will simply call Cora's Market and request groceries and sundry items. Returning to the telephone receiver, she initially insists that she is cutting back on cigarettes, and finally succumbs to order a whole carton of them, as well as eggs, mints, cheese, mayonnaise, milk, flour, butter, sugar, salt and pepper. She then proceeds to call the meat market. Affecting an East Indian speaking accent, she makes a corny, improvised joke regarding "New Deli" ("New Delhi"), in relation to "Old Deli" (23:00). Here, Goldberg's improvising moves from corny to crass, as she asks the meat man about his "meat" (penis). The exasperated meat man apparently hangs up on the crank caller.

Goldberg's zany sense of humor commands the next scene, however; in that scene, Vashti temporarily leaves the telephone and enters the tiny kitchen, pretending to have all needs supplied, imagines herself a Benihana hibachi grill master of the "House of Yap." While she loudly whoops it up as a so-called grill master, a white American neighbor in the next-door apartment, annoyed by all the noise, calls Vashti a "nigger," and warns her that a phone call to the police department is imminent. Vashti responds that she is merely "entertaining" show business friends and that she is "not crazy." In this scene, the seams of Vashti's personality begin to show, with her open denial of her steady descent into madness proof-positive of the madness itself.

Further examples of Vashti's mental deterioration appear when she creates a one-woman house party, including such imagined friends as Leroy Brown, Helga, the Contessa, and Penelope Potter, "First Grand Dame of the Theater."

Here, Goldberg not only calls into being those characters, she also punctuates their theatrical existence by quoting from Shakespeare's *King Richard II*: "I wasted time, and now doth time waste me" (Shakespeare 380). Vashti illustrates the wasting of time by writing hashmarks upon the wall, totaling the number of days, to date, that she has not worked. Goldberg's delivery of the Shakespeare excerpt creates a plausible moment of temporary lucidity for Vashti.

In the next scene, Vashti briefly recalls her rational self and, returning to the telephone, acknowledges her debt, conceding to a "Mrs. Butterworth," on the other end of the line, that her acting profession places her in a "high-risk" credit category. Exasperated, Vashti ends the call to Mrs. Butterworth, and again calls her friend Jen, this time for money. The viewer hears Jen offering Vashti her wedding ring to pawn. Vashti then calls her mother, only to find that she, too, is broke (40:26). The scene ends with the viewer becoming acutely aware that Vashti has no money and very little food; nevertheless, it appears that she has tenuously strung together and hung onto electrical and telephone services — small rays of hope.

Two of the remaining scenes of the film show Vashti as broke and broken in mind, if not in spirit. At one point, Rodney, her ex-agent, comes to visit with his muse, Miss Honey Boxe, a blonde bimbo, in tow. Having seen Vashti deftly move between classical and contemporary characters, many of her own devising, the audience wonders why she has been out of work for so long. Rodney, noting Vashti's poverty (and smoking her very last cigarette, without so much as asking permission) tries to pressure her into having sex with a film producer, to which Vashti responds by mocking the Biblical Salomé (Dance of the Seven Veils), calling it "The Dance of the Seven Flatulences," and openly decrying not only Rodney's having taken her last cigarette; but also film producers' and agents' selfishness and exploitive tactics.

Vashti's lively characterizations of imagined figures and interactions with Rodney show the audience that it is not lack of talent which thwarts her acting career; rather, her steadfast unwillingness to have sex with film producers and kowtow to agents are the primary impediments. Like the Vashti of ancient times, Vashti Blue refuses to play the game (or dance the dance, so to speak); as a result, she suffers social death. The departures of Rodney and Miss Honey Boxe from the apartment result in tangible loneliness for the film's lead character, courtesy of Goldberg's nuanced interpretations.

In the closing scenes of the film, Vashti mentions first her loneliness (1:03:11) and then her dependence upon the telephone. The director of the film parallels such by making a direct reference to James Baldwin's play, *Blues for Mister Charlie*, which brings to bear the "blues" in Vashti Blue's life. Watching Diana Sands portray a lead character in the televised version of the play, Vashti concludes that Sands's authentic portrayal of the blues meant that she, too, had "probably had" a love(r) like Vashti's Larry. She then returns to the "party," pretending to entertain five people. Once again, the white neighbor screams and warns of calling the police to report Vashti's disturbing the peace. Meanwhile, Vashti, using a hair dryer, blows a fuse and first lights candles to illuminate the dark; she then uses an extension cord to "reconnect" to the larger world. Symbolically speaking, while Vashti increasingly becomes disconnected from the larger world, she uses extension cords to "borrow" electricity from a hallway socket, recalling the words of Christ on the cross, "God — why have you forsaken me?" The actor's words lose their force however, with the unfortunate, overdone choice of musical underscore: "I'm So Lonesome I Could Cry."

The final scene of the film shows Vashti Blue's final descent into madness. During that scene, the telephone company representative first demands, then forces, entry into her apartment, presenting Vashti with a double-entendre: "Are you Blue?" (as in, "Are you Vashti Blue?" and "Are you melancholy?"). The man then scolds Vashti for her use of "illegal wiring," and begins to confiscate the telephone. Goldberg imbues Vashti with a desperation not before seen, and begs the man to allow her to keep the phone, for survival's sake. The man declares that the telephone line has been dead for more than two months; moreover, the equipment belongs to the phone company, to be confiscated at their leisure. Quickly moving from desperation to action, Vashti beats the man with the telephone receiver; defending her, Bert the Owl attacks the man as well. Grabbing a knife, Vashti stabs the man to death. In operatic fashion, the man opines that it makes no sense for her to kill him over a mere telephone (1:17:33). Reclaiming the telephone receiver, Vashti "calls" the operator, calmly asking to be connected to the police. She confesses to have been "a bad girl," and then pledges to hold the line. The owl and the viewer are the only living witnesses to her crimes.

Caryn James of the *New York Times* sharply criticized the film, beginning with the title, "Sorry, Wrong Number" (a double-entendre describing the film's disconnection from audiences and making a pun regarding the 1948 Hollywood film of the same name). James says that the film is a poorly rendered adaptation of an aspect of a dramatic, unattributed play, called, *The Human Voice*. The critic continues: "The truest, most sanely existential lines spoken during the film came from the audience on Friday night. 'I want my money back,' one person yelled, which encouraged another to say, 'I hope the film breaks'" (James). Beyond the film's lack of original plot, James says that Goldberg's improvisation is shallow and "scattershot," in sharp contrast to the robust characters which the actor honed during her one-woman Broadway show. James continues by saying that not even a dozen people attended the screening. Such may have been the result of a lawsuit which Goldberg filed against New World Pictures, to stop the film's distribution, with the argument that she "had approval of the final cut" (James). Goldberg's lawsuit was unsuccessful, however (James). Regardless of the legal issues, the film critic says that editing could not have saved the film. Neither the original audience, nor today's general audience, could fully appreciate the film; its references to Shakespeare and the Bible make it more suited to specialized audiences, such as that which appreciated the original stage play upon which the film is based. Audience is key, especially where popular film is concerned.

Black American audiences sharply criticized Goldberg's role as lead character Clara Mayfield, in *Clara's Heart* (1988). Goldberg explains: "I never said I wouldn't play a maid. I said that I wouldn't *just* play maids. But in the words of Hattie McDaniel, 'Better to play one than to be one'" (Sheff). She reminds us that the roles offered to black actors are not usually the most desirable; that neither McDaniel nor she had been regularly offered epic dramatic roles; and that black actors then and now must make the best of very slim pickings. Continues Goldberg, "I've never played a maid who wasn't a lead in the movie. And the story of these women, who clean other people's houses and take care of their children, is a worthy one to tell" (Sheff). She concludes by saying that she must seek work for herself in order to find worthwhile roles (Sheff).

Clara's Heart tells the story of Clara Mayfield, a Jamaican immigrant and single mother of a mysteriously absent son, who works as a maid for a white, wealthy family living the good life in the suburbs of Baltimore. Goldberg's portrayal of Clara Mayfield, and the complexity of the story, shows that Clara is much more than a maid; rather, Mayfield initially becomes the confidant of the white woman who employs her, and later the absolute lifeline for the woman's little boy, David, who becomes Clara's "heart." Strictly viewed from a stereotypical standpoint, one may hastily conclude that Goldberg is simply playing another mammy figure; in literature and film, a mammy always ignores her own family while strictly attending to every whim of her white employers. John McWhorter reminds us, however, not to jump to conclusions regarding racial stereotypes, even when the typical ingredients for such appear to be present:

> The "New Double-Consciousness" imperative to seek rot behind all black success has led to a tradition among black thinkers to numbly frame all black popular performances as "stereotypes" ... The saddest thing is when the "stereotype" obsession relegates valuable work to footnotes when it does not fit the program [McWhorter 206–207].

Such is the case with reviews of *Clara's Heart*. Janet Maslin of the *New York Times* praises Goldberg's performance: "Directed by Robert Mulligan in an unapologetically sentimental style, 'Clara's Heart' succeeds in tugging the heartstrings only when Clara herself is on screen" (Maslin). Maslin further says that other characters in the film appear predictable and lifeless. Black audiences saw the film through a different lens, however; summarizing such a phenomenon, Donald Bogle says, "Goldberg gave a well-crafted, convincing performance. But the script desexed her character, presenting the black woman once again as a mighty nurturer — an updated mammy — without enough of a life of her own" (Bogle 298). Taking McWhorter's admonishment into account, and viewing the film through today's lens, Bogle's words regarding the story's structure are unduly harsh, and do not take into account the on-screen chemistry between Goldberg (as Clara) and Neil Patrick Harris (as David).

In one crucial scene in *Clara's Heart*, while Clara is away visiting friends in Baltimore, David unpacks Clara's hidden suitcase, only to find personal correspondence. Reading the correspondence, he learns that Clara had a son in Jamaica, who had raped her and later committed suicide by jumping into the ocean. He also learns that such an experience tainted Clara in Jamaican society, leading her to forge a new identity in the United States; in fact, as viewers (and later, David) come to learn, some of Clara's Jamaican acquaintances, also émigrés to the United States, continue to ridicule her in Baltimore.

In another, related scene, taking place after Clara returns from her solo sojourn into Baltimore, David enters Clara's room, where he finds Clara seated upon the side of her twin bed, fully clothed, but wearing a shift which exposes her legs. After the two have a very basic, everyday conversation, David slowly moves his hand up Clara's bare leg, in an apparent attempt to explore Clara sexually. Clara, shocked, immediately scolds him, and banishes him from her room. It is clear that Clara feels violated on several levels: first, because her private correspondence has been read without her permission; second, because her room is subject to search and seizure; and third, because her employer's young son threatens the sanctity of her body. How Bogle can proclaim that Clara is "desexed," after watching the aforementioned scene, is puzzling. Actually, the scene establishes Clara as a sexual being, and David as a boy experiencing and expressing sexual awareness.

Goldberg said of *Clara's Heart*: "It's a nice movie, without any violence. It's not going to cure cancer, but it's a nice movie. And they killed it. The critics killed it. They said it wasn't funny enough. When you do the fun ones, they say it's not serious enough. And when you do the serious ones, they say it's not serious enough. God, you get to the point where you know what? ---k you!" (Chutkow). She keeps strutting along, regardless.

One of the movies in which she struts her stuff as capable actor is *Homer and Eddie* (1988) — a typical Hollywood buddy film, with the exception that Eddie, edgily played by Goldberg, opposite Jim Belushi's sensitive "Homer," is a woman. Throughout much of the movie, gender differences take a backseat to the overall quest that each has to find his or her "home." While Belushi's even characterization of Homer is, at times, lightly reminiscent of the character Lennie Small in John Steinbeck's novel, *Of Mice and Men* (1937), Goldberg's Eddie is completely and refreshingly offbeat, striking a necessary balance.

Homer and Eddie concerns Homer, a special-needs man on a mission to visit his terminally ill father in Oregon, and his chance encounter with Eddie, a self-described "escaped mental patient" (45:11) with a debilitating brain tumor, who becomes Homer's vehicle toward Oregon and a renewed sense of self. As the story begins, we see Homer asking a favor of God, to allow him to hitch a ride to Oregon; at the start of his sojourn, he twice becomes a victim of theft; thieves steal his last $87. Afterward, hopping about, alone, on a dirt road, he obtains a ride from an oil truck driver, who makes a pit stop at a restaurant. While there, Homer, homeless and hungry, tries to steal snack foods; the lady who catches him releases him. Exhausted, Homer seeks shelter in an old Lincoln Continental. The next morning finds the car's owner, Eddie, reclaiming her vehicle and confronting Homer.

After physically striking Homer, she commences to rummage through his pockets, looking for money; finding none, she pointedly asks him where he is going, especially given the fact that he, like she, is penniless. When she learns of Homer's situation and plan, she brokers an agreement with him: she will take him to Oregon, and, while en route, confront the thieves who stole Homer's money, as payment for the ride.

The evenness of Belushi's characterization of Homer contrasts sharply against the erratic, insistent nature of Goldberg's Eddie; in fact, Belushi casts Homer in feminine terms, while Goldberg portrays Eddie with a masculine tone. Gender identity specifically comes to the fore in Scene 2, when we learn that Eddie is short for "Edwina," which Eddie declares is a "girl's name"; she then teases Homer by insinuating that he is homosexual: "Homo; Homo Lanza — that's you." The interplay of feminine/masculine aspects help to convey the complexity of Belushi's and Goldberg's respective characterizations and the overall story.

Goldberg adopts a convincing overall masculine stance, as Eddie, ranging from her physical appearance to her behavior; such is in sharp contrast to her innate sensitivity, which, like her illness and poverty, she deliberately masks. For example, at one point, Eddie facetiously declares that she is a Christian Scientist; at another point, Eddie passes a stolen Diner's Club credit card, pretending that she does not know that the account is overdrawn. Later, viewers also learn that she feels the pain of being a motherless child. An Oakland native, Eddie has not seen her alcoholic mother, Linda Cervi, in a decade; Cervi, Eddie learns, has died, having foreseen her own death and written her own epitaph. While visiting her grave, Eddie hallucinates that her mother (played by Beah Richards), comes to visit her, asserting the goodness of death and beseeching Homer to "take care of [Eddie]."

Homer symbolizes the regular, normal aspects of life, while Eddie represents the storms of life. For example, at a restroom stop, Homer's simple offer of a toothbrush to Eddie is met with a brusque brush-off; belligerent, Eddie offers a wide-eyed response, babbling about attorneys, psychiatrists and nuns "out there" and bashing her head against a bathroom mirror. (Goldberg, as Eddie, effectively illustrates the irrelevance of such normal activities as teeth-brushing, against the backdrop of a world weary with pestilence, hurricanes, disease, and the like.) Homer patches Eddie's bloody head, caring for her as family — their caring relationship, emphasizing shared humanity, creates stability amid very turbulent circumstances.

In *Whoopi Goldberg: Fontaine ... Why Am I Straight?* (1988), Goldberg returns to her roots in live comedic improvisation, revisiting one of her most beloved characters. Fontaine had been nationally unveiled in her HBO special, *Whoopi Goldberg: Direct from Broadway* (1985). In *Fontaine ... Why Am I Straight?*, Goldberg deliberately blurs the lines between class and gender, beginning with the title of the performance. The term "straight," as Goldberg uses it in reference to her character Fontaine, alternately and simultaneously refers to gender (as in, *Why is Fontaine not a homosexual?*); drug use (as in, *Why is Fontaine not doing drugs?*); and finances (as in, *Why is Fontaine financially solvent?*). Fans of Fontaine soon come to learn that all of the previous questions are purely rhetorical, with Fontaine's nonchalant attitude toward life prevailing. For Fontaine has an earned Ph.D. in American literature from Columbia University, and, given her lack of social status as a black person and junkie, no possible way of gaining social status through its use, either inside or outside the formal classroom. Instead, Goldberg uses Fontaine as a cautionary tale, to teach audiences what social marginalization and prejudice can do to people.

Playing the role of Sarah Collins in *Kiss Shot*, Whoopi Goldberg effectively characterizes a hard-working single mother who revives her competitive skills as a pool shark to help save her family from financial ruin. In Chapter 1, viewers learn that Sarah, a Dunsley Electronics employee, has suddenly lost her job due to outsourcing in Taiwan, only to end up waitressing. Visiting the Bank of the West, Sarah learns that unless she is able to make a balloon payment of $7500 within four months then she and her daughter will lose their home. Sarah matter-of-factly tells Mr. Cloy, the bank officer, that the ultimatum that the bank offers is not "fair." Afterward, while recounting her experience, Sarah garners sympathy from her restaurant colleagues — but no cash.

Chapter 2 finds Goldberg effectively bringing to life the additional conflicts that Sarah endures: beyond the issues of employment and housing, she also illustrates Sarah's conflicts with her parents, who are angry that she has kept her 13-year-old daughter, Jenny (their granddaughter), from them. Sarah's father is especially bitter and refuses to loan her the money she needs, while her mother loans her all the ready cash she has on-hand: $80. A thankful Sarah reluctantly accepts the funds and strengthens her resolve to be self-reliant. The film's title comes into play as Sarah, with Jenny in tow, enters Westside Billiards Coffee Shop — the place where Sarah met her daughter's father; it was there that she learned to shoot pool, in an effort to get him to notice her. Passing on the family tradition, Sarah teaches Jenny to "shoot at 1 and sink the 9" — perform the "Kiss Shot." The resolve of Whoopi Goldberg, as Sarah, parallels that which Sarah has already brought to bear in her exchanges with the officers of Dunsley Electronics and the bank, respectively. When Jenny applauds her mother's billiards skills and laments, "Too bad you can't get paid for it," the actor's tangible shift of focus from playing billiards to playing the larger game is palpable. Future scenes show Goldberg, as Sarah, broadening her scope.

In Chapter 3, she convinces her longtime family friend, the Westside Billiards' bartender, Billy, that she is ready to compete professionally, on a part-time basis. While he doubts her readiness, she convinces him that she is a quick study and has no choice. In Chapter 4, Sarah is on the road, facing off with a variety of billiards competitors, in honky-tonk joints — she fends for herself fairly well, but does not fit in, as a woman and as a black person. Securing an agent, whose name is Max, enables Sarah to seek upscale, more lucrative venues, where, arguably, her growing billiards skills would overshadow gender and race. At one point, however, while shooting pool at the home of a wealthy businessman, she falls for a black man whom she mistakenly assumes is the doorman — Kevin Merrick (Dorian Harewood), a wealthy insurance company heir and an amateur billiards player. Tension ensues when Sarah throws a game, enabling Kevin to win the $1,000 prize. Kevin wishes to date Sarah, but she effectively conveys her independence and determination to make her own way. She calmly and convincingly explains to Kevin that she does not wish to be his dessert (Ch. 5). Tension ensues as Kevin tries to help Sarah; meanwhile, her daughter Jenny and co-workers at the restaurant encourage her to pursue the relationship with Kevin. Later in the film, the ultimate showdown has the two billiards enthusiasts facing off against each other, for a cash prize of $7,500 — enough to enable Sarah to keep her home. Will Sarah win at billiards and love? The acting chemistry between Goldberg and Harewood, as well as the unusual story line, keep viewers engaged.

Goldberg made history when she played the role of Oda Mae Brown, the corny, sensitive psychic who gains confidence in herself and her latent soothsaying skills by working on behalf of Sam, the banker, in *Ghost* (1990). Had it not been for the stalwart support of lead actor Patrick Swayze, however, the film would have been very different, and Goldberg's 1991 Best Supporting Actress Oscar win never would have happened. Ironically, Swayze was not the favorite for the part of Sam–in fact, he had heard "through the grapevine"

(Leigh 122) that the director, Jerry Zucker, was envisioning someone else for the part — Kevin Kline, who was working on another project at the time. Nevertheless, in the spirit of friendship, Zucker allowed Swayze to audition for the role; Swayze, stereotyped as a unidimensional actor because of his convincing cowboy role in *Road House*, gave the audition his all, seeing it as a "challenge" (Leigh 124) to prove his acting range. Moreover, Swayze also deeply believed in the film's overall theme of life after death: "I am convinced," he said, "that people who are dead can come back and visit loved ones. Death is a beginning, not an ending" (Leigh 121). During the audition, Swayze convincingly conveyed his undying love for the character Molly, played by Janet Hershenson (Leigh 122). Concluded Zucker, after witnessing such a stellar audition, "There's no one who can deliver a heartfelt line like Patrick" (Leigh 123). In the film, Demi Moore replaced Meg Ryan "who turned down the part of Molly"; moreover, "Molly Ringwald and Nicole Kidman also auditioned for it without success" (Leigh 124). The on-screen chemistry between the principal actors of *Ghost*— Patrick Swayze, Demi Moore and Goldberg — resonates through generations.

The irony of Swayze's nearly missing the pivotal role, combined with his enthusiasm for Goldberg's energy, creates an interesting backdrop for exploring how she finally landed the character. Originally, producers preferred Tina Turner and Oprah Winfrey for the role. Goldberg says, when her friend, also an actor, told her that "they have dug up black women out of the grave" to cast the role, she wondered why she did not know about it. Upon contacting her agent, she learned that she was not informed about the role because, the agent said, "They don't want you" (A&E Ch. 4). But, Goldberg says, Patrick Swayze "knew I was right for this part. You know, we had never met. But he liked what I did and he knew I was right and there was some resistance" (Leigh 123). At the time, she was on location in Alabama filming *The Long Walk Home* opposite Sissy Spacek. Swayze had to convince reluctant producers that Goldberg could play more than just comedy; she could also play serious drama. "Patrick managed to persuade Jerry to reconsider Whoopi, and together they flew to Alabama ... to discuss the possibilities" (Leigh 123).

> "Whoopi and I had an incredible rapport during the visit," Patrick recalled, "and after I left, I called her to let her know that over my dead body would anybody else do that role." A grateful Whoopi later elaborated, "Patrick said, 'I'm not doing it unless she does it.' He fought, stomped, kicked, and screamed, to make sure I got the part and I won an Oscar because of Patrick Swayze.... I love being with Patrick," she went on. "He's easy to be around, great to be with. Not in the biblical sense, of course. But it did cross my mind" [Leigh 123].

The rapport between Goldberg and Swayze was palpable, both on and off-screen. In recalling the experience, Swayze quipped, with a grin, that if he were not already married, he would have considered marrying her; besides, he explains, "She does like white boys. So, I thought I had a chance" (A&E Ch. 4).

Chemistry between the actors notwithstanding, shooting scenes in which Oda Mae Brown senses, but does not actually see, Sam's presence, was difficult. "Not looking at Patrick was very hard and sort of crazy-making," Goldberg remembered. "Every once in a while we would do a scene and he would tell me I was looking at Patrick. I would tell him, 'No, I'm not.' So we would shoot the scene again, and I would be looking all around trying not to look at Patrick" (Leigh 124). Such offers a stark contrast against her earlier work in *Jumpin' Jack Flash*, in which there were scenes that required her to pretend she was speaking to an actual person, when in reality, all that appeared before her was a computer screen.

A classic scene from *Ghost* shows Goldberg seated in front of a bank executive, wearing a ladies' suit and a wig of long, dark, relaxed hair, topped with a lavender-colored fez/pillbox hat, requesting a major withdrawal of funds, on behalf of Sam. (Such clothing is in sharp contrast to the stereotypical dashikis and bold costume jewelry that usually adorn Oda Mae's body.) As Sam "speaks" to her, standing behind her chair, Oda Mae interprets his requests with a playful seriousness that nearly ruins the exchange. At one point, when Oda Mae requests a withdrawal of $4 million, she tells the bank officer that she prefers that the funds be disbursed in "tens and twenties." The viewer is encouraged to laugh; but the intensity of Swayze's glare and whisper of a voice, demanding that Oda Mae instead request a "cashier's check," reins in the laughter, creating tension. Says Goldberg, "Patrick and Demi are different types of actors than I am. They need more space and quiet between scenes. But I like a lot of noise and bad jokes" (Leigh 124). Her comedic timing, in concert with Swayze's intensity, creates a kind of beautiful "noise," fostering an enjoyable theatrical "dance" between the actors. Winning the Oscar did not mean, however, that she would abandon non-starring roles, however.

On the heels of *Ghost*, Goldberg played a small but meaningful role in *Soap Dish* (1991). For 15 years, Rose Schwartz (Goldberg) has worked as head writer on *The Sun Also Sets* (a pun on the title of the Hemingway novel, *The Sun Also Rises*). Hilarity ensues when Celeste Talbert (Sally Field), the longest-lasting actress on the daytime drama, worries that her real-life adult daughter, who plays a mute on the show, may be falling for an older co-star, Jeffrey Anderson (Kevin Kline). A ladies' man formally written off the show, Anderson has recently returned from starring as Willie Loman, in a faraway dinner theater production of Arthur Miller's *Death of a Salesman*, staged especially for retirees. (Unknown to all, except Celeste, is the fact that Anderson is actually the biological father of the young woman.) Meanwhile, a younger actress on the show, determined to steal Celeste's thunder, surreptitiously works with a junior writer, to rewrite the scripts for the show, to highlight *her* acting abilities and thwart Celeste's on-screen time. Caught in the middle is Rose Schwartz, longtime friend of Celeste, who tries to calm Celeste and struggles to make the on-screen storyline make sense and take precedence over backstage antics. At one point, the unauthorized script calls for a beheaded character to be brought back to life. Even though she did not write the script, Rose, as head writer, is required to make such happen. Rose emphatically exclaims that, while she is a very good writer and has years of experience, even *she* cannot convincingly bring a beheaded character back to life.

Goldberg's convincing delivery of her lines, combined with stereotypically Jewish comedic hand gestures, offer a sharp contrast to Rose's generally calm, cool, collected, professional demeanor (also a departure from stereotypical portrayals of black women on the big screen). Beyond noting the humor of Goldberg, a black woman, portraying a Jewish woman, original audiences of *Soap Dish*, identifying with Celeste, undoubtedly recalled the decades-long work of Susan Lucci, who for decades made the *All My Children* character Erica Kane one of the soap opera world's most loved/hated mavens.

The Player (1992) tells the story of Griffin Mill (Tim Robbins), a successful, smug Hollywood studio executive, who, having rejected a film treatment, unwittingly plays a role in helping an unknown writer blackmail him. As Detective Avery, Goldberg begins by appealing to the viewer's sense of irony, in Chapter 13, "Pasadena PD": visiting the movie studio where Griffin Mill works, Avery awaits his arrival in an executive meeting room, which includes a small table, upon which two Oscar statues stand, flanking an unidentified lucite statuette. As the camera focuses upon the awards, Avery asks permission to hold one of the Oscars. The camera catches her hands gently and eagerly gripping the left statue with both hands; from off-camera, the audience hears her exclaiming how heavy the statue is; the camera then focuses upon a wide shot, showing Detective Avery holding the Oscar, flanked by her partner and another studio executive, giving an extemporaneous acceptance speech as Griffin Mill enters. The studio executive explains to Mill that this time marks the detective's first opportunity to visit an actual movie studio. Avery then wanly expresses her desire to direct Hollywood films, as she has so often taken her family on the Universal Studios tour. (This scene undoubtedly left original viewers with a comic sense of irony; most filmgoers would have known and remembered Goldberg's recent Oscar win.) As the scene unfolds, Avery and her partner are ushered into another part of the office, away from the awards, and viewers are introduced to a very serious detective, wearing a wig of mid-length, naturally curly black hair, black pencil skirt, oversized, shoulder-padded cinnamon-patterned boyfriend jacket, coordinating solid blouse and faux pearls, brown wooden-soled clogs and heavy black knee socks. It is clear that Detective Avery is a middle-class, hard-working, hard-nosed cop, hardly star-struck, and determined to get to the bottom of a murder case in which Griffin Mill is a person of interest. Avery's battery of questions directed toward Mill indicates Goldberg's ability to smoothly shift gears within a scene — no longer the star-struck visitor, Detective Avery is in her element, asking tough questions. Goldberg's matter-of-fact stance brings gravitas to the situation and actually makes Mill seem like a visitor on his own turf.

Goldberg's creative process, scope and position remind us of Henry Louis Gates's insistence upon the centrality of the black poet-musician as interpreter and projector of culture. Gates says, "Because of the nature of black poetic expression ... the black poet is far more than a mere point of consciousness of the community. He or she is a point of consciousness of the language ... transcend[ing] his or her political reality and arriv[ing] at the core of the community's values and way of life" (Gates 178). Gates's statement applies to Goldberg in many ways; a self-described "comic" (Goldberg 6) and "actor" (Goldberg 33), she uses a poetic, nuanced approach to realizing the fictional character. Such is not a contradiction, however; for Black American literature emerges from the oral/aural tradition; its earliest manifestations include riddles, rhymes, cries, hollers, songs, poems, and narratives — the very literary forms upon which Goldberg especially based her early stage work and continues to draw. A global citizen, her "community" extends beyond her Chelsea, Manhattan, beginnings to encompass America and the larger world.

In "Whipping Whoopi," in *Toms, Coons, Mulattoes, Mammies & Bucks* (2008), Donald Bogle writes that, despite Goldberg's consistent starring roles in Hollywood films of the 1980s, few "stars have been as thoroughly and embarrassingly trashed time and again in their features as Whoopi Goldberg" (Bogle 297). Bogle goes on to mention such films as *Jumpin' Jack Flash* (1986) and *Burglar* (1987), in which she is "defeminized" (Bogle 298); *The Telephone* (1988), where New York audiences, responding to the evident "waste" of Goldberg's talent (Bogle 298) reportedly cried out, "I want my money back!" and "I hope the film breaks!" (James 1987); and *Clara's Heart* (1988), in which Goldberg plays Jamaican housekeeper Clara, whom Bogle regards as a contemporary (and therefore contemptuous) mammy figure (Bogle 298). In the face of such criticism, Goldberg keeps on keepin' on, determining her own path as she goes. "When it's time to leave Hollywood, *she'll* write her own script. She always has" (Randolph 116).

Good, mixed and sometimes even poor film reviews did not stop Goldberg from succeeding. During the early 1990s she became the highest-paid Hollywood actress (Chutkow); in 1991, she was awarded the Best Supporting Actress Oscar for her role as Oda Mae Brown in *Ghost* (JPC, *WG: Second Black Actress* 54). Upon Swayze's death from pancreatic cancer in 2009, Whoopi Goldberg stated, "Patrick was a really good man, a funny man, and one to whom I owe much that I can't ever repay. I believe in *Ghost*'s message, so he'll always be near" (ABC.com).

Goldberg's Oscar win made her the first Black American woman to garner the Best Supporting Actress prize since Hattie McDaniel won for her portrayal of Mammy in 1939's *Gone with the Wind*. Goldberg's win ushered in a new era, during which Hollywood began casting its net for Oscar contenders more widely and deeply than ever before. Black American actors whose performances garnered American film acting's top prize, include: Cuba Gooding, Jr., who in 1996 won Best Supporting Actor for his work in *Jerry Maguire*; Halle Berry, who in 2001 won the Best Actress award for her work in *Monster's Ball*; Sidney Poitier, who won the Lifetime Achievement Award at the 2001 Oscars (his first was in 1963: Best Supporting Actor, for his work in *Lilies of the Field*); Denzel Washington, in 2001, for Best Actor in *Training Day*—Washington's first Oscar statue had been conferred in 1989, for his work as Best Supporting Actor in *Glory*; Jamie Foxx, in 2004, for his portrayal of the lead in the biopicture *Ray*; Morgan Freeman, who won Best Supporting Actor for his work in *Million-Dollar Baby* (JPC, *Black Oscar Milestones* 96, 98); and Mo'Nique, who in 2010 won the Best Supporting Actress prize for her work in *Precious* (Kaltenbach).

Mo'Nique, who began her career in stand-up comedy, segued into the television sitcom world with *Moesha* (1999–2000) and its spin-off, *The Parkers* (1999–2004), and has starred in such varied Hollywood film productions as *Baby Boy* (2001), *Good Fences* (2003), *Phat Girlz* (2006), and *Welcome Home, Roscoe Jenkins* (2008) (IMDb) is especially appreciative of Goldberg's example. Long before her dramatic starring role as the abusive mother in *Precious* (2009), the film adaptation of Sapphire's novel, *Push*, Mo'Nique explained the incredulousness of people openly and repeatedly criticizing Goldberg for her determination to be herself (by presenting herself as an intelligent, working woman instead of the typical Hollywood glamour queen) and participating in interracial romance. Says Mo'Nique, "How dare us [Black people] tell her who she can love?" (A&E Ch. 5). Mo'Nique also expresses a long-held hope that she, too, can rise to the status of Oscar winner. Because of Goldberg's example, Mo'Nique says that she told her "child self": "Okay, little girl in Baltimore; you can have this [the Oscar], too" (A&E Ch. 4). Mo'Nique explains that Goldberg made brown skin, natural-textured Black American hair and women wearing comfortable clothing a normal, expected part of the Hollywood scene, paving the way for a wide range of Black American actors to be taken seriously in the world of popular film. Mo'Nique's declaration of hope for an Oscar win, à la Whoopi Goldberg, came to fruition in 2010, when she received the Best Supporting Actress statue for her work as Mary in *Precious*.

Goldberg explains her determination to work while stretching the boundaries of society's (and Hollywood's) preconceived ideas about race: "I love the idea of working. You hone your craft that way. To sit around and wait for something that someone tells you is a Black film is ridiculous" (Collier 58). The wide-ranging themes of *Jumpin' Jack Flash, Burglar, Fatal Beauty, The Telephone, Clara's Heart, Homer and Eddie, Whoopi Goldberg: Fontaine: Why Am I Straight?, Kiss Shot, Ghost, Soap Dish*, and *The Player* formed a substantial proving ground for Goldberg, whose wide-ranging talents and focused diligence helped her pave her way toward achieving even greater Hollywood success. She says, "I got lucky. I know that. So I'd like people to remember that all I've gotten is a little bit of recognition and not to be afraid of me. Please cool out" (Rensin 157). Her innovative approach to acting and open-minded view of related possibilities for self and craft transformed Hollywood, creating new spaces for actors with unconventional looks and talent. When viewed simply from the surface, she may have seemed "whipped," but in the long run, she whipped Hollywood into a different shape. She didn't stumble; she strutted. And her example paved the way for others to strut their stuff, too.

4

Black and Blue(s)

Celie as Blueswoman in The Color Purple

> "There was nobody else alive in the world, in 1984, that could have possibly been Celie. She was the only Celie."
> — Steven Spielberg (A&E Ch. 4)

The blues tradition provides fertile ground for exploring Black American sensibilities regarding the irony and possibilities of freedom. An American music form born(e) out of the experiences of newly freed slaves of African descent, the blues sprang from its folk moorings in the spirituals, creating new paths, to reflect new perspectives, disappointments and hopes. "The musical genre is called the 'blues' not only because it employs a musical scale containing 'blue notes' [the pentatonic scale] but also because it names, in myriad ways, the social and psychic afflictions and aspirations of African Americans" (Davis 33). The flip side of the spirituals, which are rooted in the slave experience and show piety and reverence for God, the blues — a post–Civil War musicopoetic expression, echoes baseline truths for many Americans of African descent, who, in the midst of expressing their faith in the Almighty, also sometimes "*ignore* God, by embracing the [everyday] joys and sorrows of life" (Cone 99). "The spirituals were created in the church; the blues sprang from everyday life" (Work 28). Thus, the blues are a "secular spiritual," which "flow from the same bedrock of experience" as the spiritual; the two music forms complement each other (Cone 100) musically, experientially and culturally.

"The blues are about black life and the sheer earth and gut capacity to survive in an extreme situation of oppression" (Cone 97) in which the "divine promises of the Bible," as reflected in the Black American spirituals, were not a "satisfactory answer to the contradictions of black existence" (Cone 97). At times, pious American Christians, chattel slaves and former slaves included, defined the blues as "'non-religious' ... anti-religious and 'devil songs'" (Cone 98). Above all, the blues represents the crossroads — the place where crucial decisions are made. Decoding the crossroads and related symbols, according to traditional Yoruba, West African norms, helps us to understand the blues, its varied philosophies and manifestations, and its connections to Alice Walker's Pulitzer Prize–winning book *The Color Purple* (1982) and Goldberg's work and life.

Robert Ferris Thompson's *Flash of the Spirit: African and Afro-American Art and Philosophy* (1984) reminds us of the African moorings of the blues and related symbols.

> One must cultivate the art of recognizing significant communications, knowing what is truth and what is falsehood, or else the lessons of the crossroads — the point where doors open or close, where persons have to make decisions that may forever after affect their lives — will be lost. Eshu ... came to be regarded as he very embodiment of the crossroads.... So it was that Eshu-Elegbara became one of the most important images in the black Atlantic world [Thompson 19].

Eshu-Elegbara, also known as Llegba, is the Yoruba deity of the crossroads, symbolically represented by an elder (usually a man) walking with a cane, his legs simultaneously walking in, and representing, this life and the afterlife. In popular American vernacular, Black American bluesman Robert Johnson's relatives mention his having "sold his soul to the Devil" at the crossroads; hence his transformation from typical guitarist-troubadour to full-fledged bluesman — a "rumor" which Johnson himself "probably encouraged" (Palmer 113). The term "Devil," in this case, is not to be taken literally; instead, Johnson's family was likely applying Christian terminology to explain traditional West African cultural retentions. Johnson's "Devil" is not the embodiment of evil, as in Christianity; rather, he is the embodiment of Llegba, who, standing at the crossroads, grants one's most fervent desires. As desires are often at odds with needs, "Be careful of what you wish for" is a common admonishment and lesson of the blues. The blues also highlights the crossroads with its themes of travel, physical points of transition and related vehicles; intersections, railroad tracks, locomotives, cars, doorways, windows, ladders, pathways, waterways, natural landmarks, Southern foodways, and even the crucifix itself all symbolically relate to the crossroads and related, potentially life-altering choices. The true bluesman or blueswoman, however bruised and battered, continues his or her journey, taking the "lumps" of life along with the "sugar," savoring the victory of survival and the ability to tell others of his or her struggles and bittersweet triumphs.

Such blues philosophy informs much of Goldberg's big-screen interpretation of the character Celie Johnson, which sprang from the pen of celebrated American Southern author Alice Walker. Goldberg achieves such

4. Black and Blue(s)

sensitive, accurate interpretation of Celie's blues not only because of her considerable devotion to craft, but also because she herself, having traveled, forged and voiced a rough road to success, embodies the spirit of the modern blueswoman.

The philosophy of the blues stems from and embodies the traditional Black American adage, "You have to take the bitter with the sweet": whatever one encounters along life's journey becomes (part of) the person. The belief also holds that one can take even the most difficult moments and tragedies and transform them into rich experiences and utterances of triumph. Such trumpeting of triumph over adversity is especially ensconced in the work and life of Black American blues musicians; among early 20th-century popular blues-based musicians, perhaps none experienced and voiced such as distinctively as Louis Armstrong, the King of Jazz; and Bessie Smith, the Empress of the Blues.

Louis Armstrong, the gravelly voiced cornet-turned-trumpet player and King of Jazz, recorded Andy Razaf and Fats Waller's famous song, "What Did I Do (to Be So Black and Blue)?" A New Orleans native, Armstrong's plaintive, yet forceful, intonation highlights the dueling voices of his horn and himself. After playing through the entire song with the band (as is typical of early jazz recordings), Armstrong answers the cry of his own horn, with the inimitable sound of his voice. Playing the role of the narrator of the song, Armstrong, as the narrator, explains that he is human, just like any other person; but that the majority culture notices only his (the narrator's) brown skin/blackness and thus mistreats him (*Louis Armstrong*).

Thereafter, Armstrong briefly scats and returns to sing the next verse. The narrator's forceful determination not only to stay alive but also to openly protest unjust circumstances, captures the very essence of the blues and the irony of the song. True to form, the heroic Armstrong ends the song on a "high note," of sorts: a wailing cornet solo.

Similarly, Bessie Smith, Empress of the Blues, also traveled a hard road to(ward) success, voicing her struggles and disappointments, becoming an icon for scores of hard-working, everyday Black American people moving from plantations to cities in search of employment and better lives during the Great Migration. Far more than a Southern heritage reminder for displaced Black Americans in the North, who at times felt wistful about their former lives in the American South, Bessie Smith

> assisted in the creation of a new consciousness of African American identity, a consciousness that was critical of the experiences of exploitation, alienation — and for women, male dominance — in the North, which had been the focus of people's hopes and dreams since the earliest days of slavery. Her songs, more than any other blues performer of the era, constructed aesthetic bridges linking places and time and permitting a collective *prise de conscience* encompassing both the unity and the heterogeneity of the black experience [Davis 89–90].

In keeping with her exalted stature among Black American people, Smith dressed, comported and transported herself on her own terms, wearing only the finest clothes, both on-stage and off. She refused to be treated as a second-rate performer, eschewing travel by Jim Crow ("coloreds only") railway cars; instead, she purchased her own private, luxury railway cars, outfitted specifically herself and her lover, her band and their instruments and related equipment. Popularizing such original songs as "Baby Doll," in which the narrator openly declares sexual desire (Davis 261), and "Backwater Blues," where the narrator cries, after a natural disaster resulting in a flood, that she has nowhere to go, and no prospects for rebuilding (Davis 263–264), Smith symbolized freedom of movement, speech and sexuality, at time when Black Americans, while free of the yoke of slavery, nevertheless were bound by grinding poverty, Jim Crow and de facto racial segregation. Through the blues, Smith humanized Black experiences and created community. In "Washwoman's Blues," for example, Smith "identified with the countless numbers of Black women for whom domestic service was the only available occupation" (Davis 98).

The blues philosophy is not limited to music, it also abounds in Black American literature. Tied to, and emanating from, the oral/aural tradition, such works as Langston Hughes's *The Weary Blues* (1927); Zora Neale Hurston's *Their Eyes Were Watching God* (1937); Ralph Ellison's *Invisible Man* (1952); Toni Morrison's *Sula* (1973); and Alice Walker's *The Color Purple* (1982) are just a few key literary examples of the blues manifested. All of the aforementioned are based upon the blues philosophy and employ related symbols: the crossroads (intersections, trails, waterways, doors, windows, staircases, bridges, etc.) paired with the characters' journeys and related public revelations.

Nor are the blues relegated to expressing self-pity. Langston Hughes's classic poem, "The Weary Blues" (1927), chronicles the defiance of a Black American ragtime pianist. Set during the ragtime era (1890–1917), the time when Scott Joplin was King of Ragtime, but published during the Jazz Age (also known as the Roaring Twenties), Hughes's poem is often misconstrued as a jazz piece; actually, when carefully read, it decidedly reflects the ragtime era and its reliance upon earlier blues structures and philosophy. According to the narrator, through the sounds of the man's "soul" (Hughes lines 14–15), his very essence, the black man declares his vitality and relevance in the midst of his loneliness (Hughes lines 19–22). According to the narrator, the bluesman drones and plays a ragtime song (Hughes line 13). Ragtime, an American music form of syncopated piano music blending the manual dexterity of European classical keyboard music with the traditional West African blues aesthetic, heavily relies upon the black keys — the minor keys, or "blue notes," of the piano keyboard. The subject of Hughes's poem effectively uses the minor keys to "strike" notes of defiance against a society that ignores and shuns him.

4. Black and Blue(s)

The blues retains its significance, especially in the midst of the Great Depression (1930–1939). Zora Neale Hurston's *Their Eyes Were Watching God* (1937) pairs two blues figures: Tea Cake, the obvious bluesman, and the less obvious, but no less blues-tinged, lead character Janie, who goes from being a blues apprentice to blues master in her journey to find and articulate her self in rural 1930s Florida. Tea Cake, a traveling gambler who works as an itinerant, seasonal bean picker, plays both blues guitar and blues piano to accompany his songs concerning everyday struggles and triumphs. Taking Janie as his apprentice, Tea Cake encourages her to wear a blue dress and blue overalls (symbolizing the working class and the celestial sphere), and also encourages her to adopt the blues philosophy. Janie "takes the bitter with the sweet" with Tea Cake (whose name pairs the bitterness of tea with the sweetness of cake). Whether sharing cold Coca-Colas near Eatonville, or platefuls of beans in the Everglades, their fortunes change constantly, depending upon Tea Cake's gambling luck and the will of God. Regardless, Janie forges ahead, gaining rich memories and her own voice to console her when Tea Cake, the love of her life, dies—a cruel twist of fate. "Ah done growed ten feet higher from jus' listenin' tuh you, Janie!" (Hurston 284) her best friend, Phoeby, exclaims upon hearing Janie's story of trials and triumph. Janie's blues apprenticeship ends when she finds the words and the feelings to express the significance of her journeys, especially her love of Tea Cake, to Phoeby; Janie becomes a full-fledged blueswoman.

The blues makes its presence known in the prologue of Ralph Ellison's *Invisible Man* (1952), referencing Louis Armstrong's performance of "What Did I Do (to Be So Black and Blue)?" at the outset:

> Then somehow I came out of it, ascending hastily from this underworld of sound to hear Louis Armstrong innocently asking,
> *What did I do*
> *To be so Black*
> *And blue?* (Ellison 12)

The intense irony of the story presents itself at the outset, as the Invisible Man protests his invisibility without directly acknowledging such: "I am not complaining, nor am I protesting, either" (Ellison 3). Yet the entire story concerns the lead character's coming to terms with the double-edged sword of blackness, which both cuts him off from the larger society (hence, his "invisibility"), and renders him acutely self-conscious. At a pivotal point in the story, while gripped with homesickness (a yearning for his roots, so to speak), the Invisible Man stands at a literal crossroads, where an old man selling baked sweet potatoes offers him one, even providing the necessary butter for its proper savoring: "I'll give you some butter since you gon' eat it right here. Lots of folks takes 'em home. They got their own butter at home" (Ellison

264). When the Invisible Man tells the old man that he can tell that the tuber is sweet just by its looks, the old man, symbolizing the Yoruba deity of the crossroads Eshu-Elegba (Llegba), warns him, "You right, but everything what looks good ain't necessarily good.... But these [yams] is." The Invisible Man publicly tastes "a bite [of yam], finding it as sweet and hot as any [he'd] ever had ... feeling ... an intense sense of freedom" (Ellison 264). Having passed through a bitter phase of his life, he embraces sweet simplicity; no longer acutely self-conscious of his blackness and southern roots, the Invisible Man riffs, "I yam what I am" (Ellison 266), a declarative statement affirming his heritage as an American citizen of African descent. A master of the blues philosophy, he also masters the art of negotiating his way through hostile circumstances and territories, using, as his compass, his emerging sense of self.

The lead character of Toni Morrison's *Sula* (1973) adopts the stance of the blueswoman, leaving her community to gain a college education; but, instead of returning home to help her community, as the community expects, she deliberately sabotages relationships between men and women, simply because she can. Such sabotage includes the destruction of her best friend Nel's marriage, by having an affair with Nel's husband, Jude. Adopting a cavalier, masculine stance, Sula comes to symbolize destructive, impulsive aspects of the blues philosophy: capriciousness, selfishness and thoughtlessness. Echoing folklore concerning Black American women blues singers, a purse placed upon the ground symbolizes Sula's sexuality. In blues lore, the purse symbolizes the vagina/womb; and its placement upon the ground signifies emptiness, carelessness and bad luck. Moreover, like the folklore surrounding real-life blueswoman monarch Bessie Smith, and anticipating Walker's fictional character Shug Avery, Sula contracts an undisclosed illness, presumably a type of venereal disease, which lays her low, eventually resulting in her untimely demise (Morrison "1940").

Other literal interpretations of the blues manifest in Black American Southern cooking forms springing from chattel slave experiences: Louisiana creole, and soul food, respectively. In the American South, foodways literally manifest the blues, so that, in Black American culture, one actually "takes the bitter with the sweet," alternately and purposely ingesting and incorporating bitter and sweet elements. Take, for example, the use of Creole tomatoes (sweet) and okra (sweet) in relation to spiced shrimp (pungent/salty), andouille smoked sausage (pungent/salty) and mustard greens (pungent/salty) in Creole cooking. Similarly, in soul food, fried chicken (spicy/salty) is often paired with collard greens (pungent/salty), sweet potatoes (sweet), corn bread (sweet/salty) and red Kool-Aid (sweet), symbolizing vitality and consanguinity and often spiked with fresh lemon and/or lime slices (sweet/sour). In the motion picture adaptation of *The Color Purple*, true to its setting in early 20th-century rural Georgia, sweet-sour lemonade is served in the scene called

"Old Mr.'s Cool Drink" (Scene 16). In that scene, Sofia (Oprah Winfrey), Mr. _____'s (Danny Glover) son Harpo's (Willard Pugh) very pregnant girlfriend, takes the verbal barbs from Mr. _____, along with the lemonade, determined to stand her ground as a young, big and beautiful woman not ashamed to carry Harpo's child out-of-wedlock. Undeterred and unshaken, Sofia stands, reaches for, and drinks all of Mr. _____'s tall glass of lemonade, with several deep swallows; she "takes the bitter with the sweet," and comes out refreshed and stronger as a result.

Like Janie in Hurston's *Their Eyes Were Watching God* (1937), Celie, as blueswoman in the film *The Color Purple*, forges her own path toward happiness by redefining some social roles and rejecting others. Also like Janie, whose best friend, Phoeby, is her confidant and confidence-booster, Celie has three "sisterfriends" who help her find and project her best self: Nettie (Akosua Busia), her younger, prettier sister; Sofia (Oprah Winfrey), her daughter-in-law; and Shug Avery (Margaret Avery), traveling blues singer and mistress to Celie's husband, Mr._____. In the film, Nettie, a budding teacher, encourages Celie to develop her reading skills, by posting small vocabulary notes throughout Mr._____'s home. Later, she also writes to Celie in the hopes that her sister will know of her survival and wellness and that of Celie's two estranged children, Olivia and Adam. Initially in the film, Sofia embodies the boldness that eludes Celie; she speaks her mind and flaunts her round, heavy body, proud of her robustness and fertility. Shug Avery is all that Celie wishes she could be: smart, witty, pretty, sexually confident, and famous; her ability to sing the blues and bring many men, Mr. _____ included, to their knees, captivates Celie to the point where she fantasizes about having a romantic relationship with Shug.

Celie's journey from second-hand wife and stepmother to full-fledged person, mother, property owner and community activist fully manifests the blues philosophy. Indeed, Celie reaches several crossroads, or proving grounds, in the story—the first two by circumstance; the third, and most important, by choice. The first comes when her children, Olivia and Adam, are forcibly taken from her shortly after their birth (the story implies that the children are the result of incest; audiences, and Celie, later come to know that the children's biological father was actually Celie's stepfather). The second comes when she is married off against her will, to Mr. _____, because, according to her father, she "been spoiled" (her reputation is ruined, as she has borne children out-of-wedlock); Celie becomes Mr._____'s second wife, as his first wife has died, ostensibly due to maltreatment and overwork, leaving three unkempt, bratty children, the oldest barely younger than Celie. The third—and the most profound—proving ground comes when Celie decides to fully occupy and master the small space made available to her, transforming herself into an ideal wife and homemaker.

Realizing that Mr._____ and the children will never love her, and accepting Mr._____'s public declaration that she is "black," "poor" and "ugly" (Ch. 13), Celie uses self-determination to raise her social currency by rendering herself the community's best wife, housekeeper and household manager. Scene 4, "Married to Mr. _____," shows how, single-handedly, she transforms the filthy, unkempt surroundings into which she has been thrust into a model of cleanliness, orderliness, efficiency and economy. Celie turns Mr. _____'s house into a home. In the story, mastery of such housekeeping tasks as cleaning, cooking and basic household management provide her with the requisite experience, confidence and skills that she later uses to great advantage in the social sphere and in developing her Miss Celie's Folkspants shop. Enterprising and diligent, Celie quickly capitalizes upon her status as consummate homemaker to become the ideal hostess for her sister, Nettie, and later, Shug Avery (played by Margaret Avery).

Nettie (Akosua Busia) is Celie's younger, prettier, smarter, virginal sister. Studious and college-bound, she comes to visit Celie after running away from their cruel stepfather's sexual advances, only to find that Mr._____ has similar intentions of deflowering her. In fact, Nettie and Celie come to learn that Mr._____ had already asked their stepfather for Nettie's hand in marriage, and that Celie instead was offered to Mr. _____ as a poor substitute. The bond that Nettie and Celie share goes far beyond biology; Nettie is determined to share all of her book-learning with Celie, to show her that the sky is the limit, while Mr. _____ decidedly and repeatedly interferes with Celie's formal studies and sisterly connection. In fact, Mr. _____'s unwanted sexual advances are the reason Nettie must keep running — so far away, in fact, that she joins missionary work in West Africa. Nettie promises to write to Celie to keep their connection strong. Hating to see Celie have any love of her own, and determined to crush her spirit, for decades Mr. _____ intercepts the letters from the rusting mailbox — a symbol of the crossroads, which the film's director, Steven Spielberg, considers "the eighth character of the film" (*Cultivating a Classic*). Mr. _____ transfers them to a secret box, telling Celie that there is no mail for her. Meanwhile, Celie composes simple yet profound pleas to God to "maybe ... give [her] a sign letting [her] know what is happening" to her" (Walker 1). In the absence of Nettie, Shug Avery becomes Celie's substitute "sister" and master teacher.

Shug Avery becomes Celie's "sister" several times over: first, as the rival for Mr._____'s sexual attentions; Shug (short for "sugar," symbolizing the sweetness in life) eventually becomes Celie's sister in struggle, confidant, lover, church sister and blueswoman-master teacher. The dramatic flowering of their relationship begins in Celie's "classroom"— the successful home and hearth that she has forged against all odds. In Celie's "classroom," the guest bedroom becomes Shug's sickroom — it is rumored that Shug has contracted a "nasty woman's disease" (Walker 43). Through Celie's uncommon kindness, Shug comes to forgive herself for leaving home to pursue her blues music career; along the way, she also learns to love and see the beauty in Celie. Similarly, by feeding, bathing and consoling Shug, Celie begins a process of self-discovery, all the while nurturing a woman whose father, the respected community preacher, no longer recognizes as his daughter. In the film, the blues theme of the crossroads is invoked from the very first time Shug enters into Celie's life.

In Scene 13 of *The Color Purple*, Shug Avery enters the doorway of Mr._____'s home, under cloak of night and unannounced. Celie, who excitedly comes to the door to finally meet the regionally famous blues singer, is crushed when Shug, having just seen Celie's face, loudly exclaims, laughing with hysteria, "You sho' is ugly!" (Scene 13). At this point, Celie (whose name connotes life's "ceilings," or limitations), takes the bitter words along with Shug's sweet, earthy beauty, ingesting them whole; Shug's open indifference becomes yet another bitter pill for Celie to swallow. Margaret Avery, who played Shug, says that she recognized that the laughter in the scene was key to the scene and overall story, so she "practiced" that scene many times; moreover, she says, the scene had been shot thrice (*A Collaboration of Spirits*). The nuanced call-and-response between actors Margaret Avery and Whoopi Goldberg in this scene is palpable; viewers see Margaret Avery's seemingly spontaneous, loud, confrontational fullness, self-assurance and haughtiness, in sharp contrast to Goldberg's dramatic facial expressions, which move from over-excited anticipation to a deep sorrow and pain — the rawest depiction of expectancy violation/unfulfilled expectations — a cornerstone of the blues experience. Margaret Avery's authentic delivery of the line and the laugh wring the fullness of meaning from the text and fling them into Celie's face. As Celie, Goldberg's dynamic response to Margaret Avery's performance, by means of body language and facial expressions, bespeaks the hopes and pains of generations. Goldberg's performance is all the more remarkable as she had had no prior Hollywood filmmaking experience (*A Collaboration of Spirits*). As the film adaptation of Walker's story progresses, Celie comes to appreciate Shug and herself; a lesson that she masters, by successfully meeting one challenge at a time. Goldberg's and Avery's acting chemistry bring the novel's storyline to life on the big screen in refreshing ways.

In the film, the first challenge that Celie meets in relation to Shug is shown in Scene 14, "Cooking Breakfast." In this scene, Shug literally "takes the bitter with the sweet," with unpleasant bitterness initially offered by her lover, Mr._____. We hear Shug Avery's drunken intonations about being hungry; we see Mr._____ feebly presenting her with a mishmash of his own, home-cooked burnt offerings; we see Shug throwing the tray, food untouched, against a hallway wall in protest; and we see definitive homemaker Celie saving the day with a masterfully cooked Southern-style breakfast. Goldberg, as Celie, narrates, her deep, resonant voice expressing the excitement of anticipation, nearly verbatim, from Walker's novel:

> Dear God,
> I ast Shug Avery what she want for breakfast. She say,
> What yall got? I say ham, grits, eggs, biscuits, coffee, sweet milk or butter milk, flapjacks. Jelly and jam.
> She say, Is that all? What about orange juice, grapefruit, strawberries and cream. Tea. Then she laugh.
> I don't want none of your damn food, she say. Just gimme a cup of coffee and hand me my cigarettes [Walker 51–52].

Shug then demands a glass of water. While fetching the water for Shug, Shug begins to eat, albeit in very small bites. Upon her return, Celie notes, "Look like a little mouse been nibbling the biscuit, a rat run off with the ham" (Walker 52). Later, when Mr. _____ asks how Celie convinces Shug to eat, Celie responds, "Nobody living can stand to smell home-cured ham without tasting it. If they dead they got a chance. Maybe" (Walker 52). Goldberg's matter-of-fact, self-assured tone makes the line that Celie delivers thoroughly believable, reassuring the audience that Shug and Celie are both on the road to recovery.

The aforementioned scene illustrates Shug Avery's literally ingesting the blues—"taking the bitter with the sweet," and beginning the process of achieving a sort of balance of body, mind and spirit. Bitter, or sharp-tasting foods, such as buttermilk, grapefruit and coffee, are balanced against the sweetness of pan-seared ham, sweet milk (condensed milk), orange juice, and strawberries and cream, with the delicate flavors of biscuits, grits and eggs holding the middle ground. In Scene 16, "Old Mr._____'s Cool Drink," showing her sense of humor, and echoing Celie's sensibilities, Goldberg (as Celie) calmly narrates, thinking aloud about how Mr._____'s father seemed to love that glass of water which she served him, into which she had spit: "Next time, maybe I put a little Shug Avery pee in his glass. See how he like that" (Walker 55). In the story, Celie slyly spits into the glass, stirring it into the water with her right index finger, in retaliation against Old Mr._____'s open denigration of Shug. The visual aspects of the scene, highlighting Celie's subtle delight at seeing Old Mr. _____ ingest her retaliation show Goldberg's ability to appear at once devilish and innocent; Celie literally "gives the blues" to Old Mr._____, via a glass of spit-water. Later, "Miss Celie's Blues" (Scene 18) and "Beautiful Celie" (Scene 20) crystallize the blues as a vehicle for empowerment.

"Miss Celie's Blues" (Scene 18) shows Celie's growing infatuation with Shug Avery and Shug's affinity for women. The scene's title song, emoted onscreen by Shug, who, wearing a sequined red dress and rhinestone crown, and waving a large fan of crimson-dyed ostrich feathers, singing directly to and about Celie in Harpo's Juke Joint, is a paean to Celie's sweetness and healing hands. In this scene, Margaret Avery, as Shug, projects renewed strength and confidence, opposite the humorous, fluid Goldberg, who, as Celie, alternately delights in, and shies away from, Shug's advances. As the song and Shug's attitude shows, Miss Celie cared for the shunned Shug Avery, when Shug was stricken with an undisclosed illness (the story implies that venereal disease laid her low), bathing, clothing, feeding and grooming Shug back to health over several intense weeks of intensive homespun therapy. In many ways, Celie's human(e)ness and kindness are medicines which cure Shug's homesickness, the apparent root of her physical ailments and the second reason (beyond seeing Mr.____, who is good enough to be Shug's sometimes lover, but too "weak" to become her husband) Shug comes to town. Viewers learn that, in addition to having traveled far from home, building a name for herself on the blues music circuit, Shug is not welcome at home, as her worldly status as blues queen shames her father, a local minister and head of the community's most influential Christian church. Drowning her sorrows in alcohol, while Celie bathes her in a deep tin tub, filled with hot, sudsy water, Shug cries that her father loves her, but "he don't know it" (Scene 18). Hearing Shug's confession sparks Celie's compassion. In time, Shug responds by helping Celie learn self- and physical love.

"Beautiful Celie" (Scene 20) illustrates Celie's growing self-awareness and sexual awakening. Using the color red, a primary color signifying consanguinity, heat, sensuality and sexuality, and a component (along with the primary color blue) of the secondary color purple, Spielberg achieves his goal of creating a "poetic" (*Conversations...*) scene, which emphasizes the "sweetness" of the kiss between Shug and Celie, as opposed to the raw sexuality which also appears in the book. The aspect of sweetness, or tenderness, is also shown in the verbal and body language exchanged between the two characters, as reflected in the mirror—a prop used to great effect. In this scene, the facial expression of Margaret Avery, as Shug, shows deep love and concern for Celie; while Goldberg, as Celie, alternately shows bashfulness and boldness. Reflected in the mirror, the audience sees Shug slowly removing Celie's hand from Celie's mouth, encouraging Celie to show her "pretty teef" with a smile. Instead of "cracking" the mirror (as, according to folklore, "ugly" people do), Whoopi, as Celie, shows her beauty, while "cracking herself up" (laughing, with gusto). Sharing a mutual understanding of the frailties of Mr. ____ and the power of deep friendship and love, Shug and Celie kiss. According to Steven Spielberg, his goal was to use a "poetic" approach to expressing Celie's "emancipation." Alice Walker agrees that the scene "captures the sweetness of their relationship" (*Conversations...*). "...The sole bedroom scene between Celie and Shug plays as an innocent, friendly encounter between two very nice people, and it ends with a shot of wind chimes" (Maslin). It must be remembered, though, that *The Color Purple*, despite its brutality and sexuality, was rated PG-13 — given that reality, Spielberg's directorial choices for the scene make sense. Observant viewers realize that the film, like the book, explores lesbianism in connection with the blueswoman experience, echoing the legend of Bessie Smith, who, according to blues lore, used her luxurious, custom-designed private train car to house and travel with her female lover. Just as Smith made space in her life for a woman lover during hard days on the road with her band, so Celie makes space to love and be loved by Shug Avery, physically and emotionally.

Beyond the obvious use of blues music, and Shug Avery's status as traveling blues singer, several additional elements also symbolize the blues. Housecleaning and the threshold (points of transition); the exchange of letters, the train, and pants/trousers (freedom of movement/traveling great distances); foodways ("taking the bitter with the sweet"); and bells, wind chimes and white stones along the pathway, leading to and from the house, which (re)call the ancestors, all bespeak the crossroads and the blues. All of the aforementioned elements emanate from Walker's seasoned, Southern pen; but it is Goldberg, who brings Celie, the crux of the story, to life on the big screen. Janet Maslin reflects, "Miss Goldberg is limited at first, forced to shrug and cower in a manner that seems highly improbable in someone so evidently savvy. But she eventually grows into a tremendously compelling figure, with a huge, radiant smile that's even more powerful [than] her formidable scowl" (Maslin). Maslin's critique misses the point of much of Goldberg's performance; a real-life blueswoman and trained actor, she achieves poetic expression of Celie by applying the traditional West African masking tradition; as the Black American folk expression states, "Got one face for the world to see; another for the one I know is me." In turn-of-the-20th-century Georgia, the setting of Walker's novel, masking in the form of blackface minstrelsy, was popular entertainment; blackface performance traditions even extended to include Black American troubadours, who "blacked up" because such was the norm, thus expressing double-irony onstage. Goldberg's interpretation of Celie draws upon such cultural knowledge; as Celie, she wears a "mask" to hide ingenuity and awareness in order to survive. Such explains her dynamic performance as Celie; in sharp contrast to Janet Maslin's comments, Goldberg, the woman, is not being disingenuous when she portrays Celie's shyness; rather, she is acting. Her calculated, intentional performance of Celie recalls, for observant viewers, the experience of millions of talented, quick-witted Black Americans during the Jim Crow era, who were forced to occupy the lower stations in life and pretend to like it — or at least pretend not to know better.

In a pivotal scene, Celie removes the mask, revealing her true self; the

4. Black and Blue(s)

scene also reveals another aspect of traditional West African cultural retentions in rural Georgia. In Scene 32, "Celie's Curse," Celie verbally and physically commands Mr.____ to refrain from hurting or following her, and declares, in effect, that "what goes around comes around"—(another traditional West African philosophy that survived the Middle Passage and is reflected in the pan–African world). Wearing a drab, blue dress (bordering on battleship grey, and adorned with a cornflower-like pattern) and grey suede high-heeled shoes, Celie stands on the running board of a bright, shiny, taxicab-yellow luxury car, en route to a piece of land and home that she has inherited from her late father. The visual contrast shows Celie clearly on the verge of embarking upon a journey with Shug Avery and her new husband, Grady. Leaving behind the shock and sorrow of Shug's having found another mate, and the pain of having raised Mr.____'s ungrateful children, and the home that she has made, against all odds, she expresses the reflexive nature of evil. Celie stands powerfully at the crossroads, putting the juju (hex) on Mr. ____, with her left hand outstretched, simultaneously pointing toward him and reaching into the spiritual realm, saying, "Everything you done to me.... Already done to you." Mr. ____'s eyes flash deathly fear, but his mouth mutters a bit about her not being able to curse him. Meanwhile, Celie climbs from the running board and into the trunk of the car, among the luggage. Standing firmly in the luggage hold, as the car begins to move away from the house she calls out to Mr. ____ with clarity, and raising her right palm to the Almighty: "I'm poor, I'm black, and I may even be ugly.... But I'm here! I'm here!" (Scene 32). In this scene, Celie symbolically channels the Llegba figure, expressing power and wisdom at the crossroads.

Portraying the character Celie in the film adaptation of *The Color Purple* brought Goldberg international acclaim, resulting in a Golden Globe and an Academy Award nomination. Actually, *The Color Purple* received 11 Oscar nominations, overall, including Best Picture of the Year; Best Screenplay Adaptation; Best Cinematography; Best Art Direction; Best Costume Designs; Best Makeup; Best Original Score (co-producer Quincy Jones, along with gospel artist Andraé Crouch, were nominated in that category); Best Original Song (for Jones's "Miss Celie's Blues/Sisters"); Best Supporting Actress (for Margaret Avery and Oprah Winfrey, respectively); and Best Actress (Goldberg) (JPC).

Goldberg initially had favored portraying a different character, however. Against her initial misgivings, Steven Spielberg insisted that she play the role of Celie. Having read the book, and having heard Walker narrate portions of the novel, via a National Public Radio broadcast, Goldberg contacted Walker, by mail, to express her appreciation of the book. Walker responded with a letter enveloped in purple, telling the actor that she was familiar with Goldberg's stage work in the San Francisco Bay area, and had sent the actor's profile to Hollywood insiders (*A Collaboration...*). Walker recommended that Goldberg play Celie because of her "indomitable quality" and "wicked sense of humor" (*A Collaboration...*). Goldberg actually thought that she would make a better Sofia; to her way of thinking, based upon her knowledge of Walker's novel, Sofia was more akin to characters that she had already played, while Celie was a bit beyond easy reach. Goldberg, confident in her acting skills, but a novice with respect to Hollywood filmmaking, feared that she would ruin the film (A&E Ch. 4).

Accolades aside, the film nevertheless received mixed reviews, especially from black American audiences:

> During a screening, an entire audience of Black media professionals was at times moved to laughter, anger, disgust, pity and sympathy. But even before the tears were dried, a majority of the viewers expressed concern about the overwhelming impact of the negative images. While most point to the obnoxious male characters, it must be noted that there aren't a wealth of positive Black female characters either, and Celie is constantly told how "Black" and "ugly" she is [Norment 150].

We must take such criticism in light of DuBois's "double-consciousness" theory, as well as the array of talented artists involved in the film's production. In *The Souls of Black Folk* (1903), W. E. B. DuBois posited that Black Americans never could see their true selves, because the politics and realities of race rendered their consciousness in such a way that they could only see themselves through the lens of the other (the majority culture).

DuBois describes such an experience as being akin to looking at the self through a "veil," of sorts:

> The Negro is a sort of seventh son, born with a veil, and gifted with second sight in this American world — a world which yields him no true self-consciousness, but only lets him see himself through the revelation of the other world. It is a peculiar sensation, this double-consciousness, this sense of always looking at one's self through the eyes of others, of measuring one's soul by a tape of a world that looks on in amused contempt and pity. One ever feels his twoness, — an American, a Negro [DuBois 6].

While some reviewers perceived and projected double-consciousness upon *The Color Purple*, Goldberg saw herself as an actor who had hit the big time. While she had honed her acting chops on the stage, she was a newcomer to Hollywood film, especially when compared to such seasoned actors as Danny Glover (Mr.____), Adolf Caesar (Mr.____'s father), and Margaret Avery (Shug Avery). Thus, Goldberg spent the initial days of filming feeling starstruck (*A Collaboration...*). Her settling into and fully occupying the role of Celie was, in part, the result of the actor becoming more comfortable with the Hollywood filmmaking process, as well as Spielberg's insistence upon the cast using improvisation, one of Goldberg's strengths, within and between takes. According to Spielberg, scripted readings created "tension" between seasoned film actors and novices and sapped the cast's creative energies (*A Collaboration*). Quincy Jones and Steven Spielberg co-produced the film (moreover, Jones composed the score, while Spielberg directed the film); award-winning photographer Gordon Parks "did special still photography for the movie" (Norment 155); and Alice Walker wrote the first film treatment (adaptation) for the novel, serving as creative advisor throughout the film's development (*Conversations*). Reading *Ebony Magazine*'s review of *The Color Purple*, it is almost as though the film had been criticized for what it is not, as opposed to having been appreciated for what it is. Nor was the criticism of the film solely a Black audience issue.

Janet Maslin, of the *New York Times*, notes several inconsistencies with respect to the film: Celie and husband Mr. _____ mature, yet their children do not appear to age; costuming which seems too new to have been worn for as many years as the film describes; and comedic scenes interspersed between heavy drama and sexual innuendo, resulting in a "broad simplification" that "suggests caricature" (Maslin). Maslin says that such is the result of Spielberg's having to make the abrupt switch from directing such fare as *E.T.*, to directing *The Color Purple*. Spielberg notes his initially having felt uncomfortable with directing historically based, aspects of Black American life and culture, as a self-described "white Jewish kid" (*Conversations...*). Nevertheless, his experiences with anti–Semitism, as well as conversations with Alice Walker, who reminded him that, if he could make an extraterrestrial (*E.T.*) "comfortable" for viewers like herself, then he could find and document the human element in Black fiction, and translate such to film, helped him to claim his space as the film's director. Moreover, Quincy Jones also reminded him that, just as he need not have traveled to outer space to direct *Close Encounters of the Third Kind* and *E.T.*, he (Spielberg) need not be a Black American in order to direct a film starring a largely Black American cast (*Conversations...*). Nevertheless, international views of *The Color Purple* were more accepting and far less critical. For example, a reviewer for *Australian Doctor* praises the manner in which the film encourages viewers to seek growth through inner peace: "The movie highlights our ability to change our paths in life — to learn, find strength and grow from our experiences" (RBI).

Goldberg says that, for five years, the commercial and artistic success of the film had an unintended effect of hurting the range and availability of acting jobs for black actors in Hollywood as so few serious all-black motion pictures were being developed (*A Collaboration*). In fact, says Goldberg, "Everybody says, 'Well, why aren't you doing more *Color Purples*?' But that's not what people are asking me to do. It's not like somebody handed me another *Color Purple* and *Jumpin' Jack Flash*, and I said, 'I choose *Jumpin' Jack Flash*.' At the time, however, I was just amazed to be doing what I was doing"

(Sheff). Rae Dawn Chong, who played Squeak, explains that the nearly all–Black cast of *The Color Purple* really functioned as an ensemble, a game-changer in the realm of Hollywood filmmaking (*Cultivating a Classic*). The *Color Purple* also marked the first since *Roots* (a made-for-television miniseries, also based upon Black fiction) had captured mainstream popular American interest, in Black American culture. Perhaps one of the reasons Goldberg initially saw herself as playing Sofia is because the novel *The Color Purple* actually includes several blueswomen at different stages of development. Beyond Shug Avery, the obvious blueswoman, Walker's novel also includes several others: Sofia, Squeak and Celie; aspects of the blues tradition color the film adaptation of each character.

Sofia's open defiance of race and gender limitations places her at the crossroads of abuse and redemption; her determination to fight oppression breaks her, physically, emotionally and psychologically. Scene 23, "Sofia's Tragedy," shows Sofia (the character Harpo's first wife, played by Oprah Winfrey) balling her fist and physically knocking down the mayor, who has slapped her across the face, in recompense for her open refusal to become his wife's maid. Sofia, literally standing at a crossroads with her prizefighter beau, Buster, and three well-kept children — the whole family "looking like somebody" (Walker 84), protects Buster by redirecting his attention from defending her against a growing mob, and yelling to him to take the children home. Beyond the considerable social strife aspect, Sofia's punishment includes being savagely beaten by the mob, serving years in jail, being forcibly separated from her family and friends, and, following her incarceration, ironically serving a lengthy sentence as servant to Miss Millie, the mayor's wife. Scene 24, "Driving and Shopping," illustrates literal and figurative crossroads, showing Sofia serving as driving coach for Miss Millie, a terrible driver, who, exiting the car with Sofia following behind, thrusts a lengthy Christmas holiday grocery list into Sofia's hand. Sofia, her eyesight dim from age and the savage mob beating, can barely process the complex request. Meanwhile, Celie coincidentally meeting Sofia at this crossroads grocery store, volunteers and quickly gathers all of the needed items for her, saving her friend the time and trouble. In the film, Sofia's broken posture serves as a cautionary tale, symbolizing the price that Black Americans paid for trying to maintain their pride, in a time and place where pride was reserved "for Whites only"; while Celie's fortified, fortuitous disposition illustrates the power of God to "make a way out of no way." Nearly a year later, Sofia gets her comeuppance, however, during Thanksgiving; in Scene 31, "Dinner Table Revolt," Sofia is at first "confused," but later encouraged, by Celie's open defiance in speaking her truth, calling Mr._____ a "lowdown, dirty dog," and more. Sofia, laughing hysterically and wearing a blue dress (symbolizing the blues) adorned with white daisies (symbolizing life/death), ad libs blues lines encapsulating a lifetime of struggle, as family and friends look on:

4. Black and Blue(s) 73

Set in that jail,
Set in that jail,
... I know what it like wanna sing,
And have it *beat out ya* [Scene 31].

Drawing strength from the intensity of Goldberg's vocal delivery, (self-)restraint, and intense eyes, Winfrey's improvised performance, encouraged by director Steven Spielberg, earned Winfrey an Oscar nomination for Best Supporting Actress (*A Collaboration of Spirits*). Sofia's ability to give voice to her struggles transforms her from victim to victor, in the blues tradition. Squeak also finds her voice as blueswoman apprentice.

In the film, during the "Dinner Table Revolt" scene, Squeak, Harpo's second wife, loudly exclaims, "I'm fixin' to sing!" reclaiming and proclaiming her Christian name, Mary Agnes (Scene 31). Such declarations of victory are out of context for the viewer, however; the movie audience does not see the crossroads (trials) that Mary Agnes, née Squeak, has endured. The novel fully articulates her journey, however. The novel tells readers that Squeak (so nicknamed because of her mouse-like vocal delivery and shyness) is actually the person who stands at the crossroads of bondage and freedom, retrieving Sofia from prison. Squeak has endured trials of her own, however: "She look a little haggard, with all Sofia and Harpo children sprung on her at once, but she carry on. Hair a little stringy, slip show, but she carry on" (Walker 90). Readers come to learn that her uncle is the white prison warden who works where Sofia is incarcerated; in the novel, Celie and Odessa (Sofia's sister) outfit Squeak, literally and figuratively, to "make him see the Hodges" in her (Walker 93) and thereby gain Sofia's release. But the plan goes awry when Warden Hodges rapes her; Squeak "Come home with a limp. Her dress rip. Her hat missing and one of the heels come off her shoe" (Walker 93). After a bit of supportive prodding from the community, Squeak tells Celie and all in attendance that "he saw the Hodges in me. And he don't like it one bit," alluding to rape. Harpo openly states what all can see: that "Squeak," as he calls her, has been beaten and raped (Walker 95). Squeak, clearly having earned the right to be called by her Christian name, determined to know whether Harpo really loves her or her bright skin color, and following Celie's earlier advice to "make Harpo call [Squeak] by her real name.... Then maybe he see you even when he in trouble" (Walker 84), rises and insists that Harpo call her Mary Agnes (Walker 97). Having used and abused Squeak's body as bail, the warden releases Sofia from bondage.

Six months after Sofia's release from prison, Squeak "begin to sing. First she sing Shug's songs. Then she begin to make up songs her own self" (Walker 98). Releasing her sorrows and voicing her triumphs, Mary Agnes, a mixed-race person whom her community often describes as "yellow" (Walker 99) sings a blues song in the form of a word-play questioning how the color yellow could be used to define a person (Walker 99). Walker's use of the word "yellow" places a real-life racial term in a fictional context; in the real world, since slavery, Black Americans have used the word "yellow" to describe light-complexioned, mixed-race members of the community. With her "little, high ... sort of meowing" (Walker 98) voice, Mary Agnes's blues describes her experience of being a "yellow" (mixed-race) Black American woman, prized in some circles for being of mixed-race ancestry, and condemned in others, for the same reason. Echoing the fact that the spirituals and the blues spring from the same fount, Mary Agnes's reclaiming of her Christian name serves as a conduit for the blues, empowering her to give voice to everyday trials and triumphs.

As Walker's novel and the related film show, it is Celie, however, who undergoes the fullest transformation from powerless to powerful, within and extending the blues tradition. A former wallflower and regular victim of several layers of abuse — sexual (first, at the hands of her stepfather, and later, her husband, Mr. ____), physical (at the hands of Mr. ____ and her wicked stepchildren), and verbal (from her stepchildren, her father-in-law and Mr. ____), Celie nevertheless blossoms. She (pro)claims her space as superlative wife and housekeeper, her right to love and be loved (note her strong relationships with sister Nettie and sisterfriend-turned-lover Shug Avery), and her American right to pursue and proclaim happiness, on her own terms. To be sure, the film adaptation of the novel blunted much of the aforementioned; yet we must remember that the novel was the primary fount of the film and the primary source of information for actors to craft their respective characters. During the early 1980s, Walker's novel held perhaps even more sway in the initial adaptation for the screen than its subsequent, successful adaptation for Broadway, some 20 years later. The emotional impact of Goldberg's experience working on *The Color Purple* is clear: according to Goldberg, "Seeing the cast of *The Color Purple* for the first time in 25 years on *Oprah* was definitely a highlight [of 2010] for me" (Marr).

Beyond the direct influence of Walker 's novel, Goldberg's preparation for the role of Celie began with her early work interpreting the life and comedic genius of Jackie "Moms" Mabley. Like blues singers, Mabley traveled an uncertain road through the "chitlin' circuit," a loosely organized vaudeville theater network, through which many Black American performers gained fame, but at considerable cost. (The irony of the term, "chitlin' circuit," is clear: "chitlins," or pork chitterlings, are pig intenstines — the generally unappetizing entrails of animals, regularly fed to Black American chattel slaves, which the slaves transformed into palatable fare. By extension, "chitlin' circuit" performers likened themselves to waste being moved through the colon; in this sense, Black American performers were "the s — t," in the fullest sense of the word.) Similarly, Goldberg says that she "saw at lot of irony" as a "shy" grade-schooler in New York City's Chelsea, Manhattan neighborhood (A&E Ch. 2) and later capitalized on it by creating her own fictional characters, which captivated audiences and created vehicles for unique self-expression.

First attending Catholic school, Goldberg then named Caryn Elaine Johnson, later attended the Hudson School, where she began formal studies in acting (A&E Ch. 2). By 1973, however, she had dropped out of school, participated in the city's drug culture — "part of the era," says Goldberg; got pregnant and married the baby's father — her drug counselor, Alvin Martin (A&E Ch. 2). After her daughter, Alexandrea, was born, she divorced Martin and migrated to San Diego, with her baby girl in tow. There, she and her daughter lived in a tree house, of sorts: a rented wooden, stilted house into, and through which, a tree grew; the tree and its odd placement within the home may be considered a symbol of the crossroads. To support herself and her daughter, she worked as a bricklayer, restaurant dishwasher, cosmetologist trainee, and, while taking acting classes, a mortuary cosmetologist (A&E Ch. 3). For a time, financial exigency forced the divorced mother to rely upon welfare, an experience which continues to affect her. "I still have my Medi-Cal card," she says, "because I wanted to make sure that I never forget this" (A&E Ch. 3). Medi-Cal is the common name for the California Medical Assistance Program, a program administered by the Department of Health Care Services (CDHCS). "DHCS works closely with health care professionals, county governments and health plans to provide a health care safety net for California's low income and persons with disabilities" (CDHCS). While in San Diego, she also helped to found the San Diego Repertory Theater, acting in such plays as *Mother Courage* (A&E Ch. 3); she remains a member of the organization's board of advisors (San Diego Rep.).

A real-life blueswoman, Caryn Elaine Johnson came to another crossroads, choosing to leave San Diego and relocate to the San Francisco Bay area, where Whoopi Goldberg, actor, was born, literally and figuratively. Joining the Blake Street Hawkeyes avant garde theater group (A&E Ch. 3), she gained the freedom to occupy any space with any character of her choosing. Characteristically, Goldberg chose to create new characters, to occupy new space, such as Fontaine, the junkie with a Ph.D., and the Girl with the Long Blonde Hair, both of which figured prominently in her one-woman stage show, *The Spook Show* (1984), which she later transformed into *Whoopi Goldberg: Direct from Broadway* (1985), the audio recording of which garnered her a Grammy (A&E Ch. 3).

Reminiscent of the legacy of blues queen Bessie Smith, who traveled in style, and on her own terms, using ground transportation, Goldberg also travels by private train and bus. A native New Yorker, she is accustomed to taking public transportation, taxicabs and the like. She has regularly bussed between

Los Angeles and New York, saying that, as a native Manhattanite, she drives, but "badly" (Cavett). Thus, she regularly relies upon engineers and drivers to shuttle her from place to place. Even though she is not in the driver's seat, per se, she says, "I'm in complete command of my life [when traveling the open road]" (Cavett). She says that, when she told people about her road-tripping adventures, many compared her to a country singer (Cavett). In fact, Goldberg prefers road tripping to flying. She "didn't mind flying, but she preferred the safety of a train car when not in a hurry" (Samuels 46). Likening her train car to an "apartment" and "parlor," reporter Allison Samuels explains that the train car included "a couple of bedrooms, a private bath, a fully equipped kitchen, and a private chef"; and that it also contained "personal effects like blankets, lamps and family photos scattered about" (Samuels 46). Goldberg's private bus is similarly equipped, and also quiet, by design; says the actor, "I travel by bus, so I'm the only kid on it — no screaming" (Marr). She recently quelled aerophobia by successfully completing Virgin Air's shortened course on flight safety; as a result, she has flown to California and London (ABC News).

Despite Goldberg's accolades, roles with the dramatic intensity of Celie were hard to come by. Beyond the issues of race and gender, generally speaking, Hollywood simply was not making films like *The Color Purple*; instead, it churned out such uneven fare as *Jumpin' Jack Flash* (1986); *Fatal Beauty* (1987) and *Burglar* (1987), in which she starred, among others. Still, Goldberg does not fret about the choices that she made, as an actor, especially given the very limited selection available; for example, she says that she was turned down for the lead in *The Princess Bride* because she was told that she did not look the part. She argued that the princess "doesn't look like anybody else.... Why can't it be me?" (Sheff). She says that she learned a lot about the politics of movie-making, especially how one's looks impact the choices that actors have. Goldberg concludes, "So I took the stuff [roles] that nobody seemed to have a problem with me doing" (Sheff).

The Hollywood machine also affected how Goldberg, and the characters that she portrayed, were projected. "I was neutered in many respects," She says of her screen roles (A&E Ch. 1). Such "neutering" had a profound effect upon her public image. Nevertheless, she took the lumps along with the sugar, forging a public persona and related characters which decidedly played with, and through, such constrictions to forge a unique American voice. Replacing Shelley Long as lead character Teresa "Terry" DoLittle in *Jumpin' Jack Flash*, Goldberg played an asexual computer programmer in a masculine environment (she is even mistaken for a man, as her handle, "Terry," is mistakenly assumed to be that of a male programmer). In *Fatal Beauty*, she replaced Cher to capture the co-starring role of gritty Los Angeles undercover police officer Rita Rizzoli (opposite Sam Elliot, playing Mike Marshak). In *Burglar*, she

4. Black and Blue(s)   77

played ex-convict and professional burglar Bernice Rhodenbarr, who is blackmailed into attempting one last heist, only to become the sole witness to a murder; even the character (originally to have been played by Bruce Willis) is addressed in the masculine "Bernie," for short. As Edwina (Eddie) Franklin in *Eddie* (1996), she again takes a masculine role, playing an ultimate New York Knicks fan-turned-real-life coach. In *The Associate* (1996), she plays both Laurel Ayers, the savvy, but overlooked, Wall Street analyst; and Robert Cutty, her fictional white, male alter-ego, who gets all the credit. In *Call Me Claus* (2001), Goldberg plays Lucy Cullins, a home shopping channel television producer, who fulfills her destiny of becoming Santa Claus, taking over the reins from none other than Nigel Hawthorne, who portrays the film's original, and retiring, St. Nicholas. In *Absolutely Fabulous in New York* (2002), a special episode of the BBC comedy, *Absolutely Fabulous* (starring Jennifer Saunders as Edina, and Joanna Lumley as Patsy), Goldberg plays Goldie, a counselor working at a hip New York LGBT center, presiding over the open-air, sham "marriage" of best friends Edina and Patsy, who leave London for New York in search of Edina's long-lost gay son, Serge. During that episode, Edina and Patsy, making a snap decision, immediately assume that Goldie is a "T" (transgendered person). Meanwhile, Goldie stereotypes Edina and Patsy as a lesbian couple. So Goldie plays with the concept of homosexuality, encouraging Edina and Patsy to experiment with woman-on-woman physical love, and admonishing the uptight Edina (who is wearing a T-shirt emblazoned with the phrase *ENGLISH MUFFIN*—a double-entendre, describing a type of toasted breakfast bread, as well as her vagina) to manually lift her own breasts to the sky, and ululate.

Many of Goldberg's acting roles decidedly place her at the crossroads of gender. Not surprisingly, the American press incorrectly labels her a lesbian, ignoring her status as birth mother to daughter Alexandrea, and grandmother of three, as well as serious relationships with men, with a select few culminating in marriage (A&E Ch. 2). Accentuating the gender issue is actor Kenan Thompson, an NBC *Saturday Night Live* (*SNL*) ensemble cast member — perhaps best known as half of the Nickelodeon comedy duo Kenan & Kel; he was also the co-star (with Kel Mitchell) of *Good Burger* (2003), and star of the live-action film *Fat Albert* (2004). Thompson regularly parodies Goldberg's stint as moderator of ABC's *The View*. Thompson, as Goldberg, clearly admires her and takes great pains not to laugh at her, but rather with her. For example, the *SNL* episode, "The Ladies of *The View* Welcome Alec Baldwin" (NBC Television), includes many current *SNL* ensemble cast members, each doing his or her over-the-top impressions of the ladies of *The View*. Wearing no makeup, a rasta wig, a woman's black, collared, long-sleeve button-up shirt, African-patterned orange vest, jeans, orange Crocs and round-rimmed wire glasses, Thompson's characterization of Goldberg deliberately counters the crazy clothing, emphasizing her level-headedness to the extreme. At the other extreme is Fred Armisen, who, also in drag (wearing pasty pancake makeup, bright red lipstick, a styled auburn wig, and a red floral patterned rayon dress), overemphasizes Joy Behar's New York accent. Meanwhile, Kristen Wiig, wearing a typical working mom's outfit featuring a simple yellow sweater, deliberately over-emotes as she interprets Elizabeth Hasselbeck. Also during this scene, actor Ben Affleck openly parodies Alec Baldwin as a self-absorbed star. Taped in New York City, like *The View*, *SNL* capitalizes upon New York humor, with the broadcasts letting the world in on the jokes. Regarding Thompson's comedic portrayal of her, Goldberg says, "I love them [the impressions]. I love Kenan. I've known him since he was a little kid." She explains that she even gave him a pair of her signature eyeglasses to be used for the comedy sketches (ABC News). Viewed from the perspective of one working actor to another, the eyeglasses are more than a mere prop — they symbolize mutual respect, lend an air of authenticity, and serve as a reminder to Thompson about the real-life woman behind the lenses.

About balancing the myriad roles that she plays on stage and screen and in life, Goldberg says, "You do what you need to do and keep it moving forward" (Marr). The road that she travels twists and turns, at times, yet Whoopi Goldberg, blueswoman and consummate actor, forges ahead, connecting with audiences, maintaining her sense of humor, and telling her stories along the way — her survival and her successes are continued evidence of victory. Clearly taking pride in her breakout role as Celie in *The Color Purple*, as well as the groundbreaking work of Alice Walker, Steven Spielberg, Quincy Jones and the film's cast and crew, she declares that the film's "universal story" — its ability tell truths transcending race, gender and nationality, makes it "human" (*Cultivating a Classic*). Culminating in her sensitive, dynamic portrayal of Celie, Goldberg bespeaks the blues and beyond.

5

The Impact of Richard Pryor and Bert Williams

> My persona, my *humanity*, is based on that man [Richard Pryor].
> — Whoopi Goldberg (*Richard Pryor: I Ain't Dead Yet!*, Bonus Ch. *Then & Now*)

> I do not believe there is such a thing as innate humor.... It has to be developed by hard work and study, just as every other human quality.
> — Bert Williams (Forbes 35)

(Re)defining humanity is a purposeful, regular activity for Whoopi Goldberg. Says the actor, "I was raised to think that anything is possible in America" (Smith and Goldberg). While here she speaks about the possibility of the election of the first black president of the United States (prior to the actual election of Barack Obama), her words also apply to her liberal sense of possibilities for acting. Is there any role off-limits to a contemporary American actor and world citizen? As Goldberg and the world have come to know, scriptwriting for blackface minstrelsy is one such area, especially when the writer is a black woman. As American history shows, however, the tradition of blackface minstrelsy, and related counterpoint, forms a cornerstone of black arts. Without these, such legendary performers as Richard Pryor (1940–2005) who, according to Morgan Freeman, seemed "to transcend comedy when he spoke to us" (Pryor 207); and Bert Williams (1874–1922), "The greatest comedian on the American Stage" (Forbes xii), among many others, could not have succeeded. Both Pryor and Williams painstakingly articulated humanity through the challenges that they faced and the characters that they created, and their legacies paved the way for contemporary artists like Goldberg, who, while not a comedienne, pointedly uses humor to carry themes and color characters. In 1993, when trying to vault the line of race with her self-styled, ribald blackface humor, Goldberg unwittingly intensified both race and gender divides; such an experience perhaps distracted the audience from recognizing the common human element linking the intention of her words to those of her predecessors and generations of performers yet to come. Her disappointment, as well as the audience's disillusionment, recall for us the significance of the blues tradition, in which one literally and/or figuratively *takes the bitter with the sweet*— ingests and incorporates the disappointments and disillusionments, and voices them as part of a shared human condition.

Reaching beyond music to encompass poetry, dance, foodways and beyond, the Black American blues tradition provides fertile ground for exploring the concept of humanity in relation to blackface minstrelsy. Transmitting a philosophy of life rooted in traditional West African belief systems, filtered through the chattel slave system and making its initial impress upon American culture in the years just prior to emancipation, the blues articulates individual and community identity while reflecting unfulfilled expectations (typically at a literal and/or figurative crossroads). Including such themes as travel, the blues also protests against injustices and advocates and exemplifies freedom of expression. Thus, the blues is revised, as necessary, to anticipate and respond to people, events and circumstances. Far from articulating stereotypical downtrodden images, as commonly believed, the blues exhorts listeners to (re)call and (re)invent themselves as human beings, despite demoralizing, dehumanizing experiences. If nothing else, the very fact that the bluesman or blueswoman can openly protest his or her circumstances represents a kind of victory.

Take, for example, Langston Hughes's "Madame and the Phone Bill": a blues poem. In that poem, the narrator, a Black woman unable to pay her phone bill, protests not the phone bill per se, but rather the fact that she has substantially increased the bill by foolishly taking a collect call from a man named Roscoe, at whom she is now upset (Hughes 353). Speaking to the bill collector, an exasperated, embarrassed Madame says that he could excuse her for paying the bill and instead pursue her ex-boyfriend Roscoe for payment (Hughes 353).

The narrator's embarrassment about being unable to pay the bill pales in comparison to her being on the outs with her ex. Madame begs the bill collector's extra consideration, not because of financial dire straits, but because of her romantic crisis.

Goldberg's origins give us a clue into her sense that American traditions, from homespun improvisation to blackface minstrelsy, are also part of her cultural inheritance. She was born in Chelsea, Manhattan, home of Tin Pan Alley, the legendary locale where songwriters wrote and copied vaudeville and early Broadway tunes. She credits her mother, Emma Johnson, with fostering an early appreciation for creating a wide variety of characters: "It all began with my mother and her funny accents. When I was little, my mom and her cousin Arlene did dialects all the time, just to make themselves laugh" (Thomas

338). She mentions that her mother, usually a very serious person, and Arlene sometimes pretended to be "little, old Jewish ladies, or Spanish guys, or Hungarians ... but neither of them had ever left the country. I just loved that. I wanted to go to the places their accents were from" (338). Moreover, the remnants of blackface minstrelsy remain part of the fabric of New York culture: from 1865 through the 1880s, the minstrel show dominated American entertainment and was enormously popular in the British Isles and Europe as well: "Giant minstrel troupes roamed the landscape the way the dinosaurs had ruled the Jurassic. All the big cities had their resident troupes; at one point, New York City had ten" (Strausbaugh 126). Moreover,

> Minstrel music also took over the middle-class parlor room. Sheet music for minstrel-show hits sold as many as 100,000 copies. In minstrelsy's final years, piano rolls and phonograph cylinders disseminated sentimental late-model minstrel ballads like "Bless My Swanee River Home," "The Pickaninnies' Paradise" and the iconic "My Mammy." What had begun as noisy youth music achieved, in its mature years, something very like Victorian respectability, suitable for the whole family. As it did, the blackface mask became increasingly transparent [Strausbaugh 126].

In 1890, a Black American minstrel and vaudevillian, Ernest Hogan, sparked a national sensation with his hit song, "All Coons Look Alike to Me," spawning the coon craze, which lasted until World War I (Strausbaugh 134–135). Moreover, in 1893, an issue of the *Brooklyn Eagle* reported the activities of a group of white American "society ladies," who were planning to stage an amateur minstrel show to raise funds for a children's hospital. The "anonymous author imagined the typical boorish male telling the women, 'Oh, well, there's one thing you women can't do. You can't run a nigger minstrel show.' Which of course only made the ladies more determined to black up, grab the tambourine and bones, and prove him wrong" (Strausbaugh 127). Blackface minstrelsy paved the way for vaudeville, the precursor of Broadway — a mainstay of New York culture and a venue through which Goldberg eventually achieved Tony-winning status, through her *Whoopi: Direct from Broadway* (1985) one-woman show. Nor were stereotypes regarding race, ethnicity and women limited to Broadway; they also found their way into Hollywood film — stereotypes which Goldberg confronted directly upon her arrival in Hollywood in the 1980s.

For example, she found that blacks described her physical appearance as that of a "pickaninny"— one of many instances where Goldberg says that her "feelings were hurt" (A&E, Ch. 5); that same racial epithet was directed at her while she worked. For example, in *Burglar* (1987), white character Ray Kirschman, a former San Francisco police chief (G.W. Bailey), seeking a buyer for a stolen stamp, confronts character Bernice ("Bernie") Rhodenbarr (Goldberg), an ex-convict, with the racial slur, "pickaninny!" Bernie promptly parodies Mammy, flashing her eyes and demanding that "Massa Ray" find a buyer for the stamp, or else use it to mail himself away (*Burglar*, Scene 9). The scene is especially curious, as the screenplay originally was written for Bruce Willis; surely, the word "pickaninny" did not appear in the early version of the script; undoubtedly, the term was specifically chosen because of Goldberg's presence as headliner. Her 1993 foray into blackface minstrelsy, supplying both the majority of the script, as well as identifying the makeup artist for Ted Danson's performance (JPC, *Whoopi Goldberg Defends* 13) symbolically confronts that challenging workplace experience, as well as other stereotypes of Black Americans. In effect, Danson, transforming into the blackface minstrel, became a mask expressing Goldberg's ideas. So popular did Jim Crow Rice's act become that, not only did it serve as the gateway for blackface minstrelsy throughout the United States, the actor's stage name became associated with legalized racial segregation in the American South. While the original blackface minstrels were white variety show men, black troubadours (after emancipation) also came onboard, with the catch that they, too, had to blacken their features with burnt cork—a double-irony creating a double mask, of sorts, for the often ignored and perpetually misunderstood former chattel slaves and their descendants. "Blackface stood in for a black body presumed to exist beneath—or even instead of—the performative mask. The mask then became the means by which the character, through the songs the comedian sang or the darky dialect in which he sang them, could be thought realistic" (Forbes 25). "By far, the most famous Black performer associated with antebellum minstrelsy was the reel and jig dancer William Henry Lane, who went down in history as Master Juba" (Strausbaugh 123).

> Without the minstrel show there would have been no American works of literature such as *Uncle Tom's Cabin* (1852), no *Adventures of Huckleberry Finn* (1884), [no] Norman Mailer's 'White Negro' (1957); [and no] John Howard Griffin's *Black Like Me* (1961). [Moreover, minstrelsy is also tied to the development of American cinema,] in such landmark films as *Uncle Tom's Cabin* (1903), *The Birth of a Nation* (1915), *The Jazz Singer* (1927),... *Swing Time* (1936), in which Fred Astaire, in blackface, pays tribute to Bill 'Bojangles' Robinson; Melvin Van Peebles' *Watermelon Man* (1970); [and] *Soul Man* (1986) [Lott 5].

As a child, performing on the vaudeville circuit, Sammy Davis, Jr. also performed in blackface. The son of Elvera Davis, the daughter of a Cuban immigrant and Harlem chorus girl, and Sam Davis, Sr., a renowned vaudeville performer, young Sammy eventually became a featured member of the Will Mastin Trio, managed by Will (his father's close friend, whom Sammy was instructed to call "uncle"), and his father, Sammy Davis, Sr. (Haygood 68–69). By the time the lad was six, "They put white chalk around Sammy's lips, enlarging them. In blackface, he resembled a miniature Al Jolson"—a real crowd-pleaser; "times were hard; laughter was a tonic" (Haygood 69). Standing in the wings, young Sammy also watched his "uncle" Will and his father dance, as well as The Nicholas Brothers, and Bill "Bojangles" Robinson; by observation, he learned firsthand about the business of show (Haygood 69). Whether wearing blackface, or displaying his own natural face, Sammy Davis, Jr., like all Black American performers, could not escape the impact of race.

"The black was the truly inassimilable individual in society. As [white] performers blacked up, expressively pointing to what they were not, nothing could seem or be more opposite than the African American. By gesturing to the ultimate outsider, the [white] performer himself found inclusion and acceptance in his ironic embodiment of blacks" (Forbes 23). Nevertheless, "As vaudeville and minstrel shows intersected, minstrels white and black performed on both stages. Blackface singers and comedians were featured on virtually every vaudeville bill through much of its reign" (Strausbaugh 130). Ironically, no matter how well received or wealthy a black performer became, he or she was still subject to racial discrimination and segregation offstage. Amateur blackface minstrelsy retained its popularity among mainstream Americans until the 1970s (Strausbaugh 145).

Blackface is also part of the New Orleans Carnival tradition, where King Zulu (representing Afro-Creoles) faces off once a year against Rex (representing the Anglo-French) during Lundi Gras (the day before Mardi Gras, when Rex symbolically, and temporarily, cedes power to Black New Orleanians for the day). In 1949, Louis Armstrong, the "King of Jazz," donned the symbolic blackface and grass skirt of King Zulu, achieving a lifelong dream shared by many Black New Orleanians, including Sidney Bechet (Teachout 323), a jazz clarinetist/soprano saxophonist.

> As a boy Armstrong had watched the Zulus march through the streets of New Orleans and dreamed of being their King: "All of the members of the Zulus are people, for generations,— most of them — brought up right there around Perdido and Liberty — Franklin streets.... So finally, I grew into manhood — ahem — the lifelong ambition never did cease.... I have traveled all over the world.... And no place that I've ever been, could remove the thought, that was in my head,— that, someday, I will be King of the Zulus" [Teachout 323].

Along with his Hot Fives, in 1926, Armstrong even recorded his wife Lil's song, "The King of the Zulus (At a Chit' Lin Rag)," revisiting and rearranging it with great aplomb decades later for *Satchmo: A Musical Autobiography* (Teachout 323). While scorned in certain circles, garnering the position of King of Zulus meant gaining a special type of social currency, designed to openly parody Rex and racism — if only for a brief time during the Carnival season.

So ingrained was American minstrelsy that "on May 29, 1935, at the Golden State Theater in Oakland, the NAACP promoted an all-black minstrel show as a fund-raiser. At that point, whiteface minstrelsy moved to radio with Amos 'n' Andy, and then managed a rebirth in the 1950s on television"

(Hill and Hatch 134). Most recently, Spike Lee's *Bamboozled* (2000) deals with blackface minstrelsy, critiquing the manner in which racial stereotypes form an expected, rarely questioned and readily replicated part of the American entertainment landscape. By far, the most famous 20th-century blackface performer of African descent was Egbert "Bert" Williams, a Nassau, Bahamas, native. In 1884, at the age of ten, he immigrated with his family to the United States, fleeing "the depression that had plagued the Bahamian economy" to forge a new identity among workers in California citrus groves, which were connected to the larger country via a growing American railway system (Forbes 4). Of Williams, Booker T. Washington is said to have noted in a 1910 tribute, "Bert Williams has done more for the race than I have. He has smiled his way into people's hearts. I have been obliged to fight my way" (Defrantz 534). "[Williams] would spend his career rearticulating and refining the Jim Crow stereotype, resolutely imbuing it with humanity, dignity, and individuality"; for such efforts, audiences alternately applauded and hated him (Forbes 25). The double-edged sword of blackface minstrelsy cut both ways.

The double-meanings of blackface minstrelsy are ensconced in Paul Laurence Dunbar's poem, *We Wear the Mask* in which the narrator describes how Black Americans often deliberately employ laughter and grinning to hide the pain of chronic, pervasive socioeconomic exclusion. Dunbar's figurative mask mirrors aspects of black performance art in the signature solo works "Fontaine, the 'Junkie with a PhD,'" by Goldberg, "Wino and Junkie," by Richard Pryor and "Nobody," by Bert Williams. All three articulate humanity through studied application of the blues philosophy and the masking tradition; from the wretched to the exalted, they create universal characters which become real to audiences, via the performers' extreme attention to their respective characters' details and peculiarities. They demand that the audience reconsider self and society.

Expectancy violation is the rule, with Goldberg's Fontaine, Fontaine first appears in the American national consciousness in the HBO special *Whoopi Goldberg: Direct from Broadway* (1985), a televised, one-woman show originally staged in San Francisco under the title *The Spook Show*. This title likely was revised to introduce Goldberg to a national audience and sidestep potential public outrage regarding the word "spook"—a term which describes fear and a ghost; the term is also used in the pejorative sense to describe Black people, who, according to racist folklore, cannot be seen in the dark. *Direct from Broadway* (the audio recording of which received a Grammy for Best Comedy album) features several of Goldberg's original characters. She masterfully uses comedic elements to convey the character's story—Goldberg's fictional Fontaine seems to have been inspired, at least in part, by Richard Pryor's fictional character Willie the Junkie.

5. The Impact of Richard Pryor and Bert Williams

Born in Peoria, Illinois, in 1940, Richard Pryor became the 20th century's most famous and influential American comedian, culminating in *The Richard Pryor Show* (1977), a television vehicle which showed Pryor's versatility as an actor and writer, fashioning outrageous skits with Paul Mooney (who later appeared as the mythical black philosopher Negrodamus on *Chappelle's Show*), among others. Given the political volatility of the times during which Pryor's show was produced, as well as the show's irreverence, Pryor believed that his show would be canceled at any moment. In fact, *The Richard Pryor Show* was blacked out of several cities, including NBC's WOTV in Grand Rapids, Michigan and an affiliate in Winston-Salem, NC, during its first two airings because of "offensive material" (JPC, *Three Cities Reject* 59). Thus, he resolved to go for broke and be as outrageous as possible. His daughter, Rain Pryor, explains:

> He wasn't a regular father. He was an artist, and he was hugely successful, and most of the time he was consumed by his up-and-down career.
> In 1977 ... when I was eight years old, he had a series on NBC — *The Richard Pryor Show* — and right from the start it seemed to be in trouble. I was too young to know what was going on, but from what I heard he was a little too "out there" for the censors. It really pissed him off. One night, back at the house, he was addressing his entourage, and he was fuming. "This nigger's not going to let anyone tell him what he can and cannot say," he said. "I'm not changing a ... word for those people" [Pryor 82].

Ironically, the more outrageous the show became, the more popular both Pryor and his show became. Nevertheless, major disagreements with the show's censors led him to cut the contract from 10 episodes to "four, plus two specials a year for three years" (Robinson 117). Pryor said that, as an artist, he specifically addresses "the people in the streets. Twenty-five million Black people" — not middle-class white viewers (Robinson 122). Moreover, he said, he did not work in the formulaic way in which typical American television comedy had been presented; instead, he prized and thrived on the "sporadic and spontaneous" aspects of comedy, which, when done well and honestly, can convey world-changing "truth" (Robinson 117).

On the heels of his television comedy series, he co-starred with Gene Wilder in the wildly successful Hollywood comedy, *Stir Crazy* (1980). *Stir Crazy* is a buddy flick directed by Sidney Poitier, in which two New Yorkers, framed for bank robbery, end up in a California prison. The movie contains a famous scene, recalling blackface minstrelsy, in which Harry Monroe (Pryor), "blacks up" Skip Donahue (Wilder) in an effort to help him "be cool" and avoid detection as the two try to escape prison. During that scene, Harry convinces Skip that wearing blackface is not only acceptable, but profitable; Harry tells Skip that Al Jolson became a millionaire by doing just so.

Pryor's convictions regarding using the art of comedy to advance truth on stage and screen made him the first recipient of the Mark Twain Prize for Humor in 1998, the first national prize recognizing the significance of humor in American culture. In 1995, Peter Kaminsky (who eventually became the executive producer of *The Mark Twain Prize for American Humor*) and friends approached the Clinton administration with an idea to honor George Burns with the first prize; Burns died, however, before the Clinton administration finalized the prize (Twain and Kaminsky xiii); thus, Pryor became the award's first recipient. Other humorists so honored include "Carl Reiner, Jonathan Winters, Bob Newhart, Goldberg, Lily Tomlin, Lorne Michaels, Neil Simon, Steve Martin, Billy Crystal, posthumously to George Carlin in 2008, and to Bill Cosby in 2009" (Kaminsky and Twain xiv). Pryor died in 2005, at the age of 65, and his legacy resounds in the comedic stylings of Eddie Murphy, The Wayans (especially Keenan Ivory and Damon), D. L. Hughley, Carlos Mencia and Dave Chappelle, among many others.

Pryor details his concept of humanity in *Richard Pryor: Live on the Sunset Strip* (1982). In that stand-up comedy film, recorded shortly after he survived and recovered from self-inflicted wounds suffered during a freebasing accident, Pryor describes the significance of humanity in overcoming the vice of greed. Reflecting on his unparalleled popularity among white and black audiences, and related wealth, he mentions how his conscience (which he calls his "humanity") prevents him from simply cashing in on the enthusiasm of audiences during times when he knows that his mind/spirit connection is not strong enough to enable him to give the best performance. Pryor says, "Your humanity is bigger than that.... You don't want to rip people off.... My greed does not exceed my self-respect" (Scene 2). Self-respect is another characteristic of humanity, which Pryor reveals via his fictional character Mudbone, a Black American native of Tupelo, Mississippi, whose dark, earthy "marrow" is symbolically represented by mud, which symbolically represents and binds together all humans.

Lapsing into his most beloved fictional character, Mudbone, by audience request, he further expounds upon the concept of humanity. Speaking through the voice of Mudbone, Pryor speaks of himself in the third person, saying that he lost his humanity because of money, which enabled him to tune out the world through cocaine addiction. In a slow, sing-songy, Southern drawl, Mudbone explains that Pryor lost his "hunger" and "went all the way crazy" (Scene 21) because of tremendous wealth. He tells Pryor to enjoy his life, regardless of the hardships of racism, because he will never be(come) a white man. Mudbone advises, "Don't lighten up; tighten up," to which the audience responds with howls of laughter (Scene 21). According to Mudbone, Pryor should retain his racial and cultural heritage and gain a tight rein on reality by focusing upon universal positives, like the warmth and light of the sun shining upon one's face and the ability to make love. Finally, he advises Pryor and the audience to avoid taking life too seriously (Scene 21).

Perhaps Pryor's ability to laugh at himself is the most obvious example of the marriage of his humanity and his art. In *Live on the Sunset Strip*, he jokes about his experience of accidental self-immolation during the freebasing incident, and explains how, during his hospitalization, while he was still bandaged and intubated, a Black American hospital worker and fan objectified him to the point of asking for an autograph, while "steam" was still emanating from his (Pryor's) body (Scenes 25–26). He even jokes about an errant report, issued during his recovery, that he had just died (Scene 27). Later, Pryor borrows a matchbook from a fan, and, lighting a cigarette, makes the lit match "dance," poking fun at a widely-circulated joke that fans created, in which people likened the dancing flame to reports of his having run into the street, screaming and seeking medical attention, his body aflame (Scene 28).

Richard Pryor, the man and artist, sees humor emanating largely from anger, concerning life's inequities and peoples' idiosyncrasies; his fictional character, Mudbone, however, sees humor emanating from poverty, which Mudbone calls "hunger" (Scene 21). Both Pryor and Mudbone experience hunger, but in different ways; Pryor suffers the hunger for racial justice (a hunger shared by many of his audience members), while Mudbone experiences poverty, which he calls "hardtimes" (Scene 21); nevertheless, both the comedian and his fictional character Mudbone subsist upon and exist through humor. Goldberg sees Mudbone as one of Pryor's most important gifts to the worlds of comedy and philosophy; she says that characters like Mudbone are key to humanity, because, "Those are the cats that held all the history. They knew everything and everyone. 'Cause they sat and they observed; that was their whole job in life," providing history and much-needed wisdom, down the line (*I Ain't Dead Yet* Ch. 6). When asked to describe Richard Pryor, the man, in a single word, Goldberg steadfastly refuses, on the grounds that "that would make him a one-dimensional person.... He's so many things at once" (*I Ain't Dead Yet* Ch. 3).

Pryor's skit, "Wino and Junkie," is perhaps the immediate predecessor to Goldberg's formally educated fictional character, Fontaine. One of the earliest recorded performances of Pryor performing "Wino and Junkie" appears in the film *Richard Pryor: Live & Smokin'* (1971). That film includes such skits as "Wino Preacher," in which Wino stands at the crossroads of the projects, conducting traffic and admonishing passersby to nurture their neighbors, regardless of the destruction and confusion that surrounds them. Also included is "Willie the Junkie," concerning a passerby whose loss of family as the result of his heroin addiction inspires Wino and the audience to recognize his humanity and sympathize with him.

In "Wino and Junkie," which originally appeared on Pryor's Grammy-winning LP, *That Nigger's Crazy* (1974), Wino shows his humanity by stationing himself at the crossroads, literally and figuratively. A blues figure, Wino stands on a street corner, fashioning himself a kind of cop, "directing traffic" on a Sunday morning (*Richard Pryor Anthology* Track 9). Wino implies that most black people busy themselves on the Lord's day, traditionally a day of rest, by rushing back and forth to church, historically the most important and longest-lasting institution in black communities. While no longer a church-goer, Wino nevertheless upholds the Church, and shows his moorings by unintentionally slurring and mangling a couple of self-styled hymns, all the while admonishing drivers to "slow down" (*Richard Pryor Anthology* Track 9). He has little tolerance for Junkie, however, who also crosses his path.

Wino, who tries to redeem himself through his actions as "cop," sets himself a cut above Junkie, whom he portrays as immoral and self-absorbed. For Wino, there is no shame in addiction, per se; the element of shame comes into play when a person fails to realize his or her social obligations to serve as heritage reminder and help the larger society. The implied meaning is that Junkie is perceived as offering an especial threat to young children, who are easily influenced by what they see; Junkie not only *does not* discourage young people from doing drugs; he also is a threat because he steals in order to maintain his habit (he says that his father no longer wants him around because he stole his father's television set). Wino tells Junkie that he (Junkie) "has potential"—and that such potential can help him learn how to maximize his influence and solidify his social standing. Wino tries to school Junkie on the most important lesson that a Black man can learn: "How to deal with the white man." Quips Wino, "That's why I'm in the position I'm in today" (*Richard Pryor Anthology* Track 9). The audience heartily laughs at the ironic conclusion that Wino draws, for Wino, despite his obvious flaws, still tries to make a positive contribution to society; his presence on the street corner, for all to see, also serves as a warning to church-goers about the dangers of alcohol, the power of God's grace and the possibilities of redemption. Unlike Junkie, Wino does not wallow in self-pity; he knows that racism (represented by "the white man") stacks the deck against him, but he keeps on fighting. Pryor's Wino reminds us of the Black American adage, "Got one face for the world to see/Another for the one I know is me." Appearances can be misleading; Wino, while obviously self-destructive, is far more virtuous than he appears. God sees and knows all, and Wino is a witness. Dave Chappelle's Tyrone Biggums is a hybrid subversion of Goldberg's and Pryor's characters; instead of serving as a kind of wise fool, as do Goldberg's Junkie with a Ph.D. and Pryor's Wino, Chappelle's Tyrone Biggums deliberately and unashamedly (ab)uses his status as a drug addict to take advantage of "the man" (white people/the government) and endanger youth.

Pryor believed that Chappelle was the next in line to inherit his mantle in American comedy (Williams and Williams 239–240). Chappelle describes

5. The Impact of Richard Pryor and Bert Williams   89

Pryor's influence in universal, human terms: "You've seen those evolution charts? He's the dude walking upright" (Williams and Williams 236). Such a comment is even more moving given Pryor's struggles with drug addiction, and, later, multiple sclerosis, which claimed his life at the age of 65 (JPC, *Richard Pryor Comedy Legend* 6). A native of Washington, D.C., Dave Chappelle (b. 1973) worked the stand-up comedy circuit for years, eventually appearing in the ill-fated (but aptly named) major motion picture *Half-Baked* (1998). But it was the small screen that afforded him his biggest break. His DVD releases *Dave Chappelle: Killin' Them Softly* (2003) and *Dave Chappelle: For What It's Worth (Live at the Fillmore)* (2005) extended some of the ideas that he explored in the television comedy series that he co-produced, *Chappelle's Show* (2003–2006). True to its blues moorings, the opening credits of the show begin with a Black bluesman playing acoustic guitar, along with an elderly Black man, wailing on a harmonica. The bluesmen appear against a backdrop of white; but it is clear that they occupy a street corner (any corner), as they have placed a hat upon the ground for passersby to tip them. Chappelle drops a dollar into the hat, and the old man sings about *Chappelle's Show* being the "best show on TV" (*Chappelle's Show* opening credits). Chappelle's Tyrone Biggums is one of the show's most memorable characters.

Tyrone Biggums is a crack addict who deliberately evokes the blackface minstrel image; he presents himself to viewers as a farce, while fellow characters within the skit take him seriously. So addicted to cocaine is Biggums that he freely walks about with caked white powder "cocaine" around his lips, harkening to the white chalk which blackface minstrels use about the eyes and lips. In the skit, "Tyrone Biggums" (*Chappelle's Show*, Season 1, Scene 2), a schoolteacher (a white woman) introduces Mr. Biggums as the featured speaker for Drug Awareness Week. Biggums's presentation leads the audience to question the validity of the "scared straight" phenomenon, first popularized during the 1970s. (*Scared Straight* was a documentary shown to grade school and high school students, whereby prison inmates were questioned regarding why they were imprisoned and what they could have done to prevent such experiences. The concept of the film was to make children so afraid of the horrors of prison that they would not break the law.) Through Biggums, Chappelle questions whether a practicing crack addict should even be allowed into, let alone tour, a series of American public schools (indeed, Biggums cannot tell which school he is visiting; he has visited so many that they have become a blur). While speaking to the multi-racial, multi-ethnic inner-city grade school children, Biggums tells them, in an off-hand manner, how and where to sell, obtain and take illegal drugs — a preposterous concept that draws hearty laughter from the television audience.

Through Tyrone Biggums, Chappelle implies that a practicing drug addict specializes in, and focuses on, how to deal and take drugs; such a person is not worthy of addressing the nation's youth, especially not on the government's dime. Unlike Pryor's Wino, who tries to redeem himself, and Goldberg's Fontaine, who succumbs to drugs but does not endorse or sell them, instead choosing to dispense helpful advice, Biggums is no "big deal"; he has done nothing to redeem himself, thus, there is no reason to spotlight him as a model citizen. Moreover, instead of being chastised for actively corrupting children, he is openly rewarded with an audience of impressionable youngsters and money (ostensibly, his speaker's fees help him to maintain his habit). Nor is the shame of his condition solely the fault of Mr. Biggums; Chappelle shows that society at large ignores him, instead of helping him (the cocaine caked around his mouth shows the world a man in pain and in need of help). The grand finale of Biggums's presentation shows that he knows that he (and the system) are "full of it": he pulls a plastic trash bin from the side of the classroom, places it front and center, and defecates into the bin while the schoolchildren watch, horrified. Meanwhile, the DVD's laugh track allows the viewer to hear the television studio's live audience howling with laughter. Chappelle's character teaches viewers that Drug Awareness Week programs, while well-intentioned, may very well glorify the very drugs that the programs are designed to combat.

For three seasons (2003–2006), *Chappelle's Show* rode high as a major draw for American cable television's Comedy Central. Patterned partially after the style of *The Richard Pryor Show* (one of the writers and recurring co-stars of *Chappelle's Show* was Paul Mooney, who had written jokes for Pryor and Pryor's show); Eddie Murphy's *Saturday Night Live* skits; and Whoopi Goldberg's one-woman stage shows — *Chappelle's Show* broke new ground, even for cable television. To Chappelle's surprise, despite the show's outrageous skits, not only was the show *not* canceled, it was renewed, to the tune of a two season, $50 million-dollar contract. The renewal of *Chappelle's Show* was based "mostly on the strength of explosive DVD sales. The first season's set ... sold 2.8 million copies, making it the best-selling DVD of a TV series" (JPC, *Dave Chappelle* 53). As was true when Pryor abandoned *The Richard Pryor Show* in the midst of its success, Dave Chappelle also walked away. While Pryor's concerns revolved around freedom of speech in relation to censorship on network television, *Chappelle's Show*, a solid cable television hit, was not censored at all. Chappelle realized that, ironically, instead of being counterculture, as he had intended, the power of cable television and readily available play-on-demand commercial recordings actually helped determine and disseminate the very culture that his work had always questioned.

Prior to Pryor's Wino character (the comedic "uncle" of Goldberg's "Junkie with a Ph.D."; both Pryor and Goldberg paved the way for Chappelle's character, Tyrone Biggums) was Bert Williams' signature character, "Nobody." "Nobody" epitomized Williams's ability to make something from nothing

5. The Impact of Richard Pryor and Bert Williams

and force audiences to see his humanity in ways that their seeing his natural self could not. A Nassau, Bahamas, native, Williams (1874–1922) immigrated to the United States, eventually forming a partnership with George Walker. The duo, Williams and Walker, became renowned for their quick wit and professionalism, within the realms of blackface minstrelsy and vaudeville. Walker described their roles as cultural ambassadors: "The love, the humor, and the pathos of the black race in this country afford a field for wide study, and ... the stage is the place where the character of the African race can be studied from a real artistic point of view" (Forbes 149). For his part, after the breakup of Williams and Walker, Williams scored by creating a mythical character so grounded in human emotion that it overshadowed the actor himself: "Nobody." Also, the name of the character's signature song "Nobody" began as a downtrodden black man who could not get a break; Williams's strong understanding of misfortune and disadvantage, combined with humor, created an archetype of a man who, despite impediments, and often because of them, nevertheless keeps on fighting, all the while protesting his circumstances, with the audience cheering him on. In this sense, Williams becomes the ultimate bluesman, using another bluesman (the blackface minstrel Nobody) as his "mask."

For seven years, Williams performed "Nobody" to thunderous applause and untold encores, using improvisatory skills to freshen his approach and further enliven the character. According to Williams, after the first month of performing "Nobody," he tired of the song and tried to abandon it and the character, but audiences demanded and clamored for them (Forbes 251). Toward the end of his days of performing "Nobody," Williams used a small notebook as a prop, pretending to search for new lyrics.

Muddling his way through the notebook, and at last settling upon just the right lyrics, he uttered a phrase imploring the audience to tell him who will help him obtain needed monies to purchase warm vittles on a cold winter night (Forbes 251). As per usual, the audience yelled the title and chorus of the song along with him, indicating their universal understanding that no one will offer to help him. Ironically, Williams's ability to symbolize everyman happened only when he was in blackface, and only while he was on stage.

Williams endured many hardships as a traveling actor, forced to ride in Jim Crow "Coloreds Only" railway cars (sooty, smoky passenger cars, located between the engine and the smoker); he was forbidden to fraternize with white colleagues before and after shows; and, depending upon the city, he was often barred from taking hotel accommodations in white establishments (Forbes 251). Asked Williams, "Why is it a colored passenger can sleep over or under a white passenger on a Pullman and no color question is raised; but as soon as a citizen of color applies at a hotel for a room where he could be separated by walls and doors, objection is made to his presence?" (Forbes 279). Nor was his status as a leading blackface minstrel/ vaudevillian secure. The White Rats, "a white vaudevillian organization that was 'part union and part fraternal order,'" not only railed against B. F. Keith, the Boston-based chief organizer of vaudeville venues, they also actively sought that Black Americans (including Bert Williams) and women be barred from performing as headline acts (Forbes 179). At the height of his fame (and likely due to the influence of the White Rats), Williams lost a leading role in a major vaudeville production to 16-year-old Al Jolson (Forbes 231). Such sparked the career of Jolson, now best known for his lead in the major motion picture *The Jazz Singer* (1927), and his performance of he song "Mammy" (Forbes 231). With white audiences recognizing him as human only while he was onstage, and black audiences questioning the degree to which his artistry advanced or hurt Black possibilities, Williams continued perfecting his craft; full recognition of his challenges and contributions has yet to be made, however.

In 1976, the year of the United States Bicentennial, acclaimed entertainer Ben Vereen unveiled his blackface tribute to Bert Williams, in a one-man show. He had already starred in the Broadway smash *Pippin* [written by Ossie Davis], for which he won a Tony Award, and had gained international audiences with his notable work as Chicken George in the landmark television miniseries *Roots* (JPC, *Ben Vereen* 14–15). He especially studied the contributions and sacrifices of Williams, to get a stronger sense of his own position and contributions as a performer and also as a means of educating the public. Viewing the Bicentennial as a once-in-a lifetime, prime opportunity to explore the sagging weight and ridiculousness of race prejudice by paying homage to a fellow performer who, although Black, had no choice but to "black up" in order to be seen and heard, Vereen found that "audiences had rejected" (Forbes 334) his one-man show. As a result, Vereen "felt that he had been misunderstood" (Forbes 334).

His masterful, transformative performance as Bert Williams, a command performance given for President Reagan and First Lady Nancy Reagan, originally included a preamble, of sorts, in which Vereen gave a brief history of Williams's struggles and triumphs, and the significance of the character "Nobody" to show the irony of a "nobody" actually being somebody. Yet the television broadcast of Vereen's performance omitted his preamble, resulting in "only an image of Ben Vereen, a black man, seemingly shuffling and dancing in blackface" (Forbes 335).

The outrage which black audiences expressed was matched in 1993 when Ted Danson hosted a roast at the Friar's Club, honoring Whoopi Goldberg. Typically, roasts offer ribald humor and tongue-in-cheek, off-the-cuff, rough-around-the-edges appreciation for a man who can take as well as he gives. Influential men are "roasted"; women, however influential, typically are not.

The fact that Goldberg was roasted at all shows that she had broken through the so-called glass ceiling of Hollywood. Her willingness to be roasted, as well as actively participate in the event, shows her determination to be seen as an actor first and foremost; she apparently embraced the roast as a type of role to be played, and an opportunity to try addressing a select audience in a very different way, during an era of growing political correctness. Says Goldberg, "I'm the woman who made m. f. a household word. I am no saint. I've always been known as the other side of tasteful." She also openly questioned whether the members of the audience who protested Danson's routine had ever attended a roast before (JPC, *Whoopi Goldberg Defends* 14). Members of the audience included "Michael Douglas, Robert Guillaume and talk show host Montel Williams, who stormed out of the ceremony" (14). Both she and Danson emphasized that the script was crafted out of love for Goldberg, and that no ill will or disrespect was intended (13–14). She also said that the blackface act was conceived specifically to address the "hate mail" that she received for dating a white man: correspondence which described Danson as a "nigger lover" and wished that any progeny that they may produce together would die (13). Such hate mail was in addition to that which she received for her openness in discussing such topics as AIDS and abortion (14). In a letter to the editor of the *New York Times*, Andrew Balansky of Madison, Wisconsin, wrote, "By wearing a mask, Mr. Danson entered a world where it is acceptable to say 'nigger,' and thus he may have told us some things we did not want to hear. Comedy as an art form will, at its best, challenge its audience, most disturbingly when truth is exposed.... If we cannot accept Mr. Danson's role-playing, how are we to recognize and move beyond the many guises of racial politics performed on a real stage?" (Balansky). Moreover, "Since the mid–1960s, white Americans have been assiduously schooled to associate ... feelings of shame and guilt with blackface and minstrelsy. Black Americans have been schooled to associate similar feelings about the Black artists who historically participated in minstrelsy. The blackface mask became one of this society's universal taboo symbols" (Strausbaugh 149). Goldberg and Danson forced the audience to confront that taboo. As a result, American society punished both actors with open skepticism, negative press and hate mail.

Nevertheless, the risks that Goldberg and Danson took at the Friar's Club roast opened new possibilities for women. Four years after the Goldberg roast, The Friar's Club invited Joy Behar (best known for her work co-hosting television's *The View*, long before Goldberg joined the talk show) to break the ban on women hosting a roast; in 1997, Behar became the first woman to host a Friar's Club roast, this one for actor Danny Aiello. Barbara Walters, Richard Belzer, Buddy Hackett and Sandra Bernhard were scheduled "to skewer Aiello" (Brozan). According to the *New York Times*, "The last time a woman was in the spotlight at a Friars Club roast was in 1993 when Whoopi

Goldberg was the target of the barb fest and Ted Danson, then her companion, appeared in blackface and made comments some people considered racially insensitive" (Brozan). Said Behar of Goldberg's roast, "'No matter what I do, I will never be as controversial, so the heat is off'" (Brozan). She declared that her turn as host "won't be squeaky clean.... It just won't have the same level of raunch [as Goldberg's roast]" (Brozan).

If Vereen's revival of his one-man show is a recasting of the image of Bert Williams, then Ted Danson's blackface performance, may be considered a recasting of Vereen's efforts. While separated by gender and time, both Vereen's and Goldberg's ideas had in common the determination to show the humanity of people (flaws, foibles and fascinations); moreover, both performances demanded more consideration of audiences than they could muster, unintentionally fanning the very flames of prejudice which the performances were designed to douse. Unlike Vereen's videotaped performance before the Reagans and their guests, Danson's foray into blackface minstrelsy, largely scripted by Goldberg herself, was neither videotaped nor audiorecorded. Instead, what snippets outside audiences get concerning the event are from bits and snatches of personal anecdotes of attendees as well as articles and photographs, carried on the waves of newspapers and magazines (in much the same manner that we have evidence of Bert Williams's work and related audience responses). Either way, the results were disastrous; neither Vereen's nor Danson's performance achieved desired ends and instead inflamed audiences, rather than drawing them closer together.

According to *Jet*, "Many were incensed by Danson's humor, which included stereotypes and graphic descriptions of sexual antics with Goldberg" (JPC, *Whoopi Goldberg Defends* 12). Before the event occurred, Bobcat Goldthwait, a comedian and actor who co-starred with Goldberg in *Burglar* (1987), openly asked Danson whether black audiences would find blackface humor funny in 1993. Actor Matthew Modine appreciated the fact that Danson's character could openly mention racial epithets "like Richard Pryor did," but expressed concern regarding Danson's character mentioning Goldberg's "body parts" in great detail (60). Among attendees who protested was New York Mayor David Dinkins who denounced the performance, mentioning his embarrassment for Goldberg and the audience (60). Danson finished his performance by "wolf[ing] down" a "tray of watermelon," fulfilling his part of a "dare" which he had struck with Goldberg, while she "rolled with laughter" (60). Such an act is within the realm of minstrelsy; for within minstrelsy lore, "Blacks are associated with an insatiable desire for watermelon" (Strausbaugh 131).

Gender is a major consideration especially where Danson's appearance in blackface is concerned, for, while Goldberg saw herself as an actor and scriptwriter interacting with another actor, the audience likely saw her as a black woman (and an Oscar winner, at that) being openly disrespected by a white man. Moreover, at the time, Danson was also her romantic partner (JPC, *Whoopi Goldberg Defends* 12). Danson's blackface performance happened fewer than three years after Goldberg had won the Best Supporting Actress Oscar for her work in *Ghost*. Frustrated at the Friar's Club for apologizing for Danson's performance, Goldberg said, "The X-rated stuff is a Friar's Club tradition. Should the roasters have to tiptoe around me because I'm a Black woman?" (14). The blackface mask seemed to obscure the very humanity that it was to have highlighted. The romantic relationship of Goldberg and Danson came to an end shortly after the Friar's Club performance (JPC, *Whoopi and Ted Danson* 16). The actors had only recently co-starred, to great effect and even greater critical acclaim, in the comedy *Made in America* (1993) and had planned to do a sequel (16), which never materialized. Racial issues also came to the fore in the casting process of that film. Goldberg explains, "Unfortunately, the role of Sarah was white.... I'm a real good actress, but look at me.... I ain't white" (JPC, *Whoopi Goldberg and Ted Danson Get Big Laughs* 58). As a result, the script was rewritten to accommodate Goldberg—a choice with which producer Michael Douglas agreed (58). *Made in America* ended on a very high note—just the opposite of Goldberg's and Danson's experience at the roast.

Goldberg clearly does not allow race or gender to define her. Richard Pryor and her mother, Emma Johnson, who both believed in the power of truthtelling, are strong influences upon Goldberg's artistry. She explains, "[Richard Pryor] wasn't afraid of consequences; he didn't always *like* the consequences, but he wasn't afraid of them. And that, coupled with what my Mom always told me, which was, 'You can be yourself, if you don't care if they like you'" (*I Ain't Dead Yet!* Bonus Ch. *Then & Now*). Goldberg also says that, prior to live performances, she invokes the phrase, "Babalu, Babalu, Desilu/Richard Pryor, Richard Pryor, Richard Pryor," openly paying homage to ancestors of American comedy (*I Ain't Dead Yet!* Bonus Ch. *Love of Richard*). As author of a different identity (the blackface minstrel "roasting" her), Goldberg occupies the stance of the black poet-musician. In *Figures in Black: Words, Signs and the "Racial" Self* (1989), Henry Louis Gates, Jr., argues the Black poet-musician's "mythopoeic role: to predict our future through his or her sensitivity to our past, coupled with an acute, almost intuitive awareness of the present" (Gates 177). He further explains that the black poet-musician's "truth" is inextricably tied to language, which is in itself tied to music (Gates 177). Expounds Gates: "There can be no poetry in this context without music and myth" (Gates 177). By extension, he argues that "the Black poet is a point of consciousness of the language" (Gates 178). Taking Gates's point a step further, Goldberg uses language as a form of music; the concept of the black poet-musician serves as a fitting starting point for understanding her work and personal approach.

The "music and myth" of Goldberg's Fontaine allows the poetry (truth) to shine through. As the educated fictional Junkie, Goldberg serves as the pivotal musician-poet, warning audiences about double-speak, while weaving wisdom. Fontaine first appears as a variation of the village idiot, a stock Western theatrical character dating to ancient Greece and especially capitalized on during Shakespeare's time; Goldberg's masterful delivery, however, renders Fontaine a "fountain" of knowledge and wisdom that not only belies her appearance and sound, but also makes Fontaine "real."

In her first HBO special, *Whoopi Goldberg: Direct from Broadway* (1985), Fontaine enters the Broadway stage (a kind of crossroads), wearing a long turquoise-colored bandana, tied around the head and barely containing her funky dreadlocks; dark sunglasses; a long, black cardigan layered over a long-sleeved, waffle-weave cotton thermal shirt; black leather pants; and large tan cowboy boots with brass toe-tips. As Fontaine, Goldberg struts onto the stage, grabbing her crotch, absent-mindedly singing and dancing a variation of the theme from the 1956 film *Around the World in 80 Days*, interjecting expletives between the chorus. When she turns to address the audience, it barely responds, however. Offended, and protesting, as blues figures are wont to do, Fontaine tells the audience that the introduction, like their attitude, must be redone. Here, she uses Fontaine to teach the audience a major aspect of black arts: they are participatory and draw strength from audience response. Goldberg also reminds the audience that, while they have paid to see her, she is no court jester; she will not simply "perform" for them; instead, she fully expects the audience to work along with her. The audience laughs as Fontaine leaves the stage and re-enters a few seconds later, rehashing the song, "Around the World." The audience responds more heartily to Fontaine's premature "encore," at which point she descends into the front row and raps to Broadway singer-actor-dancer Josephine Premice, asking to kiss her hand. When Premice offers her right hand, Fontaine rejects it, saying that he/she would rather kiss Premice's left hand, as it is adorned with diamonds. The audience laughs and soon learns that Fontaine not only is a junkie, but that he/she is a self-proclaimed "businessperson," who supports the habit through theft, and that he/she has an earned Ph.D. in American Literature from Columbia University, specializing in American culture "from the 1920s to present." He/she explains that illicit drug use is necessary to dissipate anger and resentment regarding having earned a Ph.D. that does not help him/her obtain gainful employment or guarantee increased social status (Chapter 2).

Fontaine is deliberately ambiguous with respect to sexual identity; he/she swaggers, brags about enticing girls with kisses, and even kisses a woman's hand. But he/she also talks about issues as a woman would. For example, he/she mentions seeing a man carrying a protest sign, reading, "Stop Abortion," and Fontaine stops and bluntly asks the man to specify when he had experienced pregnancy (Ch. 2). The audience laughs heartily. Fontaine's take on abortion echoes that of many women who, while sympathizing with men's views, nevertheless see pregnancy as a woman's issue.

Fontaine also complains about having to pay for expensive plane tickets in advance, only to be mistreated and taken for granted. He/she mentions the inedible, cold mystery meat served as part of a pre-paid meal; having to use the rest room while aboard the plane, and seeing the flap in the toilet open, showing the fair blue skies. Fontaine expresses horror that he/she cannot comfortably sit upon the toilet, for fear that the flap would open, and he/she would get sucked into the sky. Fontaine declares that people should be able to take trial flights, paying for the ride only afterward, based upon how well customer service and flight attendants treat passengers. He/she also shows the audience how it can get the upper hand, and gain some respect from snooty ticket counter personnel, by rummaging through their pocketbooks to read their IDs, and then threatening to visit them at their homes (Ch. 2). Fontaine wishes to level the field so that ticket counter personnel, like passengers, are forced to share personal information with total strangers. Such a joke, of course, makes sense only in the pre–9/11 world.

The weight of Fontaine's philosophies comes to bear in the final moments of the skit, where he/she talks about visiting Amsterdam, ostensibly to engage in the drug culture. While there, Fontaine also tours the Vincent Van Gogh Museum and Anne Frank House. While Fontaine explains that he/she is "jaded," tears of wonderment and a breaking voice indicate the power of Anne Frank's words for even the most jaded junkie: "In spite of everything, I still believe that people are really good at heart" (Merti 3). Fontaine speaks honestly and convincingly about the impact of the Holocaust upon humanity and the ability of children to see the good in people and situations, whereas adults often will not/cannot (Ch. 2).

Goldberg reprises her role as Fontaine for her HBO special, *Whoopi Goldberg: Back to Broadway (The 20th Anniversary)* (2005), in such interrelated skits as "Everything's Everything," "Bad Intelligence," "Condoleezza," "Church and State," and "Watching You." "Everything's Everything" recalls for audience members the popular 1970s Black American phrase, which basically means, "It is what it is," a variation that incorporates and anticipates the Spanish adage, "Que será, será" ("Whatever will be, will be"). Fontaine, this time more specifically female in presentation and demeanor, once again forces the audience to acknowledge her by participating at the outset, beginning and re-starting the riff, "Around the World." The lack of audience participation at the outset causes Fontaine to quip that the audience must be majority-white (Ch. 1), a comment which itself draws laughter from the mixed-generation audience of original Whoopi Goldberg fans and their sons, daughters, grandsons and granddaughters. Upon beginning her schtick, Fontaine again enters the front row of the audience, choosing to ask to kiss a woman's bejeweled hand; the woman complies, and Fontaine asks whether the man seated nearby bought the baubles for her. The woman replies in the affirmative, sparking laughter from the audience.

A major thread tying together Fontaine's riffs is the American government's lack of awareness, epitomized by what Fontaine describes as President George W. Bush's ineptitude regarding several issues. These include geography (apparently, he cannot tell the difference between Afghanistan and Iraq); an inability to locate Saddam Hussein (G.W. explains that the American government cannot find Saddam Hussein "because he's hiding") and the fact that Stevie Wonder is blind (Fontaine mentions how, during a White House concert, G.W. waved at Wonder, as if the composer could see him, resulting in a stern look of consternation upon First Lady Laura Bush's face) (Chs. 1–4). The audience laughs heartily at the aforementioned, paving the way for Fontaine's further riffs about censorship and religious fundamentalism. Fontaine considers contemporary government censorship overbearing (she compares it to rape) because it assumes that Americans do not have the common sense to simply change the channel or station when broadcasts, such as the Janet Jackson "wardrobe malfunction," offend them. Of religious fundamentalism, Fontaine declares that such represents the very opposite of the right to religious freedom upon which the United States was founded. Fontaine returns to discuss the symbol of the Anne Frank House as a site of destruction and transformation and warns the audience that free speech, as well as religious and sexual preference, are under siege. Ending on a positive note, she recapitulates the overarching lesson of Anne Frank: that good may be found in everyone; thus, Fontaine resolves to realize that mantra in everyday life, challenging the audience to do the same (Ch. 5). Fittingly, she ends her composition by singing lines from "Every Breath You Take," popularized by the band The Police, emphasizing the song's refrain concerning the watchful eye of the narrator.

Goldberg's character Fontaine is a veritable "fountain" of knowledge and wisdom, developed through years of careful, concentrated study, the very basis of humanity and humor, as Bert Williams tells us. Similarly, Goldberg also carefully studied the history and structure of blackface minstrelsy performance, and, per the related blues tradition, intentionally adapted it for the Friar's Club 1993 roast. The basic structure and content of Danson's blackface minstrelsy performance shows that Goldberg had seriously studied, and had an understanding of, blackface stage traditions. She perhaps misunderstood or underestimated audience expectations, however, as the audience saw only the myth (stereotypes), and not the truths that she wished to convey.

While blackface minstrelsy is a salient part of black arts traditions, interwoven into the fabric of American culture, audiences do not universally understand or appreciate it. John McWhorter reminds us about the dangers of simply naming and reacting to stereotypes, without fully considering their shifting meanings over time: "The fact that Bert Williams had to wear blackface makeup cannot be seen as a more urgent message for us than in 1957, Langston Hughes' *Simply Heavenly*" (McWhorter 207). In the musical *Simply Heavenly: A Comedy*, Mamie, a Black woman in a working-class Black household, declares, "I like watermelon and chitterlings both, and I don't care who knows it" (Hughes 192). She continues,

> It's getting so colored folks can't do nothing no more without some other Negro calling you a stereotype. If you like a little gin, you're a stereotype. You got to drink Scotch.... Lord, have mercy, honey, do-don't like no black-eyed peas and rice! Then you're a down-home Negro for true — which I is — and proud of it! [Hughes 192].

Hughes's deliberate, repeated use of the double-negative underscores Mamie's frustration, while causing the audience to second-guess the validity of immediately jumping to conclusions regarding stereotypes. Like the fictional Mamie, Goldberg expresses her right to be and to express herself. She embraces the right to freedom of expression, experimenting with form and function by taking chances and voicing her views, staring down, exploring, deconstructing and ignoring stereotypes, as she sees fit.

6

Sister Rhythm and Blues
Sister Act *Success*

> I have a special affection for the 1960s songs we did [in *Sister Act*]. I don't have a set of pipes like Martha Reeves or Mary Wells, but we managed to put a little bit of our own flavor into the songs.
> — Whoopi Goldberg (Collier 37)

Reared as a Catholic, Goldberg believes in God (Whoopi Goldberg, *Back to Broadway* Ch. 4), yet she is skeptical of the Catholic Church: "The way I see it, the Catholic Church has strayed from what Christ was all about. Me, personally, I've tried to hold fast. It ain't easy, swimming against the current, but I do what I can. I was schooled Catholic, but I don't take a lot of it to heart. I use the basics — do unto others, don't judge unless your own s — t is in order — because they make sense" (Goldberg, *Book* 92). A similarly serious yet lighthearted approach to everyday ethics is evident with Goldberg's work in Disney's *Sister Act* (1992) and *Sister Act 2: Back in the Habit* (1993). The success of both films not only seems to have inspired other entertainment projects, it sparked renewed popular American interest in Catholicism and the Motown Sound, while expanding the actor's popularity among audiences worldwide.

In *Sister Act*, Goldberg plays Deloris Van Cartier, a glittery rhythm and blues soul queen of Reno, Nevada, and her altar (pun intended) ego Sister Mary Clarence: a sister (female/woman/"sistah," in the Black American vernacular) who becomes a sister (Catholic nun, named after the Virgin Mary, reflecting the virtue of clarity, or truth) as a means of hiding from thugs after inadvertently witnessing a murder. Yet the cloister of nuns, whom Deloris Van Cartier initially rejects as stodgy, stilted and cold, serves as a catalyst for the emergence of Sister Mary Clarence, the woman who finds herself in the unique position of inspiring and changing a convent, all the while atoning for her sins by helping humanity. Several scenes illustrate how Sister Mary Clarence inspires and changes the convent: Chapter 16, "New Choir Director"; Chapter 17, "Hail, Holy Queen"; Chapter 18, "Reaching Out"; and Chapter 19, "My God."

6. Sister Rhythm and Blues

In "New Choir Director," the Reverend Mother is remonstrating with Sister Mary Clarence for encouraging the nuns to explore San Francisco after dark. As a penance, Sister Mary Clarence is given the responsibility of leading the choir, so as to simultaneously put Clarence's musical skills to work and also make her more visible, so that the Reverend Mother can more readily supervise her. Sister Mary Clarence deftly replaces the longstanding choir director, Sister Mary Lazarus, using her wit and a bit of diplomacy. Sister Mary Clarence convinces Sister Mary Lazarus that the choir needs as much help as it can possibly get; hence, Clarence says, Lazarus's grueling adherence to old-school norms make her especially suited to leading the choir through much-needed daily musical exercises. (In this scene, Goldberg, as Clarence, appears devilishly cute, smoothly manipulating Lazarus and showing shades of Clarence's worldly "Deloris" side.)

In "Hail, Holy Queen" (the name of the DVD chapter, which also recalls the traditional Christian hymn), Sister Mary Clarence leads the choir (including honorary choir co-director Lazarus), in a hymn with a 1960s girl-group twist. Beginning the hymn in a traditional, staid manner, the choir, under the direction of Sister Mary Clarence, segues into a spirited 1960s-style arrangement, accented by a tambourine, handclaps, boogie-woogie piano riffs, along with spirited interjections by Sisters Mary Lazarus, Patrick, Robert, and others. (This scene illustrates Goldberg's artistic commitment, in that it relies upon and expands many of the artist's skills, such as acting, singing, and dancing; moreover, she leads the choir with authentic, carefully choreographed hand and arm gestures in time with the music, while remaining in-character.)

In "Reaching Out," Sister Mary Clarence leads her posse of nuns through the tough streets of San Francisco, extemporaneously taking a turn at jumping double-dutch, and visually surveying the neighborhood. Meanwhile the sisters counsel the poor and dejected, repair an old car, and clean and beautify the neighborhood, including touching up the church's colorful outdoor mural. During this scene, the soundtrack pumps C & C Music Factory's dance club hit, "Just a Touch of Love," amplified by the earnest, ample sounds of guest vocalist Lisa Lisa (of Lisa Lisa and Cult Jam fame). This song does more than just provide an uptempo backdrop for the nuns' activism, however — it also links the East Coast to the West Coast, providing a symbolic "cure" for the East Coast–West Coast rap debate, which raged during the era of the film's original release, and, for Goldberg fans, a connection with the actor's New York City roots.

The scene "My God" cements connections between Goldberg's affections for both the Motown Sound and Broadway. In that scene, the song, "My Guy," popularized by Motown recording artist Mary Wells, becomes transformed into "My God," with Sisters Mary Patrick and Roberts "talking up" the song, in conversation and light girl-group choreography with Sister Mary Clarence, just prior to the choir joining in. The audience also hears Goldberg's solo singing voice, as she explains, in character, that while her God is no famous actor, he still thrills. Goldberg's clear vocals show her diligence in working with celebrity vocal coach Seth Riggs, founder of the "speech-level singing" (Speech Level Singing International) technique. For good measure, she ends the scene with a traditional Broadway-style flourish, smiling widely and extending both arms, while tilting her torso toward her extended right foot.

Domestic box office receipts for *Sister Act* totaled $139,605,150 (Allmovie.com), but the global market more than doubled that amount. "The film was a surprisingly big hit in the United States. As it went on to ring up worldwide receipts of $300 million, Disney decided to give the green light to *Sister Act II*" (Chutkow). By the time *Sister Act* arrived, American audiences had grown used to lighthearted portrayals of Catholicism and Catholic nuns. During the early 1960s, the Kennedy family succeeded against the odds to become the first Catholic family to live in the formerly all–Protestant White House. Moreover, while the Catholic religion remains a serious form of remembrance and expression for the family, the press also showed the Kennedys — particularly John and Jacqueline (affectionately known to the American public as Jack and Jackie, respectively) and their children Caroline and John, Jr., in casual, secular terms. Moreover, in the worlds of American television and film, two of the most popular examples of America's growing acceptance of Catholicism which seem to influence *Sister Act* and its successor, include the ABC television series *The Flying Nun* (1967–1970) and the British feature film *Nuns on the Run* (1990). So popular was *The Flying Nun* that, in 1968, Marge Redmond, who played Sister Jacqueline, received the Emmy Award for "Outstanding Performance by an Actress in a Supporting Role in a Comedy" (IMDb "Flying Nun"). Thirty-seven years later, in 2005, Sally Field won the TV Land Favorite Airborne Characters Award (IMDb "Flying Nun"). The premise of *The Flying Nun* is that Field's character, like an angel, and given a stiff wind, may "fly in" to help those in need, at a moment's notice. Such a premise partially undergirds the *Sister Act* films: Goldberg's fictional character Deloris miraculously seems to appear out of nowhere, despite her own best efforts to stay away and mind her own (show) business. Of course, the reality outside of the nunnery is none too inviting: without the protection of the nuns, and, by extension and implication, God, Deloris Van Cartier is sure to die at the hands of thugs. Her experience in and of the cloister is seen and portrayed as a blessing in disguise, for both Deloris and the nuns.

Similarly, the lead characters in *Nuns on the Run* don nuns' habits to evade their pursuers: Eric Idle and Robbie Coltrane play Brian Hope and

Charlie McManus, respectively, gangsters under the thumb of Case Casey, played by Robert Patterson. The premise of the film is that Brian and Charlie end up with monies stolen from Hong Kong drug dealers; as a result, they must flee for their lives. Coincidentally, or perhaps fatefully, Brian and Charlie's getaway vehicle stalls near the entrance of a convent, where the two quickly don nuns' habits to escape capture and certain death. While cloistered in the convent, they pretend to be women and to hail from a different order, saying that they are merely in the nunnery on a stopover, awaiting an opportunity to commence missionary work abroad. Hi-jinks continue, as Brian and Charlie explore the world of women of a completely different "order," while also evading the Chinese Triad and Casey.

Similarly, thugs trail Deloris Van Cartier all the way from Reno to Los Angeles. Yet all Van Cartier seems to bring with her, besides motherwit, is her talent and passion for music and dance, which she uses with great aplomb, both on and off the stage. Musically akin to Motown's Martha and The Vandellas (famous for recording "Dancing in the Street"), and Mary Wells (famous for recording "My Guy"), Deloris Van Cartier and her Reno-based girl group shake and groove with the best of them. Thus, it comes as no surprise to viewers that Deloris fashions the nuns into a "girl group" of a different order, adapting such American pop songs as "I Will Follow Him," "My Guy" and the like, for a rock and roll revival-style Catholic Mass. *Sister Act* was also a winning act: by September 1992, *Sister Act* had earned "about $130 million at the U.S. Box Office" (McCullaugh and Goldstein) alone. Moreover, Disney also had planned to further capitalize upon the "summer sleeper" by feeding both the video rental and retail markets (McCullaugh and Goldstein), with efforts especially focused upon fourth-quarter availability. Even with video rental and retail stores no longer being able to afford to overstock titles, Disney's market research indicated that *Sister Act*'s lead actor, story line, comedy and soundtrack attracted a niche audience so unique that the film did not compete with typical Hollywood film releases, even during the last quarter of the year (McCullaugh and Goldstein).

As Deloris Van Cartier, Goldberg is in her element, using her singing and dancing abilities while playing the double audience of secular and religious viewers. *Sister Act* presents a story within a story, one in which there are at least two audiences to which she addresses: fans of the Motown sound, and Christian music enthusiasts. Part of the success of *Sister Act* is Goldberg's believability as both Deloris and Sister Mary Clarence; her vocal range, tone and mannerisms approximate those of such 1960s Motown artists as Martha and the Vandellas and solo artist Mary Wells. Fans of Goldberg are not surprised at her ability to ride the Motown-inspired musical wave; many also recall her early foray into the Motown Sound, in *Jumpin' Jack Flash* (1986); in Scene 14, "The Party Crasher," she convincingly conveys and alternately parodies the Motown Sound, as computer programmer Terry Dolittle successfully breaking into a high society event held at the British Consulate in New York City. Declaring herself as having no need for an invitation, Dolittle calmly explains to the ticket taker (who bears an uncanny resemblance to Princess Diana) that she is the evening's headline performer. One cue, à la Diana Ross of the Supremes, Dolittle lip-synchs and sashays to an audio clip of the original Motown recording, "You Can't Hurry Love," courtesy of the Walkman clipped to her waist cincher. For insurance, she also randomly grabs another woman's husband as her undisputed "ticket" to the festivities. Nor is the popular music of *Sister Act* entirely foreign to Christian audiences; largely inspired by the Motown Sound, it is, by design and definition, partly based upon Black American gospel quartets, solo singers and big bands. "In 1959 an enterprising record-shop owner and songwriter, Berry Gordy, founded Motown Records, with the Tamla label, in Detroit.... Gordy's first priority seems to have been to establish the unique 'Detroit Sound,' a music combining elements of rhythm 'n' blues, pop, gospel, and big band" (Southern 515).

Sister Act 2: Back in the Habit (1993) again finds Goldberg portraying Deloris Van Cartier/Sister Mary Clarence; this time, however, the Reverend Mother (Maggie Smith) specifically summons her to save St. Francis Academy, the crumbling San Francisco high school that the nuns have adopted and unsuccessfully attempted to reform. To fulfill the Reverend Mother's wishes, Sisters Mary Lazarus, Patrick and Roberts (Mary Wickes, Kathy Najimy and Wendy Makkena, respectively) travel to attend Van Cartier's final performance as a headliner in Las Vegas, with the express purpose of capturing Van Cartier and bringing her to San Francisco as the school's new music teacher. At the outset, the film references not only the original *Sister Act*, but also the television show *The Flying Nun*. During the opening sequence, Van Cartier leads the same girl group, with even snazzier costumes and musical arrangements than in the first film. The group performs a medley encompassing such popular songs as "My Guy," "I Will Follow Him" and "We Are Family," while Lazarus, Patrick and Roberts, at Van Cartier's invitation, interject their voices and bodies into the performance. At one point, the sisters try in vain to help Van Cartier, as she wildly swings about overhead, wearing a sequined nun's habit, dangling from obvious suspended wires; a contemporary "flying nun" amidst a choreographed high-wire act gone wrong. Once she gains her footing, however, she returns to form as Sister Mary Clarence.

Back in the Habit shows Sister Mary Clarence whipping a group of rowdy inner-city teenagers into shape, both academically and musically, so that they can compete in state championships for much-needed prize monies to support the school. Along the way, she also inspires the fictional Rita Louise Watson (played by a young Lauryn Hill, of the R&B group, The Fugees; Hill later became a multi-platinum solo singer-songwriter in her own right) to pursue her God-given gift of song. Rita pursues her musical passion, despite her mother, Florence Watson's (Sheryl Lee Ralph, of Broadway's original *Dreamgirls* fame), staunch admonition that such is a waste of time, as evidenced by the futile attempts of Rita's late father, a singer who never achieved commercial success. Thus, Florence declares not only the vocal competition but also membership in the school choir off-limits and insists that Rita exclusively focus upon formal studies.

Sister Act 2 shifts the focus of Deloris Van Cartier from teaching nuns ("sisters") to sing and embrace the larger community, to teaching the next generation not only to sing, but to value themselves, the world, and one another. Chapter 5, "The New Music Teacher," shows Van Cartier embodying an extreme ideal of a nun, behaving in a saintly, reserved fashion, as Sister Mary Lazarus explains to her, in earshot of the class, that, having entered the unkempt classroom of unruly students, she will experience "Sodom and Gomorrah" (Chap. 5). Rita, the ringleader of the class, explains to Sister Mary Clarence that, in no uncertain terms, students expect to receive passing grades simply for attending; in addition, the audience is also introduced to such characters as Sketch, a grocery clerk who spends classtime doodling; Ahmal, a Black nationalist of implied Muslim bent; and Frankie, an aspiring rapper. Amplifying the script are the film's set design and direction. The classroom is shown as a battleground, pitting piousness against evil, with Sister Mary Clarence standing in front of the chalkboard, upon which the titles of five traditional Christian hymns are inscribed, in chalk: "Peace In The Valley," "Couldn't Hear Nobody Pray," "Mary, Don't You Weep" and "Jesus Loves Me." Meanwhile, as Sister Mary Clarence tries to hold court, she learns that the students are rebellious, in part, because they know that the school puts so little faith and money into their education. Their outdated textbooks have been transformed into spitballs lining the classroom ceiling.

Later during Chapter 5, "The New Music Teacher," St. Francis Academy students cut loose, riffing on a nonsensical musical rhyme, concerning "cold beans" and "collard greens" (Chap. 5) — foods typically associated with the poor, but which are seldom served together. Thematically and structurally, "The New Music Teacher" is reminiscent of the "Hot Lunch Jam" scene in *Fame* (1980), which takes place in New York City's High School of the Performing Arts. "Hot Lunch Jam" begins with the percussive playing of a lunch tray and segues into the sounds of two upright pianos (one played in the classical style; the other emphasizing blues chords). In that scene, Coco (Irene Cara) leads a musical ode to humble school lunches of macaroni and cheese, bologna and canned tuna — believable dietary staples of the financially poor (but richly talented) students. In the case of *Fame*, the scene inspires the audience with its portrayal of the passion of the students and their honest expression; in the case of *Sister Act 2*, however, the students' enthusiasm for rhyme and interplay of words entertains the audience, but the audience cannot take the content of the song seriously.

Nevertheless, Sister Mary Clarence conveys points of clarity, defining the character of Sister Mary Clarence as one attuned to the rhythm and rhyme of the streets; the actor takes pains to show that, while the sister is *in* a rough situation, she is not *of* it. At one point during Chapter 5, the audience is introduced to the class holding court via a rap battle, taking place on the neighborhood basketball court. During this newfangled rap battle, Sketch faces off against Rita, with Sketch holding his own and wowing the crowd (which includes Goldberg's real-life daughter, Alexandrea, playing one of the teenagers and participating in the crowd's call-and-response with the rappers) until Rita blows him away with her feminist rhyme, its tone and timbre reminiscent of Queen Latifah's and Monie Love's rap duet, "Ladies' First," a pro-women rap song included in Latifah's debut CD, *All Hail the Queen* (1989). Goldberg's decision to include her daughter in the scene did more than just provide a professional opportunity for her child; it also served as an eye-opening experience for Alexandrea, who saw firsthand how her mother "had to fight for what [she] wanted," thus paving the way for a closer relationship between the two (Campbell).

Knowledgeable of the origins and manifestations of hip hop, Goldberg, the actor, effectively and efficiently calls upon her New York moorings and, while portraying Sister Mary Clarence, does Rita one better. Sister Mary Clarence simultaneously extends and mocks the Black American freestyle rap tradition with a snappy rap of her own, complete with exaggerated gestures, commanding her students to cut recess short, grab their book bags and return to the classroom. Goldberg's mixture of seriousness and lighthearted banter about, through and around the Black American hip-hop music tradition recall that of a freestyle rap by Stevie Wonder, a member of Goldberg's generation, in his performance of *Do I Do*, an uptempo song included in his 1996 CD, *Song Review: A Greatest Hits Collection* (Disk 1, Track 16). During the closing bars of that song (which features a ripping trumpet solo by Dizzy Gillespie), Wonder raps, openly admitting that he cannot rap like some artists. Nevertheless, Wonder perfectly mimics and extends the rhythmic delivery and vocal percussion of old-school rap, beginning with actual words and ending with a self-styled scat, accompanied by his band and his own palpable glee.

Despite its rocking soundtrack, and the return of the original film's most endearing nuns (Goldberg as Van Cartier/Sister Mary Clarence; Kathy Najimy as Sister Mary Patrick; Wendy Makkena as Sister Mary Robert; Mary Wickes as Sister Mary Lazarus; and Maggie Smith as Mother Superior), *Sister Act 2* was not the raging box-office success of its predecessor. Domestic box office receipts totaled a respectable, but not earth-shaking, $57,319,029

(Allmovie.com). As further evidence of its comparatively lackluster box-office performance, Disney released *Sister Act 2* on DVD in 2000, a year prior to the DVD release of the original film. Nevertheless, like its older cinematic sister, *Sister Act 2* proves a perennial cable television favorite nationwide, especially during the Christmas and Easter holidays; stateside, Christian holidays notwithstanding, such broadcasts are made even more frequently in Catholic enclaves, such as New York City, Boston, California, Florida and Louisiana. (Having lived in New Orleans, locus of one of the United States' largest Catholic enclaves, I can attest that *Sister Act* and *Sister Act 2* are cable television staples there, year-round.) On March 8, 1999, Broadcasting & Cable reported: "Viewers got back in the habit of seeing the 1992 Whoopi Goldberg hit 'Sister Act' last week," with the broadcast receiving "a 6.2 share" (CBI).

The overall popularity of the *Sister Act* films caused scholars to question whether revision of the music of Catholic Mass, according to contemporary pop music norms, would, as in the films, forestall the decrease in the number of parishes, while increasing related parishioner support and whether, as the films suggest, a nun's habit is all that there is to being/becoming a nun. In *Music Doesn't Make the Mass* (1996), Jerry Daoust argues that, at times, the struggle to make Catholic Mass more meaningful to contemporary parishioners sometimes includes focusing upon musical entertainment in lieu of imparting and spreading the Gospel. He continues, "Ideally, music should serve as a form of prayer, preparing us to receive the grace of the Word of God and the Eucharist. The 'Sister Act' syndrome strikes when the pursuit of magnificent music becomes an end in itself, overwhelming the celebration instead of enhancing it. The Mass, rather than being a Eucharistic celebration, becomes a free concert designed to make us feel good.... Music doesn't make the Mass; the Eucharistic celebration does" (Daoust). Daoust includes an observation regarding a real-life experience at a Christmas midnight Mass, whereby a group of tourists, clearly there solely to hear the music, became "impatient whenever the priest started talking, apparently regarding it as an interruption to the real show; they left during the Consecration" (Daoust). Daoust also mentions that, during the film, *Sister Act*, Catholic Mass is described as a "show"; and that Goldberg's Sister Mary Clarence, in leading not only the parishioners but also rough-around-the-edges street children, in jazzed-up religious song, becomes "the pied piper of liturgical music" (Daoust). For Daoust, liturgical music is not to be used simply for show, and it *definitely* does not "make the Mass."

Similarly, Carole Slade explains that, while Catholic nuns have been the subject of ridicule "most of it sadistic and pornographic," for two millennia, the film *Sister Act* (which Slade found "quite funny, nevertheless") gives viewers the impression that "clothes make the nun" (Slade). Slade gives examples of Whoopi Goldberg instantaneously transforming from character Deloris Van

Cartier to Sister Mary Clarence, simply by changing her "habit." "When Whoopi dresses like a nun, she almost immediately begins acting like one" (Slade), rising after only an hour of sleep (the sliver of time between the end of her previous nightclub gig and her new appointment), to dutifully scrub floors at 5:00 A.M. Slade also observes that, in the film, the Mother Superior eventually "cede[s] leadership of the convent" to Sister Mary Clarence, because Sister Mary Clarence's outward appearance and changed behavior (including leading a chorus of nuns in song, jubilantly proclaiming their love for Christ) make her "a great nun." He concludes, "In *Sister Act*, the habit is just a costume" (Slade). Slade may be a bit hasty in his observation, however; a basic tenet of Christian redemption is not just saying that one's life has been changed through Christ, but outwardly acting and looking the part. Moreover, the "presto-change-o" aspect of *Sister Act* is a well-worn trope in American popular film; one such example is the characterization of Homer Smith, as portrayed by Sidney Poitier, in *Lilies of the Field* (1963). In that film, German Catholic nuns cajole Smith, an itinerant carpenter/contractor, into building a chapel for them, virtually free of charge (while Smith clearly expects payment in dollars and cents, the nuns instead pay him with in-kind contributions of meager room and board). Throughout the film, the nuns declare Homer a kind of savior, sent by God to help them, continually reminding him of such; the deep irony of the extended situation provides levity for viewers who realize that it is not Homer who has changed, but rather the convent itself, by his very presence.

In Robert Townsend's made-for-television film *Jackie's Back* (1999), Goldberg's role is the polar opposite of Deloris Van Cartier/Sister Mary Clarence, but nevertheless is rooted in a recognition and parody of the Motown Sound. As the aptly named Ethyl Washington Rue Owens, who "rues" the day her younger sister, "Little" Jackie Washington, was born, Goldberg perfectly embodies the discontent one feels when one's artistic contributions have been overlooked. The actor also aptly displays the character's disgust and sibling rivalry, as Ethyl believes that Jackie "owes" her nominal success as a recording artist to her. According to the story, during the 1960s, Jackie became a runaway success at the age of 14, with the fictional "Peaches" Yancy's production of the mega-hit record "Yield," a thematic parody of Berry Gordy's Motown and The Supremes' "Stop! in the Name of Love." Musically, the song and its performance also parodies Michael Jackson singing lead as a member of The Jackson Five, on such tunes as "ABC" and "Stop! The Love You Save." The film consists of a mockumentary, ably hosted by Tim Curry, as Edward Whatsett St. John, channeling Robin Leach à la television's *Lifestyles of the Rich and Famous*.

In *Jackie's Back!*, Goldberg, as Ethyl Washington Rue Owens, wears a white nurse's uniform, and appears to be sitting on a toilet (purposefully begging the question of whether any viewer can take any of this "crap" seriously), all the while answering St. John's questions concerning her famous sister. Of Jackie Washington (ably embodied by Jenifer Lewis, a breakout star of *Sister Act* who appeared in that film as one of Deloris Van Cartier's girl group singers), Ethyl cries that she, not Jackie, was the one who enrolled in the talent contest, purchasing a yellow dress and writing the song "Yield, Yield, Yield" especially for the occasion. Yet, come showtime, Jackie not only stole the dress and the song, but also America's heart and money. As a result, says Ethyl, Jackie "is trying to make a comeback," while she (Ethyl) works as a nurse (*Jackie's Back!* Chap. 2).

Goldberg's comedic genius emerges as she improvises her lines, enhancing the melodramatic tension of the story. Heightening the mock drama is Ethyl's hairstyle (deliberately covering the actor's trademark dreadlocks): an afro, bound all around by a white headband to match her nurses' attire; a homemade hairdo, worlds away from the professionally coiffed strands of her sister, Jackie. And, unlike Jackie, whose long, manicured fingernails command attention in almost every scene, Ethyl's nails are short and bare. The viewer can only assume that Ethyl has neither the time nor the money to visit the salon for a proper hairstyle and manicure. In fleshing out the character of Ethyl, Goldberg also references an ongoing refrain in the Black American community: that black pioneers of stage and screen often are forgotten, even during their own lifetimes. The insistent, frustrated tone of Goldberg's Ethyl is reminiscent of Eddie Murphy's 1983 portrayal of his original character Clarence Walker, a fictional saxophonist and self-acknowledged "Fifth Beetle," on a *Saturday Night Live* television skit. The Murphy skit illustrates a comedic story once removed from the real-life stories of Chuck Berry and "Little" Richard Penniman, both pioneers of rock and roll, the early stages of whose careers took a backseat to those of white performers borrowing and capitalizing upon their style.

The *Sister Act* series remains very popular. During early 2006, the Pasadena Playhouse staged a "reading of the musical version of *Sister Act*," in preparation for a possible Broadway run (Sheward). By November of that year, the Pasadena Playhouse had already staged a developing musical version of the show. Critic Les Spindle wrote, "Though Peter Scheider's mounting feels more like a promising workshop than it does a world premiere, the Broadway-hopeful property might have the ingredients to sprout box office legs" (Spindle). During the 2006 season, the stage adaptation of the original film was scheduled to be performed at the Pasadena Playhouse, along with such notable titles and themes as Shakespeare's *As You Like It* and *Sherlock Homes: The Final Adventure* (Spindle). Neither of the developmental productions included Whoopi Goldberg on stage. By 2008, however, Goldberg announced that she would star in the London mounting of the *Sister Act* musical, with a planned opening in June 2009. She served as producer of the London musical, while Alan Menken, an eight-time Oscar winner whose projects include *Aladdin, The Little Mermaid* and *Beauty and the Beast,* wrote featured music for *Sister Act* in London (CBC Arts 2008). With enthusiasm, Whoopi Goldberg declared: "*Sister Act* will never die. It's like *The Mickey Mouse Club,* it's never going anywhere" (CBC Arts 2008). The London production of *Sister Act* certainly took off.

Ray Bennett, writing for the *Hollywood Reporter,* describes the *Sister Act* production at the London Palladium as "a foot-stomping, hand-clapping success with great songs by multiple–Oscar winner Alan Menken and a star-making performance by American newcomer Patina Miller [as Deloris Van Cartier/Sister Mary Clarence]" (Bennett). Not surprisingly, the June 2010 stage adaptation of *Sister Act* includes a few changes: instead of Van Cartier hailing from Reno, she hails from Philadelphia. Also, new songs such as "The Life I Never Led" and "How I Got the Calling" amplify the stage adaptation's increased emphasis upon "the view that being a nun is not a great idea" (Bennett) — a concept only mildly hinted at in the motion pictures. By July of 2010, Goldberg herself was "back in the habit," on stage at the London Palladium, but this time she played the role of Mother Superior (CBC Arts 2010). Goldberg's scheduled three-week run (from August 10–31) attracted monumental attention from fans; according to *India Vision,* word of her performance "attract[ed] fans in huge numbers, so much so that people ... camp[ed] out for days in a bid to secure tickets" (Indiavision.com). By spring 2010, *Sister Act: The Musical* was ready for its Broadway debut (Itzkoff). Goldberg's London triumph was bittersweet, however, as she "was forced to cut short her guest stint and return to the U.S. ... when her mother suffered a stroke in late August" (CBC Arts 2010). On August 29, 2010, Goldberg's mother, Emma Johnson, succumbed (Brown). Returning to her daytime work on the New York-based television talk show, *The View,* Goldberg paid homage to her mother, describing her considerable achievements, including having earned a master's degree in early childhood education and having taught a generation of educators (Brown). Goldberg continued, "She lived long enough to see her granddaughter do well and her great grandchildren do well and to see both her son and her daughter do well and have a fantastic life. I think I'm just sad sometimes that I think: 'Who will love me the way that she did?' But I realize that my brother and I have each other but, she was good. So, that was my mom" (Brown). While still mourning the loss of her mother, she returned to reprise her role as Mother Superior in the London Production (CBC Arts 2010). In addition to the successful stage musical adaptation, the combined, immense profitability and popularity of *Sister Act* and *Sister Act 2: Back in the Habit* also opened possibilities for at least two projects: *The Fighting Temptations* (2003) and *Whoopi* (2003–2004).

The Fighting Temptations, starring Cuba Gooding, Jr., and Beyoncé Knowles, concerns Darrin Hill (Gooding, Jr.), a shady but initially successful New York corporate executive, who learned how to hustle by participating in the high life of gambling. His mother, a single parent, performed on stage, singing in smoky nightclubs. As the story unfolds, Darrin encounters Lilly (Knowles), a misunderstood nightclub singer who, like his mother, is shunned by the community because she sings R & B, instead of singing solely for the Lord. Deep in debt, pursued by creditors, and having lost his job, due to presenting false qualifications for a position at which he nonetheless excels, Darrin returns to his small town South Carolina roots, to collect monies bequeathed to him by his late aunt, with the catch that he must use his musical talents to lead the small church choir to success during the forthcoming Gospel Explosion talent contest. In the process, not only does he reclaim his musical heritage, honor his mother's memory and fulfill his late aunt's mandate, he also wins Lilly's heart. As is true in *Sister Act 2*, the choir is led by a lay director more rooted in the secular world than in gospel, the choir is small and functions as the underdog of the story; and yet, against all odds, the choir emerges successful, claiming the top prize.

Whoopi (2003–2004), the network television series produced by Goldberg's One Ho Productions, concerns Goldberg as Mavis Rae, a washed-up soul singer who decides to take a turn at running a hotel and reenergizing her musical career, as the hotel's premier — and only — musical act. Unlike *Sister Act*'s Deloris Van Cartier, whose music never took a serious political turn, Mavis has a razor-sharp wit, especially where sex and politics are concerned. In fact, while the show was nominated for both a 2004 Emmy Award for "Outstanding Art Direction for a Multi-Camera Series" and a 2004 NAACP Image Award for "Outstanding Actress in a Comedy Series" (IMDb *Whoopi*), it nevertheless fell off the radar and was later canceled. Arguably, the show's active courting of controversial topics both heightened viewer interest and generated complaints, leading to the show's demise. One wonders why Goldberg chose network television as the vehicle for her project, especially when cable television offers more opportunity for groundbreaking material (indeed, HBO did just that in 1985, when it made way for her television debut in the wildly successful *Whoopi Goldberg: Direct from Broadway*).

Cable television may become a bridge linking Goldberg to Célia Cruz, the Queen of Salsa. In 2001, "Goldberg approached [Cristina] Saralegui, host of the enduringly popular *El Show de Cristina* on Univision" (Cantor) about coproducing a biographical film on Cruz. In 2001, Goldberg reportedly "approached" Cristina Saralegui, of Univision's popular *El Show de Cristina*, with the idea. Cristina Saralegui Enterprises and Goldberg's shingle, One Ho Prods., inked a development deal (Cantor) and purchased the rights to Cruz's story. Samuel L. Jackson has been mentioned as a possibility for portraying

Cruz's husband, Pedro Knight, in the film (Cabrera). In addition to co-producing, Goldberg had planned to star as Cruz. Cruz herself christened the project:

> Shortly [after the passing of Tito Puente, King of the Timbales], Cristina Saralegui called to tell us that she bumped into Whoopi Goldberg at some event and that Whoopi had told her that she always wanted to make a movie based on the story of my life. I was surprised, since I didn't know how Whoopi even knew who I was. She asked me how it was possible that I didn't know how well-known I was among many Americans and that Whoopi told her that when she was a kid, she would stand in front of a mirror with a Coke bottle in hand and imitate me singing. I didn't know what to say, so I told Cristina that Pedro and I would have to discuss the idea, but that I was excited about the prospect.
>
> A few months later, at an event where I performed in Washington's Kennedy Center for the Performing Arts, and after Pedro and I decided that we should go ahead with the movie project, Whoopi and I finally had a chance to meet. She told me how much she admired and respected me. She told me that she had been studying Spanish in order to be able to portray me more accurately. I was happy to have met with Whoopi and I am sure she will do a wonderful job with the film, since she is known for being a model of professionalism and a great actress. I am also comfortable with the project since both Cristina [Saralegui] and her husband, Marcos Ávila, are going to produce the film, with Marcos writing the script. Whoopi later told me that there would be two scripts and that I would get to choose which one I liked best. I do not know when the film will finally go into production, but I am sure that it will be a great success, since it's in the hands of three extremely talented individuals [Cruz 201–202].

That Célia Cruz influenced Goldberg should come as no surprise. A native New Yorker, reared in a multicultural lower Manhattan neighborhood, Goldberg had many opportunities to encounter the diva, if not in person, then certainly on record and in concert. Cruz, a Cuban expatriate who eventually relocated to New Jersey, made herself at home in New York City, the world center of salsa, a music form named after the spicy tomato-based condiment. In New York City, traditional Nigerian rhythms, courtesy of Cuba, intermixed with global Latin music and storytelling traditions, to create a unique American music form and expression to and for the world. While Cruz regularly toured the world, she also made sure to perform in her adopted home, at such mega-venues as Madison Square Garden and even small clubs, including Sounds of Brazil (Brevard 62–63). Concerning Cruz and the film project, Whoopi Goldberg explains, "To see a rich, dark, chocolate woman in command of thousands of people with her voice and her energy made me believe that anything is possible" (Silverman).

Cruz first came to prominence in 1947, winning first-prize in a Cuban radio program *La Hora del Té* (*Tea Time*), for her performance of the tango "Nostalgia." She also studied for three years at Cuba's Conservatory of Music

(Flores), eventually becoming lead singer for a ten-piece, all-male band, La Sonora Matancera (The Matancera Sound), named after the Cuban city Matanzas. With La Sonora Matancera, Célia (whom fans often call by first name) toured constantly, from 1951 to 1959, covering the West Indies, South America, the United States, and Mexico (Flores); eventually, she became a Secco Records artist, "record[ing] 20 albums of La Sonora Matancera songs in just one year" (García-Johnson 116). With all that touring and all those men, Cruz, reared Catholic, shrewdly guarded her reputation by adopting a motherly persona and by eventually marrying one of the band members, Pedro Knight. A major aspect of her legend is that "in public, Celia belongs to the people. In private, Celia belongs to Pedro" (Flores). True to her mystical, motherly persona, Cruz never belongs to herself: she is the instrument of God, salsa music, the public and her husband.

On stage, Cruz's costumes, including one which featured "a five-foot train of more than 400 multicolored lace handkerchiefs sewn together," and her exaggerated body movements ("Onstage she leaps, flaunts, flirts and teases to the gyrating beat of salsa"), made performing duets onstage nearly impossible. Says Cruz, "Duets were the worst; my partners either couldn't stand close enough to me, like you should when doing a romantic duet, or they'd get feathers in their faces'" (Llorente in Brevard 55).

While she is a mother figure, she nevertheless is a sex symbol, signified by her elaborate, larger-than-life costuming, full stage makeup (even when offstage) and singular status as salsa's leading lady. For Cruz, costuming is a primary way to simultaneously render herself larger than life and ultra-feminine, especially since her trademark voice is often compared to that of a man. Legendary timbales player Tito Puente (who recorded eight albums with Cruz), once recalled, "'I was listening to the radio in Cuba the first time I heard Celia's voice. I couldn't believe the voice. It was so powerful and energetic, I swore it was a man, I'd never heard a woman sing like that" (García-Johnson 116). Cruz uses her resonant, percussive voice to create "inspiraciones" ("inspirations," or ad-libs), comparable to the concept of "worrying the line" in Black American gospel music traditions and scat singing in Black American jazz traditions. In fact, as musician and persona, Cruz is often favorably compared to African American artists Patti LaBelle and Ella Fitzgerald (Brevard 56, 64).

The themes of Célia Cruz's songs resonate with everyday people: respect for women and women's sensuality ("Sazón/Seasoning"); the beauty of full, red lips ("Bemba Colorá"/"Full, Colored Lips"); celebrating brown skin of all hues ("Azucar Negra"/"Black Sugar"); self-respect in the midst of change — a theme especially directed toward the poor and working classes ("Hay Que Empezar Otra Vez"/"Having to Start Over Again"); expressing the joy of life in spite of life's hardships ("La Vida Es un Carnaval"/"Life Is a Carnival"; "Yo Viviré"/"I Will Survive"); and celebration of the drums of traditional West

Africa, upon which salsa music rhythms are based ("La Negra Tiene Tumbao"/"The Black Woman Has the Beat") ("Celia Cruz: Hits Mix"). Exiled from the island of her birth and never allowed to return, per the repeated dictates of Fidel Castro, Cruz nevertheless extended her status as teacher, by using salsa music as her lesson plan to the world. Providing the closing commentary for her posthumously published memoir, *Celia: My Life* (2004), her husband, Pedro Knight, explains, "As the teacher at heart she always was, she realized the significance of giving her 'classroom' (as she called the world) one last lesson with this memoir, which is in reality a closing song" (Cruz 247). Complementing the aforementioned is Cruz' iconic, radiant, gap-toothed smile, reflecting her inner spirit and pride in African heritage (Brevard 57); and her trademark command, «¡Azucar!» ("Sugar! Sweet!"), which regularly punctuate her recordings and live performances, creating frenzy among appreciative crowds. In an interview with Wyclef Jean, Goldberg praises Cruz's universal appeal: "She's like Patti LaBelle — she has everything you need to be a great performer. [Cruz's CD] *Carnival* is one of the few universally themed albums I've heard. And I just can't play it enough" (Jean).

Beyond Goldberg's lifelong respect and affinity for Célia Cruz's persona and music, it is likely that the actor's infectious performances as Sister Mary Clarence led fans to believe that she has the chops and sensitivity to portray Célia Cruz. Selected scenes from *Sister Act* and *Sister Act 2: Back in the Habit*, reflect the kind of on-stage energy and general *joie de vivre* for which Cruz was famous. In *Sister Act* and *Sister Act 2*, audiences hear Goldberg's own singing voice; in preparation for playing Deloris Van Cartier/Sister Mary Clarence, in *Sister Act*, the actor reportedly took voice lessons, under the direction of Seth Riggs, who specializes in the "Speech Level Singing Method" (Speech Level Singing International). Moreover, like Goldberg, Cruz also has several generations of fans, as the U.S. postage stamp featuring Cruz's likeness attests. The postage stamp, part of the Latin Music Legends series, created by musician/painter Rafael Lopez, which also includes the images of Tito Puente, Carmen Miranda, Selena, and Carlos Gardel "combines a body from a 1960s photograph, a face from one taken in the 1970s, and a feathered headdress from a 1990s shoot" (USPS 2). This gives Cruz, who died in 2003, at the age of 78, a timeless quality. Regarding the passage of time and Whoopi Goldberg, Célia's husband, Pedro, muses,

> My wife was looking forward to seeing her memoirs published, but God chose otherwise. And when He did so, Celia entrusted her final project to us, so we have treated it with the respect it deserves. I must admit that reliving the story of our lives together has not been a painless task, but whenever I felt overwhelmed, I felt Celia giving me the strength to go on. Apart from this memoir, Celia entrusted me with the Celia Cruz Foundation and the movie project based on her life and starring Whoopi Goldberg [Cruz 247–248].

6. Sister Rhythm and Blues

Time is also a consideration as far as Cruz's biopic and Goldberg are concerned. As of this writing, slightly over a decade has passed since Celia gave her blessing to Goldberg to portray her in the planned film. Reportedly, Goldberg is now seeking a younger actress to portray Cruz (Acmewebpages.com); it is not clear whether the younger thespian would replace or complement Goldberg. It is possible that the biopic of Cruz would employ several actors to trace the singer's development over time; perhaps younger artists could cover the early stages of Cruz's life, with Goldberg covering the songstress' mature years. In particular, Latino audiences "cite [Whoopi Goldberg's] performances in 'Sister Act' and 'Ghost,'" as evidence that she has what it takes to portray Cruz (Cabrera). Beyond the musical and Christian aspects of the *Sister Act* films, the actor's successful turn as teacher of music and morals, in both films, undoubtedly also resonates with Célia Cruz fans. The *Sister Act* films seem to have inspired increased interest in glee clubs and choirs; one example is the popular Fox television show, *Glee*, in which "a high-school Spanish teacher becomes the director of the school's glee club, hoping to restore it to its former glory" (IMDb *Glee*).

Beyond their overall box-office and cable television successes, the *Sister Act* films also expanded Goldberg's artistic reach and audience. Designed for general audiences, and specifically appealing to Christians worldwide, the films allow her, as Deloris Van Cartier, to make musical connections between the girl-groups of the Motown heyday and the development of Black American gospel music; and, as Sister Mary Clarence, to address religious themes in a secular context. The films also encouraged scholars to re-evaluate the role of music in the church and reconsider the image of the nuns' habit in popular culture, while re-energizing American popular interest in choral singing and the legacy of salsa music's Célia Cruz. *Sister Act* and *Sister Act 2: Back in the Habit* give Goldberg continued currency as an artist and producer. She may not have the vocal chops of Martha Reeves or Mary Wells; but her voice and presence ably carry the tunes and lessons of Deloris Van Cartier/Sister Mary Clarence and resonate with the Queen of Salsa and legions of fans.

The continued cultural relevance of *Sister Act* film is evident with President Barack Obama's recent public remark, regarding how fast his two daughters, Malia and Sasha, are maturing. "At a re-election campaign fundraiser in New York City [in June 2011] featuring 'Sister Act' star Whoopi Goldberg, Obama joked that the 1992 movie helped him figure out where to send his daughters" (Superville). Basically, President Obama, while praising his daughters' sensitivity and general good natures, jested that he would send them to a convent, evidently for their own protection (as happens with the film's lead character). This not only reflects the continued resonance of the film, but also Goldberg's political ties and influence. She attended the event as herself—as an "actor" in the broadest sense of the word, lending her time and energy to political activism on the world stage; but her presence also brought to mind, at least for President Obama, one of her most popular and enduring characters.

The *Sister Act* film series is one of several projects connecting Goldberg with Disney. After *Sister Act* (1992) and *Sister Act 2: Back in the Habit* (1993), she continued to work on Disney projects. One such project was the title role in *Eddie* (1993), a major motion picture in which Goldberg plays Edwina "Eddie" Franklin, who breaks the proverbial glass ceiling, rising from an avid sports fan relegated to the nosebleed seats at Madison Square Garden, to a respected, legitimate coach of a winning New York Knicks basketball team. She also lent her distinctive voice stylings to bring to life the characters Shenzi in *The Lion King* (1994) and *The Lion King 1½* (2004); Miss Mittens in *Snow Buddies* (2008) and Stretch in *Toy Story* 3 (2010). Moreover, in 2004, she signed with Hyperion to offer children's books via its imprint, *Jump at the Sun* (Oei). Hyperion, part of Disney Publishing Worldwide, has made special efforts to reach urban audiences; Jump at the Sun is Hyperion's high-profile imprint designed to address urban audiences and named after a phrase made famous by Zora Neale Hurston, author of *Their Eyes Were Watching God* (1937). According to Disney World Publishing (DPW), "Disney-Jump at the Sun Books celebrates the rich diversity of African American culture and history through high quality books for children and teens of all races and cultures" (DPW). Disney World Publishing counts Goldberg's *Sugar Plum Ballerinas* series and E. B. Lewis's illustrated book containing Langston Hughes's poem "The Negro Speaks of Rivers" among its "recent highlights" (DWP). Zora Neale Hurston popularized the Black American traditional phrase, "Jump at de sun," via her autobiography, *Dust Tracks on a Road* (1942): "Mama exhorted her children at every opportunity to 'Jump at de sun.' We might not land on the sun, but at least we could get off the ground" (Hurston 13). Via Jump at the Sun, Goldberg published the best-selling Sugar Plum Ballerinas series—a collection of fiction books designed for young readers aged 7–10 (Kirkus Media) or Grades 3–5 (Williams 84). The series, which she co-authored with Deborah Underwood, featuring color and black-and-white illustrations by Maryn Roos, includes: *Plum Fantastic* (2008); *Toeshoe Trouble* (2009) *Perfectly Prima* (2010); *Terrible Terrel* (2010) and *Sugar Plums to the Rescue!* (2011).

As the series shows, the Sugar Plum Ballerinas are, in the manner of actual plums, tough-skinned and delicate. The girls are special, not because they seriously study ballet and regularly perform in recitals open to the general public (in fact, Goldberg refreshingly presents ballet as a normal after-school activity, much like soccer practice), but because they learn the value of expressing individuality while also respecting differences and cultivating supportive sisterly relationships. The fictional Sugar Plum Sisters (as they call themselves) appear to have symbolic ties to her actual family. One example is the character Alexandrea Johnson, whose name appears to be inspired by Goldberg's daughter, Alexandrea, and her mother, Emma Johnson. Another example is the character Jerzey Mae, possibly named after her granddaughter, Jerzey. And Maryn Roos's lively, brown-skinned, dreadlocked depiction of Brenda and triplets Jerzey Mae, JoAnn and Jessica all bear a striking physical resemblance not only to one another; but also to Goldberg herself. In addition, the character Mason appears to be named after her actual grandson, Mason, while Maryn Roos's physical depiction of Tiffany appears to have been inspired by her real-life daughter, Alex.

Plum Fantastic, the first book of the series, tells the story of Alexandrea (Al) Petrakova Johnson, a migrant from Apple Creek, Georgia, who has moved to New York City, so that her mother, a native New Yorker and widow, can pursue her own dream of designing clothes for live stage productions — and her dream for her daughter Al to become a prima ballerina. The two dreams collide when the mother creates outlandish rehearsal costumes for Al, initially making her a laughing stock at the fictional Nutcracker School of Ballet. Al's homesickness, combined with the mother's lack of contacts needed to get her design company off the ground, make for a shaky start, but situations soon improve. Al convinces her mother that it is okay to wear normal leotards and tights to dance rehearsal, and a family friend of the Sugar Plum Sisters (close ballet school buddies) requests custom church hats from Al's mother. Meanwhile, Al fears not being good enough to play the Sugar Plum Fairy lead in the new ballet. The story ends on a positive note, with Al finally mastering tricky dance moves required of the lead role in the ballet, and Al's mother establishing not only a successful company designing one-of-a-kind church hats, but also volunteering her services as costume designer for the Nutcracker School of Ballet, located in Lower Manhattan.

Of *Plum Fantastic, Publisher's Weekly* exclaims, "Forget low expectations from celebrity authors — this series opener is warm, funny and tender" (RBI). *School Library Journal* says, "Alex's voice is full of wit and determination. This fun easy chapter book develops at a good pace and creates a bit of tension and anticipation as readers follow Alex's efforts" (Lafferty 90). *Kirkus Reviews* says, "An endearing multiethnic cast of characters and a positive message of the power of friendship make this one a keeper" (Kirkus Media). The characters are warm, friendly and real, and while race and ethnicity certainly have a function in the story (in particular, Sugar Plum Ballerina Epatha, who is of Puerto Rican and Italian ancestry and fluently and interchangeably speaks English, Spanish and Italian, makes her presence known), *none* of the characters are defined by race or ethnicity. *Plum Fantastic* was nominated for an NAACP Award.

Toeshoe Trouble, the second book in the series, concerns Brenda, an eight-year-old New Yorker and self-proclaimed pre-med student, who is happy spending time with her mother, her science books and her sister Sugar Plums — that is, until her rich cousin Tiffany comes to visit. Jealous of Tiffany's computer (which Tiffany uses only to catalog and brag about her extensive wardrobe, as opposed to conducting scientific research, which Brenda yearns to do, but, alas, lacks the funds to purchase a computer), Brenda concludes that she must, for once, get the upper hand. Brenda makes the mistake of claiming that her dance instructor's prize toe shoes (original toe shoes, autographed by the fictional Black American prima ballerina Miss Camilla Freeman) are her own. Stealing the toe shoes from their special case at the Nutcracker School of Ballet, Brenda brings the shoes home, only to have them torn to shreds by Pookiepie, Tiffany's pet dog (Goldberg, *Toeshoe* 74). Pookiepie's actions place Brenda and Tiffany in a pickle; not only will Brenda get in trouble with her mother, but also with Ms. Debbé, the dance director, head of the school and a former pupil of Miss Camilla Freeman. Moreover, Tiffany explains that her mother warned that "if Pookiepie ate any more shoes, she'd give him to the animal shelter. And if she finds out about *these* shoes..." (74–75).

The situation is resolved when the stately Miss Camilla Freeman arrives to watch the Sugar Plum Ballerinas in rehearsal, and later shares a spot of tea with them. During their meeting with Miss Freeman, the girls learn not only tea-time etiquette but also forgiveness, for Miss Freeman not only forgives Pookiepie, Brenda and Tiffany, she also gifts Miss Debbé with an even more prized set of autographed toe shoes — ones actually used onstage. In the meantime, Ms. Debbé forgives the girls, and the girls forgive themselves. The many lessons of *Toeshoe Trouble* are: be true to yourself; honesty is the best policy; to have a friend, be one; when a person makes a mistake, give him or her a chance to redeem him- or herself; respect the elders and respect people's property. Like its predecessor, *Toeshoe Trouble* also was nominated for an NAACP Award.

Goldberg dedicates *Perfectly Prima*, the third book of the series, "To Mason, my favorite little man — Granny" (Goldberg, *Perfectly*). One of the story's main characters is named Mason, apparently after her grandson; the other, Jerzey Mae, is apparently named after Jerzey, Goldberg's youngest granddaughter. While briefly recounting the plot and resolution of book four, *Toeshoe Trouble*, *Perfectly Prima* concerns Jerzey Mae, one of the triplets, and a member of the Sugar Plum Sisters, whose little brother, Mason, initially makes a nuisance of himself, but later proves to be one of Jerzey Mae's and the Plum Sisters' greatest allies. The triplets, Mason and their parents live in an upscale area of Harlem, called Striver's Row.

As the title implies, Jerzey Mae insists upon gaining perfection in all areas. For example, she keeps her room clean and tidy, and her coloring pencils organized. Nevertheless, Jersey Mae considers herself a "ballet loser," especially when making inevitable comparisons to her sisters JoAnn, a "natural athlete" (9) and Jessica, who, though born with one leg slightly shorter than the other, nevertheless is "graceful" (11) on the dance floor and with respect to writing poetry and caring for her many exotic pets.

Tension ensues when Mason is left to watch his sisters, along with other Sugar Plums, participate in dance rehearsals. (Mason and the triplets' parents are an attorney and professor, respectively, and their schedules abruptly change, to the point where, temporarily, neither is home to greet Mason after school.) While watching his sisters and their friends dance, he unwittingly lets loose Jessica's white pet rat, Shakespeare, who runs about the Nutcracker School of Ballet, much to the shock and consternation of the girls and Ms. Debbé, dance instructor and head of school. Mason redeems himself, however, when he teaches Jerzey Mae, unable to execute difficult moves on the dance floor, and suffering stage fright, how to perform the intricate steps with confidence. (As it turns out, Mason has learned the steps by watching the girls rehearse.) After unsuccessfully trying to formally coach Jerzey Mae, he finally finds success when he encourages her to play basketball with him; while they play, he draws parallels between the smooth, confident movements of Jerzey Mae on the basketball court and similar aspects of the ballet's choreography. Jerzey Mae succeeds in the stage performance, and Mason is rewarded with not only thanks and praise, but also enrollment in a nearby boys' ballet program.

Lessons abound in *Perfectly Prima*: Harlem residents constitute a wide variety of people of different socio-economic backgrounds; each person is an individual (11); children can teach and learn from each other; pride goeth before a fall (57); enjoy yourself (expecting perfection in all areas is unduly stressful); ask for help when you need it; just because a plan does not go as planned, that does not mean that one should give up—instead, one should consider trying other avenues toward success (68); boys can study ballet, too (103), and books and note-taking are important (70–71). Ironically, from the very beginning, Jerzey Mae does not heed the wisdom of her own words. At one point, she stresses that, while she and her sisters are identical, each triplet has her own personality and strengths (11). In this sense, the reader is given limited omniscience to "see" what Jerzey Mae initially cannot. These lessons, while packaged for children, also resonate with adults.

Goldberg dedicates *Terrible Terrel*, fourth book of the series, to her mother, Emma Johnson: "For Ma, who always dances..." (Goldberg, *Terrible*). Terrel is the youngest and smallest of the Sugar Plum Ballerinas; and she faces off with the Sugar Plum Sisters' nemesis, Tiara Girl, a haughty rich girl who wears tiaras all the time, who also studies at the Nutcracker School of Ballet

(Tiara Girl's real name is Alice, but the Sugar Plum Sisters refer to her by the nickname that they created for her.) Tension ensues when Terrel learns that her father, Mr. Liu, a widower, has found a girlfriend. To make matters worse, his new girlfriend is Marjory, Tiara Girl's aunt. As Terrel's mother died when Terrel was only two years of age, Terrel has assumed the role of mother and organizer of the household. "Commander" Terrel, as her family calls her, calls her older brothers and her father into service for such tasks as grocery-shopping and household chores; for the first time, her role in the family is doubly threatened, first by Marjory's very presence, and by having to associate with Tiara Girl outside of ballet school.

Initially, Terrel considers herself to have been abandoned, when Epatha, a Sugar Plum Sister with Latin and Italian cultural roots, tells Terrel that Mr. Liu's recent activities (including coming home later than usual, and wearing cologne and a fancy sweater) are acceptable and indicative of his blossoming love life — a viewpoint which the Sugar Plum Sisters, with the exception of Terrel, share. When the Sugar Plum Sisters learn that Marjory is not just Mr. Liu's new girlfriend, but also Tiara Girl's aunt, they spring into action, taking Terrel's twisted view (the fact that Marjory has gifted Terrel with a tiara, à la Tiara Girl, also stokes the flames of discontent among the Sugar Plums). With the help of her Sugar Plum Sisters, "Commander" Terrel transforms into "Terrible" Terrel, deliberately trying to scare Marjory away with loud music, a stink bomb, a fake ice cube (complete with a rubber spider sealed inside) and, perhaps worst of all, a forged "Dear John Letter." Terrel finally comes to her senses when her brother Edward casually mentions that their father, Mr. Liu, a musician, has begun singing again — a sign of their father's hope and contentment, which the family has not witnessed in years, and which Terrel, in her selfishness, could not "hear."

Terrel redeems herself when she enlists her brother Cheng to accompany her on a walk to Marjory's apartment, with the hope that she can retrieve the letter by placing her hand into the mail slot in Marjory's front door. (She stops short of breaking into a mailbox, which her brother tells her is a federal offense.) Instead of Terrel intercepting the letter, Marjory intercepts Terrel and invites her and her brother inside, and has a woman-to-girl talk with Terrel (meanwhile, Marjory has Cheng play video games, using her home-office computer). During their talk, Marjory acknowledges Terrel's distress as well as the girl's organizing abilities. She promises not to intrude on family grocery shopping and asks for Terrel's assistance in organizing the upcoming Nutcracker School of Ballet party. She also explains to Terrel that her niece's haughtiness is perhaps due to stress at home. Alice's parents are in the midst of a divorce, so they have asked Marjory, an employee of the fictional Ballet Company of New York (53), to shuttle the girl to and from ballet lessons on Saturdays. Relieved, Terrel cries, realizing that she has likely misjudged Marjory and Alice. Revealing Alice's "Tiara Girl" moniker to Marjory, she promises Marjory that she will try to treat Alice with compassion. Universal lessons of *Toeshoe Trouble* include: honesty is the best policy; be yourself; do not be too quick to judge others; keep your promises; and parents are people, too. One of the most important lessons, however, is also the most subtle: people are people. One may infer from the artwork and cultural clues within the book that Terrel is of mixed-race ancestry (likely Afro-Chinese), but this is never specified.

Sugar Plums to the Rescue! is the fifth and, apparently, final, book in the series. From its very beginning, the reader hears Goldberg's voice, dedicating the text to "ALL the fans of the Sugar Plum Ballerinas who have a dream" (Goldberg, *Sugar Plums*) — this kind of dedication indicates finality, as does the basic plot and structure of the story. The crux of the story revolves around Jessica, one of the triplets, who rescues an injured stray cat from a dumpster. Enlisting the support of her Sugar Plum Sisters, Jessica takes the cat to a veterinarian, who treats the cat for her paw injury and gives the girls advice for caring for the animal. Meanwhile, Jessica names the kitten Adrienne, after Ms. Debbé, their dance teacher and head of the Nutcracker School of Ballet. Jessica and her Sugar Plum Sisters try in vain to locate a permanent home and/or shelter for Adrienne, finally hiding Adrienne in the attic of the ballet school. Meanwhile, Jessica learns that the ballet school is in danger of closing, as the original owner has died, leaving her son, Mr. Evans, in charge of the property. Mr. Evans has every intention of "raz[ing]" (Goldberg 58) the school, to build profitable condominiums; he threatens to summarily evict the school if any of the terms of the current lease are violated. This occurs when Adrienne makes her presence known, in the presence of Mr. Evans.

In a twist of fate, Jessica notices rare peregrine falcons nesting near the attic of the building (the new hiding place for Adrienne). In a flash, the Sugar Plum Ballerinas spring into action, calling local mass media outlets, locating a possible shelter for Adrienne, contacting Animal Protection agencies, quizzing the triplets' mother, an attorney, about legal rights, etc. In short, the Sugar Plum Ballerinas not only dedicate their spring performance to saving the peregrine falcons (with Al's mother altering the costumes and Ms. Debbé revising the choreography accordingly), they also save the school by making the building a special place not only for the falcons, but also for dance. Thus, their spring performance becomes a fundraiser for the falcons and the school, and a nightmare for Mr. Evans, who not only backs down from his plans to raze the building and create condos, but also conveniently adopts Adrienne.

The many lessons of *Sugar Plums to the Rescue!* include: children can make a difference; answers to problems often can be found if one looks diligently enough; people have an obligation to care for animals; and the mass media can be used as a tool to foster positive social change. All of the Sugar

Plum Ballerinas books feature glossaries of terms related not only to ballet, but also situational terms related to each story. As seen through the situations and characters of the Sugar Plum Ballerinas series, Goldberg's wisdom shows the world what little girls, a lot of imagination, and help from one's friends can accomplish.

Goldberg is no stranger to children's literature. Prior to the Sugar Plum Ballerinas series, she offered the picture books *Alice* (1992) and *Whoopi's Big Book of Manners* (2006). *Alice* offers an urban twist on Lewis Carroll's classic *Alice in Wonderland* tale. The story concerns a little New Jersey girl who embarks upon a great adventure, first by city bus, and then by subway train, to downtown New York City, to claim a cash sweepstakes prize. Accompanying her are two friends: Robin, a male who bears a physical resemblance to the Mad Hatter, and Sal, an invisible Italian rabbit (whom the narrator likens to Robert De Niro). Along the way, Alice encounters (and narrowly escapes) a menacing diner and a greedy diva, both of whom are after Alice's prize. She also makes a new friend in a soothsayer (whom she later learns is Sal's mother, in disguise). As the journey unfolds, Alice learns how to negotiate the New York City public transit system; to not be prejudiced against people from different neighborhoods (in particular, Alice finds that some people whom she encounters hold downtown New York City in great disdain); to be wary of strangers; and also that real friends are more valuable than any sweepstakes prize. Goldberg poetically dedicates *Alice*: "To my mother,/Alex and Amarah,/Maurice Sendak,/Steven Spielberg,/Mike Nichols,/'T,'/and to everyone who has ever had a dream." Her mentioning of her daughter and granddaughter (Alexandrea and Amarah, respectively) and Steven Spielberg (who insisted that she play the lead in his film adaptation of *The Color Purple*, for which she received her first Oscar nomination) are hardly surprising. Goldberg's mentioning of Sendak is particularly interesting, however, as Sendak is perhaps most famous for the bold, visceral fantasy art of his children's book, *Where the Wild Things Are* (1963).

Sendak's influence on *Alice* is especially apparent in the dark, fantastic images of characters, objects and places, courtesy of Goldberg's narrative and the art of John Rocco. Moreover, the image of Goldberg herself appears to "color" the fictional Alice, who wears pressed hair, as did the actor, during childhood. Of *Alice*, reviewer Rosemary Bray writes, "The narrative is smart and strong, and Alice is just the kind of urban heroine many of us have been looking for in a children's book: brave but not foolish, loyal and generous, absolutely single-minded and very funny indeed" (Bray). Bray describes Rocco's art as "graceful, accomplished, sometimes funnier than the text itself ... vaguely menacing and beautiful" (Bray). In 2005, she mounted a stage adaptation of the tale at the Kennedy Center, which unfortunately was not as successful as the book. Jayne Blanchard of *The Washington Times* writes,

"Why the enchanted tale needs hectically pasted-on hip-hop flourishes begs to be answered. The outcome of this adaptation of Miss Goldberg's 1992 children's book is an uneasy combination of Eddie Murphy's character in 'Mr. Robinson's Neighborhood' sketches from the old 'Saturday Night Live' and the more cynical elements of 'Willy Wonka.'" Blanchard praises the set design, which featured "graffiti-splashed letters spelling out 'Alice' that double as beds, tall buildings, construction sites and other city sights." Given the 13-year gap between the original publication of the book and its stage adaptation, it is highly likely that many theater attendees were not familiar with the book and were perhaps expecting a storyline more in keeping with the original *Alice in Wonderland* tale. Goldberg's juvenile literature follow-up, *Whoopi's Big Book of Manners*, also a Disney/Jump at the Sun book, may be seen as a precursor to her book expressly addressed to adults: *Is it Me? Or Is It Nuts Out There?* (2010), in which the author "takes on the decline of our country's civility" (Carter) including such topics as "Politics Has Gotten #$!@%! Nasty"; "Censorship"; "No Condom? No Way"; "Road Rude" and "Toenail Clipping and Common Scents," among many other topics.

Whoopi's Big Book of Manners is a contemporary etiquette book, written at a level for and including topics appropriate for children. In fact, Goldberg says that she wrote the book as much for parents as for children. She explains, "Whenever you want to give information to parents, the best way to do it is through a kids' book (Sachs). Topics discussed in *Whoopi's Big Book of Manners*, a children's picture book wildly illustrated by Alexander "Olo" Scronczynski, include: land-line telephone and cell phone etiquette; respecting the privacy of others; personal hygiene; observing local customs, especially when traveling abroad; and not "being a poor sport"—Goldberg counterbalances such wisdom for children, with a special notice directed at parents who yell at their children's coaches, thus setting a poor example for the next generation. In addition to reaching children and parents, the book also resonates with reviewers. The October 2, 2006 edition of *Publishers Weekly* opines that *Whoopi's Big Book of Manners* "will tickle youngsters' fancy, even if it imparts little advice they haven't already heard.... Goldberg fans will recognize her voice, as she wryly slips in some counsel for grown-ups" (RBI). The December 2006 edition of *Town & Country* mentions the book's "brilliant illustrations throughout" ("Whoopi's Big Book" 198); *Publisher's Weekly* echoes and extends this, praising Olo's "electric-hued, multi-media illustrations." Marilyn Ackerman, highlighting Goldberg's "informal and humorous" text, also writes that the book's illustrations "keep the mood light" (Ackerman 94).

Goldberg, savvy and industrious businesswoman, parlayed *Sister Act* success into a solid, multi-pronged setting, where several of her "jewels" shine in connection with Disney. Such gems include: her spirited portrayal of Deloris Van Cartier/Sister Mary Clarence, in the *Sister Act* film series, which paved the way for the reported Célia Cruz biopic project; her uplifting portrayal of the title character in the major motion picture *Eddie*; her flavorful voiceovers for Disney film productions *The Lion King*, *The Lion King 1½*, and *Toy Story 3*; *Whoopi's Big Book of Manners*; and her critically-acclaimed *Sugar Plum Ballerinas* children's book series. Whether she will play the lead in the announced film production regarding the life and work Célia Cruz, the Queen of Salsa, remains to be seen. Nevertheless, Goldberg reigns as a multimedia queen.

7

A Shoulder to Cry On/ A Woman to Stand Strong

> Sometimes someone needs to snap their fingers to wake you up to where you are supposed to be.
> — Whoopi Goldberg (Zhang 2010)

Throughout her career, Goldberg has worked to break stereotypes and broaden the range and scope of her acting. Nevertheless, Black American viewers sometimes openly criticize her for taking roles that they deem racially stereotypical; ironically, white viewers sometimes criticize her for taking roles that de-emphasize or flatly ignore race. Regardless of such criticism, Goldberg is determined to make her way, on her own terms. In some cases, that means learning more about the kinds of challenges that performers of past generations faced — being "snapped" into a different set of realities, as the actor says, in order to foster authenticity; this entails boldly stepping into uncharted territories, and taking artistic risks. This chapter concerns Goldberg's work in selected television series and motion pictures, where she plays roles that capitalize upon her overall believability as a solid, dependable woman. Her work in *Bagdad Café* (television 1990–1991); *Clara's Heart* (1988); *Ghost* (1990); *Corinna, Corinna* (1994); *Girl, Interrupted* (1999); *The Long Walk Home* (1990); *Ghosts of Mississippi* (1996); *Star Trek: The Next Generation* (television 1988–1993); *Star Trek: Generations* (1994); *Star Trek: Nemesis* (2002); *The Associate* (1996) and *Sarafina!* (1992) all rely upon her ability to portray strong, reliable women.

Goldberg plays the dependable, overbearing-yet-charming Brenda in the CBS comedy series *Bagdad Café* (1990–1991), based upon the motion picture of the same title. The television series, which lasted for 15 episodes, co-starred Jean Stapleton. About the experience, Goldberg says, "It was a good opportunity and a steady job.... And I figured I could learn a lot by working with Jean Stapleton" (JPC, "Whoopi Goldberg and Jean Stapleton" 58). Her comments express a constant theme in the work philosophy of the Oscar-winning actor: engaging in purposeful, regular work and respect for fellow artists who excel at their craft. Goldberg's interest in working alongside veteran actress Jean Stapleton, in a television show based upon a critically acclaimed motion picture, should not come as a surprise. Stapleton, a member of the previous generation of multitalented stage performers, not excels not only at comedy, but also drama and classical music.

Known worldwide for playing the ditzy, redheaded, middle-aged Edith Bunker on CBS's long-running television situation comedy *All in the Family* (1968–1979), and garnering "three Emmys for Outstanding Lead Actress in a Comedy and three Golden Globed for Best Actress in a Television Series (AMG), Jean Stapleton displayed talents that extended far beyond comedy, to encompass Broadway, classical music and beyond. In fact, it was Stapleton's training in classical voice, which gave her portrayal of the fictional character Edith Bunker its characteristic loud, shrill urgency, opposite the booming, deliberate, Bronx, New York, cadence of her fictional husband, Archie (Carroll O'Connor) and the sweet, baby-doll voice of Gloria Bunker (Sally Struthers). Several parallels may be drawn between Stapleton and Goldberg: both are native New Yorkers; both stared down stereotyping in and through their varied works; and both are known to multiple generations of audiences. Stapleton's body of work is impressive — long before starring in *All in the Family*, she "studied at Hunter College in New York as well as the American Apprentice Theater, the American Actor's Company, and American Theater Wing" (AMG). She appeared in such Broadway productions as *Damn Yankees* (1955) and *Bells are Ringing* (1956), later reprising her roles in the motion picture adaptations, and performed as an "original" cast member of the Broadway shows *Rhinoceros* (1961) and *Funny Girl* (1964) (IMDb "Biography"). As an original cast member of *Damn Yankees*, Stapleton's "role was small, but her lilting voice rose above the chorus singing 'You've Got to Have Heart'" (Soylent Comm.). Among many other off–Broadway productions, she also "appeared off–Broadway in *Bon Appetit*, performing as an operatic Julia Child, mixing and baking a chocolate cake" (Soylent Comm.)

Throughout her acting career, Stapleton drew upon her formal training in classical voice, as a former member of the Hunter College (City University of New York). Robert Shaw Chorale (NNDB). (Her famous off-key duet with fictional husband Archie Bunker, in the opening credits of *All in the Family*, was intentional). On the small screen, she played Eleanor Roosevelt in *Eleanor, First Lady of the World* (1982) and had a supporting role in the motion picture *You've Got Mail* (1998) (IMDb "Biography"). Stapleton's legacy demonstrates that, if one continually stretches and applies one's skill set, then a stereotype cannot hold. Goldberg's work makes for an interesting parallel to Stapleton's career, for she fought stereotypes to carve one of the most diverse ranges of fictional characters while also forging a public identity as an activist.

As Brenda in *Bagdad Café*, Goldberg draws upon frenetic energies to contrast the character's extreme philosophies against those of the sweet-mannered, reasonable Jasmine (Stapleton). With an original CBS-TV airdate of May 11, 1990, and taped before a live studio audience, the *Bagdad Café* episode titled "Art" shows her as Brenda being the fuddy-duddy, in sharp contrast to Stapleton's laid-back, hippified Jasmine. (Brenda owns the Bagdad Café and related motel; Jasmine is a stranded tourist who boards there; both are divorced). It begins with a running joke in which the café is depicted as being not the best, but rather, the only, game in town, and thus not only tolerated, but supported (the food is, according to a paying customer, barely passable, with garlic permeating the hash browns and the breath of anyone who dares eat them). The episode actually presents two parallel plots: Brenda's and Jasmine's reactions to a nude painting which a customer claims to have painted of Jasmine; and the "art" of Brenda's daughter, Debby, who successfully practices not only impersonation but also deception, to dupe her public school teachers and evade her mother.

The primary plot pits the high-strung Brenda against Jasmine, with respect to their interpretations of a painting which Rudi, a café customer, has painted. Rudi, who has painted desert landscapes in oil on canvas, wishes to win a blue ribbon in a community art fair. He enters the café, displaying his wares across the countertop, much to the chagrin of Brenda and consternation of Jasmine, who try to find redeeming qualities in the three paintings, which seem to depict the same boring "cactus in the desert" motif. Brenda's flippant response of choosing among the three by improvised lottery discourages Rudi; but Jasmine's quiet willingness to find worthwhile qualities in the painting encourage him to ask her to pose for a portrait. She agrees.

A few days later, Rudi, likening himself to Rubens, Picasso and Gauguin, brings the portrait to the café, displaying it on the countertop for everyone to see. Much to Brenda's horror, Rudi's portrait of Jasmine goes to extremes; for, while Jasmine had posed fully clothed, Rudy has painted a nude fantasy woman in her place. At once, Brenda demands that Rudi paint clothes on the figure, naming specific kinds of clothing that he can conveniently paint over specific portions of the figure's nude body. (The audience, which cannot see the painting, laughs at her recommendations.) Yet Jasmine finds the painting flattering and, since it does not actually depict her (she assures Brenda that she posed fully clothed), she likes it.

Brenda goes to the extreme, later that night, invading Jasmine's motel room and forcing her out of bed. The audience laughs as Brenda foists even more clothing upon Jasmine, whose long-sleeved nightgown already covers her from neck to ankles. Brenda's plan is to break into the local art gallery and steal the painting before the art show begins. While Jasmine doubts the need to do so, she nevertheless complies. Brenda's hot insistence, contrasted against Jasmine's coolness, makes for an engaging, funny contrast, heightened by the fact that Brenda, the younger woman, nevertheless acts grandmotherly, while Jasmine behaves like a hippy. Brenda, despite her overbearing qualities, is a staunch, dependable friend who goes to great lengths in an attempt to preserve Jasmine's reputation.

When they reach the art gallery to retrieve the painting (the art gallery is conveniently left open for the night, attesting to the area's overall desolation), they notice that many of the artworks on display show nudity and various aspects of sensuality and sexuality, implying that the desert is dry but fertile. Meanwhile, the security guard accosts them. Gentle Jasmine cannot devise a lie to get the two out of trouble, so Brenda pretends to be a streetwalker. Brenda's impromptu act deters the security guard. On their way out, Jasmine and Brenda examine the painting. Jasmine, placing the blue ribbon upon it, convinces Brenda that the painting is beautiful, especially because the form, while false, is so flattering. The tension between mother and daughter, in the relationship between Brenda and Debby, reveals another aspect of beauty.

The episode's secondary plot concerns Brenda's teenage daughter, Debby (Monica Calhoun), who has decided to impersonate her mother, by phone, in order to miss school in favor of helping her father move to a new home. The lively banter between Brenda and Debby (called Phyllis in the original motion picture), depicts genuine mother-daughter tension. Whereas Debby knows that she is wrong for impersonating her mother and lying to her about her whereabouts, she and her mother share a sense of pride in the "like mother, like daughter" aspect. (As the story unfolds, a Bagdad Café customer, a high school teacher, notes Debby's absence from school and asks Brenda if her daughter is feeling better, thus revealing Debby's subterfuge.) As the tense tenderness between Brenda and Debby shows, the tension between mother and daughter, while sometimes fraught with frustration, can also be beautiful.

Reviewing the television adaptation of *Bagdad Café*, John J. O'Connor writes that "excitable Brenda and gentle Jasmine — she does magic tricks in her spare time — are opposites but clearly meant for each other in primetime's world of insult humor. The stars seem to be enjoying themselves immensely, and Paul Bogart, a sitcom miracle worker, directs the first episode with enough aplomb to qualify himself as a master illusionist" (O'Connor). Adapting a motion picture for the small screen is no small task; it requires consummate actors who not only know and can deliver their lines, but can also roll with the punches.

Like its motion picture precursor, the television series *Bagdad Café* creates a pastiche of attitudes and possibilities against the backdrop of the Mojave Desert. As Brenda and Jasmine, respectively, Goldberg and Stapleton clearly enjoy each other's company and respect each other's artistry, the appreciation of which is enhanced by the show's taping in front of a live audience, which plays along and helps to bring out the best of each character.

In the film, Jasmine (Marianne Sägebrecht) travels across the Mojave Desert, in a large, heavy vehicle driven by her exasperated husband. Viewers quickly learn that the two are tourists from Bavaria, en route to/from Las Vegas; their spat ends with the husband driving off without her, leaving behind such relics of their time together as a large, heavy suitcase and a thermos full of traditionally strong German coffee. When Jasmine drags a suitcase filled with men's clothing (ostensibly her husband's clothes, hastily removed from the car in error) toward the Bagdad Café, she meets an overworked, exasperated Brenda (CCH Pounder), who wonders aloud how her own husband could so quickly forget buying the new coffeemaker that he was sent to buy in faraway Las Vegas. (Meanwhile, viewers see a Bagdad Café employee adopting the thermos and employing it for use at the café; the thermos and its use as a makeshift coffeemaker becomes a running joke throughout much of the film, similar to the use of the garlicky hash browns as a running joke in the television episode "Art.")

When Jasmine learns that Brenda, the owner-operator of the Bagdad Café and related hotel, is also estranged from her husband, Jasmine, a childless woman, is determined to make herself useful by providing cleaning services and helping to care for Brenda's children, gratis. Brenda's children include Salomo (Darron Flagg), a teen who constantly plays the piano, paying homage to Beethoven (much to Brenda's chagrin and Jasmine's delight), and Phyllis, a typical American teenager with a hankering for fashion and hanging out with fast boys (whose vehicles, ranging from a motorcycle to a charter bus, represent her ticket away from the desert and toward civilization). Brenda also has an infant grandchild (Salomo's son; the whereabouts of the baby's mother are never revealed to the viewer). Yet the paranoid Brenda, still reeling from her recent tiff with her husband, cannot see the beauty of Jasmine's presence and instead, threatened by Jasmine's very presence and interference, calls the sheriff. The presence of the sheriff, a Native American, representing the only original inhabitants of the area, heightens the tension and irony of the scene: who is the "real" outsider? Meanwhile, regular customer Rudi Cox (Jack Palance), a former Hollywood set painter whose original framed works grace the walls of the dilapidated hotel rooms, sets his sights upon painting Jasmine.

The scene begins with Jasmine wearing her tailored green, worsted wool Bavarian skirt set, with matching spencer and white blouse. To these, she adds a feathered green Alpine hat, characteristic of Bavarian clothing traditions typically worn by men; and then, slowly, at Rudi's suggestion, and also indulging her own curiosity/sexuality, she removes one article of clothing at a time, until she is completely nude. Rudi hangs the image of the fully clothed portrait of Jasmine in the café for all to see, reserving the nude portrait for himself.

Other scenes in the film show Jasmine helping to bring the deadened Bagdad Café to life by sharing her gift of performing such classic magic tricks as finding coins behind patrons' ears, "sawing" a hand from a patron's arm, etc. (Truck drivers, who publicize the events via CB radio, liken Jasmine's magic show and the café's growing ambiance to that of any Las Vegas magic show, only more affordable/accessible.) Later, when the sheriff, attending one of Jasmine's magic shows, insists that her visa has expired and that she must have a green card in order to remain in the United States, Rudi approaches her in private and offers to marry her so that she can remain stateside. Meanwhile, the viewer sees a change in Brenda, who has decided that Jasmine is part of the extended family of the Bagdad Café; symbolically, Jasmine becomes the desert flower, needed and wanted as much as rain in the desert.

Understandably, the pacing of the television show is much faster than that of the film, and the live audience factor, audibly present in the television series, changes the timbre from that of its film predecessor. Nevertheless, on both big and small screens, *Bagdad Café* retains its humor and grounding in the faults and foibles of humanity. With the episode "Art" making direct connections to the original film, and given the chemistry of the actors, viewers certainly can see why CBS decided to cast Goldberg as Brenda and Jean Stapleton as Jasmine in the television series. As compared with their motion picture counterparts, Goldberg's Brenda is just as zany, while Stapleton's Jasmine is just as sweet. Each actor is simultaneously true to her respective fictional character, while also allowing aspects of her natural personality to shine through. In the television version of *Bagdad Café*, two women — one a Bavarian tourist and the other an American businesswoman, meet by chance at a Mojave Desert café-motel; estranged from their husbands, they come to rely upon and support each other. The struggling café-motel, which becomes a character in its own right, bears witness to the women's growth as human beings and "sisters" in struggle. For while the American woman literally owns the café-motel, it is the Bavarian tourist who works her magic on both the café and the hearts of its growing clientele.

One overlooked gem in the Goldberg film catalog is *Clara's Heart* (1988). The charming film garnered only lackluster box-office attention, for which she blames critics. "Take *Clara's Heart*," Goldberg explains. "It's a nice movie, without any violence. It's not going to cure cancer, but it's a nice movie. And they killed it. The critics killed it. They said it wasn't funny enough. When you do the fun ones, they say it's not serious enough. And when you do the serious ones, they say it's not serious enough. God, you get to the point where you know what? F — you!" (Chutkov). The title of the film identifies Clara Mayfield, lead character in a broken household, whose job begins as live-in housekeeper, but develops into that that of mending the hearts and spirits of the white family for whom she works.

As Clara Mayfield, Goldberg is a dependable shoulder to cry on, a middle-aged black Jamaican immigrant, who works as housekeeper and heart-mender for a wealthy suburban Baltimore family. Initially, Clara tries her best to keep not only the house, but also the household, together. Leona Hart (Kathleen Quinlan) blames herself for the death of an infant daughter, and, in the midst of her all-consuming grief, forgets how to love herself, her husband, Bill (Michael Ontkean) and her only son, David (Neil Patrick Harris). As the story unfolds, Leona abandons her husband and son in favor of cavorting with Dr. Peter Epstein (Spalding Gray), her therapist and a famous author of self-help books. Meanwhile, Bill, who cavorts with several different mistresses, moves out of the sprawling Hart house and into an upscale apartment in Baltimore. As the Harts' marriage dissolves, young David Hart twice experiences abandonment: first from his mother, and then from his father. He then finds a kind of motherly love in the day-to-day caring of Clara Mayfield.

Viewers first meet Clara in her native Jamaica, where she works as a chambermaid at an exclusive resort, tending to Bungalow B, where Leona Hart has come to grieve the loss of baby daughter Edith. In that opening scene of *Clara's Heart*, we see Clara forcing open the living room curtains, against Mrs. Hart's wishes; we also see Clara gently forcing Mrs. Hart to rise out of a tubful of water in which she had been soaking, mindlessly, for hours. To nourish Mrs. Hart, who for days has not had a proper meal, Clara calls her friend who works in the kitchen to prepare a platter of traditional Jamaican foods, such as cho-cho (a starchy root) and akee (a fruit traditionally served with saltfish). Clara's detailed care for Mrs. Hart, combined with her characteristic optimistic outlook on life, causes Mrs. Hart to fire her current live-in maid (a nondescript older white woman) and hire Clara instead. Viewers quickly learn that Clara has friends in inner-city Baltimore and, therefore, a life of her own.

In Chapter 9, Clara, who by this time has secured an apartment of her own in a working-class Baltimore neighborhood, with the hopes that her estranged husband eventually may rejoin her, teaches David to sing the traditional Jamaican Calypso song, "Brown-Skinned Girl," popularized by Harry Belafonte. In that song, the narrator, a sailor about to embark upon another excursion, tells a dark-skinned black woman to care for the infant regardless of what fate befalls him. In that scene, David, who has traveled only a few miles, but what seems to be a world away from his comfortable, predictable upscale suburban surroundings, interacts with Clara and her community, singing along, forgetting his troubles and smiling. Symbolically speaking, the "brown-skinned girl" in the song is Clara, who, in Chapter 6, has already vowed to care for David for as long as he needs her. When David asks her, in Chapter 6, whether he can depend upon her forever, she wisely tells him that he will not need her for as long as he thinks.

Beyond the worthy script and film direction, Goldberg anchors the character in the kinds of realities which many women face, adapting to varied social and work situations. Like many actual women, Clara is "all business" when she is on the job, but she also reserves slivers of time and space for herself. For example, Clara's room within the Hart household belongs to her, and it is understood that no one is to disturb her or her property. Within the sanctity of her small room is a curious red suitcase — a portable home for the hundreds of unread, returned letters that she has sent to her estranged husband. In Chapters 7 and 8, David betrays her trust by reading the letters; yet Clara's anger, resulting in her initial declaration that she and David can no longer remain friends, eventually gives way to her understanding that all people make mistakes, and that children are given to crossing boundaries simply out of curiosity.

Unlike the stereotypical mammy figure who sacrifices time and attentions concerning herself and own community in favor of nurturing the white family for whom she works, Clara does not, at any point, relinquish her ties to her own Baltimore neighborhood and Jamaican identity. In addition to maintaining her friendship with best friend Blanche Loudon, owner of a Baltimore hair salon catering to Jamaican immigrants, she also regularly attends Catholic church services with a primarily Black congregation. (In Chapter 8, Clara even brings David along for one of the church services, against her own better judgment; the boy responds with glee, learning gospel songs and taking communion.) This proves to be extremely significant, especially as the scandal regarding Ralfie, which has traversed the Atlantic Ocean, continues to cloud her existence. Black Jamaican immigrants (Dora Cambridge in particular) in the city of Baltimore know full well that, back home, Clara's son Ralfie raped Dora; when Clara confronted Ralfie with the reported misdeed, he then raped Clara, his own mother. Ralfie committed suicide by jumping off a cliff into the Atlantic Ocean. Thoughtful viewers come to understand that Clara's heart needs mending as well.

Viewers' concerns about Clara's well-being are symbolically addressed in Scene 4 when young David, a grade-school student and the runt of the school swim team, jumps off a pier in the Hart family's backyard, attempting to swim beyond the safety zone. Unable to swim further, he weakly swims toward the house, climbing up the side of the pier and into Clara's strong arms, which wrap him in a blanket and a warm hug. Later in the story, David is able to swim to the safety zone and back to the pier, with Clara instinctively waiting for him behind the Hart family's screen door. This scene symbolizes David's growing maturity and David's and Clara's healing; seeing David thriving under her care restores her faith in herself, especially where the care of children is concerned. In Scene 10, in her Baltimore apartment, Clara tells David the story of Ralfie, and David, sitting across the small table, lowers his head and reaches for Clara's hand, offering support. Clara declares that she is freed of the burden of Ralfie, and viewers understand that her special relationship with David is largely to be credited with this development. Goldberg's ability to abruptly shift from playing the wise helper, to one in need of help, to one who is healed is thoroughly convincing and largely due to her facial expressions and tone of voice.

As *Clara's Heart* unfolds, viewers learn that, just as Clara becomes a means of emotional support for the David, literally and figuratively saving him from drowning, so David, who becomes Clara's "heart," saves Clara, by reminding her that she is a capable caretaker. *Clara's Heart* shows how a combination of effective acting, direction and storytelling elevates what easily could have become a stereotypical mammy role to that of a stalwart, humane heroine, raising audience expectations and emotional consciousness to new heights.

In Chapter 3, Clara quietly commands Leona Hart to deconstruct the nursery, as it has become a shrine to the dead, preventing the family from healing; Leona cries, but eventually complies with Clara's declaration. In Chapter 5, Clara openly confronts Leona, who has returned home from a retreat, to visit David — Clara declares that Leona Hart's happiness is not the same as that of her son. Clara's open confrontation pits her against her employer. Yet Clara is determined to ensure that David is properly cared for, regardless of what happens to her job. In Chapter 8, Clara refuses to allow David to become a pawn in his parents' divorce. In that scene, Clara refuses to be a crutch for Leona, while also challenging Leona Hart to reclaim her status as David's mother. Clara's words and actions clearly show Leona and viewers that, while she is a dependable housekeeper, she knows that she cannot and should not replace David's mother, and that she is aware of, and can market, her own skills and is prepared to seek gainful employment elsewhere. This makes Clara a realistic, dependable figure, not just for the Harts, but also for and upon herself.

Aldore Collier, writing for *Jet Magazine*, explains, "Ms. Goldberg incorporates the toughness she displayed in *Burglar* and *Fatal Beauty*, as well as the tenderness of her Oscar-nominated performance in *The Color Purple*" (Collier 30). Collier also mentions how Bob Mulligan, the director, allowed the actor freedom of creative expression, similar to that which she experienced during *The Color Purple*, under the direction of Steven Spielberg (Collier 32). Moreover, says Collier, Goldberg mentioned the overall lack of control that actors have over the final product, such as editing and the like, mentioning such actors as Sylvester Stallone, Arnold Schwarzenegger and Eddie Murphy as among the elite who have control over the final product — a degree of control which she eventually would have (Collier 32). Goldberg's philosophy regarding the role echoes that of Hattie McDaniel, who in 1939 became the first Black American to win an Academy Award for playing the role of Mammy, in *Gone With the Wind* (1939). Says Goldberg, "I never said I wouldn't play a maid. I said that I wouldn't *just* play maids. But in the words of Hattie McDaniel, 'Better to play one than to be one'" (Sheff).

Collier's mentioning of creative control is a political statement, designed specifically to address Black American readers concerned about onscreen portrayals of black characters. Collier tries to explain the circumstances under which Goldberg chose to portray a black maid in a major motion picture. His comments regarding how she "was given creative expression" (Collier 32) — but not creative control over the final project are a way to soften the blow for Black readers eager to see Black Americans portrayed in positive (or at least non-stereotypical) roles. When viewed squarely, however, the role of Clara Mayfield is anything but stereotypical, not only because of the unusual twist of story, but because of her determination to craft Clara as a full human being with a heart and community and dreams of her own.

Goldberg plays a different sort of dependable woman in *Ghost* (1990); to the actor's way of thinking, the character Oda Mae Brown, for which she received the Oscar for Best Supporting Actress, becomes a heroine. She says, "There's a part of me that has always wanted to be a hero and Oda Mae permits me to play someone who becomes truly heroic" (Collier, 1990, 59). "I think it's fun. It does not cure cancer. [But] if you look at it as a piece of entertainment, you'll have a great time" (Collier, 1990, 60). Goldberg's performance in *Ghost* is more than simply entertaining, however; she brings deliberate weight to the character — a balance between being over-the-top and yet anchored to reality, a feat few actors ever master.

The veteran actor may have reveled in finally getting the chance to play a heroine, but such did not necessarily lead to more or better employment opportunities in Hollywood. Goldberg says that Oscar nominations do not necessarily lead to job offers; moreover, she expresses frustrations that people in the industry claim that her Oscar win had more to do with *Ghost*'s box-office success than talent and production value (JPC, "Whoopi Goldberg, Second Black Actress" 55). The actor concludes, "I'm tired of people telling me I'm here because of some sort of fluke. I thought the idea of moviemaking was to entertain and make money.... I don't work to please critics. I work to please me" (55).

Goldberg's work in *Ghost* not only "pleased" her, it also was a testament to one of her staunchest supporters, the project's headliner, Patrick Swayze, who insisted that she be hired for the role (*Remembering...*). According to Jerry Zucker, the director of *Ghost*, a primary issue was Goldberg's quirky public persona (*Remembering...*). She had just completed a string of offbeat films which received lukewarm reviews and lackluster box office receipts: *Jumpin' Jack Flash* (1986), *Burglar* (1987), *Fatal Beauty* (1987) and *The Telephone* (1988). Such roles emphasized situational silliness, de-emphasizing her dramatic acting abilities; thus, casting agents and the director initially did not view Goldberg as a serious contender for the role of Oda Mae Brown. In fact, Tina Turner originally auditioned for the role (*Remembering...*). Ironically, Goldberg had to prove her worth as a serious actor, even after having received the nomination for an Academy Award for Best Actress in *The Color Purple*, in much the same manner that the fictional Oda Mae Brown must prove her worth as a legitimate soothsayer. A common misinterpretation is that Brown is a mere charlatan, but careful review of the film shows Goldberg giving Oda Mae more complexity and weight. When viewed squarely, her performance conveys to careful viewers that Oda Mae has a legitimate family legacy of being able to commune with the dead — a skill which she fears that she has not inherited, and, therefore, has not fully developed.

Viewers first encounter Oda Mae Brown in Scene 5 of *Ghost*. That scene, titled "Oda Mae Brown," begins with an uptempo gospel song playing in the background, while the camera focuses upon a cheesy-looking soothsayer's lair: a Brooklyn storefront featuring neon lights tracing the shape of an open palm and spelling out the words "Spiritual Advisor." As the ghost of Sam Wheat approaches and crosses the threshold via the closed front door, viewers see a darkened room filled with people hopeful to hear from their dearly departed friends and family members. For the a fee of twenty dollars, they are granted a little time with Brown. In theatrical fashion, Oda Mae's two sisters prepare the way for the grande dame's grand entrance: almost magically a door swings open to reveal the soothsayer, wearing a roomy copper-colored lamé frock and a head full of large, dark, relaxed hair. Initially, this scene gives the audience an initial impression of Brown as fraud, but it also reveals Brown's latent talents as actual soothsayer.

Careful viewers will notice that the scene reveals the dichotomy between Oda Mae, the fraud, and Oda Mae, the real psychic, when it depicts Brown deliberately conning a Mrs. Santiago while also genuinely hearing the voice of the deceased Sam. During Scene 5, viewers see Oda Mae conning Mrs. Santiago out of a succession of twenty-dollar bills, saying that she (Brown) cannot "see" Mrs. Santiago's beloved husband, Julio; the subtle social implication, carried out by Oda Mae and her sisters, is that, if Santiago paid enough money, then Brown would be able to see him. Yet Sam's verbal pleas, openly declaring the soothsayer a fraud, let the audience know that Brown is a real soothsayer (Brown and the viewers hear Sam loudly and clearly) who also happens to also be a consummate con artist. When Oda Mae openly acknowledges Sam's presence, loudly blurting out his name before running into a closet to privately commune with God, promising to never again commit fraud, viewers hear and see the "real" Oda Mae Brown. This portion of the scene depicts a repentant woman who clearly has the gift of insight into the realm of the afterlife, now summoned to do her God-given job to serve as a medium for Sam, while protecting Molly, his loving wife. Later in the scene, the light banter between Oda Mae Brown (whose voice can be heard in both natural and spiritual realms) and Sam Wheat (whose voice only can be heard in the spiritual realm), creates levity when Sam vows to haunt her forever with song, unless she agrees to help him.

Scene 6, "Molly in Danger," shows Brown hurriedly forcing her way downtown, in accordance with Sam's wishes, against her own preference to avoid the downtown area entirely. (This scene makes the most of the film's setting in New York City, as it humorously and realistically pits Goldberg, a native New Yorker, against another.) While Brown tries, unsuccessfully, to get a disbelieving Molly to buzz her into the brownstone, Brown must contact Molly the old-fashioned way: yelling into the apartment from the street, sharing intimate details that only Molly and Sam otherwise would have known, in an effort to shame Molly into eventually letting the flashy psychic into the apartment. On cue, a neighbor with pronounced Brooklyn accent hangs his head out of a window, yelling to Brown to be quiet—at which point Brown, in authentic New York fashion, openly invites the man to kiss her behind. In this scene, viewers see Goldberg, as Brown, showing not only her New York moorings, but also her ability to stand strong as a dependable character, whom the audience accepts as authentic, even while another actor on screen (Demi Moore, as Molly) does not.

Scene 6 also illustrates Goldberg's ability to embellish even the most basic costumes to achieve character authenticity, by using facial expressions. In that scene, the viewer sees Molly visiting her local police precinct, per Sam's instructions (channeled via Oda Mae), to convey Sam's message about Willie Lopez (coincidentally a neighbor of Oda Mae Brown) as the murderer of Sam Wheat. When the police officer returns to his desk with file after file regarding not Lopez, but Brown, the viewer hears the officer rattle off a litany of Brown's recorded offenses, dating to 1967 (some twenty years earlier) and including such acts as racketeering, selling false identification, numbers running, fraud, forgery and the like. While the officer speaks, the viewer sees several mug shots featuring Oda Mae Brown: the first shows Brown wearing a platinum blonde pageboy wig and matching smirk; the second shows her wearing a large, loose, afro puff chignon, accented by a countenance of resignation; and the third shows her wearing her hair in large dreadlocks, draped over one shoulder, coupled with a blank facial expression. These images show Goldberg crafting the external, fraudulent Oda Mae Brown, creating a deliberate contrast against which the actor portrays the authentic Oda Mae Brown.

As this scene shows, costuming enhances but does not "make" the character; she is careful to allow Oda Mae Brown's getup to be the character's outer shell while using the craft of acting to convey the character's substance.

In Scene 5, "Oda Mae Brown," it is revealed that Oda Mae comes from a long line of actual psychics: a native of Louisiana, her mother and maternal grandmother both were gifted psychics who declared that Oda Mae had also inherited the gift. Oda Mae doubts this until she encounters Sam's fighting spirit. While the plot of *Ghost* may seem, at the outset, to solely concern the spirit of Sam fighting to reunite with Molly, the film's second, and equally important, storyline concerns Oda Mae Brown's acceptance of her gift and ability to channel psychic energies for good instead of profit.

In *Remembering the Magic Retrospective*, a short documentary included with the *Ghost* DVD, Goldberg explains that she sees the fundamental, internal conflict of Oda Mae Brown as consisting of the fight between virtue and vice. Moreover, in an interview, she declared that the character "becomes truly heroic" (Collier, 1990, 59). Such aspects come to the fore in a pivotal part of Scene 9, "Rita Miller." During that New York City street scene, Brown openly struggles to release a fraudulently obtained four-million-dollar check into the hands of a Catholic nun, who is collecting alms to support a homeless shelter. At Sam's request, Brown endorses the check, fraudulently signing the fictional name of Rita Miller (the individual whom she impersonates, so that the blackmailers who slaughtered Sam cannot have the money). By so doing, Brown exonerates herself while also helping humanity. Yet when the time comes for Brown to give the check to the nun, the soothsayer grits her teeth and groans as though evil spirits are trying to force her to keep the money; and when the nun firmly grasps the check, Brown tries to wrest it from her. Brown's final release of the check into the nun's hands shows the triumph of good over evil and lays the groundwork for Brown as a hero of the story.

In Scene 8, "A Gathering of Ghosts," during a séance back at Oda Mae Brown's Brooklyn storefront, the spirit of Orlando, a deceased Black American man, appears (one of a score of ghosts in attendance). Intercepting Sam's urgent pleas for attention, Orlando willfully enters Brown's body, forcing the soothsayer to use her physical self to communicate with his wife, Orticia, also seated at the table. After briefly serving as medium for Orlando, Brown forcibly expels him from her body, warning him never again to take such liberties. While the scene is played for comedy, observant viewers realize that Goldberg depicts Brown as having been traumatized in the deepest way: for Orlando simply forces his way into Brown's unwilling, unready body — an act tantamount to spiritual rape.

This is in great contrast to Scene 13, "Oda Mae Brown Possessed," in which she briefly (and willingly) surrenders her body for Sam's use. Oda Mae Brown stands and approaches Molly. Channeling Sam, Brown longingly reaches for the widow's hands, and instantaneously, the scene changes to depict Sam Wheat first lovingly caressing Molly's face, then slowly dancing with her, while the audience hears the film's theme song: The Righteous Brothers' rendition of "Unchained Melody"—a popular American song which raises the spiritual and emotional significance of the scene. Thus, Oda Mae Brown completes the journey of becoming a heroic figure.

Goldberg's stint as Oda Mae Brown in *Ghost* is not the only time when she portrays a strong, dependable fictional character who must re-establish herself, however. Take, for example, her role in *Corinna, Corinna* (1994). This tells the story of Corinna Washington, a college graduate and classically trained pianist who makes her living as a housekeeper, and her bond with Molly Singer (Tina Majorino), a motherless child in mourning, and the girl's father, Manny (Ray Liotta), a widower and writer of commercial jingles. The film begins with visual shots of the 1950s style California bungalow that the father and daughter share — the viewer sees TV dinners of Salisbury steak and Tater Tots; there are no groceries in the house, however, and alcoholic beverages abound. Thus, the film's opening scene instantly leads viewers to believe that Manny needs a wife as much as Molly needs a mother.

In the meantime, however, Manny sets his sights not on a new wife, but on hiring the perfect housekeeper-nanny. Scene 2 shows Manny interviewing a succession of seven potential candidates: a Broadway-style performer; a woman carrying a creepy doll; an Asian woman (the camera angles imply that the lady's race automatically makes her a less-desirable candidate); a woman who maniacally declares that all children love her; and a cutesy, over-eager nanny (Joan Cusack) who vows to treat Molly as though she were her own child. Humorously, the cutesy nanny gets the job ... until Manny learns that, as caretaker of the household and Molly, she expects all the trappings of a wife, sex included (Scene 3). Meanwhile, Molly continues to play the opening bars of "Good King Wenceslas" on the upright piano — the melody of which has no resolution, as her mother is not there to sit beside her to play the soprano parts, and her father, a professional musician, has no time to teach her. Thus, Manny's search for the perfect housekeeper-nanny resumes, and by Scene 4, the viewer is introduced to none other than Corinna.

From the first note, Goldberg clearly understands and communicates the character's standing as a blueswoman — a black woman who has confronted many crossroads and lives to tell the story. Viewers soon come to learn that, largely due to racial discrimination, Corinna cannot ply her trade in classical music and instead makes her living as a housekeeper-nanny. Leaving the bitterness of the blues behind, and instead retaining its lessons and radiating confidence and clarity, Corinna keeps it cool and upbeat, with respect to demeanor and carriage, amplified by jazzed-up clothing and a matching musical score. When she appears on the scene, during Scene 4, Corinna emerges from a public bus, wearing high heels, dark sunglasses with lenses and frames evoking cat eyes, a navy blue skirt suit (symbolizing the Black American blues tradition) and smoking a cigarette. Meanwhile, the wailings of a jazz saxophone (an extension of the blues music tradition, symbolizing progress and urbanity) herald her arrival. She openly calls out to, and confronts, Molly, whom she immediately sizes up as the quiet type; Corinna matter-of-factly concludes that Molly's silence will not perturb her; rather, in deep, smoky clips, she tells the little girl that such silence will actually help her finish her work faster. Confidently tipping her heels away from Molly and toward the house, her body language projecting her assumption that she has already gotten the job of housekeeper-nanny, Corinna abruptly stops, turns and offers a parting shot, which functions as a bluesy grace note of sorts, dryly complimenting Molly on her new bike. In response, Molly glares at her.

The playful call-and-response between Corinna and Molly is appropriate for the setting and theme of the film, paving the way for Corinna's central role as the figure upon whom not only Molly, but also Molly's father, lean for comfort and reassurance. Goldberg's Corinna is more than just a housekeeper-nanny; as the story progresses, she becomes a central figure in a household that is not, and, as the story initially implies, never can be, hers. At one point, Molly's crayon drawing of the family clearly depicts Corinna in the place normally reserved for the mother; yet the reality is that she is not the mother and does not enjoy the family's wealth or related social standing. Viewers learn that, as much as Corinna loves helping Molly and Mr. Singer, she simply does not make enough money. Thus, she juggles several jobs; in addition to working for Mr. Singer, she washes windows for Miss Warner and babysits for her sister Jarena (Jenifer Lewis), who reminds her that working for white folks, especially Mr. Singer, who does not pay overtime, is just a lesson in hard work and heartache (Ch. 13). Jarena also implies that, because Corinna works late hours for Mr. Singer, free of charge, then she must be having sexual relations with him. Corinna corrects her, saying that she simply was calming Molly when she suffered a nightmare (Ch. 13).

As the story progresses, Molly finds her voice, courtesy of Corinna's care. This is evident in Chapter 6, when Corinna takes the time to sit at the piano beside Molly and the two play a duet of the full, opening melody of "Good King Wenceslas." (Majorino and Goldberg actually play the instrument, with correct fingerings and use of the pedals.) "Good King Wenceslas," a traditional carol heralding the Feast of Stephen (the day after Christmas), is a standard song for beginning pianists. Symbolically, the resolution of the melody indicates the beginnings of the little girl's emotional healing, courtesy of Corinna.

Corinna's solid dependability in caring for Molly manifest in everyday duties, such as learning to drive (in order to run errands and take Molly to school) and teaching the little girl to play piano and hula hoop. Chapter 6, "Winds of Change: Queen for a Day" especially shows Goldberg's ability to have fun with an acting role while interacting with a child actor. In that scene, Corinna uses the Singer family car as the vehicle for enlarging Molly's world beyond the home and its stifling memories of Molly's mother. In that scene, as Corinna learns to drive, she tries to bring a little magic into Molly's life by pretending that she has the power to use short breaths to change red lights to green ones, similar to the act of blowing out birthday candles. She even shows Molly how to do it, and praises the little girl for displaying such latent "talent." Viewers are aware, however, that Corinna, a newly licensed driver, drives at such low speeds that she can see the opposite street light changing, and therefore correctly anticipates the light in front of her changing. Goldberg's fans would also find this scene interesting, as it partially parallels her real-life experience of learning to drive later in life.

Again in Chapter 6, "Winds of Change: *Queen for a Day*," Goldberg, as Corinna, uses the Singer family car as a vehicle for fostering Molly's positive behavioral change. In that scene, Corinna takes the car through a car wash, with Molly sitting beside her. As the vehicle moves through the car wash, Corinna pretends that the percussive sounds of the water beating upon the car mimic the imagined experience of inhabiting a maraca; and when the mechanized cloths scrub the car, she squeals, pretending that she, too, is being given a bath — seemingly spontaneous reactions which draw laughter and hearty verbal imitations from Molly. Meanwhile, Manny comes to regard Corinna as a substitute mother for Molly; in Chapter 15, "Almost Like Family," Manny tells Molly to listen to her "mother," meaning Corinna. Viewers find that Corinna actually is an estranged wife whose husband abruptly left her; but there is no sense that she is pursuing reconciliation with her husband or a romantic relationship with Mr. Singer. At this point in the film, Manny and Corinna seem equally committed to ensuring Molly's happiness, merely indulging the little girl in her fantasy that Corinna and Manny will become a married couple.

The relationship between Corinna and Molly goes too far, however, when Corinna takes Molly to work with her at a wealthy white woman's home and later takes Molly to church. During that scene, Molly, skipping school with Corinna's knowledge, helps Corinna clean the white lady's house; later, when Corinna takes Molly to a restaurant for lunch, she is mistaken for a waitress (Ch. 18). Molly, a music lover and daughter of a musician, takes especial delight in the gospel church service that she experiences with Corinna, learning the gospel song, "This Little Light of Mine" (Ch. 19). Molly also registers confusion when she smiles and describes herself as a "nigger lover" (Ch. 19). Manny takes umbrage that Corinna takes liberties with Molly's schooling (Corinna explains that Molly has abandonment issues and fears leaving home); and Corinna, seeking clarity, declares that she no longer will work overtime, with which Manny agrees (Ch. 20). Later in the story, however, Corinna and Manny share a genuine kiss in the backyard. Corinna, who formally wore the blue colors of a blueswoman, is now wearing red, evoking the memory of Manny's deceased wife, who wears red in a cherished family photo (Ch. 22). Corinna's role becomes so thoroughly enmeshed in the Singer household that Manny's only logical recourse is to fire her (Ch. 24).

Goldberg convincingly plays Corinna as a woman standing strong in her knowledge of self and the times — that interracial romantic relationships are rare, remote and typically hidden; and that, as she is more than a housekeeper-nanny, and less than a wife, it is best for her to move on. The story nevertheless ends on a positive note, for Manny, having released himself from the role of Corinna's boss, is now free to explore a romantic relationship with her. (Besides, Corinna does not consider herself as having been fired; instead, she kindly quits and returns to her familiar clothing in hues of blue.) At the end of the story, Manny and Corinna experiment with romance, much to Molly's delight; Corinna will not go wanting for affection, and the viewer knows that Corinna certainly has what it takes to gain employment elsewhere.

Similarly, Goldberg's role in *Girl, Interrupted* also depicts a dependable woman whose professional skills are a source of strength. In that 1999 film, she portrays Valerie Owens, RN, as a strong, determined, focused and dependable head nurse, working in a women's psychiatric ward. Wynona Rider (who also executive-produced the film) is Susanna, a teen diagnosed with borderline personality disorder (BPD). Based upon Susanna Kaysen's best-selling 1993 autobiography, *Girl, Interrupted* garnered co-star Angelina Jolie (who played Lisa) a 1999 Academy Award for Best Actress in a Supporting Role (IMDb Awards). The impact of Goldberg's role should also be taken in context with respect to the fact that it initially emanated from a book. In this sense, the actor was returning to familiar, successful approach which she used in crafting the character Celie in *The Color Purple*.

Kaysen's autobiography describes Valerie, and Valerie's conflicts with another nurse, Mrs. McWeeney, thusly:

> Half a dozen nurses, including Valerie, and an aide or two were on duty during the day. The night staff consisted of three comfy big-bosomed Irish women who called us "dearie." Occasionally there was a comfy big-bosomed black woman who called us "honey." The night staff would hug us if we needed a hug. The day staff adhered to the No Physical Contact rule.
>
> Between day and night was a dark universe called evening, which began at three-fifteen, when the day staff retired to the living room to gossip about us with the evening staff. At three-thirty everyone emerged. Power had been transferred. From then until eleven, when the comfy women took over, we were in Mrs. McWeeney's hands.
>
> Perhaps it was Mrs. McWeeney who made dusk such a dangerous time. No matter the season, dusk began at three-fifteen with her arrival.

> Mrs. McWeeney was dry, tight, small, and pig-eyed. If Dr. Wick was a disguised boarding-school matron, Mrs. McWeeney was an undisguised prison matron. She had hard gray hair pressed into waves that grasped her scalp like a migraine. The day nurses, following Valerie's lead, wore unbuttoned nurse coats over street clothes. No such informality for Mrs. McWeeney. She wore a creaky white uniform and spongy ripple-soled nurse shoes that she painted white every week; we could watch the paint cracking and peeling off between Monday and Friday.
>
> Mrs. McWeeney and Valerie did not get along. This was fascinating, like overhearing your parents having a fight. Mrs. McWeeney cast on Valerie's clothes and hair the same disapproving eye she gave us and clicked her teeth with impatience as Valerie gathered her coat and pocketbook and left the nursing station at three-thirty. Valerie ignored her. Valerie was able to ignore people in an obvious way.
>
> As long as Valerie was on the ward, we felt safe hating Mrs. McWeeney. But as soon as her long tapered back had receded down the hall and out the double-locked double doors, we were overcome by gloom shot through with anxiety: Now Mrs. McWeeney was in power [Kaysen 88–89].

Kaysen's descriptions provided Goldberg with an initial overview of Valerie, but it is Goldberg's ability to read between the lines, to understand and project the motivations of Valerie and her patients — especially Susanna, the narrator of the story — which bring Valerie to life on the big screen.

Goldberg stands strong as Valerie Owens, the head nurse in the women's ward in the fictional Claymoor Psychiatric Hospital, a private, Massachusetts nineteenth-century edifice, with general attitudes and behaviors to match. Goldberg interprets Valerie as a hard-working professional — a take-charge individual who willfully ignores racial stereotypes and related insults while caring for a wide variety of women and keeping an especially close eye on Susanna (Wynona Rider). From the start of the film, Valerie intermingles Black Power Movement clothing and symbols with the staid, white uniform of the nurse: a rounded, shaped afro, bound by a white headband (in place of the typical nurse's cap, of the time); a hand-crocheted, fringed poncho; and rounded wire-rimmed glasses, as complements to her standard white nurses' uniform pantset. (In sharp contrast to other nurses, who wear the skirted nurse's uniform with cap, Goldberg's Valerie "wears the pants" — a nod to the emerging nurse's profession and her status as a relative outsider.) Several scenes show her as the helpful, if understandably guarded, outsider.

Valerie wears a guarded smile of welcome as she witnesses Susanna, who is of majority age, signing herself into the facility, for what her psychiatrist (an old friend of her father) believes is a much-needed moratorium. Viewers eventually learn that Susanna Kaysen, an 18-year-old from a privileged New England background, is considered a loose woman. Kaysen has reportedly attempted suicide by downing an entire bottle of aspirin, followed by a shot of vodka — an admission she makes later during the story. Kaysen is the only member of her high school graduating class who is not college-bound. Instead, much to Valerie's chagrin and disappointment, Susanna dwells in melancholy and self-pity, clearly surrounded by women with problems even more difficult to face and conquer. Polly (Elizabeth Moss) is the teenaged victim of a house fire — the mangled remains of her face make her feign sweetness so as to gain social acceptance. Daisy Randone (Brittany Murphy), in addition to being addicted to laxatives, has an eating disorder; she will only eat roasted chickens, courtesy of her father's restaurant. (Valerie allows Daisy to amass as many as five rotten chicken carcasses, all hidden from sight under her bed, before forcing the young woman to discard them.) Lisa (Angelina Jolie) is an eight-year veteran of the ward, who openly preys upon the women's obvious weaknesses, such that the women become dependent upon her social approval and attempt suicide when she no longer socially accepts them. And Janet Webber (Angela Bettis), is a young woman with an eating disorder, who plays the race card when Valerie is present, so as to deflect attention away from her disorder. (In sharp contrast to Susanna Kaysen's book, Goldberg's depiction of Valerie deliberately downplays the significance of race; fortunately, the script and direction of the film give the actor just enough space to show Valerie's racial identity, without being defined by or confined to it.)

In Scene 4, "South Bell," Janet Webber (Angela Bettis), a woman with an eating disorder, verbally abuses Valerie, calling her, in effect, a mammy who has no life. Yet Valerie takes Janet's words in stride, insisting that Janet must eat if she wishes to wear any clothes other than a hospital gown. In Scene 19, Susanna Kaysen echoes Janet's mammy remark while Valerie is supervising her bath. Goldberg's facial expression and overall demeanor in this scene depict Valerie as being obviously hurt by Susanna's words, but even more so by her disappointment in Kaysen's deteriorating, self-defeating behavior. Despite the hurt and disappointment, Valerie nevertheless takes the upper hand, showing the young woman that, while both women are tied to the ward, at least she can go home to her family at the end of the day.

In many ways, Goldberg's interpretation of Valerie, de-emphasizing race, and emphasizing the realities of femininity and work, allows for the development of the relationship between Valerie and Susanna. Most telling is Scene 23, "Empathy," in which Valerie, who normally works in the ward during the daytime, enters Susanna's room after Daisy's suicide. The scene marks a turning point for Susanna, who has heretofore wallowed in self-pity; when confronted with the possibility that she could have stopped Lisa from tormenting Daisy to death, Susanna nearly spirals out of control. Valerie offers a sympathetic ear, specifically telling Susanna that she, unlike many women on the ward, has an opportunity to free herself from her own demons, while also helping the women of the ward see themselves anew. Valerie briefly breaks the cardinal rule of no touching, offering Susanna a sincere hug. It is clear that Valerie is a serious professional with a heart and hope for a young woman caught in a mind-maze of her own making; she also provides the young woman with sage advice, which ultimately helps the young woman out of the maze. In her calmest voice, Valerie tells Susanna that, instead of simply confessing her emotions and revelations to her diary, she must verbalize her feelings, in order to gain her freedom.

As Goldberg interprets and projects the character, Valerie represents possibilities for women, regardless of race. Far from being a mammy figure stereotypically so devoted to meeting the needs of her white "children," that she regularly abandons her own, Goldberg crafts Valerie as a staunch American working woman, who, while devoted to achieving the highest level of professionalism, does so expressly to support her family. In Scene 7, "Fuzzy-Legged Women," viewers learn that Valerie is a single mother of two, who, like the women on the ward, must lose a bit of privacy on a daily basis. She reveals that she shares a single bathroom with her children.

Viewers also learn that, ironically, the hospital ward's living room is dead, while the TV room, featuring a large black-and-white floor model, controlled by the nurses in the ward, is alive. The ward's communal television serves as a symbolic connection to the outside world, broadcasting such images as the Kennedys, *The Wizard of Oz* (which becomes an underlying theme for the women, who, like Dorothy, carry the ingredients for hope and healing within); Disney World, Florida; and the assassination of Martin Luther King, Jr. Of all the televised images, the reports regarding the assassination of King resonate the deepest; the camera shows all of the women in the ward transfixed, and also reveals Valerie's determination and disgust. Here Goldberg makes effective use of the prop of the cigarette and its smoke to "mask" her rage, but her countenance expresses shock, sadness, disappointment and concern; even given this brief view of Valerie, viewers understand that she cannot fully express her feelings because she is at work; nevertheless, her facial expression and overall demeanor say it all. Valerie connects the women of the ward to the outside world, not only via her commanding presence over other nurses on the ward, but also via her expressive eyes. At one point, Valerie is authoritatively presiding over other nurses when Lisa threatens to jab a sharp object into what she calls her "aorta" (actually a jugular vein; Valerie calmly corrects Lisa, and Lisa files away the lesson, apparently for later use). At another point, Valerie subdues Cynthia Crowley (Jill Armenante), a patient, commanding that a nurse administer a sedative. According to Lisa, Cynthia has been hospitalized for being homosexual.

Observant viewers will notice that Goldberg wears the same basic nurse's uniform, white bandana and afro in the Robert Townsend made-for-television comedy film, *Jackie's Back!* (1999). *Jackie's Back!* focuses upon a fictional washed-up soul diva (Jackie Washington, played by Jenifer Lewis), trying to make a comeback. As Ethyl, Jackie's sister, Goldberg deliberately uses the uniform from *Girl, Interrupted* (minus the afghan and rounded, wire-rimmed glasses) as a counterpoint, of sorts, to realize the character. (Evidently, Goldberg took the time to film scenes for *Jackie's Back!* during breaks in the filming of *Girl, Interrupted*.) Goldberg's ability to abruptly shift from playing a no-nonsense nurse to a spurned, angry sister illustrates Goldberg's nimble creativity. Obviously, for Goldberg, clothes do not "make" the character; she, the actor, makes the character, resourcefully making use of props to enhance her performance.

Notably, *Girl, Interrupted* received mention in *Jet Magazine*, one of the most popular magazines devoted to Black American audiences: "Goldberg stars as no-nonsense ward nurse Valerie, and Winona Ryder stars as Susanna in *Girl, Interrupted*" (JPC, "Movies to See" 65). This undoubtedly helped to increase the film's popularity, for among "major motion pictures of that era, featuring Black actors, *Girl Interrupted* marked a respectable fourth place at the box office, behind such films as *Next Friday* (which reached No. 1); *Stuart Little* (2nd place); *The Hurricane* (3rd place). *The Green Mile* ranked fifth" (JPC, "Next Friday" 36).

The Long Walk Home (1990) is another theatrical film in which one of Whoopi Goldberg's characters deals with real-life issues. Set in Montgomery, Alabama, during the time of the Montgomery Bus Boycott, *The Long Walk Home* gives viewers an atypical set of perspectives regarding strife and cooperation in the city: the vast majority of the film is given from the perspectives of Miriam Thompson (Sissy Spacek) and her maid, Odessa Carter (Whoopi Goldberg). During the months-long bus boycott, Carter must regularly walk to and from her demanding housekeeping job; upon her return home, she performs the very same wifely and motherly tasks, with exhausting repetition. Key scenes of *The Long Walk Home* illustrate varied views of women working: Scene 5, "Christmas Dinner"; Scene 8, "Taking Sides"; Scene 9, "You'll Have to Walk"; and Scene 10, "Determined Mind."

Scene 5, "Christmas Dinner," shows Odessa and Claudia, the Thompsons' two Black American maids, serving a formal dinner to the family and guests. As Claudia carries a pitcher of ice water, Odessa carries a tray of homemade dinner rolls, offering and serving them to each guest who desires one. During that scene, several guests make disparaging remarks about the bus boycott, to the effect that it must be crushed or else "niggers" will gain a sense of entitlement to the point where they will not work. During that conversation, a woman seated around the table declares that "niggers" do not work as it is, and that any civil rights that they may gain will result in a spread of "communism." The pointed nature of the woman's words, which are stated as Odessa and Claudia continue working, sparks temporary shock from guests, who, while likely agreeing with the woman, are uncomfortable that she speaks so freely in front of the help.

Scene 8, "Taking Sides," concerns community reactions to the Montgomery bus boycott. The scene begins with a brief shot inside the civic center, where white citizens have gathered to discuss the impending crisis. But the majority of the scene takes place in a Black American Protestant church, where we see Odessa and her family (including her son, who has been beaten in a race-related scuffle while trying to protect his sister, who secretly has tried to date a white youth from the other side of town) recommitting to God and community. While the pastor reminds congregants about Moses's 40-year fight against the Pharaoh to gain the freedom of his people (a parable employed to teach the community about steadfastness), congregants learn that Martin Luther King's Montgomery home has been bombed. The pastor quells the congregation, entreating them to pray for King and his family and continue to fight for civil rights. During this scene, Odessa's countenance conveys tiredness coupled with a resolve to fight.

That resolve comes to the fore in Scene 9, "You'll Have to Walk." Miriam's husband, Norman, home from work due to a head cold, learns that Miriam has been shuttling Odessa to and from work. Norman yells at Miriam, telling her that her actions will cause him to lose social standing; thus, he insists that she call and tell Odessa that she should walk to work. Odessa dutifully follows suit, walking for miles in a dress and high heels (standard clothing for respectable women during that time) during a rainstorm. This scene shows a pivotal role reversal, in that Odessa, upon arriving at the Thompsons, is treated like a guest: she is offered dry clothes, comfortable seating in the living room and a hot cup of tea, courtesy of Miriam (who explains to her that Norman has allowed his anger to force him out of bed and back to work). With diplomacy, Odessa graciously accepts Miriam's kindnesses. She needs the income, she says, but the working conditions and walking distance are too harsh. Odessa tells Miriam that she must seek employment closer to home. Beyond illustrating Odessa's determination to work, this scene also highlights the common humanity and lady-like decorum that Odessa and Miriam share. Odessa and Miriam depend upon and are strong for each other.

Scene 10, "Determined Mind," shows the individual and collective chutzpah of Miriam Thompson and Odessa Carter, set against the backdrop of growing unrest in Montgomery. In that scene Miriam openly confronts Norman, telling him that, just as she does not interfere with his day-to-day work, so he has no say in the management of the domestic sphere. She tells her shocked husband that, should he force her to abandon her plans to drive Odessa to and from work during the bus boycott, it would then become his sole responsibility to hire another maid who can make the cross-town trek to and from their house. Moreover, she tells him, since she determines her own work priorities, she has no problem with the idea of using her college education to find gainful employment, working as a secretary, if necessary. Miriam's ladylike confrontation introduces a set of potentially embarrassing possibilities for Norman; Miriam working outside the home would bring far more shame upon him than Miriam using her car to shuttle one of her maids to and from the house (the social implication, in such case, would be that Norman cannot afford to have a stay-at-home wife). This scene also shows Odessa's determination to maintain her dignity while expressing her fervent desire for citizens' rights. During the same scene, Miriam takes Odessa to work, even insisting that Odessa ride up front with her. Odessa tells Miriam that the bus boycott will open the door not only to Black Americans being legally allowed to pay first-class fare for first-class accommodations, but also other citizens' rights, such as being able to use public parks and vote in elections, during which Black American officials will be elected. In the face of such revelations, Miriam resolves to become even more involved in the bus boycott, serving as a driver for the citywide carpool, knowing that white supremacists will follow her car and that she will be harassed and, at the very least, labeled a troublemaker. Miriam and Odessa convey a shared understanding of the complicated nature of race relations and the power of cooperation to bridge gaps; neither plans to become a heroine or martyr—instead, both women embrace work, resolving that their extreme plans are necessary actions to try to restore some sense of normalcy.

Whoopi Goldberg reflected on the eye-opening experiences she had while preparing to portray a Black American maid, in a story set in the segregated American South during the Civil Rights Movement:

> And then I started talking with some of the black women from the area, the women who worked as maids and nannies, who swallowed their pride and did what they had to do to raise their families and carry on. They sat me down and set me straight. "Look," one of them said, "you wouldn't have done it any differently. You just have a different sensibility. The world is a different place. When we were coming up, if you made any noise, they'd hang you. No questions asked. They'd come in the middle of the night, and they'd take your family, and they'd kill you." She was right. I was wrong.... You had to find ways to do what you did and stay alive [Goldberg 111].

Jet Magazine, one of the most popular and influential periodicals directed toward Black Americans, describes *The Long Walk Home* thusly: "Because she was not the smile-in-your-face-all-of-the-time servant, Odessa was thought of by some of Miriam's White friends as an 'Uppity Nigger.' She managed to hold on to her dignity and calm demeanor when racist remarks are made and those she loves are violently attacked.... Ultimately, it is Odessa's strength and courage that move Miriam to defy her husband and act on her own" (JPC, "Long Walk Home" 58, 60). *Jet Magazine* seeks to clarify that the film is in no way designed to capitalize on or extend the stereotypical mammy image in Hollywood motion pictures. Nor was the struggle to tell a racially balanced, fictional story, set during the real-life Montgomery Bus Boycott, limited to the influences of public perception and film reviews.

Behind the scenes, Miramax executives had to fight to distribute the film. When *The Long Walk Home* originally was released, other major motion pictures, such as *The Bonfire of the Vanities* and *The Godfather III*, dwarfed it; nevertheless, even when Miramax staff members recommended "drop[ping]" the film, "12 people," including Miramax co-founder Harvey Weinstein and his brother "threatened to resign" if this happened (Bernstein). Miramax is known for taking artistic and financial risks; its successful distribution of such groundbreaking fare as *Sex, Lies and Videotape*, *My Left Foot*, *Cinema Paradiso* and *The Grifters* illustrate its unique positioning and function in the marketing/distribution chain.

> Despite the film's poor commercial performance, everyone at Miramax loves it, the Weinsteins say, and they reject accusations of historical inaccuracy. They insist that it deals with an important topic and that audiences should have the chance to see movies that are not high-tech spectaculars or fantasy-fulfilling romances. And so, in a move that goes contrary to all conventional wisdom in the movie business, Miramax decided to pull *Long Walk Home* temporarily from the theaters, launch a new publicity campaign, and finally to open it a second time, which they are doing in some 15 to 20 cities on Friday [Bernstein].

The *Jet Magazine* article, highlighting aspects of the film which depict the fictional Odessa Carter in a positive light, and Goldberg's determination to play the role with historical accuracy likely helped the film gain urban audience attention.

Like fellow Oscar winner Sissy Spacek (who garnered the statuette for her leading role as Loretta Lynn in *The Coal Miner's Daughter*), Goldberg was a major box-office draw. Nevertheless, Goldberg drew criticism from film critic Janet Maslin for supposedly portraying a maid without moxie. Writing for the *New York Times*, Maslin says,

> Because Whoopi Goldberg is the most prominent black film actress of the moment, she is offered roles like this regardless of whether they suit her. In this film, in "The Color Purple," and in "Clara's Heart" (in which she played a funny, kindly Caribbean-born servant working for a white family), Ms. Goldberg has taken on roles that require her to stand by passively even when no audience can believe she would. This is especially noticeable in "The Long Walk Home," which allows Odessa little backtalk and in fact barely gives her much of a voice. She observes the injustice around her without publicly or privately expressing much indignation.
>
> Ms. Goldberg accomplishes this with dignity, reserve and a lot more credibility than might be expected. Neither she nor Ms. Spacek makes the mistake of condescending to the fundamentally unenlightened characters being played [Maslin].

Maslin, in effect, is paying Goldberg and Spacek back-handed compliments. On the one hand, she criticizes Odessa for not speaking out against the lack of civil rights; on the other, she praises Goldberg and Spacek for being true to their fictional characters' respective time and place. Maslin incorrectly stereotypes Goldberg, as a loud, confrontational person, expecting the actor to be that stereotypical person on-screen, despite the fact that Goldberg's off-screen public actions, when viewed squarely, are those of a concerned American citizen, acting on and preserving the Constitutional right to freedom of expression. Maslin also mentions Miriam and Odessa as "unenlightened characters," as if, had they been "enlightened" by post–Civil Rights era concepts, they would or could behave differently. To their credit, Spacek and Goldberg, as Miriam and Odessa, respectively, show how creativity and ingenuity enable the fictional characters to skirt the edges of civil rights, all the while maintaining "ladylike" decorum and civility.

Maslin also criticizes the saintly portrayal of the Cotter family, its church-going piousness and support of Martin Luther King's platform of nonviolent resistance, contrasted against the matter-of-fact racism which the Thompson family and their friends unabashedly display. Maslin continues, "[The film's] points are made best through startling understatement, as when a Thompson relative at Christmas dinner declares, 'Those niggers just want too much and they're not willing to work for it.' Odessa, serving dinner, overhears the remark, then blankly offers this woman a roll. The woman stares back at her without a trace of an apology" (Maslin). When viewed with respect to the story's immediate, actual setting, the film is startlingly true to its time and place. Odessa's "blank" offering of the dinner roll is not a denial of the cruelty of the remark, nor is it an invitation for the white woman to apologize. It is, instead, a reflection of Odessa's dire circumstances and determination to make a way for herself and her family, against obvious odds. The stalwart, resolute Odessa Carter symbolically "snaps her fingers" to awaken thoughtful viewers to stark realities of the system of racial oppression and the fight for civil rights in 1955 Montgomery, Alabama.

Ghosts of Mississippi (1996) is another important film which squarely sets itself at the crossroads of American history and Civil Rights. On the historical significance of the film, Goldberg says that she was a child when Civil Rights activist Medgar Evers (1925–1963) was assassinated; thus, it was not until she began researching his role, as well as that of his wife, Myrlie Evers, that she realized just how pivotal Evers's role was in the Civil Rights Movement (Fuller). She says that, in essence, Medgar Evers's assassination helped to pave the way for Martin Luther King's ascension to power. On the overall significance of Civil rights Movement activists, Goldberg explains, "People like Rosa Parks, Martin Luther King, Jr., and Medgar Evers fought for me.... They are part of the reason I feel I can be whatever I want to be in this country" (Campbell).

Myrlie Evers says that she "never thought of Whoopi" playing her; nevertheless, she praises Goldberg's acting abilities, and says that "the spirit of

Myrlie [is that of] a very angry, determined woman who didn't let anything turn her around" (Campbell). As an actor, Goldberg clearly identifies with the situation in which the real-life Myrlie Evers found herself. Despite her best efforts, however, Goldberg does not convincingly portray the activist; perhaps the physical proximity of the real-life Evers during the film's shooting made the actor self-conscious. Viewers see Goldberg, as Myrlie, caring for several small children, while ironing her husband's shirts; Goldberg, as Myrlie, crying out Medgar's name, when she hears the fatal gunshot; Goldberg, as Myrlie, crying tears of sorrow and outrage, her hands holding the dying Medgar (James Pickens, Jr.) close; Goldberg, as Myrlie, scrubbing her husband's blood off the driveway with a wooden scrub brush and soapy water; Goldberg, as Myrlie, in a flashback courtroom scene, depicting the State of Mississippi being openly swayed by white supremacists, allowing defendant DeLaBeckwith (popularly called "Delay"), to delay justice, instead of following the letter of the law; and Goldberg, as Myrlie, speaking tersely, by phone, with Assistant District Attorney Bobby DeLaughter (Alec Baldwin), only half-believing DeLaughter's sincerity in wishing to bring a long-dead trial to life and DeLaBeckwith to justice. Throughout these scenes, it is clear that Goldberg has studied the real-life story, personality and perspectives of Myrlie Evers; but she does not fully convince viewers that she *is* Myrlie Evers.

Perhaps the most glaring oversight is Goldberg's lack of Mississippi accent. It is in the scenes when Myrlie connects with Assistant District Attorney Bobby DeLaughter that the oversight becomes most evident. For example, in Chapter 9, DeLaughter telephones Evers to express sincere interest in reawakening the case and bringing DeLaBeckwith to justice. During that scene, viewers connect with DeLaughter, while feeling disconnected from Myrlie's controlled rage. In Chapter 11, DeLaughter calls Myrlie's office to provide a brief update on the case. The scene nevertheless conveys the humanity of DeLaughter, while also strangely conveying coldness on the part of Mrs. Evers. In Chapter 15, viewers learn that DeLaughter deliberately denies Mrs. Evers the knowledge that his team has recovered the original murder weapon — the kind of new evidence that a third trial for suspected assassin Brian De La Beckwith (James Woods) requires.

Perhaps Goldberg was wary of attempting a Mississippi accent. The actual Evers does not have a heavy Mississippi accent — she speaks with lightly gospel-infused, stately lilt. Her manner of speech correctly conveys the (out)rage, intelligence and political savvy of Evers, but does not convey Evers's characteristic sweetness of tone, lightly imbued with the musicality and phrasing of Black American Protestant preaching traditions. In fairness to Goldberg, the film largely concerns the assistant district attorney's fight to resurrect a court case that had been tabled nearly 25 years earlier. Thus, the viewer sees the Myrlie Evers character only intermittently; the film's editing and direction are also important factors to consider.

By far, the most striking scene featuring Goldberg and Baldwin is Scene 20, which takes place in the district attorneys' offices after hours. A frustrated, nervous Bobby DeLaughter paces about the office and adjacent hallway and later takes the elevator to the ground floor. When the elevator doors open, Mrs. Evers appears, standing tall, with a determined countenance, her hands gripping a large stack of papers. For the first time in the film, camera angles force the viewer to see Myrlie from DeLaughter's perspective. When viewed from such a perspective, Goldberg seems to project a stronger image of Myrlie Evers's determination; in her hands, the documents — the only copy of the original transcript known to exist, symbolically function as an anchor for the scene, contrasting against the newly buoyed hopes of DeLaughter. When Myrlie tells DeLaughter, in a straightforward voice, that she is willing to risk losing such rare and important papers for the sake of possibly bringing De La Beckwith to justice, and that he no longer need worry about the black community possibly stymieing the court case, there is a noticeable twinkle in her eyes. That twinkle denotes underlying humor regarding the likelihood of justice finally being served, tempered with a keen understanding of the politics of the situation. Toward the end of *Ghosts of Mississippi*, Goldberg finds and delivers a necessary balance, depicting Myrlie Evers as a determined, serious activist with a wry sense of humor.

Always seeking meaningful work opportunities, Goldberg frankly asked *Star Trek* creator Gene Roddenberry to create a role for her in the television series, *Star Trek: The Next Generation* (1987–1994). NiChelle Nichols recalls Roddenberry's reaction to that request.

> Gene said, "Well, I'll just ask you one question and I'll make my decision on that. You're a big screen star, why do you want to be on a little screen, why do you want to be in *Star Trek*?"
> And she looked at him and she said, "Well, it's all NiChelle Nichols' fault."
> That threw him, he said, "What do you mean?"
> She said, "Well when I was nine years old Star Trek came on," and she said, "I looked at it and I went screaming through the house, 'Come here, mum, everybody, come quick, come quick, there's a black lady on television and she ain't no maid!'" And she said, "I knew right then and there I could be anything I wanted to be, and I want to be on *Star Trek*."
> And he said, "I'll write you a role" [BBC].

Gene Roddenberry may have written the role of Guinan for the television series, but it was Whoopi Goldberg brought it to life.

As Guinan, Goldberg drew on her previous dramatic roles. Much of her acting has more to do with effective facial expressions and body language than actual spoken dialog. Guinan is female; the oration of her name includes a variation on the prefix "gyn," denoting the "female reproductive organ: ovary," as derived from the "Greek *gyn-*, from *gynē* woman—more at QUEEN" ("gyn"), but the feminine realm is not the only source of her powers. As the fictional Guinan, Goldberg's actions and words vault the gender divide and also encompass the duality of the Irish roots of the name Guinan. "Irish: reduced Anglicized form of two distinct Gaelic names, which have now become confused: Ó Cuinneáin 'descendant of Cuinneán,' a personal name from a diminutive of conn 'chief,' and Ó Cuineáin 'descendant of Cuineán,' a personal name from a diminutive of cana 'whelp'" ("Guinan"). The fictional character Guinan "was named after famed bartender Texas Guinan, who ran a saloon during the prohibition" (Okuda 180). Portraying Guinan, Goldberg embodies authority and vulnerability, tempered by ageless wisdom. Goldberg shows that it is not how much one speaks, but rather what one says, and how one says it that makes all the difference in the universe.

At first glance, Guinan, who works onboard the *Starship Enterprise-D* as a bartender in the Ten Forward lounge, seems an unlikely source for wisdom of, and beyond, the ages. Yet her history as a former refugee and survivor of the Borg (a single-minded swarm of cyborgs, which deliberately destroyed her advanced civilization, scattering the few remaining El-Aureans throughout the galaxy) makes her a sturdy vessel not to be tampered with. Her lineage as an El-Aurean (a race of beings with superior listening skills), combined with her advanced age (her actual age never is revealed; however, she is at least 500 years old) (180) enhances her status. In addition, she "has been married several times, and has had many children. She said that all of them turned out all right, except for one who [ironically] wouldn't listen" (180). These experiences give Guinan a unique vantage point from which to understand and interpret a wide range of situations. Moreover, as "a bartender on the *Enterprise*, Guinan is where she *chooses* to be" (Brevard, F.). Guinan deliberately places herself in a position to interact with the Starfleet crew in a casual setting, revealing aspects of their true natures and problems.

In this vein, one very funny scene takes place in "Yesterday's Enterprise" (Season 3, Episode 15). During the opening scene, Guinan has a serious, private conversation with Worf (Michael Dorn), a Klingon warrior and member of Starfleet. During that conversation, Guinan, her countenance expressing an understanding of the depth of Worf's loneliness, tries to convince him to expand his horizons by dating a woman. During this scene, Worf, imbibing prune juice (which Guinan has especially prepared for him; Worf, liking the taste of the thick, purple liquid, quickly dubs it a "warrior's drink"), loudly declares that he must find a Klingon female, as human females are not built to withstand the rigors of sexual intimacy with Klingons. In response, Guinan turns a wizened eye toward Worf and calmly explains that human women are sturdier than he thinks. The humor in this scene emerges largely because Worf and Guinan are so seriously adamant about their views; Worf's prejudices sound preposterous, making Guinan's extreme proposal (at least, from Worf's perspective) sound feasible. Moreover, the symbolic significance of the drink, signifying that Worf is "full of it," albeit perhaps not for long, given the laxative properties of prune juice, gives viewers hope that Guinan's wisdom may bear fruit for Worf, in that he very well relieve himself of misperceptions and find a suitable companion in a Starfleet woman.

Given her very specialized skills and wide-ranging experience, Guinan could easily have become a high-ranking Starfleet officer, yet such runs counter to her nature and purpose of using her skills to help as many as she can, in whatever way she can (Brevard, F.). Politically, such a stance makes sense, for, as a Starfleet officer, she would be bogged down with procedures and politics; ironically, therefore, Guinan, as bartender, actually "has more influence over *Starship Enterprise* happenings, and the galaxy, than a Starfleet officer would" (Brevard, F.), especially as she regularly has the ear of Captain Picard (Patrick Stewart). Several instances during the run of *Star Trek: The Next Generation* and its culminating feature film, *Star Trek: Generations* (1994) show Picard seriously considering—and following—Guinan's recommendations, even when his considerable experience and sense of logic run counter to her wisdom and intuition. Guinan helps to "snap" members of the *Starship Enterprise* back to reality, in such key episodes as "Q Who?," "Deja Q," and "Yesterday's Enterprise."

"Q Who?" (Season 2, Episode 16) places Guinan in a pivotal position to help Captain Picard question Q's sincerity and understand the modus operandi of the Borg. When the *Enterprise-D* encounters a gigantic, living cube in uncharted space, Starfleet initially tries to seize an unprecedented opportunity to learn more about its functions and inhabitants. The results are singularly destructive: the Borg, symbiotic inhabitants of the huge, living cube, quickly subdue the *Enterprise*, resulting in the deaths of several Starfleet members. At one point, Q kidnaps Picard, trying to force him to appoint Q as a member of Starfleet (viewers come to learn that Q has willfully brought the *Enterprise-D* into contact with the Borg in order to show his superiority and to force Picard to accept his "help" in countering the Borg). And later, speaking with Picard in private, Guinan repeatedly warns Picard about the Borg, the "swarm[ing]," single-minded entity that destroyed her civilization, scattering El-Aurians throughout the galaxy. When Picard mentions that he wishes to "reason" with the Borg, Guinan, using a calm, controlled, authoritative tone of voice, tells him that there is no reasoning with the Borg. She tells him that the Borg sees the *Enterprise-D* and its crew as raw material to be studied and dissected and used, as needed, to fulfill its singular mission of self-preservation. Illustrating the dualism of her name, she describes her triumph of having survived the effects of the Borg a century earlier, as well as her vulnerability as one of the scattered survivors of their relentless attack. She pointedly warns him not to visit the Borg's lair; instead, she says, the *Enterprise* crew should leave for home, immediately.

Picard's initial decision to ignore Guinan's shrewd advice, and send an Away Team to the Borg's lair, results in near-total destruction for the *Enterprise-D*; 18 crew members die, and Picard is forced to beg Q for assistance. In finally fleeing the Borg, Picard eventually follows her, but at considerable price. Had Picard followed her advice at the outset, casualties would have been avoided, and he would have remained a step ahead of Q and the Borg.

The television episode "Deja Q" (Season 3, Episode 13) again dramatically showcases Guinan's powers and Goldberg's unique suitability for the role. In that episode, Q, an alien superior in intellect to most other life forms in the galaxy, has been temporarily relieved of his powers and expelled from the Q Continuum and rendered human as a form of punishment. The *Enterprise-D* has been summoned to help restore a moon to its rightful orbit in order to save the inhabited planet Bre'el IV from sure destruction; almost magically, Q appears, with the goal of convincing the captain to allow him (Q) to help the *Enterprise-D* crew stabilize the moon's orbit. (Not surprisingly, Picard blames Q for creating the odd circumstance.)

As the story progresses, Guinan appears. Not only is Q visibly frightened by her very presence, he dismissively calls her a "creature" and quips that she is but one of many names which she has used during the course of her lifetime and their shared history. The two oppose each other, with Guinan taking an atypical offensive stance, her body poised to pounce, her hands becoming "claws" positioned to strike. Q responds in kind, his body occupying a defensive stance, like that of a frightened dog in relation to a spitting cat. Q's words imply that, given her many guises, Guinan is not to be trusted. In response, she openly calls Q's sincerity and dependability into question; she illustrates the fact that he has been relieved of his powers by stabbing him in the hand with a fork, forcing him to bleed, as any human would.

This brings to mind the scene in *The Color Purple* (1985), when Goldberg's character, Celie, fends off the curses of Mr. ____ (Danny Glover) with quick flexes of her wrists, simultaneously deflecting his anger away from her and back towards him, calling upon a higher power to give her strength to build a life away from his decidedly destructive influence. In the *Star Trek* universe, Guinan's influence reminds Picard and the *Enterprise* crew not to trust Q; that despite his human form, he remains the proverbial wolf in sheep's clothing. The *Star Trek: The Next Generation* saga never reveals the full, shared history between Guinan and Q; viewers know only that their venom is mutual, and that there is no bridging the gulf between them (Brevard, F.).

In "Yesterday's Enterprise" (Season 3, Episode 15), Guinan plays a pivotal role in reminding Picard that a temporal rift has placed people from the past into the present, and that the people must be returned to their own place in time in order for history to right itself. In that episode (set in an alternate timeline), *Enterprise-C*, responding to an SOS from the Klingon outpost (which has been attacked by the Romulans), tries to rescue the Klingons; in response, the Romulans attack the *Enterprise-C*, the resulting blasts of which force members of the *Enterprise-C* crew 22 years into the future and onto *Enterprise-D*. Captain Picard, at the helm of *Enterprise-D*, must make a difficult, but crucial, decision as to whether to return the members of *Enterprise-C* to their own time and face sure destruction, or allow them to remain alive, in his time. Guinan detects the anomaly even before the *Enterprise-D* crew does. Looking through her window, she sees a rift in space; her facial expressions and unsettling body language communicate that something "isn't right," even before she utters the phrase. Periodic camera cuts featuring Guinan show her working in Ten Forward, encountering Tasha Yar, an *Enterprise-D* crewmember who has already died. Guinan speaks cordially, but guardedly, with her. Eventually, she reveals to Yar that she "should not be" on the *Enterprise-D*, as she is dead; moreover, Guinan tells Yar the painful truth: that her death has no significance.

When Guinan meets with Picard to plead her case that the crewmembers be returned to their own time, Picard reasons that she has no proof, that she is operating only on instinct. Guinan counters that she is "right," and that, unless he returns the visitors to their own time, then the number of deaths, already considerable, will reach catastrophic numbers. In another scene, Data, an android and an *Enterprise* crew member, tells Picard that Guinan's knowledge transcends "linear time," and that her instincts and vast experience are as solid as any facts. Against his initial misgivings, Picard decides to return the *Enterprise-C* crew to its own time; He also honors Tasha Yar's request to accompany the *Enterprise-C* to its own time, so that her death will have meaning. Picard's decision, carried out by the *Enterprise-D* crew, on the advice of Guinan, restores history, saving billions of lives and making Tasha Yar's short life meaningful.

Guinan is indeed a strong figure upon which many *Enterprise* crewmembers lean for support and advice. "To most crew members who encounter her, Guinan is the twenty-fourth-century equivalent of the classic bartender, who not only serves up just the right variety of synthehol [synthetic alcohol], but also lends a caring ear and freely gives a touch of humane wisdom wherever and whenever it is called for" (Van Hise 82). Goldberg also got the chance to portray Guinan on the big screen in *Star Trek: Generations* (1994) and *Star Trek: Nemesis* (2002).

Guinan shows the range of her powers and authority to especially good effect in *Star Trek: Generations*. In that film, Dr. Soren, a fellow El-Aurian and displaced survivor of the Borg, plans to return to the Nexus at any cost. In fact, he has invented a cloaked device, which enables him to capture an energy ribbon and ride it into the Nexus. Despite the fact that the process described will ruin an entire civilization, Soren continues with his plans, undaunted. (Observant viewers recognize that Soren is not necessarily evil; rather, he is addicted to the Nexus because it temporarily, yet falsely, restores his long-lost family and sense of belonging in the universe.) Guinan's experience of surviving the Nexus, a realm where one's deepest desires are fulfilled in the form of realistic fantasy, makes her a pivotal figure in the film.

Guinan patiently describes to Picard the near perfect sense of peace which she experienced while in the Nexus; she also describes a painful kind of withdrawal process that those severed from the Nexus experience. It is Guinan who educates Picard not only regarding the appeal of the Nexus and Soren's addiction to it, but also the utter necessity of Picard's avoiding the Nexus altogether, for his own good and that of *Enterprise-D*. This knowledge gives viewers a sense of foreboding when Picard visits the Nexus and lives his fantasy of having a wife and children and seeing his late brother, René, again. During this fantasy, which appears real (save for a few odd flashings of bulbs on a Victorian-style Christmas tree), Guinan appears to remind Picard that what he experiences on the Nexus is not real; and that he, as a commanding Star Fleet officer, has a sworn obligation to return to his crew. Guinan's strength of vision is especially potent in this scene, as it not only encourages Picard to leave an ideal "life" in favor of a challenging, real destiny of his own choosing, it also shows her strength to choose when and how to enter and exit the Nexus. Faithful *Star Trek The Next Generation* viewers realize that Guinan, having been set adrift after the Borg's attack, initially found addictive solace in the Nexus — a place which she initially did not wish to leave — and yet she made a similar choice to leave the Nexus to foster the greater good, as a staunch supporter of Starfleet. Beyond her considerable dramatic acting skills, Goldberg's sincerity in conveying Guinan's addiction to and recovery from the Nexus perhaps also draws upon her personal experience of surviving drug addiction. She says, "There ain't no joy in a high — *none*. You *think* there's a joy in a high because it feels good temporarily. But it feels good less and less often, so you've got to do it more and more often. It ain't your friend" (Randolph 111). Goldberg made many attempts to wean herself from drugs, calling the experience "hard"; using her personal wisdom, she advises youth, "Save the money and just kill yourself because [if you're using drugs] that's what you're doing" (111).

Star Trek: Generations also distinguishes Guinan's ageless wisdom from the empathic abilities of Counselor Deanna Troi. Guinan provides wisdom through the ages, successfully calling Picard to focus upon the greater good, by embracing and leading his Starfleet family. Meanwhile, Troi uses her abilities to help Picard come to terms with the recent loss of his younger brother, René, and René's family. Fearing mortality, Picard tells Troi that he regards the loss of his younger brother not only as the loss of a "son," but also the "end of the Picard family line," as Picard chose to forego having a wife and family of his own, in favor of pursuing a career with Starfleet. While Troi focuses upon helping Picard heal his emotional state, Guinan helps him restore faith in himself and recommit to his Starfleet family.

Goldberg's solidness and dependability as Guinan also helps symbolically cement a key relationship in *Star Trek: Nemesis* (2002) in the scene popularly known as "Blue Skies," (named for the Irving Berlin song with which Commander Data serenades happy couple, accompanied by a band of musicians). Seated together at a table across from the newlyweds, Geordi La Forge (LeVar Burton), and Guinan smile approvingly at the union and the song. La Forge, his vision fully restored, "sees" happiness ahead for the couple; meanwhile, Guinan smiles and looks downward, humbled by the couple's glow.

Goldberg describes her character Guinan as "a cross between Yoda and William F. Buckley," to which she also added her own unique twist (Van Hise 82). Goldberg's purported description of Guinan offers humorous nods to both the *Star Wars* universe and the university, respectively. About her experiences of landing steady acting work, including a coveted, recurring role in the *Star Trek* constellation, Goldberg explains,

> Work doesn't come to me; I go out and look for it. I call [people] up and say, "Can I have a job? Can I work with you?" Sometimes it works, sometimes it doesn't. Black folks get really pissed off about my choices, white folks get really pissed off, and sometimes everybody's mad. But you can only do what you can do, and explain yourself if you choose to. And people have come to understand that me doing *Star Trek: The Next Generation* didn't hurt me. I still got an Oscar for *Ghost*. [laughs] It's being willing to walk away that gives you strength and power — if you're willing to accept the consequences of doing what you want to do [Jean].

Goldberg's frankness about the politics of work makes its way into the major motion picture *The Associate* (1996). The story concerns Laurel Ayers (Goldberg), a Black American business executive passed over for a promotion in favor of a white male subordinate who takes the credit for all of her efforts and ideas. Although she objects to this, Laurel is ignored. This is, after all, a Wall Street world in which the image of white male power is almighty. In

Scene 3, "A Business Night," Laurel Ayers (whose first name symbolizes the "laurels" upon which she is technically entitled to stand, but is consistently denied; the character's surname, "Ayers," is a variation on the Spanish term, «ayer,» meaning "yesterday") trying to present her marketing research during a Manchester Investments boardroom meeting. During that meeting, Frank Peterson (Tim Daly), a young white man, boldly uses good looks and charm to steal Laurel's ideas and sell them to the firm's leaders, while also "selling out" Laurel. Later, when Laurel and Frank are invited to present a proposal (the invitation is really for Frank, but as Laurel has all the research and paperwork, she gets to tag along), the presentation takes place in a Manhattan strip bar, where barely-clad women offer the men drinks and light physical touching. Laurel's colleague Sandy (Allison Janney), a white woman who deliberately modulates her tone of voice in masculine fashion, tells Laurel (over the sounds of The Commodores' hit song "Brick House," and amid flashing disco lights) to show some cleavage so as to gain the partners' attention. Laurel bristles at the concept. As one acutely aware of the politics of sex in the business world, Sandy also tells Laurel about her plans to undergo breast augmentation. Laurel responds by first briefly glancing down at her own breasts, then glaring at Sandy with concern and consternation. Laurel tries to get the partners to review her business proposal, but the men are far more interested in the drinks and the scantily clad women. Speaking over the din of the party atmosphere, Laurel complains to Frank that the partners are not interested in hearing her proposal. He assures her that the partners are happy with her and that she has already made a strong impression upon them. In fact, he tells her that she should just relax and go home — advice that she takes, much to her detriment. The next morning, Laurel learns that Frank closed the deal — *her* deal — during the wee hours of the morning, securing top billing in an 8:15 A.M. board meeting, to which Laurel was not even invited.

In Chapter 4, "It's a Woman Thang," Laurel learns that Frank, her trainee, has received a promotion based upon the very proposal that she had tried to present. Angered but undaunted, Laurel attends the meeting and then finds that Frank, now her new boss, is more interested in having her and the department secretary, Sally Dugan (Dianne Weist), use the Manchester credit card to buy the firm's owner, Walter Manchester, a thank you gift. When Laurel bristles at the concept, Frank frankly tells her that women are best suited for shopping; that Laurel, not Sally, has official access to the company credit card; and that Laurel should be thankful that he is now her supervisor, because he is now in a position to shelter her.

In this scene Laurel shows moxie as she loudly and directly questions Frank's gall at obtaining the promotion using her ideas and proposal. When Frank dismisses her again, saying that she should be upset with Manchester, not him, and that she must be premenstrual, Laurel shoots back that she has no problem venting her frustrations at Manchester (who, Frank tells her, is conveniently aboard a jet and cannot be disturbed) and that, had she *really* been suffering from PMS, she would have killed him. During this scene, the turning point of the story, Laurel Ayers resigns her post at Manchester Investments and decides to create a firm of her own: Laurel Ayers Investments. Laurel Ayers is also the owner, landlord and resident of a six-unit Brownstone. Her tenants include Mrs. Cupchik (Helen Hanft), a retiree who lives on the top floor, who bemoans Laurel's long hours at work and lack of family, while regularly offering hot cocoa and marshmallows to the beleaguered businesswoman; and Bissel (Lee Weikoff), a professional female impersonator.

In Chapter 4, we see Laurel trying to build her business by securing meetings with Manhattan businessmen, using the Rolodex she secured during her tenure with the former firm. Time and again, the businessmen tell her that they love her ideas, but that their respective "partners" will not approve — a repeated brush-off (it seems that none of the men actually have business partners). Just as the viewer begins to think that the businessmen ignore Laurel because of her race, it presents scenarios showing that gender is the primary detriment. For example, in Chapter 4, Laurel secures a meeting by promising a potential client that she can treat him to desirable seats at a Rangers/Detroit hockey game; during the game, while Ayers tries to sell him on her proposal, the businessman is more concerned with eating popcorn and watching the game. Ayers also visits a female-owned-and-operated bank to present a prospectus, with the hopes of gaining $150,000 in startup funds. When the loan officer requests collateral, Goldberg, as Laurel Ayers, plays dumb, sheepishly mentioning such laudible attributes as diligence and fortitude, to which the officer turns a cold shoulder. She reminds Laurel that a woman-owned bank is still a bank and must follow standard business practices. Laurel quickly changes demeanor to acknowledge the loan officer's point and then offers the six-unit apartment building, which she inherited from her deceased father, as collateral. Later, Laurel Ayers meets a potential client on the golf course, but the man is clearly more interested in spending time bonding with his fellow male golfers than talking business deals with her. (While they are standing on the green, the businessman, clearly more interested in male bonding, walks away from her, and toward male colleagues, while she is talking.) Stymied by sexism, Laurel invents a fictional male business partner, Robert S. Cutty, spontaneously named after she spots a bottle of Cutty Sark situated behind the potential client.

In Chapter 5, Robert S. Cutty moves beyond a mere name to become a fleshed out (if not flesh and bone) character when Laurel creates an outlandish webpage for the fictional partner. Before long, potential clients are demanding to meet the eccentric, wealthy Cutty. Laurel employs Sally Dugan (who has left Manchester Investments), and the drag queen Bissel to bring Cutty to life. Using Bissel's makeup and hair techniques, Laurel Ayers becomes Robert S. Cutty, an elderly white man who resembles Marlon Brando. At one point, Laurel singlehandedly saves Syntonex, a high-tech firm on the edge of bankruptcy, owned by the innovative and brilliant Aesop Franklin (Austin Pendleton) yet of course Cutty receives the credit. When Frank Peterson, Laurel's former trainee, realizes that he cannot navigate the shark-filled waters of Manchester Investments, he publishes doctored photographs so that he and Cutty appear to be close business associates.

While the overall storyline of *The Associate* is clearly farcical, the roots of the fictional Laurel Ayers's frustrations are very real. While filming *The Associate*, Goldberg encountered a similar real-life scenario.

> In January 1996, a phalanx of William Morris agents poured into a room in a Long Island mansion during a break in the filming of *The Associate* to explain to a new client, Whoopi Goldberg, the actress and comedian, how they could expand her career. Ms. Goldberg, between scenes portraying a Wall Street financial analyst stymied by sexual and racial discrimination, pointed to the lone female agent in the group, Cara Stein, and said, "Let her go first." Then, she relentlessly peppered Ms. Stein with questions and ideas.
>
> "I just thought," Ms. Goldberg recalled, "they're probably not going to let her say anything, and I'll probably be dealing mostly with her."
>
> Nearly two hours later, the meeting ended with barely a word from any of the men. Since then, the two women have talked many times a day, and Ms. Stein has helped guide Ms. Goldberg's growing Hollywood production business. "I had a feeling she would work as hard as I would," said Ms. Goldberg, known socially to be rather laid back, but very competitive when it comes to business [Koch].

That the above experience took place during a hiatus of *The Associate* illustrates the timeliness of the film and its cultural accuracy. Nevertheless, one *New York Times* critic misunderstood and panned the film:

> If you're a star who is dying to explore the cross-dressed land of "Tootsie," "To Wong" and "Mrs. Doubtfire," you had better choose an amusing character of the opposite sex to play. That's one of the lessons of "The Associate," the movie in which Whoopi Goldberg finally takes the plunge into comic transvestism and misses the mark.
>
> If "The Associate" is entirely unbelievable (it makes "Working Girl" seem like neo-realism), it still has fun parading assorted caricatures. Mr. [Tim] Daly and Bebe Neuwirth obviously relish their roles as different types of yuppie scum. Mr. Daly's Frank is a duplicitous corporate climber with the face of the boy next door and the soul of Machiavelli. Ms. Neuwirth is the kind of slinky, sleep-your-way-to-the-top schemer who gives new meaning to the slogan about power being the ultimate aphrodisiac.
>
> Ms. [Dianne] Wiest is endearing as a pleasant, sleepy-eyed secretary who is a secret powerhouse of wisdom and capability. The movie is nearly stolen by Lainie

Kazan as an intrepid gossip columnist named Cindy with a basso profundo voice and bosom to match. Ms. Goldberg is her usual omnivorously friendly (and, when necessary, bluntly feisty) self, a living breathing smile button, with dreadlocks and smart, dancing eyes.

"The Associate" is admirably if oddly color blind. There are only two allusions to Laurel's being black, and they are both made in passing [Holden].

Holden's blunt, racist statement, describing Goldberg as a "living, breathing smile button, with dreadlocks and smart, dancing eyes," as though she were a kewpie doll, misses the mark. The purpose of the film is not to increase the number of popular American films devoted to exploring transvestitism or racism; it is to show how the glass ceiling and gender divide create, uphold and replicate double standards for even the most diligent, effective, enterprising American working women. When viewed through this lens, *The Associate*, despite its over-the-top scenes, showcases Goldberg's wide-ranging acting skills to great effect, while inspiring viewers to take note of gender inequality and root for Laurel and Sally.

True to its title, *Sarafina!* (1992) is all about Sarafina ("fine little Sara"), played by Black South African Leleti Khumalo. Initially, Sarafina embodies all the fire and none of the experience of a true leader, but she latches on to her teacher, Mary Masembuko (Goldberg), who by example teaches Sarafina and her colleagues more about the world and a woman's place and possibilities than any book ever can. Focusing not only upon one, but two, black women heroines is atypical of Hollywood's depiction of South Africa; typically, the emphasis has been upon male heroes, especially the "White savior," says Jerry Mofokeng, a Black South African drama specialist (Whitaker 114).

> Getting the story of Black South Africa's march toward freedom on film ... has posed something of a problem. Of the 10 or 12 movies depicting South Africa that have been made in the last decade, the vast majority have had white characters as their dramatic centerpiece. The often-cited example is Richard Attenborough's 1987 movie *Cry Freedom* in which Denzel Washington played Stephen Biko, the Black nationalist leader who was battered to death in police custody. The star of the film, however, was Kevin Kline, who played Donald Woods, the white journalist who befriended Biko and investigated his death [Whitaker 114].

Symbolically speaking, the made-for-television movie *Bopha!*, also set in South Africa, balanced the scale a bit, by placing Black American actors Danny Glover and Alfre Woodard in starring roles. But the film, while well produced and well received, was *not* a major motion picture and thus did not have an appreciable impact. Moreover, it did not usher in a groundswell of change on the racial front, where the depiction of South African culture is concerned (Whitaker 114).

That the major motion picture *Sarafina!* breaks the mold as far as the depiction of Black South Africa is concerned, should not come as a surprise. The story, centered upon historic protests among Black South African students in 1976, began as a successful play written and staged by Mbogeni Ngemi, with music by Hugh Masekela, Black South Africans widely respected for their art, featuring a nearly all-black cast. "Slated for a 10-week stint at New York's Lincoln Center in 1987, the show wound up running for more than two years before it was made into a movie featuring Whoopi Goldberg" (Whitaker 114). The stage production's success, as well as its prominent placement among New York cultural destinations, made it a natural choice as a major motion picture. Nevertheless, it took six years for Ngemi to raise the necessary funds to bring the stage play to the big screen. The project received South African monies as well as backing from a French company and funds via the BBC (British Broadcasting Company) (Collier "Whoopi Goldberg Stars" 55). American investors initially were reluctant, because, as Ngemi explained, "Musicals haven't done well recently because they haven't been made well" (57). Goldberg's high international profile (especially with her then-recent success with the film *Sister Act*) and willingness to play the key role of Mary Masembuko may have turned the tide and encouraged American investment. Initially, Goldberg expressed surprise that South Africa had such a well-developed major motion picture tradition (55). Upon reading the script of *Sarafina!*, courtesy of film producer Anant Singh, Goldberg loved it and wanted to be part of the film project. She did express concern, however, about potentially taking a film part away from a native South African (55). "But the people on that end [in South Africa] said I should come" (56). Goldberg explained that "the role was so well-written and said such good things that I had to do it" (56). Ngemi praised Goldberg's willingness to participate in the film, given the real-life strife that characterized much of South Africa during the film's production (56)

Billed as the film's star, Goldberg plays the fictional Mary Masembuko, a progressive history teacher in a Soweto school. "Progressive" means global—to underscore this, the film opens with a scene showing Black teenage schoolboys throwing Molotov cocktails into a schoolroom at dusk. A worn world globe blazes away atop a schoolteacher's desk. Masembuko tries to instill Black pride among her students, Black South Africans who disdain the system of apartheid and its decidedly limited curriculum. Conflicts of race, gender and the generations are brought front and center in Scene 4, "More Than This," in which the internationally renowned singer-songwriter Miriam Makeba (popularly and affectionately known as "Mama Africa") plays Sarafina's mother, Angelina.

In that scene, Angelina tells her daughter to get on with her life, and stop romanticizing Hollywood, the freedom struggle and Nelson Mandela (The opening scenes of the film also shows the fictional Sarafina alternately worshipping a portrait of the real-life Nelson Mandela, and fantasizing herself a big Hollywood film star, with other schoolchildren ["paparazzi"] following her every move). When Sarafina speaks frankly about wanting to obliterate the whites in power, her mother pointedly tells her that not all whites are evil; that some — particularly the ones for whom she works, are "good people." When Sarafina fantasizes aloud that her father died in the battle for human and civil rights, Angelina gives her a reality check, explaining matter-of-factly that her father went to Mozambique and died of illness; not a hero's death, but rather the death of a common working man. When Sarafina protests her mother's servile status and the family's resulting meager vittles, her mother pointedly explains that she must work and that meager food is better than none at all. She also reminds Sarafina that she is but one of four children, and that she should mind her own business (taking care of her three younger siblings and excelling at her studies), or risk death. Sarafina says that she prefers death to a life of servitude, to which the mother replies that she cannot waste time complaining and that, unlike Sarafina, she must work instead (Scene 4). The conflict between Sarafina and her mother is an ongoing refrain running parallel to the larger conflict of apartheid and Black South African self-determination.

Masembuko's home is a small, red brick edifice — definitely a step up from the shanty in which Sarafina and other members of her class live, but a far cry from the well-heeled world of the whites, in which Sarafina's mother labors. In Scene 5, "Soweto's Children," Sarafina consults with Masembuko, to gain wisdom as to how she may help the freedom struggle. In particular, Sarafina says that, while boys can engage in physical fighting, she is at odds with such as a female (there is an inference that Sarafina, the eldest of four children born to Angelina, must set an example for her siblings). By the time this scene occurs, Sarafina has resisted the sexual advances of the constable, a Black South African named Sabela. While cruising past the schoolchildren on the streets of Soweto, he tries to charm her into giving up her virginity as well as the names of her comrades who committed the school bombings (Scene 2).

In the orderly setting of her home, Masembuko calmly tells Sarafina that she must have a destination in mind before embarking upon any plans. Sarafina honestly and intently asks about Masembuko's deepest wishes. This conversation takes place at the kitchen table. Having recovered a hidden rifle from near Masembuko's stove and placing it in the center of the table marks a turning point the women's relationship. Masembuko responds by saying that she wishes an end to war; she longs for the return of her lover, Joe, a family of her own, and harmony at home (Scene 5). She confides that the rifle belongs to Joe; that he has used it, ostensibly, to kill. She insists that her hands have not touched the firearm and that she does not condone killing and questions her ability to do so, even when her home and personal safety are at stake. Masembuko's words foreshadow the evening capture of Sarafina's teenaged schoolmate, a young man tortured into revealing the names of key players in the school bombings (Scene 5).

In Scene 6, "The Informer," the Mary Masembuko character comes full-circle. In the opening scene of the film, we see her leading the students in "The Lord's Prayer," with the hand gestures of a trained choir director, and hybrid Black American/Black South African choreography. In Chapters 2 and 5, Masembuko navigates the narrow strip of limited freedom, which formal education, popularity among students and a modicum of money can buy. By Scene 6, however, after having experienced an inquisition of sorts, conducted by the Black South African school principal, under the direct influence of a white South African police lieutenant, Masembuko returns to the classroom to remind students that she does not teach subversive behavior. Rather, she teaches history in such a way that students are able to explore options other than hurting others and burning down schools. Goldberg strikes a proper tone in this scene, as the Miss Masembuko character appears at once authoritative and yet one with the Black South Africans, to which the school children positively respond. Throughout the film, Goldberg affects Black South African mannerisms, facial expressions and dialect, so as to appear authentically Black South African — a necessity, since the majority of cast members are Black South African.

Masembuko actually appears in only five of the film's 11 chapters: Chapter 1, "Opening Titles/Sarafina"; Chapter Two, "Mary Masembuko"; Chapter 5, "Soweto's Children"; Chapter 6, "The Informer"; and Chapter 7, "Teacher Arrested." Nevertheless, the character's significance to the story is that her influence, like that of Mandela, continues, and even increases, during her absence. First, she is led from the classroom to the tenth floor of the jail for alleged subversive acts against the apartheid government, in the form of people's empowerment lectures deviating from the state-sponsored syllabus. Later, she jumps to her death, refusing to succumb to a no-win situation. Paralleling Sarafina's narration (Sarafina imagines that she is speaking to her idol, the imprisoned Nelson Mandela), upon the teacher's death we hear the steady voice of Masembuko, ringing in the consciousness of Sarafina, resonating Masembuko's deepest desires for peace, harmony and a family of her own (Ch. 10).

Healing occurs in the story when Sarafina literally (to borrow from the traditional Black American spiritual, "Down By The Riverside") "studies war no more," throwing the old rifle into the bush and walking away. She then returns to her mother, Angelina, begging forgiveness for her childishness. In *Sarafina!*, Mary Masembuko serves as a catalyst for change, and also as a bridge between Sarafina, her mother and the Black Soweto township at-large: the end of the film finds the schoolchildren singing of burgeoning liberty, voicing the song, "Freedom Is Coming Tomorrow!"

Whether playing fictional maids, nurses, a teacher or even a real-life civil rights activist, Goldberg shows us her characters' underlying humanity. Her work transports us to different times and places.

8

Crossing the Lines
Acting and Activism

> I can't speak for Hollywood — I'm not Hollywood, I live in New York. So I can speak for me.
> — Whoopi Goldberg, interviewed in *The Advocate* (Stockwell 68)

When Goldberg speaks, people listen. Sometimes, audiences respond with words and deeds of support; at other times, they "doth protest too much" (Shakespeare, *Hamlet* 133). Defining herself as an "actor" gives Goldberg an active stake in the drama of stage, screen and the larger world. If, as Shakespeare says, "All the world's a stage" (Shakespeare, *As You Like It* 38), then Goldberg takes that concept literally, "acting" as artist and American citizen. As a result, she at times courts controversy, but she always, *always* remains true to herself.

In her lengthy career as a film actor, Goldberg has played a wide variety of roles, ranging from an inquisitive computer technician (*Jumpin' Jack Flash*), to a professional thief (*Burglar*), to a narcotics detective (*Fatal Beauty*), among many others. Such roles, with their strong masculine edge, extended to Goldberg a false, stereotypical image of being either non-sexual or homosexual; she mentions that her womanly sexuality was simply ignored; or that she was presumed to be gay (Randolph 114). None of the aforementioned drew as much ire and consternation from black viewers, however, as did her roles as maid/housekeeper, however. Many black moviegoers considered the servile aspects of her roles in such Hollywood films as *The Color Purple* (1985), *Clara's Heart* (1988) and *Corinna, Corinna* (1994) as a throwback to the mammy image created by Hattie McDaniel in *Gone With the Wind*. Of her portrayal of Clara Mayfield, in *Clara's Heart*, for example, Donald Bogle writes, "The script desexed her character, presenting the black woman once again as a mighty nurturer — and updated mammy — without enough of a life of her own" (Bogle 298).

Goldberg sees the situation much differently, however. In preparing for her role as maid Odessa Cotter, playing opposite Sissy Spacek (as Miriam Thompson, Odessa's employer) in *The Long Walk Home* (1990), she says that she interviewed black women who had worked as maids in white households, in the Montgomery, Alabama, area. They explained to her the "life and death situation" (Zhang) which they faced during the 1960s. They explained to "Hoopi," as they called her, that her initial plan to play the role in a more openly confrontational manner ran counter to the politics of the era and place during which the film is set (Zhang). Goldberg admits that she learned a valuable lesson by speaking with the ladies, who had dealt daily with the realities of race, class and gender while working as maids for white families: "Sometimes someone needs to snap their fingers to wake you up to where you are supposed to be. I've gotten better at that to figure out eras and what was going on" (Zhang). Moreover, she has always maintained that, while she recognizes her African biological roots, she is a quintessential, natural-born American. In speaking with Wyclef Jean, she explains, "I can do anything. And I don't believe that I have to stay on one side of the fence or the other. I don't believe that there is any good career move or bad career move. I believe there are only the things that make me happy" (Jean 66). Among these "things" is her determination to make a difference, both on-stage and off, to emphasize humanness in the context of global awareness. Toward this end, she boldly steps toward and crosses lines of race, class and gender, as her varied roles demand.

In *Eddie* (1996), she portrays Edwina "Eddie" Franklin, a New York City limousine driver, who wins a rigged contest to serve as the New York Knicks' guest coach. In moving from limo driver to honorary professional basketball team coach, Eddie moves from one typically masculine role to another, placing her unique stamp on each. Wild Bill Burgess, a billionaire Texan (played by Frank Langella, with whom Goldberg later developed a close, personal relationship) buys the team and sponsors the contest, as a way of boosting New York Knicks fandom; once the contest ends, however, Wild Bill fully intends to discard Eddie and the team. A life-long Knicks fan, Eddie will not allow either plan to take root; she openly refuses to be Wild Bill's flunkie: instead, she flips the script, and actually leads the team to a national championship, cementing her status as a "real" coach, and the team members' ties to their beloved New York.

Reviewing the film, Janet Maslin says, "*Eddie* is savvy and good-humored, without too many of the soggier sports movie clichés. There's only one point at which Ms. Goldberg, microphone in hand, makes an inspirational speech in the middle of Madison Square Garden" (Maslin). Harvey Araton is not quite as convinced: "What would a real coach-devouring star in the National Basketball Association say if the likes of Whoopi Goldberg walked into the locker room, clipboard in hand? In the immortal words of Derrick

Coleman, the former New Jersey Net known for ignoring the simplest request, like participating in a game: "Whoop-de-damn-do." Araton's disparaging remarks aside, Goldberg convincingly works opposite "49 N.B.A. players [who] will convey authenticity even to viewers who recognize only one of them (Dennis Rodman, thanks to the magenta hair)" (Maslin). In addition, cameos by such New York icons as Donald Trump and Mayors Giuliani and Koch lend the film an air of authenticity. Vindication for Eddie (and Goldberg, for that matter) comes in the form of Knicks who actually care about more than their profiles and paychecks; players who actually *play* basketball; surging grassroots campaigns in support of Eddie and the team; and street vendor kitsch, including miniature replicas of the Statue of Liberty made in Eddie's likeness, complete with dreadlocks. By its conclusion, the film exhorts moviegoers to cheer along with Eddie and the Knicks. Goldberg also successfully crosses the lines of gender and race expectations in *The Associate* (1996).

In *The Associate* (1996), Goldberg plays Laurel Ayers, a high-powered Wall Street executive, who, despite continually producing worthwhile campaigns for her otherwise white, male firm's clients, repeatedly gets passed over for much-deserved promotions. In frustration, she devises a plan to temporarily impersonate a fictional Wall Street tycoon; take the credit for the fictional tycoon's successes and establish herself as a major player. Ayers's life is turned upside down, however, when she learns that the persona of her white, male fictional character, Mr. Cutty (whom she names, on-the-fly, after Cutty Sark scotch, enlisting the aid of a drag queen to help her bring Cutty to life) ironically overshadows her own. Film reviews were mixed: Stephen Holden says, "[Mr. Cutty] looks like a cross between George Washington with a ponytail and John Houseman in one of his Smith Barney commercials [and] turns out to be a monosyllabic bore" (Holden). Holden speaks most harshly about Goldberg herself, in stereotypical kewpie doll-golliwog terms: "Ms. Goldberg is her usual omnivorously friendly (and, when necessary, bluntly feisty) self, a living breathing smile button, with dreadlocks and smart, dancing eyes" (Holden). Actually, Cutty strikes more of a comical, yet grounded, George Washington-meets-Marlon Brando tone; in her able hands, Cutty is reclusive, elusive and eccentric. Critic Edward Levine is more charitable toward the film, saying that, at least, the film acknowledges the fact that Wall Street no longer offers lifetime job security; hence the plausibility of "Ms. Goldberg's character leav[ing] a big company to start her own computer firm" (Lewine). Goldberg infuses her character with a hip, real "New York-ness" that makes Laurel Ayers' skills believable, regardless of how she packages herself.

The gravity of the film centers upon the scene toward the end, where "Cutty" removes the mask to reveal the real Laurel Ayers. That scene, masterfully commanded by Goldberg, who modulates her voice from the deep, booming tones of Cutty to the normal New York cadence that is uniquely

Goldberg's, with dramatic, self-styled choreography to match, recalls her early solo Broadway stage work, where she transforms from "Crippled Girl" to free-flowing woman. Her work crystallizes the film's overall theme of not simply taking people at face value; of valuing the real person and his or her talent. A plus is the twist at the end of the film, where Laurel Ayers rescues the secretary (aptly played by Dianne Weist) from wasting her talents and instead makes her a full partner in their new financial venture. In another film, Goldberg literally takes the reins, playing one of the most famous white male roles, in *Call Me Claus*.

In *Call Me Claus* (2001) she plays Lucy Cullins, a home shopping cable television executive scarred by an experience during her youth. She had asked Santa to bring her daddy, a soldier away at war, home for Christmas. Instead, her father's untimely death casts a pall on the holiday, rendering Lucy a nonbeliever. That is, until, however, Old Saint Nicholas himself (played by the venerable Nigel Hawthorne) calls upon her to replace him after 200 faithful years of service. Lucy's ability to believe in Christmas again signals her belief in humanity; Goldberg transforms into an enthusiastic — and believable — St. Nicholas, making the rounds with her sleigh and trusty, antlered steed.

Part of Lucy's transformation, beyond that of opening her heart to the possibilities of the Christmas season, is Goldberg infusing her own infectious sense of humor into the character. When St. Nicholas transfers his powers to Lucy, she inherits his Santa uniform. She insists, however, that her Santa coat be altered to specifically fit *her*, as she is "short-waisted"; Lucy also says that she does not mind having a few white dreadlocks ("here and there"), but that she does not wish to change her overall appearance. St. Nicholas agrees, telling her that her basic essence and appearance will remain the same. After he waves his hand, a taxicab is transformed into a sleigh, complete with eight reindeer at the ready, and Lucy is now in full Santa attire (sans the wide belt), and wearing faux white dreadlocks attached to her Santa cap.

Once again, Goldberg's acting skill allows her to play what is usually a male character. Adding another feather to her cap, she also served as executive producer of *Call Me Claus*, along with co-producers Lisa Sanderson and Garth Brooks.

Years later, Goldberg returned to the theme of Christmas, with her personal essay addressed to children, "Christmas and My Magic Mom," illustrated by Elise Primavera, and included in the anthology *Marlo Thomas and Friends: Thanks and Giving All Year Long* (2004). In another Christmas-themed project, she also appears as Daniel's boss (ostensibly, God) in *It's a Very Merry Muppet Christmas Movie* (2002).

In the made-for-television movie *Good Fences* (2003), Goldberg plays Mabel Spader, the wife of Tom Spader (portrayed by Danny Glover), both of whom are socially severed from the larger world, due to their success. Tom's successful law practice allows him to move his family from their small home in a black community in Lovejoy, Illinois, to an exclusive, nearly all-white neighborhood. There, Mabel is constantly mistaken for a maid; after all, the only black women seen at the grocery store are those shopping for their employers. Mabel's insistence upon performing household chores, presents an ongoing embarrassment for the maids whom she encounters. Eventually, Tom insists that she hire a Hispanic maid. Meanwhile, Tom's success at work comes at a severe price, in that he is afraid to show ties to his former life. A lonely Asian housewife takes their teenage son, Tommy-Two, as an exotic boy toy (he eventually rebels further, attending the historically black Morehouse College instead of Princeton, his father's preference). Mabel, in loneliness and despair, retreats into drugs and disillusionment.

Good Fences presents a tragic switch on the popular American theme of social climbing, epitomized by television's *The Jeffersons* (1975–1985). In *The Jeffersons*, George (Sherman Hemsley), a businessman, and his wife, Louise (Isabel Sanford), a former maid, move from a working-class Queens neighborhood (a neighborhood which included the bigoted character Archie Bunker (Carroll O'Connor); *The Jeffersons* was a spin-off of television's *All in the Family*) to an upscale Manhattan apartment, to live the good life. In Manhattan, George's successful dry-cleaning company makes him a bigger fish in an even bigger pond. Louise's charm and easy elegance, balancing George's gruffness, helps smooth the couples' way into new social situations.

In *Good Fences*, relationships within the Spader household become strained when Tom (a former Civil Rights Movement freedom fighter-turned modern version of Uncle Tom—a sellout), paranoid that neighbors will see him only as a color, and not as a successful businessman, forbids his wife to socialize with the Crisps, the only other black family in the exclusive neighborhood. This new black family gains access to the neighborhood by winning the lottery. The family matriarch, Ruth (Mo'Nique), insists on perpetuating urban traditions, such as holding outdoor barbecues for old friends, and blasting music for all to hear.

Good Fences has as its theme the age-old adage, "Good fences make good neighbors," popularized by Robert Frost's poem, "Mending Wall" (1915). Defining boundaries, responsibilities and opportunities, fences also can be used to build walls of suspicion and misunderstanding, as *Good Fences* shows. Tom Spader becomes so incensed by Ruth's "ghetto" ways tainting the neighborhood, that he torches her mansion. Mabel tries to atone for Tom's sin by reaching out to Ruth, in sincere neighborly fashion. *Good Fences* shows how social atavism can take root and flourish, even in the midst of what appears to be an ideal setting.

With its diversity and varied pace, New York is the perfect setting for Goldberg's NBC situation comedy, *Whoopi*. In fact, the show was not only taped there, it was also set in New York (as was *The Cosby Show* [1984–1992], which had been set in Brooklyn). From 2003 to 2004, Goldberg produced and starred in the eponymously titled show, portraying Mavis Rae, a "one-hit wonder who now runs a small New York hotel.... Critics have generally praised the show and have compared the prickly, politically incorrect Mavis Rae to the Archie Bunker character in *All in the Family*" (Mask 345). Crafting the character of Rita, the white woman who is "blacker" than any black character on the show, including her boyfriend (Mavis's brother, Courtney Rae, played by Wren T. Brown), Goldberg steps out on a limb, bringing to the fore the universality of the formerly all-black hip-hop experience. She relates that Eminem is a real-life example of the universality of hip-hop: "Eminem is a viable, strong male character who is both white and black.... There's no right or wrong of it, no judgment of it, but it's what's happening in our [American] culture" (Dreisenger). Goldberg also broadens the scope of racial identity beyond basic black and white, to have her character Mavis Rae playfully trade jabs with Nasim (Omid Djalili, a native Londoner of British-Iranian extraction).

Goldberg acknowledges that television critics have a strong impact upon whether a television show will be successful. If they write disparagingly about a show, they sink it; conversely, their positive reviews can keep a new show afloat while it finds it audience. The actor explains: "When I used to do the Oscars, we hadn't even shot it, and it was already the worst show. I hadn't even gone into the theater, hadn't even found a dress, hadn't even signed a contract. But already, it was going to be a sh- -ty show" (JPC, "Whoopi Goldberg Challenges" 65).

Over a decade earlier, the actor had also spearheaded another short-lived show named after its founder: *The Whoopi Goldberg Show* (1992), a television talk show that may simply have been ahead of its time; *TVOne on One*, a successful interview show currently hosted by TVOne network owner Cathy Hughes, legendary radio broadcaster; founder of RadioOne, and "the first African American woman to have a publicly traded company on the New York Stock Exchange" ("Catherine 'Cathy' Hughes" 391). seems to largely draw its stylistic inspiration from Goldberg's example. In *TVOne on One*, Hughes sits in a comfortable, well-appointed private setting, chatting for an hour with a single black star of stage and/or screen. Similarly, Goldberg's talk show had

> no studio audience, no band or posse, no announcers. Ms. Goldberg does not follow the "monologue, question, answer, film clip, move down, next guest" routine. (There is only one guest per show.) It is an anti-talk show in much the same way that Ms. Goldberg is an anti-celebrity, with just a piano player and mellow, often gushing, never confrontational conversation between her and people she's intrigued by [Wilkerson].

Unlike Cathy Hughes, Goldberg did not restrict her interviewees to black stars; her guests are "drawn from lineups that each week set up juxtapositions that might have Ice T one night, Al Gore the next" (Wilkerson). Goldberg wanted her guests to feel "comfortable" and be themselves; they need not feel forced to "perform for an audience" (Wilkerson).

Part of the success of the Hughes, show, beyond its cadre of stars, is the host's credibility in radio broadcasting, as well as her approachability and willingness to probe beyond surface issues to learn more about her guests as human beings. In this regard, *TVOne on One* is also reminiscent of Goldberg's talk show, where the "personality" of the guest is more important "than the latest book or hit single" (Wilkerson). Hughes's show specifically targets a black, upwardly mobile demographic, the very same demographic that she continues to reach with her mammoth, metropolitan D.C.-based *RadioOne* network (WOL radio is its flagship station). In sharp contrast, Goldberg was trying to reach middle America. Goldberg's foray into the talk show format may have stalled for a time, but it paved the way for her later success as radio co-host for the morning radio show, *Wake Up with Whoopi*, and, eventually, moderator on ABC's *The View*.

Broadcast on ClearChannel satellite radio, *Wake Up With Whoopi* featured "music, call-ins and topical issues," reflecting Goldberg's New York moorings. The actor says that, from the time that she was a child, she always considered radio "cool"; she planned to bring more of the casual aspect of her personality to the show: "I want to be the voice that says we're O.K. today" (Lee, May 2006) — a voice that provides positivity in a world of confusion and uncertainty. Eventually, she shared the WKTU (103.5 FM, New York) radio booth with broadcast buddy "Paul Bryant, known as Cubby" (Lee, "Whoopi Gets Cubby").

In 2007, Goldberg's selection to serve as moderator for ABC television's *The View* came with considerable fanfare, from fans to co-stars alike. "Rosie O'Donnell's name wasn't mentioned on 'The View' Wednesday morning. But a few moments after Barbara Walters introduced Whoopi Goldberg to a live television audience as the show's new moderator, replacing Ms. O'Donnell, Ms. Goldberg left no doubt that a new era was dawning" (Steinberg). Rather than get into the details of why O'Donnell left the show, or discuss reported feuds between co-stars, Goldberg offered the even-handed view that people can agree, or even agree to disagree, but that long, drawn-out feuds are not worth the time and grief: "Life is way too short" (Steinberg). *The View* was in its tenth season when Goldberg was tapped to serve as moderator; during that time, she had stepped in, at the last moment, to substitute for no-shows; her background in comedy and improvisation, along with her strong work ethic, made her a "go-to guest" (Steinberg).

Since joining such regulars on *The View* as Elizabeth Hasselbeck, Joy

Behar and Sherri Shepherd, Goldberg has shown her healthy appetite for civil debate. Two of the most recent examples are her reaction to the Roman Polanski trial and the BP oil spill debacle. Goldberg drew jeers from many viewers when she said, "It wasn't rape-rape," when responding to Roman Polanski's 1977 guilty plea for "unlawful sexual intercourse" with a 13-year-old girl, following his arrest in Switzerland on September 26, 2009 (*That's That*). She also mentioned that, in some societies, some 13-year-old girls are married (Long). John Long wrote sarcastically about Goldberg:

> Whoopi Goldberg, perhaps our greatest living American philosopher (look at all the sage advice she gave [*Star Trek's*] Captain Picard through the years) also came down on the side of protecting our Precious Celebrity Resource.... Before I was enlightened about the infallibility of our entertainment elite, I might have considered such a comment reprehensible" [Long].

Long makes the mistake of saying that Goldberg assumes that her point of view has more merit because she is a Hollywood "star." To the contrary, her authority is vested in her status as an American citizen. On the September 30, 2009, episode of *The View*, Goldberg clarified her position regarding the controversial director. Polanski, she reminded viewers, pled guilty to a lesser charge of "engaging in unlawful sexual intercourse with a minor"—not rape. She also said that her original comments were not meant in any way to condone Polanski's behavior (ABC). Meanwhile, Samantha Geimer, the person whose rights Polanski violated so many years ago, has moved on; now a bookkeeper, and mother of three, she considers the matter closed: "He did something really gross to me, but it was the media that ruined my life" (Kennedy). For Geimer, unrelenting media attention exacerbated an already-delicate situation.

Of the BP oil spill, the worst man-made disaster in U.S. history, caused by an oil rig explosion and its subsequent collapse into the Gulf of Mexico, Goldberg shouted, pointing into *The View* studio camera, "I don't care about the politics! ... Fix it" ("Goldberg Blasts BP Bosses"). The audience cheered. Goldberg has a built-in fan base of New Yorkers proud to see one of their very own having a say on the national stage. Instead of relying on that, she relies upon common sense and her unwavering belief in the power of discussion and debate. Her daring and sense of timing, evident in her work on *The View*, was honed, in part, by her successful runs on Broadway—another New York venue celebrating the interplay between performers and live audiences.

In the 1997 revival of the Broadway play *A Funny Thing Happened on the Way to the Forum*, Goldberg successfully tackled the role of Pseudolus, the Roman slave whose goal was to obtain freedom by forging a romantic connection between the master and the object of the master's affections.

Goldberg was slated to play succeed Broadway legend Nathan Lane, who had just snagged the Tony for the role. Understandably, she worried about following in Lane's footsteps; besides, she had not starred on the Broadway stage in 13 years (Swarns). Such backstage jitters, Goldberg explains, are her way of forcing herself to grow as an actor. She explains, "It's like walking on water. Sometimes you make it halfway through and then you sink. It's very scary. But I need to be nervous. I need to stretch" (Swarns). Goldberg had fun with the role and the novelty of playing it. At the beginning of the play, she makes tacit reference to her then-boyfriend, actor Frank Langella. Referring to an elderly man in the play's opening scene, she turns and asks the audience, "What am I going to do with that old white man? I got one at home" (Brantley). Later, when "a doll representing an infant is flung onto the stage (part of the narrative that establishes the play's backstory), she shrieks, 'I don't want that blond baby. That's another movie, honey'" (Brantley). Goldberg's comments ostensibly address the criticism, which she faced, for playing such roles as maids in Hollywood films. Such ad libbing, while characteristic of her improvisational training, is rare, in this play, for her "presence is less frantic and more deliberately centered ... [she is] the sardonic straight woman to the chaos around her" (Brantley). To assist with adapting the play to Goldberg, a "global replacement of pronouns" took place; and she, playing Pseudolus, "makes clear that she is helping her master shop" for a whore, rather "than ogling the merchandise for herself" (Grimes). Such minor accommodations helped foster the continuity of the storyline without squashing her unique contributions to the role.

In *Book* (1997), Goldberg speaks with frustration regarding the double-standard of race, with respect to the right to freedom of expression. She says that Jewish comedians, such as Jackie Mason, can joke about Jewish identity, but that same consideration, oddly, does not apply to her: "If I step onstage and start talking about, 'Oh, there goes an old Jew,' then there's trouble. I become a black person, speaking negatively to describe another person. I cross a line" (Goldberg, *Book* 185). Here, the actor is speaking out against the use of racism to silence, and the American tradition of having race trump all other aspects of American identity (including Goldberg's own admitted Jewish ties). As she views the odd social construct, even gender takes a backseat to race. It can be argued, therefore, that Mason's relative freedom to discuss Jewish identity is not only tied to his Jewishness, but also his status as a man.

This should come as no surprise. Sojourner Truth's famous speech *Ain't I a Woman?* (1851) showed Truth, a slave occupying a rung on the social ladder comparable to that of cattle, fighting for the right to be considered a woman; she also claimed her right to free speech at a women's rights rally.

Ironically, during her speech, she also had to fight off rumors that she was, in fact, a man. Truth's hardened physical appearance came from performing manual labor; she also bore 13 children:

> That man over there says that women need to be helped into carriages, and lifted over ditches, and to have the best place everywhere. Nobody ever helps me into carriages, or over mud-puddles, or gives me any best place! And ain't I a woman? Look at me! Look at my arm! I have ploughed and planted, and gathered into barns, and no man could head me! And ain't I a woman? I could work as much and eat as much as a man — when I could get it — and bear the lash as well! And ain't I a woman? I have borne thirteen children, and seen most all sold off to slavery, and when I cried out with my mother's grief, none but Jesus heard me! And ain't I a woman?
>
> Then they talk about this thing in the head; what's this they call it? [member of audience whispers, "Intellect"]. That's it, honey. What's that got to do with women's rights or negroes' rights? If my cup won't hold but a pint, and yours holds a quart, wouldn't you be mean not to let me have my little half measure full? [Truth].

Although informed by Christianity, Goldberg is not specifically religious; moreover, she is not given, or asking for, her "little half measure"— instead, she takes it, and then some. She once spoke out against the pope, saying that she does not think he has the right to make decisions that only God can make, regarding such matters as homosexuality, abortion and divorce (Goldberg 92). As a pro-choice activist, Goldberg does not advocate abortion, but she does believe that a woman should have the right to obtain "a clean, safe abortion, with dignity and respect," if she so chooses (157). She also advocates personal choice regarding euthanasia (178).

In 1994, the actor donated $75,000 to relief organizations assisting Rwandan refugees (Brozan). Such an announcement is not an example of Goldberg's self-aggrandizement; rather, it represents her efforts to publicize the genocide and poverty from which Rwandans fled, and serves as an open challenge to people around the globe to do what they can to help the needy. In a similar vein, in 1997, she raised $233,000 for Broadway Cares–Equity Fights AIDS. She also supported the Los Angeles AIDS benefit, by way of a videotaped appeal to audiences attending *Howard Crabtree's When Pigs Fly*. Ironically, she "lauds Broadway Cares as she announces that the use of cameras and recording devices is strictly prohibited in the theater" (Brozan). Journalist Nadine Brozan calls her "a fundraiser's dream" (Brozan). Similarly, she also co-starred with Billy Crystal and Robin Williams in the successful *Comic Relief* comedy fundraiser series: "Back in 1986 ... [they] teamed up to emcee the very first *Comic Relief* special — a star-studded HBO telethon for the homeless, dreamed up by comedy writer Bob Zmuda, that became [an annual] tradition until 1998" (Pienciak). In 2006, the trio teamed up again, to honor the benefit's 20th anniversary and also raise funds to assist victims of Hurricane Katrina (Pienciak).

Similarly, she has also openly assisted with AIDS awareness and welfare-to-work campaigns. In her preface to *Breaking the Walls of Silence: AIDS and Women in a New York State Maximum-Security Prison* (1998), Goldberg writes, "In this book lives facets of my life that were too close to share with other people.... Everything in the book is applicable to you or someone you know. You'll be glad it wasn't you and sad that others have had to live this so that you might read and learn from it and, perhaps, slow the mighty flow of AIDS."

After fighting to get the courage to write, and then find a publisher, for her manuscript *Farewell, Welfare* (1992), Mary Waterhouse initially struggled with the idea of asking Goldberg to write the book's foreword. Says Waterhouse, "I needed some help in getting some attention for the book. I had heard that Whoopi Goldberg had been on welfare and was passionate about the issue" (Waterhouse 87). Waterhouse is referring to Goldberg's open acknowledgment of her temporary reliance on public assistance to try to make ends meet, as a young divorcée with a toddler daughter. During those transitional times, Goldberg studied cosmetology and hair, while also training as an actress, as part of a National Endowment for the Arts community theatre program in California. Goldberg marvels that the cosmetology school did not require her to pay tuition for her studies there. She mentions offering to do odd jobs around the academy, to work off her debt; but the school asked only that she study hard and complete the training. "How cool was that?" she asks (Goldberg, *Book* 132). In another context, Goldberg mentions as a point of pride being able to personally return a check to the welfare office, after five years of receiving public assistance, saying, "Here. I don't need this anymore" (Randolph 111). Waterhouse, inspired by Goldberg's example of moving up and out of welfare, surprised herself by reaching Goldberg's assistant after making only three cold-calls to Los Angeles-based talent agencies. She then sent a handful of sample chapters to Goldberg's assistant: "A few weeks later," Waterhouse relates, "Whoopi sent me a letter of support! I was thrilled and amazed. I eventually got her permission to use the letter as the foreword to the book, which meant that I could also put her famous name on the cover" (Waterhouse 87).

Goldberg's foreword for *Farewell, Welfare* compares the goal of welfare-to-work with that of Neil Armstrong's pioneering walk on the moon. She says, "*Farewell Welfare* ... is a second small step for women and men, a second giant leap for humanity. We've reached the moon–we must now reach our neighbors" (Goldberg, "Foreword" 9). Declaring herself "lucky" to have been able to leave the welfare system, she supports Waterhouse's book as a means for welfare recipients to rewrite the scripts of their lives and become self-supporting (9). Waterhouse may have been surprised that Goldberg supported her project, but such generosity is not unusual for the actor; it also is in keeping with her global view of self in relation to the larger society. In *Book* (1997), Goldberg says that one of her fervent goals is that of "narrowing the gap" between the haves and the have-nots, during her lifetime (136). Her experience of being, first, a married mother, then a divorced mother, then a single mother and welfare-recipient, in addition to the strong example of her own mother, shapes Goldberg's view.

Motherhood remains one of Goldberg's most important roles. She does not, however, consider herself a good mother, because, as she says, "I don't have those nurturing mommy skills that you need" (Randolph 115). Nevertheless, her laudable example of being forthright seems to have made a favorable impression on her daughter, Alexandrea, who, determined to bring her own baby into the world, helped Goldberg to learn that "pro-choice means either way" (A&E Ch. 4). Also a proud grandmother, she declares that her granddaughters, Amarah Dean and Jerzey Dean, are poised to rule the world: "Just look in their eyes!" she shouts (Cook 42). A black-and-white photograph, dated 1997 and shot in Los Angeles, shows Goldberg's mother, Emma Johnson; Goldberg; Goldberg's adult daughter, Alexandrea; and Alexandrea's daughters, Amarah and Jerzey, peering straight at the camera, with Amarah's and Jerzey's eyes showing a kind of wisdom beyond their years. Little Jersey, naked and held in her mother Alexandrea's elegant, strong, manicured hands, plays with a strand of her grandmother's hair. This photograph is a portrait of three strong women — and two strong women in the making. Goldberg says that one of her mother's "greatest" lessons is "to work hard at whatever you do and always keep it real" (Cook 42).

Keeping it real is another way of expressing the kind of motherwit which Emma Johnson instilled in her daughter. In Denzel Washington's book, *A Hand to Guide Me* (2006), a compilation of select musings on lessons that contributors' mothers had taught them, Goldberg recounts a grade school experience, in which her mother's keen insight helped to teach ethics and forgiveness. She says that one of her childhood friends, a boy named Robert, generally had been outside the social circle, as had she; but for a brief time, during a school trip, she became part of a constellation of "popular folks." As a result, she adopted their stance, which was to simply ignore Robert. Says Goldberg, "It wasn't overt.... He just didn't exist. It's like I left him behind" (Washington 96). The irony was that the young Caryn didn't even realize her abuse of privilege, until her mother queried her about the trip, and, through her own brand of child psychology, forced her to admit to not only ignoring Robert, but her obligation to make amends with him. Says Goldberg, "It never occurred to me that I had done to my friend what these folks had always done to me" (Washington 97). Robert accepted Caryn's sincere apology (97).

Goldberg says that her mother's lesson even influences her work on *The View*. During one taping, when she unknowingly discredited an invited guest on-air, she apologized profusely to the actress, and gifted her with chocolate (Washington 98). Acknowledging human frailty and foibles, Goldberg says that her mother's teachings empower her to admit when she is wrong, to reach out to make amends, and to forgive herself.

Goldberg's own motherly challenges and successes echo those of many mothers who simply do what they must in order to survive and to ensure the safety and happiness of their children. Yet, in the face of her very real commitment to motherhood stands the stark reality of her status and work as stage and screen performer. In a candid interview on A&E's *Biography* (2002), Goldberg admitted that, as much as she loves and supports her daughter, she could not — and would not — deny her own need to explore and capitalize upon her own creativity and growth (A&E Ch. 4). In a related interview (also part of the DVD), Alexandrea admits to experiencing a kind of jealousy for having to share her increasingly famous mother not only with Hollywood figures but also with total strangers (A&E Ch. 4). In the midst of such understandable tensions, Goldberg remains determined to be both a very good mother and a consummate stage and screen performer; this is not surprising, given the balancing act her own mother had sustained.

Emma Johnson had worked as a Head Start teacher and a nurse (Davis 205) while raising her son, Clyde, and daughter, Caryn Elaine, in Chelsea, Manhattan. Nevertheless, Johnson maintained her "eccentric" (Davis 205) ways, including riding her bicycle to and from school (205). According to Goldberg, in Patti Davis's *The Lives Our Mothers Leave Us* (2009), one of the strongest aspects of her mother's personality is being authentically herself while also maintaining a respect for her own privacy: "My mother's like a clam. She's told us nothing about herself" (204). This is not for lack of her children trying: Emma Johnson's philosophy is simply rooted in the belief that people must find and make their own way. Goldberg summarizes her mother's philosophy thusly: "I don't need to tell you about me, because it is what it is. But what are you going to do for *you*?" (204). Johnson's philosophy encouraged her children to develop healthy introspection and a respect for self, others, and personal boundaries — keys to Goldberg's authenticity and humanity.

The motherly aspect of Goldberg's public persona speaks through many channels, ranging from interviews to children's books and endorsements. In *The Lives Our Mother's Leave Us* (2009), she, speaking with Patti Davis, once again recounts her grade school shame of ignoring Robert, and her mother's corresponding lesson of humility; she also mentions how her mother taught her that lying is its own unsatisfying reward. One weekend, when *The Nutcracker Suite* ballet was being presented in New York, young Caryn asked her mother if she could attend the show. Johnson said that her daughter may attend the show, but only if she cleaned her own room first. Caryn promised to follow her mother's edict, but the moment her mother left the apartment on an errand, Caryn simply went to the show, ignoring her mother's requirement.

Caryn's lie got the best of her, however, when she returned from the show, and learned that she had misplaced her key to the apartment: "I had no keys. I'd gotten into the building, but I couldn't get into the apartment" (Davis 208). She imagined herself climbing out of the hallway window and onto the ledge to access the apartment from the outside; meanwhile, standing helplessly in the hallway, she anxiously awaited her mother's return (208). When her mother arrived, and asked Caryn if she had cleaned her room, Caryn lied and said that she had. Goldberg says, "That was the first and last time my mother waled on me [whipped me]." Emma Johnson was doubly insulted, not only because of her daughter's defiance, but also because, as Goldberg explains, "It was a stupid lie.... I didn't think enough of her to at least be amusing" (209). In other words, Goldberg says, she had insulted her mother's intelligence.

As the author and co-author of several children's books and short stories, Goldberg does not condescend to children, nor she does not adopt a motherly stance; instead, she takes the role of the wiser, older friend. For example, in *Whoopi's Big Book of Manners* (2006) wholly written by Goldberg, and effectively illustrated by Olo, she cautions children against such social taboos as interrupting others' conversations; picking one's nose; leaving behind a mess; not covering one's mouth when coughing or sneezing; barging through a door without knocking; using one's cell phone in such places as churches, restaurants and movie theaters; and ignoring basic social customs abroad (Goldberg, *Whoopi's Big Book*). Goldberg also explains the importance of observing such social graces as saying "Please" and "Thank You." Unfortunately, the book was not kindly reviewed. Daniel Handler wrote, "Whoopi Goldberg's philosophical principles are sounder [than many other children's etiquette books] ... [but] "the book is a litany of mannerly observations, presented in slapdash style that suggests they've just popped into the author's head. The advice is good; the book is not" (Handler). The primary focus of Goldberg youth-oriented books is to encourage children to see themselves as part of the larger fabric of society, and to behave accordingly. For example, In *Sugar Plum Ballerinas: Plum Fantastic* (2008), Goldberg focuses the reader's attention upon fictional lead character Alexandrea (Al) Petrakova Johnson, who, at her mother's will, must leave her suburban home in order relocate to Harlem, and take ballet lessons there, at the Nutcracker School of Ballet. Conflict ensues when Al, a newcomer, gets the coveted role of Sugar Plum Fairy (prima ballerina), in the ballet's annual performance of *The Nutcracker*

Suite, a story vaguely reminiscent of Goldberg's real-life childhood experience. Goldberg's fictional work also echoes the energy of Debbie Allen's semi-autobiographical children's book, *Dancing in the Wings* (2003), concerning a young Black dancer named Sassy, who strives to become a prima ballerina.

In May 1999, in a tradition forged by Oprah Winfrey, Goldberg and Rosie O'Donnell lent their celebrity status to advocate reading (Canedy). "In a campaign designed to make reading cool to young people — and, by extension, to sell more books ... Goldberg and O'Donnell are ... featured in ads promoting reading as hip," promoting the Association of American Publisher's "Get caught reading" slogan (Canedy). Symbolically, Goldberg's endorsement of reading is all the more significant, as she is dyslexic. Her condition was not diagnosed until after she reached adulthood (Randolph 111).

Goldberg has made many celebrity endorsements for a wide variety of products. For television ads reintroducing the brand to a wider, younger audience, she became the voice of the "Avon calling" slogan (Elliott). She also endorsed Flooz, an "online gift currency" system (Cox) and precursor to gift cards and PayPal. In 1999, she wore a milk mustache in print ads for the now-iconic California Milk Processor *Got Milk?* ad campaign.

Goldberg's Slim-Fast endorsement was much heralded at its start; the Slim-Fast Company hired her to be its no-nonsense celebrity face and voice, after losing sales to followers of the Atkins Diet (Day). She starred in at least two commercials: "Whoopi/Low Carb," in which she "runs around a swanky apartment and calls herself a 'big loser' who has big news about the Slim-Fast plan"; and "Whoopi/Lose Twice," in which she "encourages consumers to 'shake the notion of 'just shakes' out of your head" (Day). Both ads rely on her ability to ad lib, while also making connections between her persona and the audience; "Whoopi/Low-Carb" displays her typically self-effacing humor; "Whoopi/Lose Twice" shows Goldberg's willingness to make fun of herself by mentioning her headful of dreadlocks. Such ads were designed specifically to target Wal-Mart and Sam's Club shoppers. Her Slim-Fast endorsement went swimmingly until she made comments regarding President George W. Bush during a political rally. Goldberg, a Democrat, repeated the term "Bush," ostensibly making a reference to the vagina, implying President Bush lacked manly fortitude. Such comments drew such ire from the American public that Slim-Fast executives quickly rescinded Goldberg's contract and removed all ads featuring her. Goldberg responded, "The fact that I am no longer the spokesman for Slim-Fast makes me sad, but not as sad as someone trying to punish me for exercising my right as an American to speak my mind in any forum I choose" (Ives).

The Slim-Fast funk did not stop Goldberg from being tapped to tout the virtues of the myTouch Android phone. Emphasizing authenticity ("100% Jesse. 100% Whoopi. 100% Phil"), the myTouch's ad on the back cover of the October 19, 2009, issue of *Newsweek* shows Goldberg sandwiched between master bike builder Jesse James and coach of the Los Angeles Lakers, Phil Jackson. Both men assertively put their phones in the viewers' faces; for her role, Goldberg takes a different, although equally assertive stance, staring directly at the viewer, while glancing over her round, purple-tinted shades; her phone daintily and firmly balanced, from top-to-bottom, between the palms of her hands.

Perhaps her most challenging endorsement role to-date is her multifaceted "take" on famous (and infamous) women through the ages, for Kimberly-Clark's Poise Pads "LBL (Light Bladder Leak)" campaign. During ads widely promoted via the Internet, Goldberg portrays the Mona Lisa, Helen of Troy, Joan of Arc, Lady Godiva, Cleopatra, and the princess of *The Princess and the Pea* fame. The historical figures memorably complained about their "spritz" (a term which Goldberg successfully ad libbed for the campaign), and how Poise Pads gave them their freedom. "I don't want to be painted," says Goldberg's Mona Lisa, speaking with a French accent. "I want to be dry." As Cleopatra, she says, "I have a problem — I've been leaking for years" (Kimberly-Clark). Her down-to-earth personality and willingness to laugh at herself make her a likely endorser of Poise Pads. Besides, says Anne Jones, marketing director for Poise, "Women want clarity in their communication and for us to be open and honest.... But they also want to identify with a term that doesn't make them feel like they're incontinent, a term that is attached to their fear of aging" (Newman). Poise's formal phrase, "Light Bladder Leakage (LBL)" and Goldberg's folksy term, "spritz," fit the bill.

Goldberg seems to be most in her element, however, endorsing the 2009 *Toys "R" Us Toy Guide for Differently Abled Kids*, a "complimentary, one-of-a-kind guide" that addresses the "individual needs" of differently abled children, by helping readers select Toys "R" Us products that are geared toward children's special abilities (Toys "R" Us).

The complete list of previous celebrities featured on the cover of *Toys R Us Differently Abled Toy Guide* include:

2008: Meredith Vieira (Host of *Who Wants to Be a Millionaire?*); 2007: Maria Shriver (Author and First Lady of California); 2004: Dionne Quan (Voice of Kimi on *The Rugrats*); 2003: John Ritter (Actor); 2002: Mattie J.T. Stepanek (Poet/Author/2002 Muscular Dystrophy Association Goodwill Ambassador); 2001: Maria Shriver (Author and First Lady of California); 2000: Chris Burke (Actor, Spokesperson for the National Down Syndrome Society); 1998: Doug Flutie (Buffalo Bills Quarterback); 1997: Marlee Matlin (Actress); 1996: Heather Whitestone (Miss America, 1995); 1995: Jim Abbot (Major League Pitcher) [Toys "R" Us].

In explaining Goldberg's selection as 2009 celebrity endorser, a spokesperson for Toys "R" Us described her as a "mother and grandmother; Oscar, Tony, Grammy and Emmy Award-winner, and child advocate." The cover of the 2009 *Toys "R" Us Toy Guide for Differently Abled Kids* shows an alert, happy Goldberg, holding a special-needs child on her lap, the little girl clapping her hands and laughing, as Goldberg pretends to serve "cookies" (ostensibly, it is tea time). Her enthusiasm is palpable, and mirrors that of the little girl to the point where one barely notices racial differences (Goldberg is black; the little girl is white). Her love for children is obvious, as is her determination to use her celebrity status to help make a positive difference.

Goldberg was tapped to serve as UNICEF international ambassador, and was appointed September 17, 2003, for her work in combating HIV/AIDS. As a worldwide UNICEF ambassador, she records public-service announcements, offering information on HIV and AIDS prevention, as well as how communities can work together in the face of HIV/AIDS. In particular, UNICEF appreciates the fundraising and social awareness impacts of "her public service announcements following the 2004 Indian Ocean tsunami and in support of the Unite for Children, Unite Against AIDS campaign" (UNICEF).

While Goldberg's name and persona have been used to achieve positive ends, they also periodically have been used as the basis of ridicule. For example, the name Whoopi, which connotes flatulence, can be heard on the South Park episode "Spontaneous Combustion," which originally aired April 14, 1999. During that episode, people randomly explode, the reason being that too many South Park residents are deliberately stifling their flatulence. The South Park geologist who solves the conundrum is awarded a trophy for his efforts; the host for the "42nd Nobel Prize Awards" is none other than Whoopi Goldberg, ostensibly because she had hosted the Oscar Awards on numerous occasions. The subtext of the *South Park* episode is that she has nothing better to do with her time and skills than to host awards ceremonies; and the more eccentric and upscale her audience, the better. In "Spontaneous Combustion," she is presented as a cross between a blackface minstrel and a golliwog, with an exaggeratedly dark skin tone, bulging eyes, fuchsia-colored lips, gleaming white teeth, ridiculous zebra-patterned outfit and outlandish hair ornament. While standing at the podium, she continually repeats the phrase, "I hate Republicans," to the delight of her stuffy audience.

Goldberg says that she has endured undue scrutiny for dating and marrying white men. She explains that black men often have problems relating to black women in power: "A woman with power is a problem for any man, but particularly a Black man because it's hard for them to get power.... I have to have a life, and that means dating the men that want to date me" (JPC, "Why Some Blacks Choose" 49). She has dated such high-profile Hollywood film co-stars as Ted Danson (*Made in America*) and Frank Langella (*Eddie*). Her first marriage to a black man (her former drug counselor, and the father of her daughter, Alexandrea) was not questioned. Yet her relationships with white men have been subjected to much scrutiny (A&E Ch. 5). Her daughter, Alexandrea, as well as acting colleague Mo'Nique agree that Goldberg has the right to love whomever she wishes, regardless of race. Mo'Nique especially defends Goldberg against the extra scrutiny which black communities give her interracial romantic choices (A&E Ch. 5). The white men Goldberg married are on the production side of the film industry, and therefore largely unknown to the public. During the mid–1980s, after reportedly knowing him "for only a few days," she married David Claessen, a Dutch cinematographer, whom she met "while filming a documentary on the homeless" (JPC, "Whoopi Goldberg Talks" 1986). In 1994, she married Lyle Trachtenberg, a "movie-industry union representative ... whom she met on the set of *Corinna, Corinna*" (Brozan). While both marriages ended in divorce, they illustrate Goldberg's belief in romance and family.

Goldberg's influence even extends to fashion. This is understandable given her flair for the dramatic (dressing, looking, acting the part), as well as her certification as a cosmetologist. In fact, her many credits include a stint as hair stylist for the production of the film *Golden Dreams* (2001) (IMDb). Goldberg's foray into fashion is as much her privilege as a New Yorker as it is her chance to encourage emerging talent and to market her own wares and sense of style. As of this writing, she is marketing her own line of sensuous bedding, via her "G. Beds by Whoopi Goldberg" line (QVC). According to the distributor, QVC, each bedding ensemble symbolizes a major turning point in her life (QVC). The line includes coverlets and fancy pillows covered in velvet and satin, with earth and jewel tones balanced by cool white.

On April 8, 2010, the *New York Examiner* profiled the living area of Goldberg's SoHo loft, showing its spaciousness and well-appointed details. On view were the white furniture and walls, ceiling-mounted track light-ing, three large windows (each draped on either side with narrow, unadorned white panels to allow natural sunlight to shine through), and an expanse of warm hardwood flooring. All form a fitting backdrop for her collection of art — framed oil paintings of various sizes, sculptures, and folk art, with a unifying Asian influence. Tanvier Lee, Manhattan Interior Design columnist for *The Examiner*, aptly describes the loft as "airy, personal, and livable" (Lee). This is not the first time that Goldberg's digs have been heralded as exhibiting style; the cover of the August 1994 edition of *InStyle Magazine* touts "Whoopi's Hideaway: an Exclusive Look at The Elegant Retreat" (*In Style Magazine*).

Goldberg regularly attends New York Fashion Week, and spends time with such fashion luminaries as André Leon Talley, "*Vogue*'s editor at large and a regular at the Sugar Bar, the upper West Side club owned by the singing duo Nickolas Ashford and Valerie Simpson" (Holson). (Ashford and Simpson are perhaps best known as the songwriters of such Diana Ross staples as "Ain't No Mountain High Enough" and "Reach Out And Touch Somebody's Hand.") While paying a visit to the Sugar Bar after New York's Fashion Week had concluded, Goldberg whooped it up with Talley and other patrons, openly appreciating the vocal artistry of such established performers as CeCe Penniston, as well as the work of such emerging performers as Damara Lynn Greene and Andre Henry, whom she told, "You're great." She also graciously agreed to allow her fans to photograph her while holding a sign that said, "Happy Birthday, Gloria" (Holson). Both Talley and Goldberg have homes in the outskirts of the city and cultivate an appreciation for home décor and hospitality, as an escape from the hustle and bustle of New York (Holson).

In 1992, after eight years of experimentation, Nor'east Miniature Roses, Inc. perfected a hybrid rose, which horticulturist Harm Saville named the "Whoopi" for its "free-blooming and cheerful" nature (Yang). The "Whoopi," named after Goldberg, features beautiful, deep red and white blooms no larger than two inches in diameter, with the plant itself standing to a maximum height of 16 inches (Yang). Other roses which the company named for famous people include the "Barbara Bush," the "Bing Crosby" and the "Christian Dior" (Yang). Shakespeare wrote, "That which we call a rose/By any other name would smell as sweet" (*Romeo and Juliet* 26). Amid the thorns and thistles of American debates and possibilities, a rose called Whoopi proudly stands.

9

Playing the Part
The Actor as Sidekick and Supporter

> We all need help from each other — in one way or another, at one time or another — And yet there's something awful happening out there, where people think asking for help is not a good thing.
> — Whoopi Goldberg [Goldberg 238]

In *Book* (1997), Goldberg tells readers that there is no shame in needing and requesting assistance. She specifically discusses the National Endowment for the Arts (which, like the projects and institutions that it supports, requires help in the form of funding for its very existence); welfare, affirmative action, and Dan Paisner, the ghostwriter whom she hired to help her organize transcripts of her original talks, to help make *Book* a reality. On the other side of the equation, the implication is that helping others is a virtue. Goldberg's philosophy regarding the importance of helping others makes its way into some of the fictional characters that she portrays. This chapter explores Goldberg as sideliner or supporter in such motion pictures as *Homer and Eddie* (1989), *Boys on the Side* (1995), *Moonlight and Valentino* (1995), *The Deep End of the Ocean* (1999), *How Stella Got Her Groove Back* (1998), *Homie Spumoni* (2006), *Theodore Rex* (1995 V) and *Racing Stripes* (2005). This chapter also examines special projects like the fundraiser series *Comic Relief;* the song, "Bowwow to the Beat," included in the Disney CD, *Mickey Unrapped* (1994); and *Rodrigue: The Man and His Dog* (1992), an independent film featuring the work of George Rodrigue, a Louisiana visual artist.

Lightly reminiscent of John Steinbeck's novel, *Of Mice and Men* (1937), *Homer and Eddie* offers aspects of the traditional buddy/coming of age stories, with a twist: instead of featuring male bonding, viewers are instead introduced to a man (Homer, played by Jim Belushi) and a woman (Eddie — short for Edwina, played by Goldberg). The end result is the bonding of two complex human beings, who look beyond each other's faults to emphasize commonalities and support each other.

Homer Lanza (Jim Belushi) is a 30-plus-year-old special-needs person, whose demeanor is lightly reminiscent of the character Lennie Small in *Of Mice and Men*. In Steinbeck's novel, Lennie is described as a "huge companion" (Steinbeck 3) — a lumbering man, whose intelligence has been blunted, since childhood, by the sudden, swift kick of a horse to the head. Instead of being a drifter, Lennie wants to "live off the fatta the lan' ... An' have rabbits" (Steinbeck 14). Homer, in *Homer and Eddie*, is intentionally set adrift, hailing from a wealthy family who abandoned him. (Homer's eccentricities are largely due to an accidental head injury, which he received in his youth at the hands of another child.) Similar to Lennie's pastoral visions of being rooted in an abundant geographic place with his best buddy and protector, George, and a garden and "different color rabbits" (Steinbeck 16) to keep him company, Homer's primary goal is to reclaim his place and sense of belonging with his family.

Not surprisingly, Homer's new best friend, Eddie Cervi, evokes the fictional character George Milton in *Of Mice and Men*. In Steinbeck's novel, George is described as "small and quick, dark of face, with restless eyes and sharp, strong features" (Steinbeck 2). This also describes Goldberg, as Eddie. Like Lennie, George is a drifter — an itinerant worker, who seeks opportunities for work, food and lodging along the way. Eddie is also a drifter, of sorts — a homeless, quick-witted, if at times misdirected Black American woman whom Homer first encounters living in a late-model Lincoln Continental. Symbolically speaking, Eddie is "on the move," using the vehicle as temporary lodging. (Eddie, it is eventually revealed, is psychotic, having recently been released from a mental institution and suffering a malignant brain tumor.) Homer and Eddie complement each other well: Homer has no money and no car and cannot drive; and Eddie has a car and drive (willpower), but nowhere to go. Thus, the two set out from Las Vegas to find Homer's family, with the understanding that, upon arriving in Oregon, Homer will compensate Eddie for her efforts.

Eddie's family includes a madame with a whorehouse located in Beatty, Nevada — a stopover en route to Oregon. Eddie correctly assumes that Homer is a virgin. Homer denies this, claiming that he has had sexual relations "5,000 times." Eddie declares that Homer is "not a man," until he has had sexual relations with a woman. She pays the required $30 (no family discount is allowed) for Homer to use the services of a prostitute. Eddie later declares that Homer is "not a man" unless he can drive a car, and promptly places him behind the wheel of her beloved Lincoln.

In a role reversal at the end of the story, Homer pledges to take care of Eddie. By that time, Eddie's deep-seated emotional problems have come to the fore. She has lost touch with reality. Upon reaching Oregon, Homer learns that his parents had willfully left him behind, as they no longer wished to care for him.

Casual viewers of *Homer and Eddie* may be tempted to recall the antics of *Bonnie and Clyde*. But unlike Bonnie and Clyde, who scheme together as part of their complicated romance, Homer and Eddie are two best buddies simply making their way in the world together. As Homer and Eddie are not a married couple or even romantically involved, Homer's pledge to support Eddie is far beyond the norm, yet wholly believable in the context of the story. Janet Maslin, of the *New York Times*, praised the film: "This is the kind of film in which Homer and Eddie, hitting the road in search of life's big answers, will locate not just their respective long-lost parents, but also the childhood friend of Homer's who pitched the fateful ball" (Maslin *Homer and Eddie*). Belushi's and Goldberg's masterful, sensitive portrayals of Homer and Eddie, respectively, effectively convey the overarching concept that the journey is more important than the destination, and that humanity transcends gender and wealth. Far more than a typical "buddy" flick, *Homer and Eddie* shows two actors who greatly respect the craft of acting and each other.

In *Boys on the Side* (1995), Goldberg portrays Jane, a bluesy lesbian nightclub singer who supports not only herself, but also her struggling New York–based band, and, eventually, Holly (Drew Barrymore), a straight, quirky, pregnant friend, and Robin (Mary-Louise Parker), a recent acquaintance with a deadly secret. In Scene 1, "I'm one," Jane performs Janis Joplin's song, "Piece of My Heart," onstage. (During the performance, Goldberg's actual singing voice is heard, belting out the pain of the fictional character Jane.) Jane signals a white woman seated at a table near the stage, and when the musical set is over, approaches the woman, whose boyfriend has already left the table. The woman, clearly not catching on to Jane's signal, and having ignored her spirited stage performance, mistakes her for the club's waitress. Jane struggles to save face by pointing out an unsightly bit of mucous around the woman's nose. Dejected, she returns to her band, which the club has once again stiffed of its take. Shortly thereafter, Jane leaves the band, with plans to leave New York altogether, to try a new life in San Francisco. This scene sets the stage for the remainder of the film, focusing on the intertwined theme of journeys, women and personal revelations.

Initially, Jane and Robin present themselves as a typical odd couple: Jane is earthy and frank; Robin is aloof and obtuse. In fact, the only reason why their paths cross is that Jane responds to Robin's *New York Times* ad, seeking a partner to ride cross-country, and Jane, eager to leave town and start a new life, is the first to respond. Jane, a rock-and-roll enthusiast and true New Yorker, accepts a degree of dishevelment and grime as part of life; yet Robin, a neatnick and germophobe, carefully labels every object in her apartment, carries tissues to wipe down surfaces before touching them, and forbids Jane from smoking in the vehicle. As the two travel cross-country, Robin reveals that she is a real estate agent; she has been through a divorce; she is chronically ill (although she attributes periodic coughing to "allergies"); and she is sentimental. In fact, while Jane laughs at Robin's incurable romanticism, Robin makes no excuse for her abiding love of The Carpenters' interpretations of the popular ballads "Close to You" and "Superstar," and the film, *The Way We Were*, starring Robert Redford and Barbra Streisand.

During a stopover in Pittsburgh, Jane introduces Robin to Holly, her longtime friend. Jane and Robin learn that Holly is trapped in an abusive relationship with Nick, her boyfriend and the probable father of her unborn child — and that Holly, blinded by what she sees as love, refuses to leave him. In Scene 7, "Jogging Nick's Memory," Nick verbally and physically abuses Holly in their squalid Pittsburgh apartment, claiming that Holly has stolen his drug money (no longer a drug addict, according to Holly, Nick simply deals drugs, and she attributes his aberrant behavior to drunkenness). Yet Jane does not accept such behavior and steps in to protect Holly. An enraged Nick calls Jane a "dyke," punches her and throws her against a wall. While this scene shows the physical strength and determination of Jane, it also shows the strong side of Robin who negotiates a way for Nick to learn the whereabouts of his funds (by telephone call to a drug supplier), calming the situation long enough for Holly to regain her composure and take half of the drug money stashed in the freezer. Before they leave, the three women strap Nick to a chair and tape his mouth shut with duct tape. Later, on the road, they learn that Nick has died, and that Holly is the chief suspect in his death. Robin helps Holly obtain legal assistance, and Jane helps Robin obtain necessary health care and communicate with her estranged mother.

As the story progresses, viewers see Jane falling in love with Robin, a straight woman who, it turns out, has full-blown AIDS. Nevertheless, Jane sacrifices her own feelings to ensure that Robin's romantic needs are seen to by arranging for her to have a sexual encounter with Alex, a bartender in Tucson. (She also reveals Robin's HIV status to Alex, which leads to a rift between the two women). Jane also helps Robin, whose mother has taught her to be ashamed of her body, to be proud of herself. In Scene 18, "Words Will Make You Free," in the kitchen of their shared Arizona home, Jane challenges Robin to be frank in expressing the realities of women's bodies, and Jane complies. This touching, funny scene shows Goldberg imitating Mammy from *Gone With the Wind*, telling Robin (whom she jokingly calls "Mis' Scarlett") that she is "free!"

In one particularly poignant scene, Jane softly serenades the dying Robin. Holly, having been released from prison, assumes a new life as mother of a baby daughter. Her new husband, Abe (Matthew McConaughey), an honest Arizona policeman, had turned her over to Pennsylvania authorities, so that she could serve her time, clear her name, and live an honest life. Jane is facing yet another breakup with a dearly loved one — this time all the more devastating, because she barely has the chance to have a normal relationship with Robin, before AIDS complications destroy Robin's frail body. Goldberg's fierce, wistful performance as Jane reminds the viewer of the adage, "'Tis better to have loved and lost/Than never to have loved at all" (Tennyson).

Writing for the New York *Times*, Janet Maslin praises Goldberg's work in *Boys on the Side*:

> Ms. Goldberg, still reigning as Hollywood's most uncategorizable star, finally finds a role that suits her talents. Jane changes almost as drastically as Robin, and Ms. Goldberg brings immense amounts of heart and humor to this story. (She also sings, and does it to surprisingly touching effect in the film's final moments.) Ms. Goldberg is able to accommodate all manner of jokey outbursts without obscuring the essential seriousness of her performance. "You free, Miz' Scarlett, you free!" she exclaims sarcastically, after prompting the buttoned-down Robin to finally say a few sexually frank words [Maslin].

Robin's euphemisms for the vagina, as well as Jane's frank words concerning the organ, in *Boys on the Side*, are reminiscent of Eve Ensler's *The Vagina Monologues*. In that book, Ensler declares that she is "worried about vaginas, what we call them and don't call them" (Ensler 5), and she rattles off a quick list of euphemisms for the vagina, which she collected during her travels, interviewing women from all walks of life. Ensler concludes that it is necessary for women "to love women, to love our vaginas, to know them and be familiar with who we are and what we need" (Ensler 118). Such is a basis for understanding the complex story lines of the film, *Boys on the Side* and the strong voice of Whoopi Goldberg, as Jane. Goldberg also lends her voice to the Arista Records' 1995 CD release, *Boys on the Side Original Soundtrack*.

In addition to Goldberg, the *Boys on the Side Original Soundtrack* (1995) features tracks performed by Bonnie Raitt, Melissa Etheridge, Sheryl Crow, Indigo Girls, Stevie Nicks, Pretenders, the Cranberries, Annie Lennox, Sarah McLachlan, and Joan Armatrading. Bonnie Raitt actually makes two appearances on the disk, with her version of Roy Orbison's song, "You Got It," serving as auditory bookends for the project. Sheryl Crow offers her song, "Keep on Growing," which appears during Scene 10, "Cruising #1." Indigo Girls not only appear on the soundtrack offering, "Power of Two," they also have a cameo in the film, as performing artists on the fictional Teatro Carmen nightclub stage (at one point, Goldberg, as June DeLucca, even joins Indigo Girls Band as a percussionist). Stevie Nicks's bluesy anthem, "Somebody Stand By Me," communicates loss in the midst of moving on. Pretenders' lead singer Chryssie Hynde's haunting vocals on the mid-tempo song, "Everyday Is Like Sunday," communicates wistfulness. Annie Lennox's ballad "Why?" amplifies Scene 2, "Not Close to Robin," in which Jane packs her personal belongings, facing the fact that her career in New York is over. Sarah McLachlan's "Ol'

55" appropriately pays homage to Route 55, the route which the fictional women in the film take — a route which runs east to west across the continental United States. Joan Armatrading's powerful song "Willow," and the voice of Dolores O'Riordan, of the Cranberries, singing "Dreams," amplify Scene 3, "On Their Way," in which Jane and Robin begin their westward trek together. "Crossroads," performed by Jonell Mosser, deepens the meaning of Scene 8, "Fast Exits," in which Jane helps Robin tape shut Nick's mouth while Holly takes half of the available cash from the freezer. Goldberg's touching performance of Roy Orbison's "You Got It," while in character as Jane DeLucca, appears as Track 12, the second-to-last track on the *Boys on the Side* soundtrack. The placement of that song fittingly reminds listeners of Scene 38 of the film, in which Jane serenades the dying Robin, while family and friends celebrate Robin's life and the homecoming of Holly and her baby. Goldberg's urgent, plaintive intonation of "You Got It" was recorded live on the film's Tucson, Arizona, set; it stands in sharp contrast to Tracks 1 and 13, Bonnie Raitt's upbeat studio recording of the song, backed by a full rock-and-roll band. (While Goldberg appears to play the piano in the film, the *Boys on the Side Original Soundtrack Album* credits Lon Hoyt as the actual pianist whom the audience hears.) The *Soundtrack Album* liner lines include the following acknowledgment: "Special thanks to Whoopi Goldberg for singing live with passion and commitment over and over and over and over and over...."

In *Boys on the Side*, Goldberg plays a lesbian who deliberately evades outing herself, in favor of expressing non-sexual love for another woman. (The story implies that Robin's ex-husband is a philanderer and introduced the AIDS virus to the marriage.) Such a viewpoint is lightly reminiscent of her stated views regarding sexuality. She says, "People always seemed shocked that I have a private life, that I have a child, three grandchildren, that I'm straight.... Everybody seemed to think I was gay for years. I didn't — and don't — care" ("Rants and Raves"). In the case of the fictional Jane, it is not that she does not care about sexual labeling; rather, Jane cares so much about Robin that she would rather cast the spotlight upon Robin and Robin's love for Alex, a local bartender, than risk losing the platonic love of Robin by revealing her romantic love for her. In this film, Goldberg creates the perfect balance between portraying the wistfulness of a love that could be, in favor of emphasizing the love that is. Empowering and offbeat, *Boys on the Side* offers lessons in love, beyond sexuality, beyond the bars of prison and beyond the realm of death.

In *Moonlight and Valentino* (1995), Goldberg plays Sylvie, best friend of Rebecca ("Becky") Lott, a 30-plus-year-old childless poet and professor, suddenly rendered a widow (her husband Ben, a scientist at the local university, had been struck and killed by a car while jogging around their quiet upstate New York neighborhood). Sylvie is an artist — a potter, wife and mother of three, who can mend broken pots and even Becky's broken heart, but she cannot seem to mend her own.

In Scene 1, "Credits/Shocking News," Rebecca searches by car for her husband, who has not returned from his regular morning jog. Upon seeing a police officer, he informs her of an accident, and, upon describing the fallen man, describes her husband's general profile and clothing. Dazed, Rebecca drives to the hospital emergency room, only to learn from a nurse that her husband has died. A flurry of phone calls between Rebecca and Sylvie, Sylvie and Alberta, and Alberta and ex-stepdaughter shows the interconnectedness of the characters, who individually and collectively resolve to help Rebecca deal with her loss. Symbolically speaking, it is Sylvie's presence and support which become the primary rock upon which Rebecca leans.

Also during Scene 1, viewers see Sylvie taking the reins, driving Rebecca Lott about town. When Sylvie reaches across the front seat of the car to comfort Rebecca, she recoils from her touch. Later, during that same scene, as Sylvie opens the front door to the Lott house, Rebecca does not wish to touch any object, for fear that she will disturb the picture of her life. Rebecca's life picture is not perfect, but rather familiar and therefore comforting. Viewers come to learn that she is torn about the fact that she delayed having children, much to Ben's consternation. Her body and her spirit recall having made love with Ben just before the accident, and Rebecca renders her body, and the entire house — Ben's vision for their life together — a shrine to his memory.

In Scene 2, "Tea and Sympathy," Sylvie tries to support Rebecca's wishes by not touching her, and by trying to shield her from her overbearing, controlling ex-stepmother, Alberta (Kathleen Turner), a corporate executive. When the headstrong Alberta enters the Lott household, she bounds up the stairs and immediately begins to express sincere sympathy by embracing the "untouchable" Rebecca; meanwhile, Sylvie asks that Alberta respect Rebecca's wishes. Goldberg's work in this portion of the scene illustrates her ability to convey the kind of friendship that supports a friend even when she does not fully understand her.

Also during Scene 2, Sylvie diligently works in the kitchen, alongside Rebecca's younger sister Lucy, trying to find just the right blend of tea, to soothe Rebecca's soul. Sylvie rattles off the choices, including black, peppermint and chamomile teas, reminding Lucy that the gesture of taking tea will be one which Rebecca always will remember; yet the flighty Lucy is of very little help. Once again taking control of a situation affecting her best friend, Sylvie chooses the tea and the cup — a custom-made pottery vessel featuring an odd, standing monster grafted onto and leaning against the cup's side; a quirky example of Sylvie's creative handiwork, reminding them of all of the "monsters" that make life unpredictable. As the story unfolds, viewers come to learn that Sylvie has monsters of her own with which to grapple.

Sylvie actually has problems with her marriage to a white man named Paul (played by an unbilled Peter Coyote), although race has nothing to do with the problems. Sylvie explains to Rebecca that she and Paul have not had sexual intercourse for three months, and that she feels disconnected from him and fears that Paul will leave her. Alberta helps Sylvie come to terms with the fact that Sylvie expresses herself to her friends and through her art, but not to her own husband. When Sylvie openly fantasizes about a housepainter, Alberta asks her why Sylvie does not simply share such desires for creative sex with Paul. Goldberg interprets and projects Sylvie as a typical American wife and mother who loves her husband and children, and has somehow lost little pieces of her self, to be found through wisdom and time spent with women friends.

In the motion picture *The Deep End of the Ocean* (1999), based upon the best-selling novel of the same title by Jacquelyn Mitchard, Goldberg portrays the fictional Detective Candy Bliss. Candy Bliss is a no-nonsense, Chicago-based investigator charged with the responsibility of finding and returning missing three-year-old Ben Cappadora (Michael McElroy) to his Madison, Wisconsin, family: birth parents Beth (Michelle Pfeiffer), a professional portrait photographer and Pat (Treat Williams), a budding restaurateur, and siblings, older brother Vincent and baby sister Kerry (Cory Buck and Alexa Vega, respectively). When Beth Cappadora brings her growing brood to her 15th high school reunion, her son Ben disappears from a crowded Chicago hotel lobby. Initially thinking that Ben is simply playing hide-and-seek (his favorite game), the family comes to the realization that he may have been kidnapped; a half-eaten sandwich, found on the floor several feet away from where Ben had been standing, is the only visible clue as to his whereabouts. While threads of the novel tie together all of the characters, it is clear that Goldberg's performance, while informed by the novel, is not slavishly bound to it; the actor makes the character Candy Bliss her own, as the following dialogue makes clear:

> "Beth, this is my boss," Jimmy told her. "This is Detective Supervisor Bliss."
> "I'm not really his boss — who could boss Jimmy? I just head up the detectives," said the woman, smiling.
> "You're a police chief?" she asked stupidly.
> "No, just of detectives.... Well, my name is Candy Bliss."
> Beth laughed, snorted; she couldn't help it, but was instantly mortified.
> The woman's green eyes lighted with a kind of conspiratorial joy. "I know — it sounds like a stripper, huh? My sister's name is Belle, can you beat that? Belle Bliss? I'm the stripper; she's the gun moll. The stuff parents can do to you, huh?"
> She stopped, and pressed one slender finger against a deep line just between her arched brows. "I can't believe I said that. Mrs. Cappadora, I want you to know, we are going to find your little boy. Can we sit down?" Jimmy drifted away [Mitchard 40].

Later in the book, there is this exchange:

> ... "You look just like Gloria Steinem," Beth said....
> "So says everyone," Candy replied ... [(Mitchard 97].

During a section of the book which takes place at the fictional Chapel of Our Lady, Bliss although raised in the Jewish faith, now finds parallels to the Christian world: "Guilt. Misogyny. You name it," she tells the Catholic Beth, reminding her that Christ's mother was" a Jewish mother, you know? And if anyone would help you now, maybe it would be a Jewish mother" (Mitchard 81).

When Beth questions her own faith, Candy tells her,

> "Maybe you don't have to believe everything. Maybe you don't have to know how to pray. Maybe you have all you can do right now just to hold on. Maybe holding on is enough."
> Beth looked up at the statue of the Virgin. "Hold on, huh?" she whispered. "To what? To *her*?"
> "If you want. Maybe."
> "And what if there's nothing there?"
> "Then ... you can hold on to me." [Mitchard 81].

Throughout the novel and in the film adaptation, Beth "holds on" to and leans against Candy Bliss for stability and strength; symbolically speaking, Bliss helps save Beth from drowning.

The concept of the "deep end of the ocean" refers to young Ben's admitted fear of water; his penchant for playing hide-and-seek — and, ironically, burying/drowning himself in many different small spaces so as to evade his family, especially his older brother, Vincent. Until Ben's disappearance, Vincent almost always seems to find him; the "deep end of the ocean" also refers to Ben's whereabouts. The concept of drowning is also a metaphor for Ben's disappearance and Beth's related guilt; Ben disappears, as though drowned forever; meanwhile, his mother "drowns" herself in sorrow, forgetting (how) to love her husband, son and daughter.

In the film, Bliss functions as cultural reminder for Beth, helping her surface from the "deep end of the ocean" of grief. Imbuing Candy Bliss with a seriousness balanced by a quick, strong sense of humor, Goldberg makes detective work seem delicious. As the story unfolds, Beth begins openly questioning her own mothering abilities, to the point where she regularly and willfully abandons her husband and children, instead obsessing ("going off the deep end") about how she could allow her youngest son to simply disappear; alternately, she obsesses about how to find Ben and return him to his family.

In Scene 6, "Sedating Beth," Bliss's participation is brief, but effective. The scene takes place in a Chicago hotel lobby, just hours after Ben's disappearance. Pat Cappadora reunites with his wife, Beth, while Bliss quietly asks

Beth for a recent photograph of the little boy. When Beth retrieves the color photo of a smiling, blonde-haired, blue-eyed Ben, wearing a red baseball cap, T-shirt, blue jeans and sneakers, poised to hit a home run with a baseball bat, she begins to sob, beginning a steady descent into self-doubt and self-pity. Detective Bliss, Goldberg respectfully takes the photo from Beth's hand. Beth descends into nervous exhaustion, with medics administering a sedative by injection.

Scene 8, "Not Giving Up," takes place in and around Detective Bliss's Chicago office. There, Beth awaits the opportunity to meet with her, to discuss the case. Meanwhile, as Beth serves herself coffee in an adjoining hallway, she overhears Bliss talking with Detective McGuire (Wayne Duvall), explaining the need to call in the FBI, as the case is interstate. McGuire's loud response — that Ben is dead, and that calling in the FBI is an unnecessary administrative formality — is met with Bliss's stark reply that the case is not over. Beth overhears this exchange and is reeling with the thought that the case may be over before it even begins. When Bliss leaves McGuire's office, she immediately invites Beth into her own office, leaving the door wide open. (Such symbolism paves the way for the viewer's better understanding of the politics which Bliss confronts and manages as the department's only Black, woman, gay detective.) Bliss immediately tells Beth that even though her fellow detectives are reluctant to continue the search, she remains on the case, which, she declares, is still open. When Beth reaches to touch Bliss's hand in a show of thanks and solidarity, Bliss quickly recoils, then offers quick apologies to Beth, explaining matter-of-factly that her status as a gay detective makes her a target for sexual harassment claims, especially from female clients. Bliss, recognizing that she has gone overboard with caution, then offers Beth a peace offering of sorts, in the form of Gummi Bears — an unconventional offer which Beth makes laugh. When Beth seems uncomfortable about giving in to reality during a crisis, Bliss looks straight into her eyes and calmly tells the bereaved mother that laughter is okay, and that she still has two beautiful children who need her. She also reminds Beth that there are many paths toward survival.

In Scene 13, "Nine Years Later," takes place at Cappadora's, an authentic Italian restaurant in Chicago, which Paty Cappadora founded with his father. The restaurant, like the Cappadora's new Chicago home, heralds new beginnings, but Detective Bliss, touring the restaurant alongside the Cappadora family and other family friends, tells Beth that the new restaurant and home are mere symbolic trappings of success — not necessarily signs or symbols of the family's progress in finding or surviving the loss of Ben. The number nine evokes the gestation period of a human; symbolically speaking, as the story unfolds, the kidnapped Ben becomes "reborn" as Sam Karras (Ryan Merriman), over a nine-year period. The 12-year-old boy, one of Kerry Cappadora's schoolmates, shows up at the family's front door one day, asking if they need someone to take care of their lawn. Beth takes a picture of Sam and tells her husband and Bliss that he bears an uncanny resemblance to Ben. Thus, the investigation is revitalized.

In the film's denouement (Scene 15), Bliss calmly brings the deception of Cecil Lockhart (Maryanne Summers), Beth's high school friend, to light. Cecil, who had committed suicide five years earlier, was a television personality who had given birth to a child, who died. To compensate for her loss, she kidnapped Ben to raise him as her own. Later, she married a man named George Karras (John Kapelos), leaving him in the dark concerning Ben's origins. In Chapter 17, "Cecil Lockhart," Detective Bliss blames herself for not having identified Lockhart as the kidnapper, since she had interviewed her during the early days of the investigation. Bliss explains that she did not do her job of finding Ben; that, despite her diligence, the Cappadoras actually found him. Beth and Pat refuse to accept Bliss's admission of guilt, saying that she could not have known Cecil's deception, and that it was Ben (Sam) who found them.

New York Times film critic Janet Maslin praises Goldberg's portrayal of Bliss: "Ms. Mitchard may have described Detective Candy Bliss as looking just like Gloria Steinem, but she's played sturdily by Whoopi Goldberg here" (Maslin). Goldberg's sturdiness extends beyond the manner in which she delivers her lines. Her Detective Bliss is detached just enough to be convincing on and at the job, and tender enough to reach, sympathize with and encourage Beth Cappadora. Bliss, in essence, becomes Beth's long-term supporter and sister in struggle.

In *How Stella Got Her Groove Back* (1998), Goldberg plays Delilah Abraham, a sister-girlfriend to Stella Payne (Angela Bassett), a 40-plus-year-old woman who falls in love with a man half her age. The on-screen chemistry of Goldberg and Bassett actually brings more to bear than the Terry McMillan novel on which the film is based. In the novel, Bernadette, the narrator, describes her relationship with Delilah thusly:

> I wish I could call Delilah. But I can't. She'd only been my best friend since college and we only talked on the phone every other day and she was the most brilliant person I ever met and we could talk about anything and she lived all the way in Philly and then last year she decides to surprise me and die suddenly from some stupid liver cancer that she didn't even tell me she had until she was in the fucking hospital and then she was gone the next week and there was a lot of shit we still needed to talk about. A whole lot of stuff. Years and years' worth of stuff. She knew I was going to miss her ass and I *do* miss her black ass and the only way I can make the hurt go away is to do one of two things: pretend that she's still alive and that we're just not on speaking terms, which we went through from time to time, or pretend that she never existed. Trying to do both has required a great deal of effort and imagination and whenever I'm not looking my heart plummets down real low and I can hardly tolerate longing.

So over these next few weeks I want to try to do some make-Stella-feel-good stuff. Which is why I'm planning to do some things I've been meaning to do but I haven't for one reason or another. Mostly because I'm always too busy. Always doing something. Work alone has been kicking my ass. It's been said before, but I'm here to give new meaning to the phrase, "I hate my job" [McMillan 29–30].

These words form the skeleton around which she fleshes out the character Delilah. Terry McMillan and Ron Bass may have adapted the novel for the big screen, but it is Goldberg who brings the character to life. Viewers get the first taste of Delilah's playfulness in Scene 4, "Come to Paradise," in which Stella, having seen an ad on television beckoning tourists to Jamaica, impulsively calls Delilah to get her to "buy into" the idea of a girlfriends' vacation. Stella gets the answering machine, on which Delilah has recorded a purring Eartha Kitt voice message. In Scene 5, "Delilah," viewers first see the bubbly Delilah, bounding across a busy Manhattan street, calling Stella on her cell phone, responding positively to the idea of a trip to Jamaica. (It is raining in the San Francisco Bay area, where Stella, a securities analyst, lives; Delilah's audible optimism brings light and life into Stella's dreary world.) As Delilah hurriedly traverses the crowded street, speaking in insistent clips, en route to her work as a window dresser for an upscale department store, viewers latch onto Goldberg's enthusiasm for the acting role, as well as the possibilities that await Delilah and Stella. She also forewarns Stella not to be jealous that she (Delilah) has lost weight, and will therefore mesmerize Jamaican men with her self-proclaimed dangerous curves. In an improvised bit of business, Delilah ties a red scarf around the neck of a Calvin Klein mannequin; a moment later she stuffs the scarf in the mannequin's underwear, creating an exaggerated bulge, which she excitedly shows to passersby.

Delilah is the catalyst for Stella actually following through on the plan "to try to do some make-Stella-feel-good stuff" (McMillan 30). She tells Stella that money and childcare are no excuses for not traveling—in fact, Delilah reminds her, Stella has the necessary seniority at work, funds, and child care to cast down her cares and take a much-needed two-week vacation. Besides, Delilah pointedly reminds her even if Stella does not think herself worthy of a two-week vacation, Delilah certainly is. Moreover, Delilah reminds Stella that Stella's son and Delilah's godson Quincy (Michael J. Pagan), is visiting his father, Stella's ex-husband, Walter Payne (James Pickens, Jr.).

Scene 6, "Welcome to Jamaica," shows Stella flying to Montego Bay; when she reaches the hotel, she asks the concierge for Delilah, and, almost magically, she appears, hollering and running across the vestibule to embrace Stella. During this scene, the first of the film's two specific references to black hair is made: while Delilah shows her full dreadlocks (bound by a colorful bandana placed at the nape of her neck), Stella has hired a master braider to manifest a mane for her, replacing the high-maintenance relaxed hairstyle, which she usually wears at the office. When Delilah sees Stella's braided mane, she compliments her by saying that they take two decades off Stella's appearance. (From a sociocultural perspective, Black American viewers [the targeted audience for the film] especially appreciate the dreadlocks and braids as low-maintenance hairstyles.) Later, when the women visit Stella's room, Delilah quickly fishes into Stella's personal belongings, selecting a pair of black lacquer hoop earrings, which she asks to borrow. The two women, who behave like sisters, pledge to meet for breakfast the following morning. Humorous contrasts between the two sisterfriends come to the fore during the next morning, when Stella begins an intense workout of her well-toned body on the beach; meanwhile, Delilah openly fakes workout enthusiasm. When Stella energetically runs off camera, stage left, Delilah exits stage right, moving her hips as though running, while actually dragging her feet. (The actors genuinely seem to delight in each other's company, making the scene socially and culturally authentic.)

In Scene 8, "Buddy and Jack," Delilah takes charge by snagging two potential (if decidedly temporary) Black American suitors: Buddy (Barry Shabaka Henley) an overweight, out-of-shape, over-eager man whom Delilah has decided is good enough for Stella; and Jack (Richard Lawson), a handsome, well-built, if socially awkward, stutterer, whom Delilah decides is good enough for herself. Delilah's plans go awry, however. In Scene 9, "The Pajama Disco," hotel guests party, wearing only their pajamas and underwear (at one point, the Jamaican woman emcee entreats women to remove their tops, and some comply). Stella warms to the advances of Winston Shakespeare (Taye Diggs), while Delilah, at first dancing with Jack, then somehow swept into dancing with first one white (and apparently gay), woman, then another loudly takes mock umbrage at the fact that Stella is dancing with Winston instead of Buddy.

Scene 19, "Life Is Too Short," depicts another supportive phone call between Stella and Delilah. Once again, Delilah initiates the call. This time, however, the call takes place while Stella, who has decided to extend her vacation, is in Jamaica; meanwhile, unbeknownst to Stella, doctors have hospitalized Delilah. During the phone call, Delilah decidedly deflects attention away from herself and urges Stella to make the most of life, including following up on the budding relationship with Winston — when Stella expresses fears of being too experienced for Winston, Delilah pointedly tells her that there is no harm in loving, and being loved by, a younger man. In this scene, Delilah verbally paints herself as a bored monarch, referring to the attending nurse (whom only she and the audience can see) as a kind of lady-in-waiting; meanwhile, Delilah irritatedly fends off the nurse's efforts, just long enough for her to impart wisdom to her friend.

Scene 21, "Cancer," confirms Delilah has advanced-stage cancer. Far from allowing only the storyline to communicate such information to viewers, however, Whoopi Goldberg's performance subtly and consistently drops hints to this effect. In Scene 6, "Welcome to Jamaica," Delilah plays with Stella's jewelry, looking at herself in the mirror, her facial expressions alternately mocking the puckered lips of fashion models and channeling the funkiness of James Brown. Yet, for a brief moment, Delilah also looks upon herself with seriousness, while casually mentioning to Stella that she has not been feeling well. In Scene 10, "Delilah's Opinion," when Delilah flops down upon Stella's hotel bed, ostensibly to chide Stella for taking interest in Winston), but it is actually because she is simply too exhausted to return to her own room. Delilah laughs as she addresses Stella; then, looking at the ceiling, she briefly registers a countenance reflecting fatigue and physical pain.

Scene 22, "The Hospital," shows Stella visiting Delilah, which is by far the most poignant scene in the film. Initially Stella talks and dances about, reminding the bedridden Delilah about friends at a college going-away party (including Johnny, who, according to school legend, reeked of body odor), as well as popular dances and songs of the women's shared past. While Stella lightly increases the portable radio's volume, they hear Marvin Gaye's disco hit, "Got To Give It Up (Part I)." While Stella, wearing a grey business suit and heels, dances The Skate, Delilah plays along, "dancing" in her hospital bed, until the physical pains become unbearable, at which point Delilah asks Stella to administer a quick dose of morphine. During this scene, Delilah refers back to their friend Johnny's body odor and says only half-jokingly that she probably smells pretty bad herself. Stella simply tells her friend that such is not the case, and curls up beside her in the hospital bed. The two then take turns singing "Row, Row, Row Your Boat," with the emphasis falling upon the song's concept of the dream in relation to life. Stella and Delilah effectively express individual and shared understandings of the temporality and frailty of life.

Unfortunately, at least one film reviewer misses the point of the aforementioned scene and Goldberg's acting. Writing for the *New York Times*, Stephen Holden says, "A mawkish death-bed scene awkwardly tries to camouflage the movie's lack of interest in Delilah, whom Ms. Goldberg plays with her customary down-home gusto. That twinkling crocodile grin hasn't lost its power to charm, shtick though it may be" (Holden "How Stella"). Holden's lack of appreciation for the scene reveals his lack of understanding of Black American social ties, as believably represented in the scene, as well as his general disdain for Goldberg as actor and black woman. Thoughtful viewers (especially those who have read McMillan's novel) delight in Delilah and feel genuine sadness at her untimely passing.

Scene 23, "Who'll Be My Best Friend Now?" takes place in a church memorial service for Delilah. While Stella stands at the pulpit, offering words of remembrance, and the concept of the "dream" in relation to life, Winston surprises her by walking into the sanctuary. Viewers come to realize that, while Delilah has been Stella's sidekick for 22 years, she also paved the way for the re-awakening of Stella's soul; moreover, the women's pet name for each other is "Bertha." "Bertha" is akin to "Birther"—one who brings forth life.

The acting chemistry and respect between Goldberg and Bassett is palpable and not surprising, given their accomplishments. Bassett is a Yale School of Drama graduate, nominated in 1994 for an Academy Award (Best Actress for portraying Tina Turner in the 1993 drama, *What's Love Got to Do with It?*) (IMDb "Awards..."); in 1991, Goldberg won the Best Actress award, for playing Oda Mae Brown in *Ghost* (1990)—in 1986, she also was nominated for Best Actress in a Leading Role, for her work as Celie in *The Color Purple* (1985) (IMDb "Awards ... Goldberg").

Goldberg is secure enough in her skills to try a wide variety of projects, including *Homie Spumoni* (2006). The story concerns a black couple, George (veteran stand-up comedian and comedy writer Paul Mooney) and Thelma (Goldberg), who are awarded a trip to Italy when George wins a sandwich-naming contest.

While taking a gondola ride with their two young sons, the gondola hits a rough patch and nearly capsizes. George saves himself and, by grasping Thelma's dreadlocks, saves her as well. He also manages to grab hold of their eldest son, Dana, saving him, thus leaving their baby, Leroy, to float down the Adige River in a basket. Many miles later, Leroy's basket entangles itself in the marsh (an obvious parody of the Biblical Moses story). A childless Italian woman named Maria (Lina Felice) takes the child home. Her husband, Enzo, a poor deli owner, strongly believes that they would face discrimination for having a black child. So, upon Mary's recommendation, the couple immigrates to the United States, via Ellis Island, with their newly adopted baby—whom they have christened Renato—in tow.

At the American immigration office, Maria holds the cloaked baby close to her body, thus preventing immigration officers from noticing that the baby is black. Thus begins Renato's re-introduction to American life. In the company of his Italian and Italian American relatives, Renato casually uses racial epithets to describe Black Americans. A musicophile, he spontaneously lapses into "That's Amore" and "Volaré," in the manner of Dean Martin. Still living at home, and working for Enzo's, his adopted father's deli, Renato's bedroom is awash in Italian flags, colors and posters featuring Italian and Italian American icons. Despite such cultural moorings, he nevertheless violates his family's fervent expectations of marrying a Catholic Italian woman, and instead becomes engaged to a stereotypical Jewish American princess, Ali Butterman (Jamie Lynn Sigler). A conflict arises when a photograph of Renato, taken at

Enzo's deli, appears in a nationally distributed magazine, which his birth parents use to track him down in the hopes of reclaiming him.

The plot, while weak, predictable and even insulting, at points, nevertheless provides worthwhile opportunities for viewers to see Paul Mooney acting opposite Goldberg. Chapter 9, "Baltimore, Part of Italy," shows Mooney and Goldberg, as supportive life partners George and Thelma, traveling to Little Italy, New York City, to see and reclaim their long-lost Leroy. (Real-life legal issues never come into play — viewers must suspend disbelief.) In Chapter 9, viewers see Renato, awakening to face a new day, descending the staircase and into the kitchen, drinking milk straight from the carton, passing gas and pretending to grade its rank smell like the grading of wine. Unbeknownst to Renato is the fact that his adoptive and birth parents are in the next room, witnessing the entire scene. Nevertheless George and Thelma register surprised, yet supportive facial expressions. When Thelma rises from the sofa to reclaim her son, the doubly shocked Renato begins bounding back up the stairway, away from his birth mother and toward his comfortable room. Thelma repeatedly calls out her son's first Christian name and lunges toward him. George rushes to her side and tries to calm her. Thelma's over-the-top response to Renato's presence is, indeed, like the dead rising from the grave.

Chapter 10, "Family Dinner," introduces viewers, and Leroy/Renato, to George and Thelma's comfortable, upper-middle-class home. The subdued, orderly setting spoofs *The Cosby Show*, in which Bill Cosby and Phylicia Rashad, as obstetrician Heathcliff and attorney Claire Huxtable, respectively, raise five children in a respectable Brooklyn brownstone. George and Thelma's household is quite different. Instead of the avant garde jazz music tracks which punctuate *Cosby Show* themes and transitions, George and Thelma's household is awash in pseudo gangsta rap, courtesy of their eldest son Dana, who still lives there and is determined to make his parents acknowledge him. Moreover, George and Thelma's living room still sports a "Welcome Home" banner, consistently in place for 22 years, symbolizing a mother's incessant belief in the ultimate return of Leroy. When George hears the rap music, he instantly shouts to Dana to turn off the music, and tells Leroy that he is part of a respectable family, not a family of "niggers," as the music implies. George, Thelma, Leroy and Dana sit around the family table, eating a traditional fried catfish soul food dinner, accented by George's sacred Louisiana hot sauce. Thelma lapses into wholesome mother-mode, making sure that her boys are well-fed and happy — even though it is obvious to viewers that Renato does not appreciate catfish, and Dana, jealous of the attention that Leroy has always gotten, does not appreciate him.

In Chapter 15, "Parental Righteousness," María and Enzo visit George and Thelma, with María making a peace offering of *milangiani* — traditional

Italian eggplant casserole. Once the couples have finished dinner (in a quick comic quip, George compliments María's cooking, likening the taste of the eggplant to that of chicken), María and Thelma retreat to the kitchen, ostensibly to wash dishes. While the women are away, the men make peace, while the women make war. In the kitchen, María criticizes Thelma for losing Renato; meanwhile, Thelma criticizes María for "stealing" Leroy. Then María says that Thelma did not take good care of Renato, and must not have breastfed him, because Renato had a cold when María found him. Then Thelma, with controlled rage, explains that she indeed not only breastfed Leroy, but also baptized him, to which María replies that he should have been baptized Catholic, not Lutheran. At this point, Thelma rises from her seat at the kitchen table and grabs a bottle of Louisiana hot sauce, threatening to cut María with the bottle's jagged, cracked-open end. Meanwhile, María also stands, grabbing her chair to shield herself, while loudly yelling in Italian. (Thelma's posture mocks that of Hollywood film scenes, in which, during barroom brawls, a man cracks the bottom of a wine bottle, using the neck of the bottle as a handle, the bottle's jagged bottom becoming a sharp weapon.) While she wields the broken bottle of hot sauce, Thelma speaks gibberish, imitating scat singing and traditional Black South African click-songs, and ending with a Latin-tinged phrasing of "your Mama." The film ends with Leroy/Renato marrying Ali Butterman (whose true birth identity as a Catholic Cuban refugee is exposed) and all characters, now forming an extended family, agreeing to disagree. *Homie Spumoni* is a very weak film; but Mooney and Goldberg aptly portray supporting characters George and Thelma, intermittently and temporarily raising the bar for viewers.

Goldberg also temporarily raises the bar in *Theodore Rex* (1995), a direct-to-video release, which seems to have been doomed from the start. Prior to the shooting of the film, she was sued for $20 million for alleged breach-of-contract. According to the September 20, 1993, issue of *Jet Magazine*, "T. Rex Productions [filed the suit against Goldberg] for allegedly reneging on a verbal contract to appear in the film" (JPC 38). According to the August 29, 1993 issue of *Variety*, her legal representative, Ralph Loeb, said: "Goldberg was offered scripts all the time and although she expressed an interest in 'T. Rex,' she had by no means committed" (Reed Business Information). None of that seems to matter when one watches Whoopi Goldberg play "straight man" to Theodore (Teddy) Rex, a fictional, cloned Tyrannosaurus Rex (voiced by George Newbern). Set in an undetermined future (where such animals as elephants and raccoons are extinct, their DNA housed in Kane's laboratory, a cavernous place which he calls an ark), the plot concerns Theodore Rex's attempt to solve mysterious deaths connected to Elizar Kane (Armin Mueller-Stahl), thus revealing Kane's plot to exterminate humankind. Elizar Kane is a billionaire who seems to be a curious combination of the Biblical Noah, Mary Shelley's Dr. Frankenstein and Dr. Evel of *Austin Powers* fame. Kane is also the man who cloned Teddy Rex and brought him back to life; Kane's latest plan is to launch a missile which will start the next ice age, decimating the human population (save for himself and a few others of his choosing), and enable him to re-populate the earth with cryogenically frozen pairs of all bacteria and non-human animal species. The film's plot is utterly ridiculous, but Goldberg gives the role of a futuristic burned-out veteran grid police officer (lightly reminiscent of the lead character in *Robocop*), her best efforts.

As Katie Coltrane, Goldberg supports Teddy Rex's unorthodox detective work, remaining serious and calm throughout most of the film, despite having to wear a ridiculous, ill-fitting, likely uncomfortable costume, consisting of a too-tight black diving suit, complete with unconvincing vinyl overlay (supposedly computerized body armor). Coltrane's support of Teddy Rex is, at first, begrudging, and solely based upon professionalism—she is far too advanced and he is too much of a novice for her to want to partner with him. But as she begins to see his loneliness and social needs as a member of an extinct species, her support becomes more like that of a thoughtful friend than mere co-worker. The film ends with Coltrane and Teddy Rex being, if not best buddies, then at least friends. In the closing scene, as the commissioner publicly promotes Teddy Rex, the hero of the film, to Detective First Class, Teddy declares that, given his new status, he now can choose his own partner—and he chooses Katie Coltrane—a distinction with which Coltrane does not fully agree. The audience is led to believe that Coltrane appreciates Teddy Rex as a friend, but prefers to work with an officer of equal caliber.

Whoopi Goldberg effectively narrates the role of another kind of best friend in the major motion picture *Racing Stripes* (2005), a family-friendly movie which, at times, evokes a *National Velvet*-meets-*Charlotte's Web* sensibility. The story concerns a baby zebra inadvertently left behind by a regional traveling circus during a vicious rainstorm. A beautiful teenaged daughter, Channing Walsh (Hayden Panettiere), adopts the animal and raises it as a racing pony. Channing's father, Nolan Walsh (Bruce Greenwood), owns a small subsistence farm in Kentucky, near the race track where the fictional Kentucky Open is annually held. Prior to the untimely death of Mrs. Walsh, resulting from a horseback riding accident, the small farm had been the legendary training ground for Kentucky Open winners. When Channing decides to make the zebra her own special project, she names it "Stripes."

Because Stripes (voiced by Frankie Muniz) has grown up in a largely equestrian community, he believes that he, too, is a horse. Yet the horses shun him, refusing to accept him as one of their kind; and other animals on the Walsh farm also initially treat him condescendingly because he does not look or act like any "horse" they ever have seen. Moreover, neighbors, including

Clara Dalrymple (Wendie Malick), the owner of the Kentucky Open, openly shun the Walshes, as the Walshes are no longer training winning horses. So poor are the Walshes that, when their tractor dies, Mr. Walsh trains Stripes to pull a plow, to prepare the ground for seeding—a sight which neighbors interpret as being simultaneously innovative, resourceful ... and *desperate*. Stripes is also at a disadvantage as far as racing is concerned, because, as a wild animal, his flight response is heightened at the expense of gaining or maintaining the necessary endurance for racing competitions. Stripes certainly earns his, in the form of regular, open criticism and lack of opportunity to prove himself—but Franny (voiced by Goldberg), a wise and sensible goat, gives Stripes moral support for the long haul.

Viewed squarely, Franny, from her positioning on the sidelines of the farm and the actual equestrian races, serves as heritage reminder for the Walsh's barnyard animals. For example, when she first encounters Stripes, whose basket had been placed on the floor of the barn in the middle of the night, Franny openly compliments the strange creature's looks, while other animals — including Reggie the rooster (voiced by Jeff Foxworthy) and Franny's husband, Tucker, a Shetland pony (voiced by Dustin Hoffman), look at Stripes askance.

Behind the scenes, while Stripes independently tries his skills against ponies during secret impromptu races after dark, Franny persistently goads Tucker (who had endured criticism similar to that which Stripes faces) into training Stripes for competitive racing. (Goldberg's use of voice is particularly believable here, as she adopts the stance of the nagging wife; quite apropos for a fictional middle-aged nanny goat.) Meanwhile, Channing decides to honor her late mother by following in her footsteps as a competitive equestrian jockey. When the family truck breaks down, threatening her meager livelihood, she successfully rides Stripes to her job at the site of the Kentucky Open, much to her father's consternation and Ms. Dalrymple's chagrin.

Stripes received positive reviews, including the following: "The vocal talent is top-notch: Dustin Hoffman, as a gruff Shetland pony named Tucker, is so precise in his delineation of the character that by the end of the film, the animal has come to resemble the bewigged Hoffman in [the 2004 film] *I ♥ Huckabees*. Other celebrity beasties include Mandy Moore as a sexy filly, Whoopi Goldberg as a levelheaded goat and Joe Pantoliano as Goose, a big-city pelican on the run from the mob" (Stevens).

Several scenes show Goldberg, as the sidelined Franny, positively asserting her influence. By Scene 10, Franny learns that Tucker has been quietly coaching Stripes; Goldberg's sunny intonation further encourages Tucker to reclaim his status as co-trainer on the Walsh farm. In Scene 15, Franny plainly declares that a little encouragement can go a long way and pledges to encourage Stripes in his bid to become a Kentucky Open winner. In Scene 17, Franny delivers on her promise; viewers see Franny calmly leading Stripes (who suffers from a lack of self-confidence), to the part of the Walsh barn displaying dusty photographs of the Walsh family (father, mother and daughter) standing beside winning race horses at the Kentucky Open. As Franny emphatically conveys to Stripes, the horses were trained by none other than Nolan Walsh and co-trained by her husband, Tucker. Scene 17 is quite significant, as it symbolically hands the winner's garland to Stripes and foreshadows Stripes's actual victory. In Scene 24, viewers see Stripes successfully winning the Kentucky Open — ridden by none other than Channing, who wears her mother's customized competition gear — a gift given to Channing by her father. In Scene 25, the announcer slips the winner's garland over Stripes' head — and, in the tradition of helping others, championed by Franny, Stripes promptly lowers his head, to slip the garland onto Tucker's neck — a gracious "thank you" gesture. Goldberg's portrayal of Franny shows that a sideliner can make a major impact on the playing field and in society — an important lesson for children, the film's primary intended audience.

In *Comic Relief I* (1986), a landmark comedy fundraiser for the homeless, Goldberg improvises comedic sketches alongside longtime friends Billy Crystal and Robin Williams, in a manner lightly reminiscent of the Rat Pack, which regularly featured Frank Sinatra, Dean Martin, Peter Lawford and Sammy Davis, Jr. Instead of performing solely to the Rat Pack's Las Vegas crowd, which generally expected to hear ribald humor and related music in an after-hours lounge environment, *Comic Relief* took place during Prime Time on a Saturday, addressing a general American TV audience. *Comic Relief I* distinguished itself by its use of intermittent video clips profiling the daily realities of homeless people. HBO, a pay-cable service, permitted its affiliates to carry the presentation as part of their basic cable schedule, without an extra charge to viewers." "Performed before a remarkably supportive audience at the cavernous Universal Amphitheater in Los Angeles, 'Comic Relief' faced, and never quite surmounted, a split-personality problem. The phenomenon of the homeless is hardly conducive to laughter" (O'Connor). Nevertheless, *Comic Relief* worked — so successful is the venture that it has a 20-year track record of raising awareness of homelessness and related funds and even spawned a British equivalent, *Comic Relief II* (1986). *Comic Relief II* was filmed in the United Kingdom, directed by Rowan Atkinson, included skits written by John Cleese (among others) and featured such luminaries as Atkinson, Chris Barrie, Simon Brint, Frank Bruno and Kate Bush (IMDb Comic Relief 1986/II).

In 1990, *Comic Relief* relocated from Los Angeles to New York City, boasting, in addition to Crystal, Williams and Goldberg, such comic talents as Louie Anderson, Bill Cosby, Elaine Boosler, Candice Bergen, and, of course, the Rockettes, among others" (Gerard). Of the experience of working with Crystal and Williams, Goldberg says, "I'm sort of the bonder.... You have to understand that to work with the two of them is a difficult thing. They're very patient with me because I'm slow. They never let me panic" (Gerard). Goldberg's mentioning of the concept of "slowness" must be taken in context: of the three, she is the only member of the trio who has not worked as a stand-up comedian; moreover, her skill of improvisation requires her to take the time to continually assess and re-assess situations, to devise situation-appropriate responses. According to Robin Williams, the authenticity of Goldberg's participation in *Comic Relief* was palpable. Early in her career, she faced hard times and homelessness herself, and, therefore, had direct knowledge of some of the homeless shelters to which the telethon's donations were sent (A&E Chap. 6). Each member of the trio brings his or her own strengths which, when done well and in concert, creates a scenario whereby the whole is even greater than the sum of its parts: Goldberg excels at improvisation; Crystal excels at impersonations and shtick; and Williams excels at spontaneously crafting the absurd—saying and doing that which most members of the audience only can imagine.

One certainly sees this aspect of bonding in the trio's work, from *Comic Relief*'s very beginnings. For example, in *Comic Relief I*, viewers are introduced to a stage set adorned, not with a typical red velvet stage curtain, but a wall of cardboard boxes, set along Any Street, USA (symbolizing the visible transience of homeless people, many of whom must call cardboard boxes and the like "home," as well as the manufactured aspects of homelessness). Against this backdrop, Goldberg, plays a professional window dresser for Bergdorf's (an upscale New York department store), and Crystal, impersonates a homeless person. When the fashion maven approaches the homeless man, she inadvertently demeans him, by praising his streetwise attire, saying that it is just the sort which should be profiled in the storefront windows. Meanwhile, the vulnerability of the homeless man, as well as the fashion maven, is amplified when Williams, as a random passerby, wearing a skullcap and long trenchcoat, "flashes" the window dresser (the audience sees only Williams' back, as he opens his trenchcoat; meanwhile, Goldberg recoils in overblown horror), while the audience howls with laughter. When viewed squarely, the trio is not making light of homelessness; rather, the group is highlighting a social problem and demanding that Americans take responsibility in addressing it.

Another skit, this one from *Comic Relief VII* (1995), has Williams dropping to his knees behind Crystal and suggestively placing his fist between Crystal's legs, simulating an erect penis, while Crystal uses voice effects to personify/give voice to the "penis." Meanwhile, Goldberg, standing by, says that the men's horseplay is off-limits to her as she does not have a penis. She responds by saying that, unlike the men, she cannot just casually imitate her vagina onstage—and she illustrates such, by using her hands to create a diamond-shaped, talking "vagina." Williams joins in and, interrupting Goldberg's vagina "talk," imitates a "vagina" on her behalf, moving from his previous place behind Crystal, to take a new position on the floor behind Goldberg, placing his outstretched hands between her legs and pretending to "act out" the part of the vagina. The audience, along with Williams and Goldberg, laughs heartily. Williams's spontaneous, outrageous acts are done with great respect for Crystal and Goldberg; he uses visual cues, quickly assessing his stagemates' overall demeanor, as well as the mood of the audience, to determine how far he can take the bit (Chap. 9).

To underscore the seriousness of *Comic Relief* efforts, on May 9, 1990, Robin Williams and Goldberg testified, alongside Connie Perez, an Outreach Worker for the Children's Hope Program of Oxnard, California, as witnesses for the U.S. Senate Committee on Labor and Human Resources Hearing on the Homelessness Prevention and Community Revitalization Act of 1990 (U.S. Senate Committee on Human Labor and Human Resources).

During 2006, the trio gathered for yet another installation of *Comic Relief*— this one specifically to benefit Hurricane Katrina survivors, New Orleans and the Gulf Coast. (The 2006 show is not the first time that *Comic Relief* assisted hurricane survivors; in 1992, *Hurricane Relief* assisted the survivors of Hurricane Irene and featured, among many other performances, Goldberg, alongside Gloria Estefan, singing a rousing rendition of the Isley Brothers' song, "Shout!") From the start of *Comic Relief 2006*, viewers familiar with the *Comic Relief* series notice a dramatic difference, with respect to the sets and staging. Unlike some of the previous shows which featured barebones, improvised sets designed to evoke realities of poverty and underscore the ad hoc character of the show, *Comic Relief 2006* boasts lush stage sets and trained dancers wearing professionally designed costumes, all with an eye and ear toward rekindling pre–Katrina New Orleans. This seemed appropriate given the show's setting at the Coliseum at Caesar's Palace in Las Vegas. The opening sequence begins with the sounds of an authentic Dixieland-style jazz band, accompanying Billy Crystal, Goldberg and Robin Williams as they ride across the stage on a float and lead a chorus of French Quarter hoofers, masked revelers, junkanoo ("John Canoe") stilt walkers, and general Mardi Gras-style revelers in "When the Saints Go Marching In." "When The Saints Go Marching In" is a song performed during the second-line aspect of traditional New Orleans funerals. It is also a theme song of New Orleans (Swenson 93, 147), popularized by Louis Armstrong, a native New Orleanian also known as the "Ambassador of Jazz" (National Portrait Gallery). Moreover, when "Trumpeter Al Hirt was part owner" of the New Orleans Saints football team, "his rendition of 'When the Saints Go Marching In' was made the official fight song" (Johnson 3).

Billy Crystal is wearing a red satin top hat, matching pants and peppermint-red striped vest, as if hosting a three-ring, big top circus. Goldberg wears a white satin sash, adorned with the title "Grand Marshall" draped across a black tuxedo, along with a black oversized top-hat, reminiscent of that of the Mad Hatter (except that it is adorned with colorful feathers). Robin Williams is dressed in a metallic court jester's outfit featuring traditional New Orleans colors of purple, green and gold (symbolizing justice, faith and power), with a twist. Echoing Williams's *Comic Relief* predilection toward phallic imagery, the actor wears an oversized, shiny gold codpiece (which also doubles as a storage pouch for props, such as packaged peanuts, that he uses for other skits). Crystal tells the audience that the codpiece shows Williams's excitement about being in Las Vegas; meanwhile, Goldberg, to the delight of the audience, chastises Williams for wearing it, while asking permission to touch it.

Fittingly, the trio's performance of "When the Saints Go Marchin' In" reflects sardonic humor. The lyrics that Crystal sings echo how Katrina took *Comic Relief* and the world by storm and by surprise, as well as the slow response from FEMA (the Federal Emergency Management Agency). The lyrics that Goldberg sings lampoon President George Bush's decision to make Mike Brown the head of FEMA, while also highlighting the fact that New Orleans remains a worthwhile a site for tourism. Singing in a gravelly manner, deliberately evoking the legacy of Louis Armstrong, Williams reminds viewers that the levees were not built to withstand the storm, and that monies are needed to restore the Gulf Coast. At the end of the song the trio offers a rousing chorus, telling viewers that they have the power to combat Katrina and help the Gulf Coast rebuild by picking up the phones and pledging their support (*Comic Relief 2006* Scene 1). Later, when the three introduce Bill Clinton, who offers a sincere, pre-recorded message detailing the impact of New Orleans on American culture and describing the work of the Bush-Clinton Katrina Fund in addressing the crisis, Whoopi sneezes — which signals Crystal and Williams to dramatize that she has actually farted a storm, generating laugher from Goldberg and the audience (Scene 6).

In addition to the trio of hosts, the show features Bonearama, an authentic New Orleans brass band ("bone," short for "trombone," retains its allusions to death and sexuality). The show also features a variety of American comedians. Ray Romano muses upon middle-class married sex life. Rosie O'Donnell talks about avoiding gastric bypass and commercial dieting as marks of distinction among Hollywood actresses. Bill Maher jokes that George W. Bush, in light of Hurricane Katrina, is a lame duck president. George Lopez criticizes the idea of addressing illegal immigration by building a wall separating the United States from Mexico and posits that, ironically, Mexicans would be called upon build it. D.L. Hughley jokingly criticizes how the national news errantly described Hurricane Katrina survivors as "refugees," instead of American citizens. Jon Stewart (*The Daily Show*) faces off against Stephen Colbert (*The Colbert Report*) who, in an over-the-top, fictional declaration, says that too many celebrities are taking advantage of Hurricane Katrina for the sake of publicity. Meanwhile, Colbert's fictional character does the same, creating an ice statue of himself; a yacht named after himself (which he claims to have used to save Hurricane Katrina survivors); faux dollars and a related casino, using the airtime to "pitch" his wares and services supposedly in the name of helping Hurricane Katrina survivors. These are just a few of the many performers who helped make *Comic Relief 2006* a success.

Goldberg's lasting influence as a member of the original *Comic Relief* comedy trio is evident in the fact that even the *Star Trek* universe recognizes her. During *Comic Relief V* (1992), members of the *Star Trek: The Next Generation* crew examine such artifacts as old *Comic Relief* T-shirts and sweatshirts, and a projected, digital photo featuring Billy Crystal, Whoopi Goldberg, and Robin Williams. While the crew assesses the significance of the artifacts, Data summarizes the fundraising efforts of *Comic Relief* and its positive impact on 500,000 homeless people. Adding a comic edge to the otherwise serious skit, Gates McFadden, as Dr. Crusher, notes that Goldberg looks eerily similar to the *Star Trek* character Guinan — a suggestion which the *Enterprise* crew quickly dismisses (Chap. 8). As sidekick to Billy Crystal and Robin Williams in the televised *Comic Relief* charity fundraising series, Goldberg expanded possibilities for women's roles in comedy, while also helping to make a positive difference in the lives of homeless Americans.

The Disney music CD *Mickey Unrapped* (1994) includes "Bowwow To The Beat" (Track 5), an upbeat rap song performed by Goldberg. In that song, she portrays man's best friend — in this case, the Disney character Pluto. The structure and thrust of the song are lightly reminiscent of George Clinton's popular song, "Atomic Dog" (1990), in which the narrator, a dog, openly ponders why he instinctively chases cats. "Bowwow To The Beat" also lightly recalls James Brown's popular song, "Papa's Got a Brand New Bag." In the Disney recording, however, Goldberg, as the narrator, mentions doggy-doo cleanup bags. The structure and theme of "Bowwow To The Beat" also tacitly recognizes the cultural influence of such Black American rappers as Li'l Bow-Wow and Snoop Dogg. In the song, written by Robin Frederick and Michael Lewis Becker, Pluto pledges loyalty to Mickey Mouse, leading a pack of dogs to dance as one. By the end of the song, the pack gets out of hand, barking loudly, prompting Pluto to serve as referee. The humorous song reminds listeners that dogs can be loyal supporters, and, like humans, they can be trained.

"Bowwow to the Beat" is not the only example of Goldberg successfully portraying man's best friend. She voiced the title role of Tiffany (AKA Blue Dog), in David Du Bos's independent documentary film, *Rodrigue:*

A Man and His Dog (1992). Blue Dog is the fictional name of Rodrigue's beloved Tiffany, a cross between a cocker spaniel and a terrier, who lived in Louisiana as part of the Rodrigue family for a dozen years. Veronica Rodrigue adopted Tiffany from a box of puppies, which a medical doctor had carried to the hospital where she worked. George Rodrigue believes that Tiffany thought herself to be human; and since she lived with the Rodrigues for five years before the birth of André, the Rodrigues' first-born child, Tiffany was especially threatened by this new addition. Yet, over time, says Rodrigue, Tiffany and André became best buddies. According to George Rodrigue, Tiffany was present when Rodrigue began his art studio, and saw every painting that he completed during the early years of the studio. Succumbing to illness, Tiffany died at the age of 12, when Andre was 7 years old. Rodrigue lived with numerous photographs of Tiffany; and when he was commissioned to complete paintings for a book of ghost stories, he interpreted Tiffany as a contemporary "loup-garou" (literally French for "werewolf"; Rodrigue considers his depiction of Tiffany a "ghost-dog," in the spirit of the loup-garou) and append the image of Tiffany onto the paintings, which otherwise depict personal recollections of traditional Cajun landscapes, life and culture. Scholars of contemporary art classify Rodrigue's stylized depiction of Blue Dog (so named by passersby who saw images of Tiffany in a French Quarter gallery display window in 1991) as comparable to that of Andy Warhol.

> Overall ... Blue Dog, whose biography entwines that of its creator, eschews comparison because it is in a category by itself. A discomforting place for the accountants of art history, who deplore the blurring of genres or the emergence of yet undefined ones. And an explanation of Rodrigue's uneasy status as a contemporary artist astride opposite worlds Warhol at least posthumously mastered, of a runaway brand and a brave new art.
>
> Like the artist himself, Blue Dog early on in its existence found itself deep in Cajun territory. Posing with the remainderd characters of Cajun tableaux, it lends once sober scenes an almost burlesque quality: before the perennial partakers of the aioli dinner, in the dazzling company of Jolie Blond; in a hollow tomb with its anonymous cross, under many oaks and moons, by a river whose blue flows from the same aqua palette as its coat, implying an intrinsic connection. But a connection, as the title of one *Save Me from the River* (1998) suggests, both artist and subject seek to break free of. Like Rodrigue at a point in his life, Blue Dog no longer, if ever, quite fit. Together, they traveled on [Danto 39–40].

Rodrigue is careful to maintain the dignity of the whimsical electric blue image of a dog with ears mimicking those of a Papillon and wide, curious eyes like yellow caution lights. Having painted over 400 portraits of Tiffany, he insists that Blue Dog is "not a cartoon" and that, having passed up numerous opportunities to mass-market the image, he is determined to preserve Tiffany's legacy in the form on "paintings and silkscreen prints only" (*A Man and His Dog— Part 2*).

Rodrigue explains that Tiffany is painted in blue to denote the spirit world, and that the dog is always "pasted on the landscape [of the paintings]. Just a spirit. Not a part of it" (*A Man and His Dog—Part I*). While the actual Tiffany was female, Rodrigue says that Blue Dog, Tiffany's spirit, is beyond gender, sometimes presenting itself in paintings as male, and sometimes as female. He also declares that Blue Dog represents contemporary Cajun culture, alongside such images as oak trees, Louisiana landscapes and alligators. In fact, says Rodrigue, while his early paintings concern traditional Louisiana landscapes and themes, the addition of Blue Dog creates a bridge, of sorts, connecting the past with the present and giving contemporary audiences not only a glimpse of a South Louisiana Cajun past, but a taste of Cajun sensibilities regarding the spirit world.

As principal narrator of Tiffany's spirit, Whoopi Goldberg has fun literally playing a bitch. At one point in the film, Goldberg, as Tiffany pasted onto a traditional Cajun scene of a Rodrigue painting, deflects off-color remarks from classically painted nude women in the painting, who ask her when she has found a man; Tiffany calls the women "bitches," and then reflexively points the word toward herself. Goldberg's eager, yet thoughtful, voice also aptly expresses Tiffany's excitement and confusion. At each stage of the journey, Tiffany is thrown for a loop, meeting all sorts of creatures along the way: a white chicken, an alligator, a pair of rabbits (one white and the other black), a red dog (which, except for its menacing color, looks like Blue Dog) and even the original Tiffany, whose presence informs Blue Dog that she is, in fact, dead. Goldberg's verbal intonation of incredulity makes Blue Dog's denial of death sound real.

The legend of Blue Dog reminds viewers of the popular children's storybook, *Are You My Mother?* (1960), in which a scrappy chick, with wild eyes, walks about, asking all sorts of animals if they are his mother; and Charles Schultz's *Snoopy, Come Home!* (1972). In *Snoopy Come Home*, the Peanuts character Snoopy, responding to a letter from a faraway girl named Lila, travels to meet her, with Woodstock as his sidekick–Snoopy meets many different characters during his quest to find Lila and return home to his worried master, Charlie Brown. As Tiffany in *Rodrigue: A Man and His Dog*, Goldberg's pronounced New York accent provides the necessary contrast against traditional Cajun voices. Other voice artists featured in the documentary include Paige O'Hara (who voices the nude women, the high society Southern Lady and the Red Headed Lady); Yeardly Smith (who voices the chicken, the alligator, the bat and the Indian chief); and Cameron Thor (who voices a pair of blue suede shoes [lightly mimicking the sounds of Elvis Presley], as well as the black rabbit, and Jacques, George Rodrigue's son).

Another connection between Goldberg and Blue Dog is that of a shared appreciation for the art and necessity of free speech. Throughout her career, and especially evident by her work as moderator on ABC television's *The View*, Goldberg has worked to create a safe space for healthy discussion and debate, preserving and extending the American tradition of freedom of expression. Similarly, Blue Dog has appeared in numerous settings, to give voice to American frustrations and possibilities. For example, post–Hurricane Katrina, Blue Dog expressed the views of Americans affected by the storm, awaiting federal assistance. Several of Rodrigue's paintings, included in his book, *Blue Dog Speaks* (2008), illustrate the American ideal of free speech. *Throw Me Something, F.E.M.A.* (2006) depicts Blue Dog wearing a mask, as during Carnival and Mardi Gras; but the intensity of the dog's yellow eyes, peering from beneath the mask transforms the basic request common of all revelers into a resolute command. Another Rodrigue painting, *Cut Through the Red Tape* (2006), shows Blue Dog beleaguered by red tape (an allusion to the bureaucracy preventing Hurricane Katrina survivors from receiving much-needed government assistance). Yet another Rodrigue creation, *To Stay Alive, We Need Levee 5* (2005), shows Blue Dog's intense yellow eyes peering over emergency tape; the emergency tape reads, "TO STAY ALIVE WE NEED LEVEE 5," and is placed such that it covers/stifles the dog's mouth and snout. Rodrigue's *Stars and Stripes and Me* (1996), completed long before the Hurricane Katrina disaster, shows national pride, with Blue Dog resolutely standing in front of the American flag.

Goldberg's appreciation for the art of Rodrigue, and vice-versa, are apparent in the final frame of *Rodrigue: A Man and His Dog*. That frame depicts an original Rodrigue painting, showing a smiling Goldberg, as herself, seated upon the ground, wearing an oversized white shirt and black pants, beneath a traditional South Louisiana oak tree, at dusk, flanked by Red Dog and Blue Dog. Two lit candles, symbolizing the novena, a Catholic tradition of mourning the dead and seeking God's grace, are also included in the painting.

In a published interview, "Dishin' with Whoopi: Whoopi Goldberg Discusses Her Latest Role on Broadway" (August 5, 2008) she briefly talks about her dual supporting roles as Aphrodite and Calliope, respectively, in the Broadway musical of *Xanadu*, while also emphasizing the centrality of free speech as an American tenet and basis of the television show *The View*. Moreover, she reminds American viewers that they also have the right to free speech, but that hate mail will not halt freedom of expression. In other words, others' dissenting opinions will not deter her from speaking her mind. Goldberg's philosophy concerning her brief (9 week) supporting roles in *Xanadu* echo her strong work ethic and belief in helping others. She says, "I like working.... [A supporting role] allows me to do my little thing and also enjoy what other folks are doing" (ABC News). Her approach allows her to experiment as an actor while also learning from others, supporting the theater production (not only by filling in for Jackie Hoffman and Kerry Butler — the show's original Aphrodite and Calliope, respectively; but also using her name to draw attention, and ticket buyers, to the show) and allowing space for fellow actors to shine. Goldberg's belief in the importance of supporting roles is evident in her 1991 Oscar win for playing Oda Mae Brown in *Ghost* (1990). Her varied supporting roles on stage and screen remind us that sidelining can be empowering, and that helpfulness can be very good indeed.

10

Returning to Her Roots
Back to Broadway *and Beyond*

> Elmo likes her hair and her skin.
> —*Sesame Street* character Elmo, speaking to special guest
> Whoopi Goldberg, on *The Best of Elmo* (1994)

Sesame Street character Elmo's statement that he "likes" Goldberg's natural hair texture and skin tone shows just how far American popular television has come in depicting a more diverse America. Through her many acting roles and social causes, Goldberg has helped to change American television and film landscapes, making black hair (especially dreadlocks) and brown skin more commonly seen and therefore, less threatening. Her determination to maintain her distinctive dreadlocks has resulted in increased scrutiny both within and outside of black communities. Goldberg epitomizes the words spoken by Lord Polonius to Laertes, in Act 1, scene 3 of William Shakespeare's *Hamlet*: "This above all: to thine own self be true; And it must follow, as the night the day, Thou canst not then be false to any man" (Shakespeare 36). Throughout her career, and culminating in her one-woman show, *Whoopi Goldberg: Back to Broadway* (2005), she lives her truth, speaking through her words, her actions and her hair.

Moreover, her training as cosmetologist shows that her trademark dreadlocks are not the result of happenstance but choice. Even today, dreadlocks are considered counterculture, even among Americans of African descent; this was especially true during the 1970s and 1980s, when Goldberg, American artist, came of age.

Frances Marie Ward, in her University of North Carolina at Greensboro doctoral dissertation, "'Get Out of My Hair!': The Treatment of African American Hair Censorship in America's Press and Judiciary from 1969–2001" (2002), explains that legal issues involving Black hairstyles emerged during the 1960s, with the advent of the Vietnam War. Generally, the U.S. military maintained that the afro hairstyle was non-regulation. Thus, in addition to fighting the Vietnam War, from the 1960s to the 1970s, "Black soldiers were fighting for the right to wear an afro hairstyle—the hairstyle of choice for some during a time of unrest and protest" (Ward 76). In 1969, the *New York Times* reported, "Airman 1st CL August Doyle, 21 years old, of Dallas, faced a special court-martial" for refusing to cut his afro; "The airman refused, explaining his hairstyle was part of his black identity" (Ward 78). Such controversies extended to lawsuits in the 1970s and 1980s concerning braided hairstyles, including cornrows; by the 1980s, press attention "turned to a new dimension of hairstyle controversy.... The spotlight moved from the military to the corporate world and from Afros to cornrows and braids" (Ward 85). The July 21, 1981 edition of *The Wall Street Journal* reported that Renee Rogers, a "veteran American Airlines ticket agent," filed a lawsuit alleging that "her employers insisted that she remove her braids or wear a wig over them during work or put her hair into a bun" (Ward 85). Rogers lost the suit, but others would follow, with varying degrees of success. By the 1990s, lawsuits concerning dreadlocks, and the associated Rastafarian religion, also emerged. In 1999, "Seven FedEx couriers, most of them Rastafarians who wear dreadlocks, were fired, even though they offered to wear their hair under a hat or in a neat, businesslike fashion" (Ward 107). According to Ward, a New York attorney general filed a lawsuit against Federal Express, on behalf of the workers, because "sincerely held religious beliefs" are covered under the Civil Rights Act of 1964 (Ward 107).

Ward's use of the phrase "hair censorship" in the title of her dissertation is especially interesting, as it shows that Goldberg's chosen hairstyle may be considered as making specific statements about the actor's sense of self and society. Moreover, she is not only bucking the trend of standard Hollywood beauty, she is pushing against the Hollywood corporate structure. Like Doyle, Rogers and the seven FedEx couriers, Goldberg demanded the right to work—to do her job while also being true to herself. By choosing to maintain the dreadlocked style, she asserts her right to freedom of expression. She also symbolically sidesteps the long, straight hair controversy among black women; for though her locks are long, they maintain their natural texture.

Scene 7, "Straight & Nappy," in Spike Lee's *School Daze* (1988) dramatizes class differences among women of African descent enrolled in a fictional all-women's historically black college in the American South. In that scene, "Wannabees" (black women with obvious caucasian features, wearing long, flowing hair; subdued grey leggings; and coordinating, fitted tops; and dancing in a hybrid classical/modern style) face-off against "Zigaboos": black women with primarily African features, who wear shorter, thick, sometimes wild, hair; and loud, streetwise clothing (bright red, ill-fitting tops, red leggings and red shoes). Accentuating the Zigaboos' status are their signature dance moves, ranging from the jitterbug of Black Harlem, to traditional West African movements. According to the Zigaboos, the Wannabees "want to be" white; the Wannabees beg to differ, however, saying that the Zigaboos are jealous of their caucasian-influenced beauty. Adding insult to injury, at one point in the dance, which functions as a kind of duel à la *West Side Story* (1961), the Wannabees taunt the Zigaboos by using Aunt Jemima masks; the Zigaboos respond by mocking the Wannabees by wearing masks of Judy Garland as Dorothy in *The Wizard of Oz* (1939). Then members of the two groups yell, screech, pull each other's hair and boldly attempt to topple each other.

The setting of "Straight & Nappy" is the fictional Madame Re-Re's Beauty Salon. The term "Re-Re" may be Spike Lee's way of tacitly mentioning the fact that hairstyles, like attitudes, must be redone, while also giving a nod to the Queen of Soul, Aretha Franklin (fondly called, "Re-Re"), and her signature song, "Respect." Throughout the film, the men from a neighboring fictional all-men's historically black college are caught in the middle. Some wish to associate only with Wannabees; some prefer Zigaboos. Either way, it is clear that the Wannabees, with the long, flowing hair, are considered the most desirable.

Hair length and texture are also issues in black American novels; take Zora Neale Hurston's *Their Eyes Were Watching God* (1937), in which the lead character, Janie, is considered a kind of prize, largely due to her Caucasian features, including a "great rope of black hair swinging to her waist and unraveling in the wind like a plume" (Hurston 11). Having stolen the prize from Janie's first husband, the crude farmer Logan Killicks, Janie's second husband, Jody, is so jealous of her beauty and how it captivates other men, that he orders Janie to bind her hair with a kerchief. This act she dutifully performs, for decades, in the small Florida town for which Jody serves as the mayor and owner/manager of the general store. Upon his death, however, Janie literally "lets her hair down," being true to herself: she tears "off the kerchief from her head and let[s] down her plentiful hair. The weight, the length, the glory [is] there" (Hurston 135). Janie's third and final husband, Tea Cake, the love of her life, tells her that he cannot sleep for want of combing her hair: "I ain't been sleepin' so good for more'n uh week cause Ah been wishin' so bad tuh git mah hands in yo' hair. It's so pretty. It feels hus' lak underneath uh dove's wing next to mah face" (157). Tea Cake's jealousy of Janie is stirred when he mistakenly assumes that, because she has Caucasian features, she would prefer an upper-class Black mate, rather than a bluesman and gambler, such as himself. Upon returning from a few days of carousing with "railroad hands an dey womenfolks," Tea Cake tells her, "Befo' us got married Ah made up mah mind not tuh let you see no commonness in me.... Taint mah notion tuh drag *you* down wid me." Janie responds, "Looka heah, Tea Cake, if you ever go off from me and have a good time lak dat and then come back heah telling me how nice Ah is, Ah specks tuh kill you dead. You heah me?" (186). Here, Janie breaks the stereotype of the exotic, haughty, upper-class mixed-race woman.

The theme of hair texture in relation to social class also makes its way into late twentieth-century Black American literature. Benilde Little's *Good Hair* (1996) tells the story of Alice Andrews, a black, Newark-based reporter, who encounters extreme class consciousness when she enters the world of the Black elite in Manhattan. A hallmark of one's breeding, in this society, is women's hair: its texture, form and presentation. At one point in the novel, Andrews attends the wedding of Laura, who, according to social standards, reaches a state of "Nirvana" (Little 101), because, instead of marrying the typical government employee "GS-12 or GS-13" (101), she marries Dr. Jeffrey Doran. Andrews, the narrator, explains: "In many Black families, being a doctor, or marrying one, is what becoming a priest is in Italian families. It's as good as it gets" (101). After exchanging pleasantries with fellow guests, Andrews retreats to the ladies' room, only to find, much to her chagrin, that her hair is not up to code:

> I sat in front of a mirror.... I looked at my hair, which was big and bushy. I looked not only as though I were from out of town, in this crowd, I seemed to be from outer space. No one here would let their hair "go back" like this. I thought it looked kinda good, but two of the bridesmaids in pink who stood in front of the mirror next to me, with perms so straight they were afraid to revert [return to their natural state], looked at me as though I had asked for spare change [101].

Among the black upper-class, Alice Andrews finds that she is merely in it, but not of it. That Benilde Little's novel became a 1996 Blackboard Bestseller (PBA.org) speaks volumes about black women's preoccupation with their hair and related class issues.

Chris Rock's documentary *Good Hair* (2009) questions Black American preoccupation with hair texture and length. While Rock creatively weaves good humor throughout the film, he also shows that the drastic measures which some take to try to achieve "good hair" are no laughing matter. According to Rock, his young daughter Zahra's preoccupation with her hair encouraged him to do the project; when she asked him why she lacked "good hair," he changed the topic of discussion, so as not to overreact (Marsh 62). In addition to surveying viewpoints of the famous (including Raven-Symoné, star of Disney's *That's So Raven*, who admits to using an East Indian hair weave), Rock speaks on camera with a white American chemist who gives a scientific demonstration, complete with protective goggles and gloves, regarding the dangers of sodium hydroxide, the basis of many hair relaxers. In Scene 3, "Relaxers," the chemist's demonstration shows that only a few drops sodium hydroxide easily eats through the layers of a large, raw chicken breast; within four hours, the chemical completely devours an aluminum soda can. When Rock tells the chemist that some Black Americans put sodium hydroxide on their hair, the chemist openly questions why anyone would do such a thing. When Rock explains that some Black women use such chemicals to straighten their hair (and, the film shows, a few even subject toddlers to such practices, in the hopes of training the hair to grow straight), the chemist responds with great concern. He goes on to describe the dangers, including chemical burns on the scalp, causing bald patches and permanent tissue damage at the molecular level; and the damaging effect of caustic fumes upon sensitive lung tissue. In Scene 8, "Cash," Rock interviews vendors of long, straight, imported East Indian hair, learning of the lucrative nature of their business. Scene 9, "Tonsure," shows Rock traveling to India, where he learns about the extreme lengths to which hair traders go in order to obtain and import the best quality, longest Asian hair. (In this instance, the traders go to religious temples to collect hundreds of pounds of hair, which is sacrificed to the gods, as part of a tradition called "Tonsure.") By the time Scene 11, "Los Angeles," is shown, the notion strikes Rock that he, too, can make scads of cash — by cornering an as-yet untapped market for unprocessed black hair. Walking up and down a busy city sidewalk, with handfuls of bushy black hair, he tries to "hawk" the hair, to no avail. Rock's humorous approach to opening and encouraging serious dialogue concerning the politics of black hair is reminiscent of Goldberg's work.

Long before Spike Lee's film, Benilda Little's novel, and Chris Rock's documentary, Goldberg's original fictional character, the "Girl with the Long, Blonde Hair," purposely reminded everyone how the Cinderella story belongs to every American. In Chapter 5, "Blonde Hair" in *Whoopi Goldberg: Direct from Broadway* (1985) (included in *Whoopi Goldberg: Back to Broadway — 20th Anniversary Edition*), Goldberg embodies a fictional, poor, overgrown, seven-year-old Black girl who lives near a nuclear reactor (hence her overly large size, in relation to her age); the girl dreams of being white, with blonde hair and blue eyes. Placing a white, long-sleeved shirt atop her head, the girl swings her "hair," showing how she can style it into a "ponytail," and says that she no longer wishes to be Black, since her mother bears no resemblance to television actresses and personalities (Ch. 5). The little girl also mentions how she tried to bleach herself white by bathing in Clorox; instead of becoming white, however, she "got burned" (Ch. 5), at which the audience nervously laughs — not so much at the child's predicament, but at her immediate, immature response thereto.

The mentioning of Clorox as a means to "bleach white" is part of Black American vernacular and experience, dating at least to the late 19th century. "Black was not beautiful, and those whose skin was light enough to 'pass' often attempted to do so. In the United States, there was an explosion of hair straightening and skin lightening among African Americans at the turn of the century" (Gilman 111). Nor is such a tactic limited to black Americans; Gerald Sider's "Struggles for History among a Native American People" documents that a Lumbee Indian, identified only as "M," described how she and some of her childhood friends "would 'steal' Clorox ... from her grandmother's laundry supplies to put in the bathwater, trying to lighten their skin" (Sider and Smith 71). Like Toni Morrison's *The Bluest Eye* (1970), in which the character Pecola Breedlove detests her black skin, and declares that she wants blue eyes, Goldberg's development of the "Girl with the Long Blonde Hair" (to borrow Morrison's description of the development of *The Bluest Eye*) "focused ... on how something as grotesque as the demonization of an entire race could take root inside the most delicate member of society: a child; the most vulnerable member: a female" (Morrison 210). For a time, Goldberg herself wore blue-colored contact lenses, but, she says, she did so for no other reason than fashion; she also says that she is unfairly targeted for having done so, because other entertainers, such as Cher and Tina Turner, who change their eye color and hair texture, respectively, are not called sellouts (Rensin 57). One person who openly criticized Goldberg's use of blue contact lenses is film director Spike Lee, who, having read Morrison's novel, commented that black people with blue eyes have an "unnatural" look; he then posed a rhetorical question concerning Goldberg's fashion choice: "What is wrong with your God-given eyes?" (Lee 57–58). Regardless of such criticism, Goldberg continues to pave her own way, on her own terms.

Like Morrison's Pecola Breedlove, Goldberg's "Girl with the Long Blonde Hair" teaches the audience a lesson about being true to oneself. While perhaps initially addressing black audiences with her skit, she is speaking to *all* people. She will not acquiesce to the standards of television and Hollywood beauty; instead, through her art and her self, she will force the media and American society to recognize her as she is. True to her American roots, Goldberg's fictional character has dreams and a determination to pursue happiness; yet, such dreams are rooted in a kind of double fantasy: the girl never will be white, nor are the television images that she extols real. In the fairy tale, Cinderella escapes the drudgery of housework, a cruel stepmother, and cruel step-sisters, to "step" into her own glass slipper and claim the prince as her prize. No such prize awaits Goldberg's tragicomic character, however. The tragedy and irony of the "Girl with the Long Blonde Hair" is that she does not appreciate her own natural beauty and charm; instead, she forfeits self-acceptance for a fantasy. Her monologue encourages audience members to sympathize with the character, and, hopefully, look beyond limited, confused and confusing social norms to find true beauty.

> For Black women, skin color is ... central to identity. Despite more than twenty years of "Black is beautiful" rhetoric, negative attitudes about women with dark skin persist. In a recent study at DePaul University in Chicago, Midge Wilson and two of her students, Lisa Razzano and Sherry Salmons, selected almost eighty people, evenly divided between males and females, Blacks and Whites, and asked them to look at photos of Black women and characterize their impressions of each. Regardless of how the individual woman's attractiveness (prejudged to be high or low), the study participants nearly always rated the dark-skinned women as less successful, less happy in love, less popular, less physically attractive, less physically and emotionally healthy, and less intelligent than their light-skinned counterparts. The only quality in which the dark-skinned females were *not* rated lower was sense of humor, a phenomenon they labeled the "Whoopi Goldberg effect" [Russell et al. 67–68].

The fact that the study specifically mentions Goldberg as a symbol of the so-called "phenomenon" is evidence of her influence upon popular culture. Beyond the influence of her deep, brown skin tone is her dreadlocked hair.

> Dreadlocking perhaps carries a more radical political connotation than any other hairstyle. Yet all it entails is growing curly hair out to the point where it 'locks,' the stage at which dreadlocks become permanent and cannot be changed without cutting. Few Whites have hair curly enough to grow into "dreads"; with rare exceptions, the style is uniquely Black. Traditionally, dreadlocks have been associated with the Rastafarians of Jamaica, and American men with dreadlocks are usually musicians or members of the counterculture. However, an increasing number of American Black women are adopting the style. They are writers and performers, like Alice Walker and Whoopi Goldberg, or professors, journalists and social workers — not exactly corporate types, but not members of a counterculture, either [Russell et al. 87].

As independent contractors, black women working in the aforementioned professions have more latitude than the average American worker, to experiment with hairstyles and make individual style choices within and for the workplace.

In the lyrical essay, "In the Kitchen," Jewelle Gomez muses on the symbol of the "kitchen" (the euphemism for the naturally tightly curled hair at the nape of the neck, which, like an actual kitchen, is often hidden and requires straightening) among black women. Says Gomez, "It was decades before I believed that those tender naps were not an insult to beauty but a natural part of it" (Gomez 257). Gomez mentions the "pressure created by unrelieved images of" popular Black American actors, singers and the professional classes, which encourage Black American women to conform to Eurocentric concepts of beauty (263). She counterbalances such information by listing the names of a few prominent Black Americans who have determined their own standards of beauty, including natural hairstyles: "I never thought

I'd live to see movie stars and notables like Rosalind Cash, Toni Morrison, Goldberg, or Alfre Woodard on public stages wearing naturals and dreadlocks, but I have" (263). Goldberg is well aware of her influence upon black women's fashion. Having admired the dreadlocked mane of actress Rosalind Cash, she decided to try the hairstyle. Says Goldberg, "I was wearing my hair a little natural and I used to braid it. And then one day ... I just got tired and I said, '...I'm never taking these braids out.' But for so long my particular package was alien to everybody. Today when I see dreads, braids, plum lipstick and women wearing flats and sneakers, I know part of that is because of me" (Campbell 102). She describes her personal fashion style as "low-maintenance" (102).

By extension, and not surprisingly, Goldberg infuses hair critique into many of her Hollywood film characters. Her very presence in such films as made black hair an issue; she says that black audiences bluntly asked her why she wore dreadlocks, saying to her, "Why are you misrepresenting us?" (A&E Chap. 5). She also mentioned how her hair and general casual attire caught fire from both blacks and whites. On the one hand, she says, she was called a "pickaninny" (Chap. 5); on the other, behind-the-scenes discussions included such talk as, "When we shoot the movie, what are we going to do with this?" "This" meant her hair, which Goldberg says people would handle as if undesirable and practically untouchable (Chap. 5). Not surprisingly, directors and cosmetologists often devised last-minute work-arounds for her hair; for on more than one occasion, she replaced white actors in title roles, including Shelley Long in *Jumpin' Jack Flash* (1986); Cher in *Fatal Beauty* (1987); and Bruce Willis in *Burglar* (1987) (Chap. 4).

Hair texture is also an issue in Hollywood films featuring majority-black casts. In Scene 4, "Married to Mister," in *The Color Purple* (1985), young Celie (Desreta Jackson) attempts to comb her stepchild's unruly hair while the girl screams in pain. Celie, visibly disgusted by the fact that Mister (Danny Glover) has neglected the child, pointedly asks him to tell her when someone actually had taken the time to comb the girl's tangled, matted hair. Mister responds by telling her to quiet the child. Celie defiantly replies that the girl is in pain. Mister responds with a swift, hard backhanded slap across young Celie's face. Trembling and sobbing, she continues combing the girl's hair with one hand, while muffling the girl's screams with the other. In contrast to the uncombed hair of the unkempt child and her own dull, dusty-looking hair are the heavy, shiny, swinging plaits of her beautiful younger sister, Nettie. Desreta Jackson's sensitive portrayal of young Celie sets the tone for Whoopi Goldberg's portrayal of the adult Celie, who is deemed "ugly," not only because of her deep brown skin tone, but also because of her odd smile and style-less hair.

In another film, making a nod to the 1970s, Goldberg, as the fictional

Ethel Washington Rue Owens in *Jackie's Back!* (1999) covers her dreadlocks with a large, black human hair afro-wig, complete with a white bandana, to match her nurse's outfit. In *Good Fences* (2003), she again covers her dreadlocks with a human hair wig, this time styled in relaxed, mid-length curls, to bring to life the fictional lead character, Mabel Spader, an upper-middle-class black woman who drowns her loneliness in alcohol and pills, while living "the good life" in the suburbs.

The politics of black hair even have meaning in outer space. While portraying Guinan, in *Star Trek: The Next Generation* (28 episodes, 1988–1993) (*Star Trek*), Goldberg's dreadlocked hair generally was covered in a futuristic polyester turban or fez. (Infrequently, her full dreadlocks can be seen in brief scenes while occupying Guinan's quarters aboard ship — perhaps the *Star Trek* powers-that-be perceived that dreadlocks were too "locked" within, or anchored to, a specific time and place, to make them part of Guinan's general aboard-ship attire.) Nevertheless, her example paved the way for other Black American actors to openly showcase dreadlocks in other science fiction television shows. For example, for 68 episodes (2000–2003), Keith Hamilton Cobb played the Tyr Anasazi in Gene Roddenberry's *Andromeda*. On that television show, which starred Kevin Sorbo as Captain Dylan Hunt, the tall, strapping Cobb sported a full head of dreadlocks as part of his fictional character's everyday attire. Malcolm-Jamal Warner, playing the role of Kurdy, wore a dreadlocked mane in 34 episodes of the post-apocalyptic television show *Jeremiah* (2002–2004). And by the time *Stargate Atlantis* hit television airwaves, Jason Momoa, playing Ronon Dex, sported full dreadlocks for 78 episodes (2005–2009). While Goldberg paved the way for dreadlocks on television shows depicting scenes from 20th-century earth, and only tangentially in the *Star Trek* universe, younger men eventually are allowed to do so, on a full-time basis, in American television's science fiction worlds.

Nor are Goldberg's references to her hair always in jest. For example, her natural hair is exquisitely coiffed, taking the form of a crown of sorts, when she accepted her Oscar for Best Supporting Actress in 1991; similarly, her natural hairstyles are ornately gorgeous in *Clara's Heart* (1988) and *Made in America* (1993). In *The Long Walk Home* (1990), however, she wears a high-quality, human-hair wig, pressed to create soft curls. Goldberg's decision to be "true to her roots," so to speak, should not be taken lightly. Early photos of a young Caryn Johnson included in A&E's *Biography: Whoopi Goldberg* (2008), show that the youngster's hair had been straightened, perhaps with a hot comb, and then "bumped" under, to create soft curls.

Nor was her work in cosmetology limited to working on the living. Goldberg's formal training in cosmetology came in handy during her stint in preparing embalmed corpses for funerals. Such work likely entailed not only applying makeup to the skin and nails, but also cutting and styling natural hair, as well as styling and setting wigs, hats, and the like. Such an experience made her quite adept at working with costumes and makeup. The actor jokes that one of the best aspects of such a job is that it paid well; and there were other bonuses: "You make your own hours, you were left to yourself pretty much, and the customer rarely talked back." On balance, and in all seriousness, she explains that death renders race irrelevant; moreover, "It was a kind of privilege to make [the deceased] look their best for the friends and families" (JPC, "What Stars Did" 61).

During the 1970s and 1980s, considerable controversy erupted concerning black women, especially where the workplace was concerned. *Essence Magazine*, which had for years billed itself as "The Magazine for Today's Black Woman," served as a major proving ground for Black women's hairstyles in the neighborhoods and beyond. Also during the 1970s and 1980s, such magazines as *Sophisticates' Black Hair: Styles and Care Guide* and *Blac-Tress* highlighted black hair artistry and pushed the boundaries of accepted hairstyles for the workforce. In 1989, even Aunt Jemima got a makeover. According to *Jet*, "The 'new' Aunt Jemima is trading her headband for soft, curly, gray-streaked hair and pearl earrings" (JPC, "Aunt Jemima" 15). Prior to that time, Aunt Jemima wore a checkered headkerchief (which revealed very little hair, around the edges); no jewelry; and a plain, white frock. The "new" Aunt Jemima, instead of rolling out of bed to make pancakes, is instead, preparing pancakes for the family, ostensibly as they prepare to go to church. Either way, she still shares the same sunny smile, with the same tilt of the head. Such a change to that image of an icon of the Quaker Oats Company showed that even major corporations were questioning the presentation of black women's hair. By choosing to remain true to her roots, Whoopi set new standards for black women's acceptance in Hollywood, both behind-the-scenes as well as in front of the camera. For example, she prides herself on being *au naturel* for her daily appearances on ABC's *The View*: "It takes six minutes for makeup.... I don't have to do the makeup, the eyelashes, and the hair. I am not the glam queen.... It's OK, because it's just Whoopi" (Waldron 58). Goldberg's philosophy echoes that of many working women, who take care of such basics as bathing and grooming and let their work-related skills, diligence and attention to detail be the focus of their day-to-day workplace experience.

Observant viewers of film credits note that Goldberg often has her own (hair)stylists on-set; in addition, she keeps her cosmetology skills fresh by working behind-the-scenes. For example, she is credited as hair stylist for the 2001 documentary film, *Golden Dreams*, concerning the cultural development and diversity of California. She also narrated the film, playing the role of Calafia, Queen of California.

Reporting for *The Advocate*, Anne Stockwell asks Goldberg to compare her experience of revisiting some of her original Broadway characters and skits to her original presentation of two decades earlier. She responded, "Well, I'm older, and so I have to keep the energy level up. It's kind of a physical show, and for an hour and a half I'm talkin' and movin' and groovin' and pontificating. Sometimes I think I'm too ... old for this!"

Critic William Stevenson was less than generous when reviewing Goldberg's 20th anniversary special, *Whoopi Goldberg: Back to Broadway* (2005):

> Goldberg has plenty of attitude, but her semi-improvised material is more tacky than witty. The second character she does is a new one named Lurleen. She's a sweet, likable Southerner, but in this section Goldberg stoops to bathroom humor in search of easy laughs. Lurleen talks about menopause, Depends [adult diapers] and erectile dysfunction. She recalls life in the '50s, '60s and '70s based on — I kid you not–what kind of sanitary napkin she was wearing at the time. She says "pudendum" [the external genital organs] frequently and claims that men check each other out at urinals. It's crass, juvenile and generally not amusing [Stevenson, 2005].

Stevenson takes her wit and craft out of context; not surprisingly, he is unable to reconcile Goldberg's current public image with her early, far-ranging, experimental acting. His criticism of the actor's use of bathroom humor misses the fact that, in her first HBO special, she described a scene in which she was sitting upon a toilet, pontificating about life and smoking a cigarette, while being interviewed.

Stevenson's misunderstanding reminds us that Goldberg has acted for so long that she now has three overlapping generations of fans. Her first fans are the Baby Boomers — her original fans, dating to the 1970s, who are fully aware of her live stage training and presence. Generation X fans are those she gained during the 1980s–1990s, largely through cable television specials; *Star Trek: The Next Generation*; *The Hollywood Squares* game show; and a string of feature films. Of that era, Goldberg quips, "There should be a Whoopi Channel, because every time I turn the TV on, one of my movies or some movie I don't even remember making is on" (JPC, "Whoopi Goldberg Says" 65). Generation Y fans consist of children and tweens (children between the ages of 9 and 12) who know her as a regular *Sesame Street* guest, movie actor and author of children's books. She addresses the first two sets of fans through her most recent work on *The View*. Far more than a typical televised anniversary special, *Whoopi Goldberg: Back to Broadway* is best appreciated as a reunion of Goldberg with her original audience and a reunion of an artist with her craft. Most importantly, *Whoopi: Back to Broadway* serves as a bridge between past and present, paving the way for future actors.

Making a nod toward women's general attitudes about menstruation and Eve Ensler's *The Vagina Monologues*, Goldberg's *Back to Broadway* offers a song and dance to the tune of "Waltzing Matilda," which she calls, "Balding Pudenda." She also rhetorically asks why male "menopause" (as evidenced by upbeat television commercials regarding prescription medications to treat erectile dysfunction) is projected as a positive experience to be effectively counteracted with medication; while women's menopause is considered a negative experience. In Chapter 7, "Women's Club," she describes how women's pains and progresses can be chronicled through the varieties of feminine hygiene products available to multiple generations of menstruating women.

Goldberg's nod to *The Vagina Monologues* is the humorous opposite of Ensler's skit, "Angry Vagina." Ensler declares war against anyone who or anything that cannot accept her vagina as it is: "That's what they're doing — trying to clean it up, make it smell like bathroom spray or a garden.... If my vagina could talk, it would talk about itself like me; it would talk about other vaginas; it would do vagina impressions" (Ensler 72–73). Instead of reflecting anger, however, Goldberg "dances" (with) her vagina, singing along with it and composing special lyrics for the occasion.

Goldberg is not alone when it comes to waxing eloquent on the subject. Rita Dove's famous poem, "After Reading Mickey in the Night Kitchen for the Third Time Before Bed" describes how the poet explains to her young daughter "what the wrinkled string means/between my legs" — the string connected to the tampon placed within her body. The narrator of the poem uses that experience as a teachable moment, connecting daughter and mother. Dove's reading of the poem during her installation as National Poet Laureate at The Library of Congress empowered the author and her audience. After receiving permission from her ten-year-old daughter to share the poem with the public, Dove has made a commitment to read it every time she gives a speech, regardless of the occasion. "But I did have a moment," says Dove, "[when] I thought, 'I am at the Library of Congress ... and The Great Hall' and I thought, 'No, I've done it before and I will do it here.' And it was very hard to do" (Cavalieri).

With her concept of the "Balding Pudenda," Goldberg also applies and extends Eve Ensler's Vagina Warriors concept. According to Ensler, Vagina Warriors are educators and "citizens of the world" who "cherish humanity over nationhood"; they are "directed by vision" and are "not ruled by ideology"; they "love to dance" and "have a wicked sense of humor" (Ensler 5). She formally defines "Vagina Warrior" as "a woman or man committed to or working toward ending violence against women and girls" (Ensler 136). This aptly describes Goldberg, whose story of the "Balding Pudenda" teaches audiences to accept themselves and work to build bridges of understanding across generations and around the world. (Her humorous openness in discussing feminine hygiene products likely led to her recent stint as national spokesperson for Poise Pads.)

Goldberg's reasoning for eliminating the "Girl with the Long Blonde

Hair" from her most recent Broadway show has as much to do with the times as her determination to continue pushing the boundaries of her craft. "Queen Latifah exists." she explains. "Regina King exists. There are so many visual reminders that we Black women come in infinite varieties" (Edwards).

Having won an Oscar for Best Supporting Actress in 1991 for her role as Oda Mae Brown in *Ghost*, and given her background in live theater, Goldberg successfully hosted the Oscars four times: 1994, 1996, 1999 and 2002. During the 2008 Oscars, she was included in the televised Best Actress montage; nevertheless, her name and likeness were omitted from a seven-minute montage honoring past Oscar Awards hosts. Said a tearful Goldberg during a live broadcast of *The View*, "Undoubtedly I pissed somebody off yet again.... You know what, I don't — I don't know" (Serpe). Her colleagues on *The View* supported her with comforting words, which she initially "tried to laugh off," but then became "overwhelmed" to the point of tears, thanking each of her colleagues with a sisterly kiss (Serpe). The montage had also omitted former Oscar host Steve Martin, among others (Serpe). According to Oscar awards show producer Gil Cates, "No harm was intended, and I feel very, very badly that she [Goldberg] was left out" (Silverman). Cates personally called her to offer his apologies for the gaffe, which she accepted (JPC, "Whoopi Goldberg Accepts" 32). Cates's omission baffles longtime Oscar viewers and Goldberg fans.

During the 1999 Oscars Goldberg appeared as Queen Elizabeth I, complete with white powder foundation, a mountainous decorated wig, a humongous ruffle neckpiece and a record-setting array of genuine jewels. During her performance, she alternately described herself as "the African Queen" and "the last twentieth-century fox" (JPC, "Whoopi Goldberg Delights" 55–56). *Jet Magazine* may have expressed it best: "Whoopi Goldberg shocked, surprised and consistently entertained the estimated worldwide audience of one billion people who tuned in and watched as she hosted the 71st Annual Academy Awards telecast in Los Angeles" (55). Moreover, "Goldberg, who was also the host that year, broke the record for wearing the most diamonds when she wore $41 million of Harry Winston jewels, the most worn by any person at the Oscars. Her collection included various pieces, including a 107-carat white diamond ring worth $15 million" (Mazgan). Afterward, "The costume, from the private collection of Bob Mackey, sold at auction for $22,800 by Christies Auction House, Tuesday, Nov. 22, 2005, in New York" (Associated Press). Each time Goldberg hosted the awards ceremonies, she entered the forum in a different, wholly unexpected get-up; yet none, however clever, would ever top that of her queenly debut.

On June 15, 2008, Goldberg hosted the Tony Awards, at Radio City Music Hall, under multiple, funny guises, including Sebastian, the red crab from Disney's *The Little Mermaid*. During that show, in fact, the host was "popping into numbers from various musicals — 'The Phantom of the Opera,' 'Spamalot,' 'A Chorus Line,' 'Spring Awakening' — to mildly amusing effect. She also flew in as Mary Poppins ('Yeah, I can watch the kids, but I won't be cleaning your house'). She was funnier taking a backhanded swipe at Clarence Thomas ('forgetting' that Thurgood Marshall, now the subject of a one-man show starring Laurence Fishburne, was not the only African American Supreme Court justice)" (Lloyd). Clearly, her sense of irony and playfulness remain sharp.

In 2001, Goldberg's wry sense of humor was awarded the Mark Twain Humor Prize. Previous awardees include Richard Pryor, Jonathan Winters and Carl Reiner (Warren). As the fourth recipient of the award, she became the first woman to gain the coveted prize; thus far, Lily Tomlin, honored in 2003, is the only other woman to have received the award. This is not surprising as Goldberg has been favorably compared to Tomlin. Five years earlier, Tomlin received her 1985 Broadway show, *The Search for Signs of Intelligent Life in the Universe*, which "ran for six months, about half as long as the original production" (Zinoman). Journalist Jason Zinoman calls Tomlin an "actress and performance artist," a phrase which also applies to Goldberg. She explains: "People think they have to write comedy for me — and I'm not a comedienne. I do not do stand-up" (Rensin 154). In fact, when she began making Hollywood films, she says, "producers wanted me to be the female answer to Eddie Murphy" (Rensin 57–58). The very fact that Goldberg became the first woman awarded the Mark Twain Humor Prize is evidence of her status as satirist; for Twain, though possessing ribald wit, was never mistaken for a comedian; he was, instead, recognized, during his lifetime and beyond, a master of words; an authentic American Southerner and a quintessential satirist. Goldberg is certainly colorful with language.

Despite her status as a star, Goldberg does not always have to be center stage. She has shown considerable interest as a producer of Broadway shows, such as the planned revival of Ntozake Shange's choreopoem, *For Colored Girls Who Have Considered Suicide When the Rainbow Is Enuf* (1975). "Goldberg has been involved in productions of *Thoroughly Modern Millie* (which earned her a Tony Award), her own *Whoopi…. The 20th Anniversary* and a revival of August Wilson's *Ma Rainey's Black Bottom*" (Associated Press "India.Arie").

That Goldberg appreciates the artistry and messages of India.Arie is understandable; singer-songwriter India.Arie is known for her natural beauty, emphasizing traditional African features, as well as her self-affirming songs, "Brown Skin" and "Video," from her debut Motown CD, *Acoustic Soul* (2001). "Brown Skin" describes a woman who loves her own, as well as her lover's, deep skin tones; "Video" concerns a woman's holistic response to social pressures of the video age: despite the forged video images of women, she remains confident in her natural beauty and unconcerned with material wealth. Goldberg willingly agreed to produce Shange's *For Colored Girls* ... since it tackles some of the most vexing social problems faced by black women. Shange's "colored girls" comprise a rainbow of American women of African descent, working their way through life's difficulties to find themselves — mirrors of some of the very challenges which she faced and is dedicated to eradicating. The Broadway revival of the show was scheduled to take place at the Circle in the Square Theatre on August 19, 2008 (Hetrick). *Essence Magazine* heralded the revival as a showcase not only for a timeless story of women's creativity and survival but also "A-list talent, including ... director Shirley Jo Finney (in her Broadway debut) at the helm, Tony Award-winner Hinton Battle providing choreography and Shange herself, who updated the text" (Bass). Despite Whoopi Goldberg's "pull[ing] out all the stops" (Bass) to make the show a success, however, the "revival was canceled when a major investor withdrew from the production" (Johnson). The organic nature of *For Colored Girls* ... is notable not only for its fierce authenticity, but also because it is reminiscent of the process by which Goldberg, artist and activist, came to be.

In the introduction to *For Colored Girls, Who Have Considered Suicide/ When the Rainbow/Is Enuf*, Shange explains how the characters and stories emerged from her experimental works in modern dance and jazz, near Berkeley, California, in December 1974. She mentions how the poetry gave way to dance, which formed a new kind of (self-) expression, which then required a new and different accompaniment to accentuate a growing, articulated sense of self. Shange says that accepting her African physical traits also enabled her to accentuate a growing sense of self. Shange says that this also enabled her to articulate herself as an artist (Shange xi). The stages of the choreopoem's development were as widely varied as the stage productions and characters themselves. Shange mentions how physical spaces with which she had become familiar became performance spaces: "Women's Studies Departments, bars, cafes & poetry centers" (Shange xiii). Each of the spaces and related, shifting audiences provided an opportunity for revisiting and revising Shange's growing list of colorful characters: the lady in brown; the lady in yellow; the lady in purple; the lady in red; the lady in green; the lady in blue; and the lady in orange (Shange 5).

Each of the women exists on the fringes of society, and each nevertheless alternately shares and takes center stage while telling her story. The lady in brown declares her love of Haitian revolutionary Toussaint L'Overture, because, despite her St. Louis "integrated home/integrated street/integrated school ... 1955 waz not a good year for lil blk girls" (Shange 27). The lady in yellow mentions losing her virginity in a Buick after becoming drunk at a party; thereafter, she associates dancing with sex. The lady in purple transforms herself into the mulatto Creole "Sechita" of the Mississippi Delta, a carnival stage performer who embodies a mélange of exotic sensualities tied to New Orleans voodoo (Shange 23–24). The lady in red expresses her (out)rage at being ignored by a man whom she doggedly pursues, hoping that he will care about her. Showing her blind dedication to a man who cares nothing for her, she describes how she has offered him houseplants, poems, and handmade cards, all to no avail. Reaching the end of her patience with this one-sided affair, she decidedly she tells the man that she has been watering his houseplant since the day they met, and that from here on in he can do it (Shange 14). The lady in green embodies many of the aspirations of Shange herself. Declaring that someone has stolen her "stuff" (the double-entendre here refers to her sexuality, true/suppressed personality and material goods), and that she is the "sole and rightful owner of all that is her(s) (Shange 50). The lady in blue, who interjects her story with bits of Spanish and salsa riffs, mentions how she and her boyfriend considered themselves Puerto Rican, until they realized that they were of mixed-race ancestry (Shange 11). Her experiences in salsa clubs, as well as through dance and blues and jazz music, provide an outlet for her vitality as an African-based person. The lady in blue claims that the spirits of salsa greats Willie Colón and Célia Cruz, as well as blues/jazz artists Archie Shepp and Billie Holiday, are being channeled through her intense experience of dance (Shange 13). Later in the story, the lady in blue mentions her sense of shame for being pregnant out of wedlock, and the jarring experience of an abortion (Shange 22). The lady in blue concludes that her own sense of inadequacy prevented her from telling anyone about the pregnancy; hence she faced the realities and agonies of the pregnancy and the abortion alone (Shange 23). The lady in orange tries desperately not to be the stereotypical bitch, and chastises herself for her frustrations and sorrows, swallowing such for so long that both burst forth as a bold confession in the form of a dirge (Shange 43).

The story ends with the "colored girls" in chorus, telling the story of Crystal, an abused woman who gives birth to a child, Kwame. Kwame's father, Beau Willie, a barely literate gypsy cab driver and Vietnam veteran suffering from post-traumatic stress disorder, purposefully drops the child out of a fifth-floor apartment window, because delicate, hardened Crystal will not marry him. Articulating Crystal's pain, the "colored girls" band together, creating a kind of rainbow, vowing to remain true to themselves.

Like Goldberg, Ntozake Shange expressed her growing sense of self through a renaming process: "Ntozake Shange was born Paulette Williams in Trenton, New Jersey, on October 18, 1948. In 1971 she changed her name to Ntozake Shange which means 'she who comes with her own things' and 'she who walks like a lion' in Xhosa, the Zulu language" (Women of Color).

10. Returning to Her Roots

Also, Shange is determined to use her art, not only as a medium for self-exploration and self-expression, but also to transform society. Both Shange and Goldberg are Baby Boomers; both came of age as artists working in the San Francisco area. For these reasons and more, it makes sense that Goldberg would choose to produce Shange's choreopoem, for a new audience, starring the next generation of artists.

Undaunted by the premature cancellation of the Broadway revival of *For Colored Girls*, Goldberg acted in Tyler Perry's major motion picture adaptation of the same title, set in New York, bringing to light a new fictional character: Alice/White. Goldberg was in good company, for the film boasted other high-profile thespians, including Janet Jackson (Jo/Red), Thandie Newton (Tangie/Orange), Phylicia Rashad (Gilda), Anika Noni Rose (Yasmine/Yellow), Loretta Devine (Juanita/Green), Kimberly Elise (Crystal/Brown), Kerry Washington (Kelly/Blue) and Tessa Thompson (Nyla/Purple).

Goldberg's character, Alice/White, functions as the neighborhood's self-styled evangelist, preaching against the evils of the city. Meanwhile, her daughters Tangie and Nyla run amok: the eldest because she can, and the youngest because she gets caught in a web of sexual activity that she mistakes for love. Tangie, a bartender by trade, freely gives of her body to men, in defiance of how "good girls" should behave; yet, when the men, mistakenly thinking that she is a whore, offer to pay her for her services, she casts them out, only to take on other temporary sexual relationships as a short-lived remedy for chronic emotional pains. Meanwhile, Nyla, a teenager poised to study dance at the college level, and eager to experience love, gets pregnant in the backseat of a car; the shame of the experience drives her further away from her mother and into the den of Rose (aptly portrayed by singer-songwriter Macy Gray), who performs a backroom abortion. (In Scene 8, "College Applications," Nyla lies to her mother and sister, saying that she needs to raise monies for "college applications"; in reality, she is trying to raise $300 for an illegal abortion.)

Scott Bowles, writing for *USA Today*, thoroughly misunderstands the film, describing it as a "lump of coal" among major film offerings during the 2010 Christmas season, and saying that "the title alone could scare off a mainstream audience" (Bowles 2D). Later, Claudia Puig, also writing for *USA Today*, describes Goldberg's performance as Alice/White as "particularly wince-inducing" and "unintentionally comic" (Puig 5D). Puig also writes that Tyler Perry's screenplay "flattens the drama" and "jumble[s]" the timeline of the story, adding, "If it's set in the present day, why would a character have to submit to a gritty back-room abortion?" (Puig 5D). More informed viewers know that such procedures, unfortunately, still take place. Moreover, Nyla's experience of abortion symbolically connects her to her mother and elder sister. For example, in Scene 15, "You Don't Know Me,"

Alice rushes into the local hospital, shocked to find her daughter Nyla there, suffering the effects of the illegally performed abortion. Relieved to know that Nyla will survive, Alice later confronts Tangie in her apartment. Alice also forces Tangie's latest lover onto the street, after which she blames Tangie not only for funding Nyla's abortion, but leaving her sister to face the harshness of the procedure, and its ramifications, alone. Tangie, in turn, blames her mother Alice for forcing her to have her own abortion. Alice defends her actions by saying that at least she was with her for the procedure.

Goldberg's work in this scene is especially noteworthy, as it shows the actor expressing emotions ranging from shock and disbelief, to relief, to horror and disgust, and to shame and anger, serving as fitting counterpoints to the dazed innocence of Nyla and the hot rage of Tangie. This powerful scene reveals that both mother and daughter had been sexually molested by Alice's father. Alice also reveals that her father, hating the "blackness" that Alice's skin tone represents, willingly "gave" her to a caucasian man, so as to ensure that his granddaughters would not be as "black" as she (Scene 15). This scene provides individual and collective catharsis for Alice and Tangie, clearing the way for the women's healing.

As Alice/White, Goldberg symbolically wears white clothing, nearly from head to toe: white turbans, white tunics, long white skirts and white shoes. Yet a quirky aspect of the costuming of the character came from Goldberg herself, who counterbalanced the white with odd, inexpensive socks of many colors (*For Colored Girls*/Special Features/ "Transformation..."/ Scene 56). Another aspect of the quirkiness of Alice is that she outwardly seeks calm, quiet and peaceful surroundings, yet she compulsively hoards objects. Her dingy apartment is overflowing with disarray and refuse, representing the emotional baggage and internal confusion that she still carries. Observant viewers note that, as the story progresses, the color white that Alice wears actually begins to appear increasingly dingy and unkempt, an example of the careful work of costumers, who intentionally used different shades of white clothing to depict the chronic, ironic impurity of Alice's actual life (*For Colored Girls*/Special Features/ "Transformation..."/Scene 56).

At a critical juncture in the film, Alice/White cries out that she has been the victim of two rapes, both at the hands of a white man — hence the very existence of her daughters Tangie and Nyla, both of whom bear distinct Caucasian features. Not surprisingly, Alice's warnings to Tangie and Nyla go unheeded, as Tangie sees Alice as a hypocrite and Nyla is too young and starry-eyed to glean the wisdom of Alice's words. There is no "Wonderland" for this Alice; for Alice/White cannot love herself. Nevertheless, she loves her daughters and desires the best for them. Goldberg's substantive, insistent portrayal of Alice/White brings to mind the Black American saying among mothers: "Do as I say, not as I do."

Goldberg is determined to live a life of substance, and to make an indelible impression upon society through her art and example. Fittingly, in 1995, she added her handprints, footprints, and impressions of her trademark braids to the forecourt of the world-famous Grauman's Chinese Theater in Hollywood. A very private person, she also recognizes the fleeting nature of Hollywood stardom, countering such with concrete expressions of humanity. She counts among her strongest supporters such humanitarian-activists as Harry Belafonte, Sidney Poitier and the late Elizabeth Taylor — Taylor especially encouraged Goldberg to "have something to show" for her efforts (Edwards). Taking Taylor's advice, she has collected works of art and first editions of favorite books. As Goldberg explains, "I have works of beauty I can point to and say, 'This is what happened while I was living my life'" (Edwards).

In Chapter 6, "Elmo's Fur," in *The Best of Elmo* (1994), Elmo sincerely compliments Goldberg's "very pretty brown" skin and "bouncy" hair, likening her hair to "fur." Adopting the stance of the older, wiser friend, she nicely, but firmly, responds that Elmo has fur — "bright, soft, red" fur, but that her dreadlocks are hair. Standing corrected, but still curious about her skin and hair, Elmo then nicely asks her if she would "trade" her skin and hair for his red fur. Goldberg, gently pulling on her skin and hair and shaking her head to show the permanence of her skin and dreadlocks, responds that she likes her hair and skin just fine, and that she would never trade her physical traits for someone else's. Elmo and Goldberg then declare their friendship in the face of obvious physical differences. In that moment, they transcend race and gender. Together, they teach important lessons of (self-)acceptance and community building. Goldberg weaves truth into her multi-layered life while encouraging audiences to (re)claim and proclaim their own heritage.

Works Cited

A&E. *Biography Channel Presents: Whoopi Goldberg*. A&E Television Networks, 2002. DVD.
A&E. *Biography: Whoopi Goldberg*. [2002]. A&E Television Networks, 2007. DVD.
A&E. *Biography: Whoopi Goldberg*. A&E Home Video, 2008. DVD.
ABC. "Hot Topics: Whoopi on Roman Polanski." Originally aired 30 Sept. 2009. Web. 7 Sept. 2010. http://theview.abc.go.com/video/hot-topics-whoopi-roman-polanski.
ABC News Video. "Whoopi: I Didn't Attack Hasselbeck. (View ladies say last week's debate about N word nothing personal)." http://abcnews.go.com/video/playerIndex?id=5417819.
ABC News. "Whoopi on 'Sugar Plum Ballerinas' (Comedienne and author talks about her new children's book series." Interview with Robin Roberts. *Good Morning America* (*GMA*) (5 May 2009). http://abcnews.go.com/GMA/video/whoopi-sugar-plum-ballerinas-7506354.
ABC.com. "Whoopi, Barbara Remember Patrick Swayze." *The View* (14 Sept. 2009). http://theview.abc.go.com/blog/whoopi-barbara-remember-patrick-swayze.
Absolutely Fabulous in New York (AKA Gay) [2002]. *Absolutely Fabulous: Absolutely Special*. Dir. Tristram Shapeero. Perf. Jennifer Saunders, Joanna Lumley, Julia Sawalha. BBC Video, 2005. DVD.
Ackermann, Marilyn. "Whoopi's Big Book of Manners." *School Library Journal* (Nov. 2006): 94, 96.
Acmewebpages.com. "Celia Cruz Project on Hold." http://www.acmewebpages.com/whoopi/news.htm.
Adams, James Truslow. *The Epic of America*. [1931]. New York: Little, Brown, 1959.
African American Lives. PBS, 2006. DVD.
African-American Registry. "Moms Mabley: Comic Pioneer." http://www.aaregistry.com/african_american_history/539/Moms_Mabley_comic_pionee.
The African Queen. [1951]. Dir. John Huston. Perf. Humphrey Bogart, Katharine Hepburn. Paramount Home Entertainment, 2010. DVD.
All in the Family: The Complete Fifth Season. [1975]. SONY, 2009. DVD.
All Music Guide (AMG). "Jean Stapleton: Biography." http://www.allmusic.com/artist/jean-stapleton-p397852/biography.
Allen, Debbie. *Dancing in the Wings*. New York: Penguin, 2003.
Allmovie.com. *Sister Act*. http://www.allmovie.com/work/44910.
_____. *Sister Act 2: Back in the Habit*. http://www.allmovie.com/work/119906.
American Historical Association (AHA). *Papers of the American Historical Association, Vol. II*. New York: G. P. Putnam's Sons (The Knickerbocker Press), 1888. 404–405.
The America's Intelligence Wire. "Whoopi Goldberg Discusses Race Issues." *The America's Intelligence Wire*. (28 Nov. 2006). General OneFile. Web. 23 Feb. 2012. Gale Document Number: A155213877. Document URL: http://go.galegroup.com/ps/i.do?id=GALE%7CA155213877&v=2.1&u=va0018_002&it=r&p=GPS&sw=w.
Andrews, William L., and Frances Smith Foster. *The Concise Oxford Companion to African American Literature*. New York: Oxford University Press, 2001.
Andromeda (TV 2000–2005). http://www.imdb.com/title/tt0213327/.
Araton, Harvey. "FILM VIEW; Spoofing a Game That's Already Cartoonish." *New York Times* (2 Jun. 1996). *General OneFile*. Web. 28 Aug. 2010. Gale Document Number A150512843. Document URL: http://find.galegroup.com/gps/infomark.do?&content

233

Set=IAC-Documents&type=retrieve&tabID=T004&prodId=IPS&docId=A150512843&source=gale&userGroupName=va0074_remote&version=1.0.

Armstrong, Louis. *What Did I Do (To Be So Black and Blue)?* Audio Companion, *The Norton Anthology of African American Literature*, 2nd ed., eds. Henry Louis Gates, Jr., and Nellie Y. McKay. New York: W.W. Norton, 2004. Disk 1: *Music*, Track 21.

The Associate [1996]. Dir. Donald Petrie. Perf. Whoopi Goldberg, Dianne Weist, Eli Wallach, Tim Daly, Bebe Neuwirth. Hollywood Pictures Home Video/Buena Vista Home Ent., 1999. DVD.

Associated Press. "Bob Mackie raises money for AIDS research." *USA Today* (23 Nov. 2011). http://www.usatoday.com/life/lifestyle/2005-11-23-mackie-auction_x.htm.

Bagdad Café (1987). Dir. Percy Adlon. Perf. Marianne Sägebrecht, CCH Pounder, Jack Palance, with Monica Calhoun and George Aguilar. Orion Pictures/Metro Goldwyn Mayer Home Ent., 2001. DVD.

Bagdad Café (1990–1991). "Art." Originally broadcast on 11 May, 1990. WBMG Birmingham, Channel 42, CBS Television.

Bagdad Café: Art 1/3. Retrieved 11 Aug. 2011. http://www.youtube.com/watch?v=NaV3IlbGx6M&feature=related.

Bagdad Café: Art 2/3. Retrieved 11 Aug. 2011. http://www.youtube.com/watch?v=ymzvBowZ5T0&feature=related.

Bagdad Café: Art 3/3. Retrieved 11 Aug. 2011. http://www.youtube.com/watch?v=HHUQKVglJGY&feature=related.

Balansky, Andrew. Letter to the Editor. "Racial Role-Playing And Guises of Politics. (Editorial Desk) (Letter to the editor)." *New York Times* (24 Oct. 1993). *General OneFile*. Web. 31 Oct. 2010. Gale Document Number:A174704589. Document URL: http://find.galegroup.com/gps/infomark.do?&contentSet=IAC-Documents&type=retrieve&tabID=T004&prodId=IPS&docId=A174704589&source=gale&srcprod=ITOF&userGroupName=va0074_002&version=1.0.

Baldwin, James. *Blues for Mister Charlie*. [1964]. New York: Vintage, 1995.

Bamboozled [2000]. Dir. Spike Lee. Perf. Damon Wayans, Savion Glover, Jada Pinkett-Smith. New Line Home Entertainment, 2001. DVD.

Bass, Patrick Henry. "True Colors: Whoopi Goldberg and India. Arie team up in a revival of *For Colored Girls...*, This fall's buzz-building Broadway event." Essence, Sept. 2008. 94.

BBC. "Interviews: Nichelle Nichols." http://www.bbc.co.uk/cult/st/interviews/nichols/page4.shtml.

Belafonte, Harry. *Calypso* [1956]. RCA, 1992. CD.

BBC News. "Gay Tinky Winky Bad for Children." *BBC News*, 15 Feb. 1999. http://news.bbc.co.uk/2/hi/276677.stm.

Bells Are Ringing [1956 Original Broadway Cast Recording]. SONew York, 1990. CD.

Bennett, Lerone, Jr. "Pioneers in Protest, Part IX: Harriet Tubman — Rebel Was Slave Activist, Union Spy." *Ebony* (Nov. 1964): 148, 150–157.

Bennett, Ray. "'Sister Act' (Theater Review)." *Hollywood Reporter* 410.4 (4 Jun. 2009): 12.

Bennetts, Leslie. "THEATER; The Pain Behind The Laughter of Moms Mabley. (Arts and Leisure Desk)." *New York Times* (9 Aug. 1987). *General OneFile*. Web. 31 Oct. 2010. Gale Document Number: A176097504. Document URL: http://find.galegroup.com/gps/infomark.do?&contentSet=IAC-Documents&type=retrieve&tabID=T004&prodId=IPS&docId=A176097504&source=gale&srcprod=ITOF&userGroupName=va0074_002&version=1.0.

Bernstein, Richard. "Miramax Films Goes Up Against the Big Guns. (Cultural Desk)." *New York Times* (20 Mar. 1991). *General OneFile*. Web. 24 July 2011. Gale Document Number: A175142135. Document URL: http://find.galegroup.com/gps/infomark.do?&contentSet=IAC-Documents&type=retrieve&tabID=T004&prodId=IPS&docId=A175142135&source=gale&srcprod=ITOF&userGroupName=va0018_002&version=1.0.

The Best of Elmo. [1994]. Dir. Emily Squires. Perf. Kevin Clash (as Elmo), Fran Bill, Jim Henson, Ruth Buzzi, Sonia Manzano, Whoopi Goldberg, Julia Roberts. Sesame Workshop, 2001. DVD.

Blanchard, Jayne. "Goldberg's 'Alice' a Mouthy Mercenary; Unfortunate Crassness Spoils Show's Fine Casting and Staging." *Washington Times* (23 Dec. 2005): D10

Blassingame, John. *Slave Testimony: Two Centuries of Letters, Speeches, Interviews and Autobiographies*. Baton Rouge: Louisiana State University Press, 1977.

Bloom, Julie. "ARTS, BRIEFLY; Whoopi to Join Xanadu." *New York Times* (15 Jul. 2008): E2(L).

_____. "India.Arie on Broadway — Produced by Whoopi Goldberg." Web. 10 Oct. 2009. http://www.baltimoresun.com/entertainment/custom/wire/sns-ap-people-indiaarie,0,2355242.story.

Works Cited

Bogle, Donald. *Toms, Coons, Mulattoes, Mammies and Bucks: An Interpretive History of Blacks in American Films* (4th ed.). New York: Continuum, 2001.

_____. *Toms, Coons, Mulattoes, Mammies and Bucks: An Interpretive History of Blacks in American Films*. New York: Continuum, 2008.

Bowles, Scott. "A Season of Thrills and Chills." *USA Today* (5 Nov. 2010): 2D.

Boys on the Side. [1995]. Dir. Herbert Ross. Perf. Whoopi Goldberg, Mary-Louise Parker, Drew Barrymore. Warner Bros. Pictures. Warner Home Video, 1999. DVD.

Boys on the Side: The Original Soundtrack Album. ARISTA/BMG Marketing, 1995. CD.

Bragg, Rick. "To Bind Up a Nation's Wound with Celluloid." *New York Times* (16 June 1996). *General OneFile*. Web. 28 Aug. 2010. Gale Document Number A150505717. Document URL: http://find.galegroup.com/gps/infomark.do?&contentSet=IAC-Documents&type=retrieve&tabID=T004&prodId=IPS&docId=A150505717&source=gale&userGroupName=va0074_remote&version=1.0.

Brantley, Ben. "Goldberg Variations on Fun in 'Forum.'" *New York Times* (7 Mar. 1997). *General Reference Center Gold*. Web. 4 Sept. 2010. Gale Document Number A150391870. Document URL: http://find.galegroup.com/gtx/infom ark.do?&contentSet=IAC-Documents&type=retrieve&tabID=T004&prodId=GRGM&docId=A150391870&source=gale&userGroupName=va0074_remote&version=1.0.

Bray, Rosemary L. "CHILDREN'S BOOKS; Curiouser and Curiouser. (Book Review Desk)." *The New York Times Book Review* (8 Nov. 1992). *General OneFile*. Web. 19 July 2011. Gale Document Number: CJ174996045. Document URL: http://find.galegroup.com/gps/infomark.do?&contentSet=IAC-Documents&type=retrieve&tabID=T004&prodId=IPS&docId=CJ174996045&source=gale&srcprod=ITOF&userGroupName=va0018_002&version=1.0.

Brevard, Frank. Personal interview. 26 Feb. 2012.

Brevard, Lisa Pertillar. *Womansaints: The Saintly Portrayal of Select African-American and Latina Cultural Heroines*. New Orleans: University Press of the South, 2002.

Briemeier, Russ. "The Spongebob Squarepants Movie (Review)." *Christianity Today* (19 Nov. 2004).

Brown, James. *Papa's Got a Brand New Bag*. Special Music, 1992. CD.

Brown, Liz. "Whoopi Goldberg's Mother Dies: 'Who Will Love Me the Way That She Did?'" Examiner.com (7 Sept. 2010). http://www.ex aminer.com/the-view-in-national/whoopi-goldberg-s-mother-dies-who-will-love-me-the-way-that-she-did-video.

Brozan, Nadine. "Chronicle.(Metropolitan Desk)." *New York Times* (3 Oct. 1994). *General OneFile*. Web. 28 Aug. 2010. Gale Document Number A174476798. Document URL: http://find.galegroup.com/gps/infomark.do?&contentSet=IAC-Documents&type=retrieve&tabID=T004&prodId=IPS&docId=A174476798&source=gale&userGroupName=va0074_remote&version=1.0.

_____. "Chronicle." *New York Times* (22 Sept. 1997). *General OneFile*. Web. (31 Oct. 2010). Gale Document Number: A150287783. Document URL: http://find.galegroup.com/gps/infomark.do?&contentSet=IAC-Documents&type=retrieve&tabID=T004&prodId=IPS&docId=A150287783&source=gale&srcprod=ITOF&userGroupName=va0074_002&version=1.0.

Bullfinch Press. *Unchained Memories: Readings from the Slave Narratives*. Foreword by Henry Louis Gates, Jr. Intro. Spencer Crew. New York: Bullfinch, 2003.

Burglar. Dir. Hugh Wilson. Perf. Whoopi Goldberg, Bobcat Goldthwait, G.W. Bailey, with Special Appearance by Leslie Ann Warren. Warner Home Video, 1987.

_____. [1987]. Dir. William A. Fraker. Perf. Whoopi Goldberg, Bob Goldthwait, G.W. Bailey. Special Appearance by Leslie Ann Warren. Warner Home Video, 1998. DVD.

C & C Music Factory. "Just a Touch of Love (Every Day)." *Gonna Make You Sweat*. SONew York, 1990. CD. Track 4.

Cabrera, Cloe. "Fans Whoop It Up Over Cruz Role." *The Tampa Tribune* (21 Sept. 2003): 3.

Cahner's Business Information (CBI). "Cable's Top 25 People's Choice." *Broadcasting & Cable*. 129.10 (8 Mar. 1999): 46.

California Department of Health Care Services (CDHCS). *About Us*. http://www.dhcs.ca.gov/Pages/AboutUs.aspx.

Call Me Claus. Dir. Peter Werner. Perf. Whoopi Goldberg, Nigel Hawthorne, Brian Stokes Mitchell, Victor Garber, Taylor Negron, Frankie R. Faison, Alexandrea Wentworth, Melody Garrett, Robert Costanzo. One Ho Productions/Columbia Tri-Star Home Entertainment, 2001. DVD.

Campbell, BeBe Moore. "Whoopi Talks Black." *Essence* (Jan. 1997): 56–58, 100–102.

Canby, Vincent. "Film: Whoopi Goldberg in 'Burglar.' (Weekend Desk) (Movie Review)."

New York Times (20 Mar. 1987). *General One-File*. Web. 22 Mar. 2011. Document URL: http://find.galegroup.com/gps/infomark.do?&contentSet=IAC-Documents&type=retrieve&tabID=T004&prodId=IPS&docId=A176181903&source=gale&userGroupName=va0018_002&version=1.0.

Canedy, Dana. "THE MEDIA BUSINESS: ADVERTISING; Celebrities join efforts to persuade people to read more books." *New York Times* (20 Apr. 1999). http://www.nytimes.com/1999/04/20/business/media-business-advertising-celebrities-join-efforts-persuade-people-read-more.html.

Cantor, Judy. "Whoopi Partners with Cruz." *Variety* 390.1 (17 Feb. 2003): B10(1). General OneFile. Web. 23 Feb. 2012. Gale Document Number: A98136151. Document URL: http://go.galegroup.com/ps/i.do?id=GALE%7CA98136151&v=2.1&u=va0018_002&it=r&p=GPS&sw=w.

Caper, William. "Whoopi Goldberg: Comedian and Movie Star." African-American Biographies Series. Berkley Heights, NJ: Enslow, 1999.

Carlin, George. *Brain Droppings*. New York: Hyperion, 1997.

———, Excerpt from "*New Release: It's Bad for Ya* (DVD)." http://www.georgecarlin.com/home/home.html.

———. *Napalm and Silly Putty*. New York: Hyperion, 2001.

———, with Tony Hendra. *Last Words*. New York: The Free Press, 2009.

Carter, Bill. "ABC Is Closing In on Two New Panelists for 'The View.'" *New York Times* (28 July 2007): B9(L). *General OneFile*. Web. 28 Aug. 2010. Gale Document Number CJ166881702. Document URL: http://find.galegroup.com/gps/infomark.do?&contentSet=IAC-Documents&type=retrieve&tabID=T004&prodId=IPS&docId=CJ166881702&source=gale&userGroupName=va0074_remote&version=1.0.

Carter, Gayle. "Five Questions for Whoopi Goldberg." *USA Today* (14 Oct. 2010). http://www.usatoday.com/life/books/news/2010-10-14-buzzplus14_ST_N.htm.

"Catherine 'Cathy' Hughes (1947–) Radio Personality, Broadcast Executive." *Encyclopedia of African American Business, Volume 1*, eds. Smith, Jessie Carney, Millicent Lownes Jackson and Linda T. Wynn. Westport, CT: Greenwood, 2006.

Cavalieri, Grace. "Rita Dove: An Interview." *The American Poetry Review* (Mar.–Apr. 1995): 11+. *General Reference Center Gold*. Web. 6 Sept. 2010. Gale Document Number A16646953. Document URL: http://find.galegroup.com/gtx/infomark.do?&contentSet=IAC-Documents&type=retrieve&tabID=T003&prodId=GRGM&docId=A16646953&source=gale&userGroupName=va0074_remote&version=1.0.

Cavett, Dick. "Whoopi Goldberg: The Host of the Oscars Chats with the Greatest Talk Show Host of All Time. (Oscars and More — Two Terrific Talkers Go at It).(Interview)." *Interview* (Apr. 2002): 62+. *General OneFile*. Web. 5 Feb. 2011. Gale Document Number: A84237675. Document URL: http://find.galegroup.com/gps/infomark.do?&contentSet=IAC-Documents&type=retrieve&tabID=T003&prodId=IPS&docId=A84237675&source=gale&userGroupName=va0018_002&version=1.0.

CBC Arts. "Whoopi Goldberg to Star in London 's Sister Act Musical." *The Canadian Broadcasting Corporation (CBC)*. 16 Nov. 2008. General OneFile. Web. 23 Feb. 2012. Gale Document Number: A189067729. Document URL: http://go.galegroup.com/ps/i.do?id=GALE%7CA189067729&v=2.1&u=va0018_002&it=r&p=GPS&sw=w.

———. " U.K. 's Hit 'Sister Act' Musical Slated for Broadway." *The Canadian Broadcasting Corporation (CBC)*. 6 Oct. 2010. General OneFile. Web. 23 Feb. 2012. Gale Document Number: A238774583. Document URL: http://go.galegroup.com/ps/i.do?id=GALE%7CA238774583&v=2.1&u=va0018_002&it=r&p=GPS&sw=w.

Celtic Pride. [1996]. Dir. Tom DeCerchio. Star. Damon Wayans, Daniel Stern, Dan Aykroyd. Walt Disney Video, 2002. DVD.

Censorship in America's Press and Judiciary from 1969 to 2001. Chapel Hill, NC: Doctoral Dissertation, 2002. Web. 8 Aug. 2009. http://kwul.kwu.ac.kr/oversea/11_3086647.PDF.

Chappelle's Show, Season 1 (Uncensored). Dir. Rusty Cundieff, Andre Allen, Scott Vincent, Bill Berner, Bobcat Goldthwait, Peter Lauer. Perf. Dave Chappelle. Paramount, 2004. DVD.

Chutkov, Paul. Whoopi's Revenge (For Years Hollywood Executives Considered Her a Talented Pain in the Neck. Now She's Making Them Pay." *Cigar Aficionado* (1 Sept. 1993). http://www.cigaraficionado.com/Cigar/CA_Profiles/People_Profile/0,2540,57,00.html. Gale Document Number: A176181903.

Cinderella (Two-Disc Special Edition). Dir. Clyde Geronimi, Hamilton Luske, Wilfred Jackson. Perf. Ilene Woods, James MacDonald, Eleanor

Works Cited

Audley, Verna Felton, Rhoda Williams. Walt Disney Home Ent., 2005. DVD.

City of Alachua. "Celebrating a Century (1905–2005): Alachua — A Good Life Community." http://www.cityofalachua.com/.

Clara's Heart. [1988]. *Whoopi Goldberg Collection: Four Film Favorites (Bogus/Clara's Heart/Made in America/Corinna Corinna.* Dir. Robert Mulligan. Perf. Whoopi Goldberg, Michael Ontkean, Kathleen Quinlan, Neil Patrick Harris. Warner Home Video, 2010. DVD. (Disk 1 of 3, Side 1).

Clinton, George. *Atomic Dog.* Capitol Records, 1990. CD.

A Collaboration of Spirits: Casting and Acting "The Color Purple" (2003). Dir. Laurent Bozereau. Appearances by Steven Spielberg, Reuben Cannon, Whoopi Goldberg, Alice Walker, Quincy Jones, Oprah Winfrey, Margaret Avery, Danny Glover, Kathleen Kennedy, Akosua Busia, Rae Dawn Chong. Warner Home Video. Disc 2 of *The Color Purple (Two-Disc Special Edition).* Warner Bros. Pictures/AOL Time Warner, 2005. DVD.

Collier, Aldore. Whoopi Goldberg Becomes a Nun to Escape Mob in Movie, 'Sister Act.'" *Jet* 82.n6 (1 Jun. 1992): 34.

_____. "Whoopi Goldberg Stars as Heroic Teacher to Leleti Khumalo in *Sarafina!* Film." *Jet* (28 Sept. 1992): 54–57.

_____. "Whoopi Goldberg Talks About Her Role in 'Ghost' and Blasts Critics Over Her Film Choices." *Jet* (13 Aug. 1990): 58–60.

_____. "Whoopi Goldberg: Tough and Tender in New Film Drama, 'Clara's Heart.'" *Jet* (24 Oct. 1998): 30–32.

The Color Purple (Two-Disc Special Edition) [1985]. Dir. Steven Spielberg. Perf. Danny Glover, Whoopi Goldberg, Oprah Winfrey, Margaret Avery, Willard Pugh. Warner Home Video, 2003. DVD.

Comic Relief: The Greatest and The Latest. Comic Relief, 2008. 2 DVDs.

"Comic Relief's Canny Comedians Trade Yuks for Bucks to Help the Nation's Homeless." *People Weekly* (3 Apr. 1989): 134+. *General OneFile.* Web. 28 Aug. 2010. Gale Document Number A7471403. Document URL: http://find.galegroup.com/gps/infomark.do?&contentSet=IAC-Documents&type=retrieve&tabID=T003&prodId=IPS&docId=A7471403&source=gale&userGroupName=va0074_remote&version=1.0.

Complete Original Motion Picture Soundtrack). [1966]. ASIN: B00005EF9Y. Audio CD, 2001.

Cone, James. *The Spirituals and the Blues: An Interpretation.* [1972]. New York: Orbis Books, 1991.

Conversations with the Ancestors: "The Color Purple" from Book to Screen (2003). Dir. Laurent Bozereau. Warner Home Video. Disc 2, *The Color Purple (Two-Disc Special Edition).* Warner Bros. Pictures/AOL Time Warner, 2005. DVD.

Cook, Mariana (photographs), Jamaica Kincaid (intro.). *Generations of Women: In Their Own Words.* San Francisco: Chronicle Books, 1998.

Cooper, Michael. "A Smoky Bar in New York? It's Just TV, Bloomberg Says." *New York Times* (7 Aug. 2003): B4. *General OneFile.* Web. 29 Aug. 2010. Gale Document Number A106375685. Document URL: http://find.galegroup.com/gps/infomark.do?&contentSet=IAC-Documents&type=retrieve&tabID=T004&prodId=IPS&docId=A106375685&source=gale&userGroupName=va0074_remote&version=1.0.

Corinna, Corinna. [1994]. Dir. Jessie Nelson. Perf. Whoopi Goldberg, Ray Liotta, Tina Majorino, Wendy Crewson, Larry Miller, Joan Cusack, Don Ameche. New Line Home Video, 1999. DVD.

Cox, Beth. "Whoopi Goldberg Stars in Flooz Commercial." *ClickZ (Marketing News and Expert Advice).* http://www.clickz.com/clickz/news/1701421/whoopi-goldberg-stars-flooz-commercial.

Cox, Gordon. "Whoopi Goldberg." *Variety* 419.8 (12 Jul. 2010): 27.

_____. "Whoopi Joins Blighty 'Act.'" *Daily Variety* 308.3 (8 Jul. 2010): 3.

Crouch, Stanley. *The Artificial White Man: Essays on Authenticity.* New York: Basic Civitas Books, 2004.

Cruz, Celia. *Celia Cruz: Hits Mix.* Sony Music International, 2002. CD.

_____. *Celia: My Life.* New York: Rayo/HarperCollins, 2004.

Cullen, Countee. "Heritage." *Norton Anthology of African American Literature,* 2nd ed. Eds. Henry Louis Gates, Jr., and Nellie Y. McKay. New York: W. W. Norton, 2004. 1347–1350.

Cultivating a Classic: The Making of "The Color Purple." (2003). Dir. Laurent Bozereau. Warner Home Video, 2003. Disc 2, *The Color Purple (Two-Disc Special Edition).* Warner Bros. Pictures/AOL Time Warner, 2005. DVD.

Damn Yankees. [1955 Original Broadway Cast Recording]. RCA Victor Broadway, 1990. CD.

Daoust, Jerry. "Music Doesn't Make the Mass." *U.S. Catholic*. 61.n5 (May 1996). 20(5).

Dave Chappelle: For What It's Worth (Live at the Fillmore). [2004]. Dir. Stan Lathan. Perf. Dave Chappelle. SONew York Pictures Home Entertainment, 2005. DVD.

Dave Chappelle: Killin' Them Softly. Dir. Stan Lathan. Perf. Dave Chappelle. Platinum Comedy Series, UrbanWorks Entertainment/Ventura Dist., 2003 DVD.

Davis, Angela. *Blues Legacies and Black Feminism: Gertrude "Ma" Rainey, Bessie Smith, and Billie Holiday*. New York: Vintage, 1999.

Davis, Patte. *The Lives Our Mother's Leave Us*. Carlsbad, CA: Hay House, 2009.

Day, Sherri. "THE MEDIA BUSINESS: ADVERTISING; Slim-Fast Bets that its campaign featuring Whoopi Goldberg and new products will lift its sales." *New York Times* (30 Dec. 2003). http://www.nytimes.com/2003/12/30/business/media-business-advertising-slim-fast-bets-that-its-campaign-featuring-whoopi.html.

The Deep End of the Ocean. Dir. Ulu Grosbard. Perf. Michelle Pfeiffer, Treat Williams, Jonathan Jackson, John Kapelos and Whoopi Goldberg. Mandalay Ent./ Columbia TriStar Home Video, 1999. DVD.

Defrantz, Thomas F. "Williams, Bert, and George Walker." *Harlem Renaissance Lives from the African American National Biography*. Eds. Henry Louis Gates and Evelyn Brooks Higgenbotham. New York: Oxford University Press, 532–534.

"Deja Q." *Star Trek: The Next Generation*. Seas. 3, Ep. 13. Dir. Les Landau. Paramount Television, 5 Feb. 1990. Amazon Instant Video. http://www.amazon.com/Deja-Q/dp/B005HES9D4/ref=sr_1_1?s=movies-tv&ie=UTF8&qid=1331661355&sr=1-1.

Disney World Publishing (DPW). "About DPW Books." Disney World Publishing. 24 Mar. 2011. dpw_lob_books_fact_sheet_032411.pdf.

Dogma (Special Edition). [1999]. Dir. Kevin Smith. Perf. Matt Damon, Ben Affleck, Kevin Smith, Salma Hayek, George Carlin. Sony Pictures, 2001. DVD.

Douglass, Frederick. *Narrative of the Life of Frederick Douglass, An American Slave, Written by Himself*. Intro. Robert B. Stepto. Cambridge: Belknap P of Harvard UP, 2009.

Dove, Rita. "After Reading Mickey the Night Kitchen for the Third Time Before Bed." *Our Mothers, Our Selves: Writers and Poets Celebrating Motherhood*. Karen J. Donnelly and J.B. Bernstein, eds. Westport, CT: Bergin & Garvey, 1996. 50.

Dreisinger, Baz. "The Whitest Black Girl on TV." *New York Times* (28 Sept. 2003): AR24(L). *General Reference Center Gold*. Web. 4 Sept. 2010. Gale Document Number A108238491. Document URL http://find.galegroup.com/gtx/infomark.do?&contentSet=IAC-Documents&type=retrieve&tabID=T004&prodId=GRGM&docId=A108238491&source=gale&userGroupName=va0074_remote&version=1.0.

DuBois, W.E.B. *The Souls of Black Folk*. [1903]. Radford, VA: Wilder, 2008.

Dunbar, Paul. "We Wear the Mask." *The Norton Anthology of African American Literature*. 2nd ed. Eds. Henry Louis Gates, Jr., and Nellie Y. McKay. New York: W. W. Norton, 2004. 918.

Eastman, P.D. *Are You My Mother?* New York: Random House, 1960.

Eddie [1996]. Dir. Steve Rash. Perf. Whoopi Goldberg, Frank Langella, Denis Farina. Walt Disney Video, 1999. DVD.

Edwards, Audrey. "Whoopi Goldberg." *Essence* (May 2005): 338.

Elliott, Stuart. "THE MEDIA BUSINESS: ADVERTISING; Avon Products is abandoning its old-fashioned image in an appeal to contemporary women." *New York Times* (27 Apr. 1993). http://nytimes.com/1993/04/27/business/media-business-advertising-avon-products-abandoning-its-old-fashioned-image.html?src=pm.

Ellison, Ralph. *Invisible Man*. [1952]. New York: Vintage International, 1995.

Ensler, Eve. *The Vagina Monologues (V-Day Edition)*. Foreword by Gloria Steinem. New York: Villard, 2001.

Essence Magazine (1 Aug. 1977–Pres.) http://go.galegroup.com/ps/aboutJournal.do?pubDate=120070601&actionString=DO_DISPLAY_ABOUT_PAGE&inPS=true&prodId=GPS&userGroupName=va0018_002&searchType=BasicSearchForm&docId=GALE%7C1264.

Fame [1980]. Dir. Alan Parker. *Double Feature: Purple Rain/Fame*. Warner Bros. Ent. and Turner Ent., Dist. Warner Home Video, 2008. DVD.

Fat Albert. [2004]. Dir. Joel Zwick. Perf. Kenan Thompson, Kyla Pratt, Omarion Grandberry. Twentieth Century–Fox Home Entertainment, 2005. DVD.

Fatal Beauty [1987]. Dir. Tom Holland. Perf. Whoopi Goldberg, Sam Elliott, Ruben Blades, Harris Yulin, John P. Ryan. Metro-Goldwyn Mayer Home Entertainment, 2001. DVD.

The Fighting Temptations. [2003]. Perf. Cuba

Gooding, Jr., Beyoncé Knowles, Mike Epps, Nigel Washington, Chloé Bailey. Dir. Jonathan Lynn. Paramount, 2004. DVD.

Flores, Aurora. "Celia Cruz: Salsera Sonera." *"Cómo yo me llamo?": Celia Cruz/A Biographical Exhibition of the Life and Artistry of Celia Cruz*. New York: Caribbean Cultural Ctr., 1990.

The Flying Nun: The Complete First Season. Perf. Sally Field. Sony Pictures Home Ent., 2006. DVD.

For Colored Girls. Dir. Tyler Perry. Perf. Janet Jackson, Thandie Newton, Whoopi Goldberg, Phylicia Rashad, Anika Noni Rose, Loretta Devine, Kimberly Elise, Kerry Washington. Lionsgate Films, 2011. DVD.

Forbes, Camille. *Introducing Bert Williams: Burnt Cork, Broadway, and the Story of America's First Black Star*. New York: Basic Civitas, 2008.

Ford, Paul Leicester. *The Writings of Thomas Jefferson, Vol. II, 1776–1781*. New York: G.P. Putnam's Sons (The Knickerbocker Press), 1893.

Frost, Robert. *Mending Wall*. Web. 4 Sept. 2010. http://www.bartleby.com/118/2.html.

Fuller, Graham. "Ghosts of Past and Present— Interviews with Whoopi Goldberg and Rob Reiner—Interview." (Jan. 1997). Brant Publications, 1997; Gale Group, 2000. http://www.findarticles.com/p/articles/mi_m1285/is_n1_v27/ai_19121817/pg_1.

García-Johnson, Ronie-Richele. "Celia Cruz, Singer." *Notable Hispanic American Women*, ed. Diane Telgen and Jim Camp. Washington, D.C.: Gale Res., 1993. 115–118.

Gates, Henry Louis. *Figures in Black: Words, Signs and the "Racial" Self*. New York: Oxford University Press, 1989.

Gerard, Jeremy J. "'Comic Relief' for a Serious Cause." *New York Times* (11 May 1990). http://www.nytimes.com/1990/05/11/arts/comic-relief-being-funny-for-a-serious-cause.html?src=pm.

Ghost. [1990]. Dir. Jerry Zucker. Perf. Patrick Swayze, Demi Moore, Whoopi Goldberg. Paramount Pictures. Paramount/Viacom, 2001. DVD.

Ghosts of Mississippi. [1996]. Dir. Rob Reiner. Perf. Alec Baldwin, Whoopi Goldberg, James Woods. Castle Rock Entertainment. Warner Home Video, 2010. DVD.

Gilman, Sander L. *Making the Body Beautiful: A Cultural History of Aesthetic Surgery*. Princeton, NJ: Princeton University Press, 1999.

Giovanni, Nikki. "Poem for a Lady Whose Voice I Like." http://www.poetryfoundation.org/archive/poem.html?id=177835.

Girl, Interrupted. [1999]. Dir. James Mangold. Perf. Wynona Rider, Angelina Jolie, Clea Duvall, Brittany Murphy, Elizabeth Moss, Jared Leto, Jeffrey Tambor, with Vanessa Redgrave and Whoopi Goldberg. Columbia Pictures. SONew York Pictures Home Ent., 2004. DVD.

"GOLDBERG BLASTS BP BOSSES." *World Entertainment News Network* (9 Jun. 2010). *General OneFile*. Web. 28 Aug. 2010. Gale Document Number A228391642. Document URL: http://find.galegroup.com/gps/infomark.do?&contentSet=IAC-Documents&type=retrieve&tabID=T004&prodId=IPS&docId=A228391642&source=gale&userGroupName=va0074_remote&version=1.0.

Goldberg, Whoopi. *Alice*. Illus. John Rocco. New York: Bantam Books, 1992.

———. *Book*. New York: Bob Weisbach Books/William Morrow.

———. *Is It Just Me? (Or Is It Nuts Out There?)*. New York: Hyperion, 2010. 1997.

———. Foreword. *Farewell, Welfare!* By Mary Waterhouse. Seattle, WA: Peanut Butter, 1992.

———. Preface. *Breaking the Walls of Silence: AIDS and Women in a New York State Maximum-Security Prison*. By the Women of the ACE Program of the Bedford Hills Correctional Facility. Woodstock: Overlook, 1998.

———, with Deborah Underwood. *Sugar Plum Ballerinas: Perfectly Prima*. New York: Disney/Jump at the Sun, 2010.

———, with ———. *Sugar Plum Ballerinas: Plum Fantastic*. New York: Disney/Jump at the Sun, 2008.

———, with ———. *Sugar Plum Ballerinas: Sugar Plums to the Rescue!* Illus. Maryn Roos. New York: Disney/Jump at the Sun, 2011.

———, with ———. *Sugar Plum Ballerinas: Terrible Terrel*. New York: Disney/Jump at the Sun, 2010.

———, with ———. *Sugar Plum Ballerinas: Toeshoe Trouble*. New York: Disney/Jump at the Sun, 2009.

———, with ———. *Whoopi's Big Book of Manners*. New York: Disney/Jump at the Sun, 2006.

Goldberg, Whoopi. *Book*. New York: Bob Weisbach Books/William Morrow, 1997.

———, with Pictures by Olo. *Whoopi's Big Book of Manners*. New York: Disney/Jump at the Sun Books, 2006.

Gomez, Jewelle. "In the Kitchen." *Tenderheaded: A Comb-Bending Collection of Hair Stories*. Eds. Juliette Harris and Pamela Johnson. New York: Washington Square Press/Pocket Books, a Division of Simon & Schuster, 2002. 257–263.

Gone With the Wind [1939]. Dir. Victor Fleming. Perf. Clark Gable, Vivien Leigh, Hattie McDaniel. Warner Home Video, 2000. DVD.

Gone With the Wind (Two-Disc 70th Anniversary Edition). Dir. Victor Fleming. Perf. Clark Gable, Vivien Leigh, Leslie Howard, Olivia De Havilland. Warner Home Video, 2009. DVD.

Good Burger. [1997]. Dir. Brian Robbins. Perf. Kel Mitchell, Kenan Thompson, Sinbad, Abe Vigoda, Shar Jackson. Paramount, 2003. DVD.

Good Fences [TV 2003]. Dir. Ernest R. Dickerson. Perf. Danny Glover, Whoopi Goldberg, Zachary Simmons Glover, Ryan Michelle Bathe. Showtime Ent., 2003.

Good Hair. Dir. James Stilson. Perf. Chris Rock. HBO Films, 2009. DVD.

Grimes, William. "On Stage, and Off." *New York Times* (31 Jan. 1997). General Reference Center Gold. Web. 4 Sept. 2010. Gale Document Number A150411026. Document URL: http://find.galegroup.com/gtx/infomark.do?&contentSet=IAC-Documents&type=retrieve&tabID=T004&prodId=GRGM&docId=A150411026&source=gale&userGroupName=va0074_remote&version=1.0

"Guinan." Ancestry.com. http://www.ancestry.com/name-origin?surname=guinan.

"Gyn." Merriam-Webster.com. http://www.merriam-webster.com/dictionary/gyn.

Haley, Alex, and Michael Eric Dyson (intro). *Roots: The 30th Anniversary Edition*. New York: Vanguard Books, 2007.

Handler, Daniel. "Children's Books." *New York Times* (14 Jan. 2007). http://www.nytimes.com/2007/01/14/books/review/Handler.t.html?pagewanted=all.

Haygood, Wil. *In Black and White: The Life of Sammy Davis, Jr.* New York: Alfred A. Knopf, 2003.

_____. "Why Negro Humor Is So Black." *The American Prospect* (10 Dec. 2001). http://prospect.org/article/why-negro-humor-so-black.

Hetrick, Adam. Broadway Revival of *for colored girls* will Arrive at Circle in the Square Aug. 19." Playbill.com. (24 Jun. 2008). http://www.playbill.com/news/article/118954-Broadway-Revival-of-for-colored-girls-Will-Arrive-at-Circle-in-the-Square-Aug-19.

Hill, Errol, and James V. Hatch. *A History of African American Theatre*. Cambridge: Cambridge University Press, 2003.

Holden, Stephen. "MOVIE REVIEW: How Stella Got Her Groove Back (1998) FILM REVIEW: He Likes Video Games? Nobody's Perfect." *New York Times* (14 Aug. 1998). http://movies.nytimes.com/movie/review?res=9C04E6DD133AF937A2575BC0A96E958260&scp=3&sq=How%20Stella%20Got%20Her%20Groove%20Back%20Movie%20Review&st=cse.

_____. "Whoopi Goldberg's Turn to Try a Gender Bender." *New York Times* (25 Oct. 1996). *General OneFile*. Web. 24 July 2011. Gale Document Number: A150446987. Document URL: http://find.galegroup.com/gps/infomark.do?&contentSet=IAC-Documents&type=retrieve&tabID=T004&prodId=IPS&docId=A150446987&source=gale&srcprod=ITOF&userGroupName=va0018_002&version=1.0.

Holson, Laura. "Fashion's Newest Odd Couple: André Leon Talley and Whoopi Goldberg." *New York Times* (28 Feb. 2010): ST1.

Homer and Eddie. Dir. Andrey Konchalovskiy. Perf. James Belushi, Whoopi Goldberg. Warner Home Video, 1996. VHS.

Homie Spumoni. Dir. Mike Cerrone. Donald Faison, Jamie Lynn Sigler, Joey Fatone, Tony Rock, Paul Mooney and Whoopi Goldberg. Perf. R-Caro Productions. Dist. by Warner Bros. Home Video, 2006. DVD.

Honeycutt, Kirk. "Preaching to the Choir." *Hollywood Reporter*. 393.50 (17 Apr. 2006): 10.

How Stella Got Her Groove Back. Dir. Kevin Rodney Sullivan. Perf. Angela Bassett, Taye Diggs, Regina King and Whoopi Goldberg. Twentieth Century–Fox Home Ent., 1998. DVD.

Hughes, Langston. *The Collected Works of Langston Hughes, Vol. 6: Gospel Plays, Operas and Later Dramatic Works*. Ed., Intro. Leslie Catherine Sanders. University of Missouri Press, 2004.

_____. "Madame and the Phone Bill." *The Collected Poems of Langston Hughes*. New York: Vintage Classics, 1995. 353–354.

_____. "The Negro Artist and the Racial Mountain" [1926]. *The Norton Anthology of African American Literature, 2nd ed*. Eds. Henry Louis Gates, Jr. and Nellie Y. McKay. New York: W. W. Norton, 2004. 1311–1314.

_____. *The Weary Blues*. In *The Collected Poems of Langston Hughes*. Ed. Arnold Rampersad (David Roessel, assoc. ed.). New York: Vintage Classics, 1995. 50.

_____. ["You Don't Know/You Don't Know My Mind..."]. *The Collected Works of Langston Hughes, Vol. 13: The Big Sea*. Ed., Intro.,

Joseph McLaren. Ed. Board Arnold Rampersad, chair, Doland Hubbard. Columbia: U of Missouri P, 1992.

Hurston, Zora Neale. *Their Eyes Were Watching God*. [1937]. New York: HarperPerennial Modern Classics, 2006.

IBDb (Internet Broadway Database). "Whoopi Goldberg." http://www.ibdb.com/person.php?id=42457.

IMDb. "Awards for Angela Bassett." http://www.imdb.com/name/nm0000291/awards.

———. "Awards for Angelina Jolie." http://www.imdb.com/name/nm0001401/awards.

———. "Awards for Whoopi Goldberg." http://www.imdb.com/name/nm0000155/awards.

———. *Comic Relief* (1986/II) (TV). http://www.imdb.com/title/tt0284008/combined.

———. "*Glee* (TV Series, 2009–)." http://www.imdb.com/title/tt1327801/.

———. "*Jeremiah* (TV Series 2002-2004)." http://www.imdb.com/title/tt0290966/.

———. Make-Up Department: *Golden Dreams* (2001) (Hair stylist: Ms. Goldberg). Web. 25 Aug. 2010. http://www.imdb.com/name/nm0000155/.

———. "Mo'Nique." http://www.imdb.com/name/nm0594898/.

———. "Paul Mooney." http://www.imdb.com/name/nm0600763/.

IMDb. "Biography for Jean Stapleton." http://www.imdb.com/name/nm0822958/bio.

———. "*Whoopi* (TV Series 2003-2004)." http://www.imdb.com/title/tt0364902/. http://www.christianitytoday.com/ct/movies/reviews/2004/spongebobsquarepants.html. http://www.nps.gov/home/historyculture/upload/GoldbergBio.pdf.

India.Arie. *Acoustic Soul*. Motown, 2001. CD.

Indiavision.com. "Whoopi Goldberg's Return to 'Sister Act' Onstage Is a Hit." http://www.indiavision.com/news/article/entertainment/93051/.

Infoplease. "Quotations from Notable American Women." http://www.infoplease.com/spot/whmquotes1.html/.

InStyle (Aug. 1994).

It's a Very Merry Muppet Christmas Movie. Dir. Kirk R. Thatcher. Perf. Steve Whitmire, Frank Oz, Dave Goelz, Eric Jacobson, David Arquette, Joan Cusack, Matthew Lillard, William H. Macy, Whoopi Goldberg. Universal Studios, 2002. DVD.

It's Bad for Ya. Dir. Rocco Urbisci. Perf. George Carlin. Home Box Office, 2008. DVD.

Itzkoff, Dave. "She Can't Kick the Habit: Whoopi Goldberg Back in 'Sister Act.'" *New York Times Arts Beat* (7 Jul. 2010). http://artsbeat.blogs.nytimes.com/2010/07/07/she-cant-kick-the-habit-whoopi-goldberg-back-in-sister-act/?pagemode=print.

———. "'Sister Act' Finds a Broadway Home." *New York Times* (6 Oct. 2010): C3(L).

Ives, Nat. "THE MEDIA BUSINESS: ADVERTISING; Marketers run to pull the plug when celebrity endorsers say the darndest things, or worse." *New York Times* (16 July 2004). http://www.nytimes.com/2004/07/16/business/media-business-advertising-marketers-run-pull-plug-when-celebrity-endorsers-say.html?src=pm.

Jackie's Back! [1999]. Perf. Jenifer Lewis, Tim Curry. Dir. Robert Townsend. Xenon Pictures, 2002. DVD.

James, Caryn. "Film: Whoopi Goldberg in The Telephone." *New York Times* (14 Feb. 1988). http://movies.nytimes.com/movie/review?res=940DE5DE113FF937A25751C0A96E948260.

Jean, Wyclef. "Whoopi Meets Wyclef—Actress Whoopi Goldberg—Interview." April 1999. Brant Publications 1999; Gale Group, 2000. http://www.findarticles.com/p/articles/mi_m1285/is_4_29/ai_54349256/pg_1.

Jefferson, Thomas. "Declaration of Independence." Web. 25 Aug. 2010. http://www.archives.gov/exhibits/charters/declaration_transcript.html.

———. "Inalienable Rights." *Thomas Jefferson on Politics & Government*. Collected by Eyler Robert Coates, Sr. http://etext.virginia.edu/jefferson/quotations/jeff0100.htm.

The Jeffersons: The Complete First Season. SONY, 2002. DVD.

Johnson, Sharon. "Literary Lion." Barnard College. (1 Feb. 2011). http://barnard.columbia.edu/headlines/literary-lion.

Johnson, Taft. *New Orleans Saints: From the Futility of the Archie Manning Years to Drew Brees and Super Bowl Glory*. Webster's Digital Services, 2010.

Johnson Publishing Company (JPC). "'Aunt Jemima' Trademark to Get 1990s Makeover." *Jet* (15 May 1989): 15.

———. "Behind the Laughter of Jackie (Moms) Mabley." *Ebony* (Aug. 1962): 88–91.

———. "Ben Vereen Critical After Being Hit by Truck Driven by Show Biz Acquaintance." *Jet* (29 Jun. 1992): 14–15.

———. "Ben Vereen Still Under Fire for Blackface Act." *Jet* (12 Feb. 2001): 14–16, 18.

———. "Black Oscar Milestones." *Ebony* (Nov. 2005): 96, 98.

———. "Dave Chappelle Reportedly Checks into Mental Facility." *Jet* (30 May 2005): 53.

———. "Goldberg, Avery, Winfrey Up for Oscars in *Purple*." *Jet* (24 Feb. 1986): 54.

———. "'Long Walk Home' Movie Sheds New Light on Montgomery Bus Boycott." *Jet* (25 Mar. 1991): 56–58, 60.

———. "Movies to See (Girl Interrupted)." *Jet* (24 Jan. 2000): 65.

———. "'Next Friday' Is No. 1 at Opening Weekend." *Jet* (7 Feb. 2000): 36.

———. "People Are Talking About....." *Jet* (22 Feb. 1999): 46.

———. "Richard Pryor, Comedy Legend, 1940–2005." *Jet* (9 Jan. 2006): 6–12, 14–18, 28–32, 36–37.

———. "Three Cities Reject Richard Pryor Show." *Jet* (13 Oct. 1977): 59.

———. "What Stars Did Before They Became Famous." *Jet* (26 Oct. 1998): 60–63.

———. "Who Are the Black Actor's Who've Made 50 Movies or More?" *Jet* (24 Apr. 2000): 60–63.

———. "Whoopi Goldberg Accepts Oscar Apology." *Jet* (17 Mar. 2008): 32.

———. "Whoopi Goldberg and Jean Stapleton: Actresses Star in TV's new 'Bagdad Café.'" *Jet* (23 Apr. 1990): 58–60.

———. "Whoopi Goldberg and Ray Liotta Go for Laughs and Love in 'Corinna, Corinna.'" *Jet* (29 Aug. 1994): 32–35.

———. "Whoopi Goldberg and Ted Danson Get Big Laughs in *Made in America*." *Jet* (14 Jun. 1993): 56–59.

———. "Whoopi and Ted Danson Issue Joint Statement Revealing They're No Longer an Item." *Jet* (22 Nov. 1993): 16.

———. "Whoopi Earns $7 Million for Role in 'Sister Act 2.'" *Jet*. 85.n9 (27 Dec. 1993): 55.

———. "Whoopi Goldberg Challenges Stereotypes in Her TV Sitcom, Whoopi." *Jet* (27 Oct. 2003): 62–65.

———. "Whoopi Goldberg Defends Ted Danson's Blackface at Friar's Club Roast." *Jet* (25 Oct. 1993): 12–14, 60.

———. "Whoopi Goldberg Delights Worldwide Audience as Host of the 71st Annual Academy Awards." *Jet* (5 Apr. 1999): 55–59.

———. "Whoopi Goldberg Says She Should Have a TV Channel in Her Honor." *Jet* (28 Sept. 1998): 65.

———. "Whoopi Goldberg: Second Black Actress to Win an Oscar in 52 Years." *Jet* (22 Apr. 1991): 54–57, 59.

———. "Whoopi Goldberg Sued Over Reported Film Pact." *Jet* (20 Sept. 1993): 38.

———. "Whoopi Goldberg Talks about New Movie, New Husband." *Jet* (3 Nov. 1986): 58–59.

———. "Whoopi Goldberg Wins 1993 Female Star of the Year Award (National Association of Theater Owners)." *Jet* 83.n4 (1 Feb. 1993): 9.

———. "Why Some Blacks Choose to Date Outside Their Race." *Jet* (17 Sept. 2001): 48–50.

Joy Behar Show. "Interview with Joan Rivers; Interview with Whoopi Goldberg." (1 Apr. 2010). Web. 6 Sept. 2009. http://archives.cnn.com/TRANSCRIPTS/1004/01/joy.01.html.

Jumpin' Jack Flash [1986]. Dir. Penny Marshall. Perf. Whoopi Goldberg. Twentieth Century–Fox Home Ent., 2004. DVD.

Jumpin' Jack Flash. [1987]. 20th Century–Fox Home Entertainment, 2004. DVD.

Kaltenbach, Chris. "A 'Precious' Oscar for Mo'Nique (Baltimore County Native Wins Supporting Actress Honor." *Baltimore Sun* (8 Mar. 2010). http://articles.baltimoresun.com/2010-03-08/entertainment/bal-monique-oscars-0308_1_baltimore-county-born-actress-mo-nique-black-experience.

Kaminsky, Peter. Intro., Ed., and Mark Twain. *The Chicago of Europe: And Other Tales of Foreign Travel*. New York: Sterling, 2009.

Kaysen, Susanna. *Girl, Interrupted*. New York: Vintage, 1994.

Keegan, Rebecca Winters. "Top 10 Awkward Moments: 4. The View Overuse of the N Word." Time.com (3 Nov. 2008). http://www.time.com/time/specials/packages/article/0,28804,1855948_1864014_1864018,00.html.

Kemp, Theresa D. *Women in the Age of Shakespeare*. Santa Barbara: Greenwood (ABC-CLIO), 2009.

Kennedy, Helen. "Roman Polanski's Victim Samantha Geimer, Now 45, 'Got Over It Long Ago.'" *New York Daily News*. Web. (28 Sept. 2009). http://www.nydailynews.com/gossip/2009/09/28/2009–09 28_roman_polanskis_victim_now_45_got_over_it_long_ago.html.

Kennedy Center. "History of the Mark Twain Prize/Past Winners." Web. 27 Sept. 2009. http://www.kennedy-center.org/programs/specialevents/marktwain/.

———. "The 12th Annual Mark Twain Prize for American Humor." http://www.kennedy-center.org/programs/specialevents/marktwain/.

Kimberly-Clark. "1 in 3 Like Me." http://web.archive.org/web/20110128142904/http://www.poise.com/1in3likeme.

Kirkus Media LLC. "Goldberg, Whoopi: SUGAR PLUM BALLERINAS." *Kirkus Re-*

views (1 Sept. 2008). *General OneFile*. Web. 19 July 2011. Gale Document Number: A184141814. Document URL: http://find.galegroup.com/gps/infomark.do?&contentSet=IAC-Documents&type=retrieve&tabID=T003&prodId=IPS&docId=A184141814&source=gale&srcprod=ITOF&userGroupName=va0018_002&version=1.0.

Kiss Shot. [1989]. Dir. Jerry London. Perf. Whoopi Goldberg, Dennis Franz, Tasha Scott, David Marciano, Reddy Wilson, Dorian Harewood. Imperial Entertainment and London Productions with Whoop, 2001. DVD.

Koch, Neal. "Funny Lady, Serious Woman. (Whoopi Goldberg Is Known to Be a Very Competitive Businesswoman)." *New York Times* (24 Mar. 2002): BU2(N); BU2(L). *General OneFile*. Web. 24 July 2011. Gale Document Number: A84158385. Document URL: http://find.galegroup.com/gps/infomark.do?&contentSet=IAC-Documents&type=retrieve&tabID=T004&prodId=IPS&docId=A84158385&source=gale&srcprod=ITOF&userGroupName=va0018_002&version=1.0.

Lafferty, Bethany A. "Goldberg, Whoopi. Plum Fantastic." *School Library Journal* 54.12 (Dec. 2008): 90.

Lee, Felicia R. "Whoopi Gets Cubby." *New York Times* (2 Jun. 2006): E5(L). *General OneFile*. Web. 28 Aug. 2010. Gale Document Number A146523609. Document URL: http://find.galegroup.com/gps/infomark.do?&contentSet=IAC-Documents&type=retrieve&tabID=T004&prodId=IPS&docId=A146523609&source=gale&userGroupName=va0074_remote&version=1.0.

———. "Whoopi Goldberg Is Taking Her Wit to the Radio." *New York Times* (9 May 2006): E2(L). *General OneFile*. Web. 28 Aug. 2010. Gale Document Number A1455011230. Document URL: http://find.galegroup.com/gps/infomark.do?&contentSet=IAC-Documents&type=retrieve&tabID=T004&prodId=IPS&docId=A145501230&source=gale&userGroupName=va0074_remote&version=1.0.

Lee, Spike. *That's My Story and I'm Sticking to It*. Narr. Kaleem Aftab. New York: W.W. Norton, 2006.

Lee, Tanvier. "Celebrity Homes: Whoopi Goldberg, SoHo loft." *The Examiner* (8 Apr. 2010). http://www.examiner.com/interior-design-in-new-york/celebrity-homes-whoopi-goldberg-soho-loft.

Leigh, Wendy. *Patrick Swayze: One Last Dance*. New York: Simon Spotlight Entertainment/Simon & Schuster, 2009.

Lewine, Edward. "The Dow Is Up: Greed Revisited." *New York Times* (10 Nov. 1996). *General OneFile*. Web. 28 Aug. 2010. Gale Document Number A150432297. Document URL: http://find.galegroup.com/gps/infomark.do?&contentSet=IAC-Documents&type=retrieve&tabID=T004&prodId=IPS&docId=A150432297&source=gale&userGroupName=va0074_remote&version=1.0.

Lewis, Jone Johnson. "Sojourner Truth: Abolitionist, Minister, Ex-Slave, Woman's Rights Activist." http://womenshistory.about.com/od/sojournertruth/a/sojourner_truth.htm.

Lhamon, W.T., Jr. *Jump Jim Crow: Lost Plays, Lyrics, and Street Prose of the First Atlantic Popular Culture*. Cambridge: Harvard University Press, 2003.

Lilies of the Field. [1963]. Perf. Sidney Poitier, Lilia Skala, Lisa Mann. Dir. Ralph Nelson. MGM Home Ent., 2001. DVD.

The Lion King. [1994]. Dir. Rob Minkoff, Roger Allers. Perf. Matthew Broderick, Jeremy Irons, James Earl Jones, Whoopi Goldberg, Niketa Calame. Walt Disney Studios Home Ent., 2011. DVD.

The Lion King II/2. Dir. Bradley Raymond. Perf. Nathan Lane, Ernie Sabella, Julie Kavner, Jerry Stiller, Matthew Broderick. Walt Disney Home Video, 2004. DVD.

Little, Benilda. *Good Hair: A Novel*. New York: Simon & Schuster, 1996.

Lloyd, Robert. "2008 Tonys: Oddly, the Speeches Were the Best Part." *The Envelope* (*Los Angeles Times*). (16 Jun. 2008). Web. 27 Sept. 2009. http://theenvelope.latimes.com/awards/tonys/la-et-review16-008jun16,0,987680.story.

Long, John. *Roman Indulgences*. Web. 15 Oct. 2009. http://www.roanoke.com/editorials/commentary/wb/222556.

The Long Walk Home [1990]. Dir. Richard Pearce. Perf. Whoopi Goldberg, Sissy Spacek, Dwight Schultz, Ving Rhames, Dylan Baıker. Miramax. Echo Bridge Home Ent., 2002.

Lott, Eric. *Love and Theft: Blackface Minstrelsy and the American Working Class*. New York: Oxford University Press, 1995.

Made in America. [1993]. Dir. Richard Benjamin. Perf. Whoopi Goldberg, Ted Danson, Will Smith. Warner Home Video, 1998. DVD.

Markham, Pigmeat, with Bill Levinson. *Here Come the Judge*. New York: Popular Library, 1969.

Marr, Madeleine. "Watch Out, Whoopi's Aiming at You." *Miami Herald* (Wed. 12 Jan. 2011). http://www.miamiherald.com/2011/01/12/v-print/2011949/watch-out-whoopis-aiming-for-you.html.

Marsh, Steve. "I Don't Want to Be Nothing But a Comedian (The Chris Rock Interview)." *Sky.* MSP Communications/Delta Air Lines. (Nov. 2009): 60–63.

Mask, Mia L. *Goldberg, Whoopi.* African American Lives, eds. Henry Louis Gates, Jr., and Evelyn Brooks Higginbotham. New York: Oxford University Press, 2004. 343–345.

Maslin, Janet. "*Clara's Heart* (1988) Review/Film: A Superior Servant." *New York Times* (7 Oct. 1988). http://movies.nytimes.com/movie/review?res=940DE2DD1F3AF934A35753C1A96E948260.

_____. "Film: 'Fatal Beauty,' With Whoopi Goldberg. (Weekend Desk) (Movie Review)." *New York Times* (30 Oct. 1987). *General OneFile.* Web. 22 Mar. 2011. Document URL: http://find.galegroup.com/gps/infomark.do?&contentSet=IAC-Documents&type=retrieve&tabID=T004&prodId=IPS&docId=A176054011&source=gale&userGroupName=va0018_002&version=1.0. Gale Document Number: A176054011

_____. "FILM REVIEW; Loud Fan Becomes Loud Coach." *New York Times* (31 May 1996). *General OneFile.* Web. 28 Aug. 2010. Gale Document Number A150517591. Document URL: http://find.galegroup.com/gps/infomark.do?&contentSet=IAC-Documents&type=retrieve&tabID=T004&prodId=IPS&docId=A150517591&source=gale&userGroupName=va0074_remote&version=1.0.

_____. "Film: The Color Purple, from Steven Spielberg (Cultural Desk) (Movie Review)." *New York Times* (18 Dec. 1985). General OneFile. Web. 30 Jan. 2011. Gale Document Number: A176458852 Document URL: http://find.galegroup.com/gps/infomark.do?&contentSet=IAC-Documents&type=retrieve&tabID=T004&prodID=IPS&docId=A176458852&source=gale&srcprod=I'].

_____. "MOVIE REVIEW: Homer and Eddie (1989) Reviews/Film: On the Road with a Homicidal Whoopi Goldberg." *New York Times* (9 Feb. 1990). http://movies.nytimes.com/movie/review?res=9C0CE6D9143FF93AA35751C0A966958260&scp=2&sq=movie%20review%20homer%20and%20eddie&st=cse.

_____. "MOVIE REVIEW: The Deep End of the Ocean (1999) Film Review; A Child Is Gone, and Then He Is Not." *New York Times* (12 Mar. 1999). http://movies.nytimes.com/movie/review?res=9C06E4DB173EF931A25750C0A96F958260.

_____. "Review/Film; A Personalized View of the Civil Rights Struggle. (Weekend Desk)." *New York Times* (21 Dec. 1990). *General OneFile.* Web. 24 July 2011. Gale Document Number: A175604720. Document URL: http://find.galegroup.com/gps/infomark.do?&contentSet=IAC-Documents&type=retrieve&tabID=T004&prodId=IPS&docId=A175604720&source=gale&srcprod=ITOF&userGroupName=va0018_002&version=1.0.

Maslon, Laurence, and Michael Kantor. *Make 'Em Laugh: The Funny Business of America.* New York: Twelve, 2008.

Mazgan, Laura. "Harry Winston Is a Girl's Best Friend." CNNMoney.com (13 Mar. 2003). Web. 27 Sept. 2009. http://money.cnn.com/2003/03/04/news/oscars_diamonds/index.htm.

McCann, Bob. "Goldberg, Whoopi." *Encyclopedia of African American Actresses in Film and Television.* Jefferson, NC: McFarland, 2010. 131–135.

McCullaugh, Jim, and Seth Goldstein. "Disney's 'Sister' Gets into the Sell-Through Act (Walt Disney Home Video's Picture, 'Sister Act')." *Billboard* 104.n38 (19 Sept. 1992): 5.

McMillan, Terry. *How Stella Got Her Groove Back.* New York: Signet, 1997.

McWhorter, John. *Authentically Black: Essays for the Black Silent Majority.* New York: Gotham Books, 2003.

Mellon, James. *Bullwhip Days: The Slaves Remember (An Oral History).* New York: Grove, 1988.

Merti, Betty. *The World of Anne Frank: A Complete Resource Guide.* Portland, ME: J. Weston Walch, Pub., 1998.

Metcalf, Geoff. "Polanski Beyond Contempt But Not the Law." *Newsmax* (1 Oct. 2009). *General OneFile.* Web. 28 Aug. 2010. Gale Document Number A208778435. Document URL: http://find.galegroup.com/gps/infomark.do?&contentSet=IAC-Documents&type=retrieve&tabID=T003&prodId=IPS&docId=A208778435&source=gale&userGroupName=va0074_remote&version=1.0.

Mickey Unrapped. Walt Disney Records, 1994. CD.

Mitchard, Jacquelyn. *The Deep End of the Ocean.* New York: Viking, 1996.

Morricone, Ennio. *Il Buono, Il Brutto, Il Cattivo: Music by Ennio Morricone (The Complete Original Motion Picture Soundtrack).* [1966]. ASIN: B00005EF9Y. Audio CD, 2001.

Morrison, Allan. "Negro Humor: An Answer to Anguish." *Ebony* (May 1967): 99–100, 102, 104–106, 108, 110.

Morrison, Toni. *Sula*. [1973]. New York: Plume, 1982.

———. *The Bluest Eye*. [1970]. New York: Alfred A. Knopf, 1993.

National Park Service. "Whoopi Goldberg: Comedian, Actress, Winner of Grammy, Tony, Emmy and Academy Awards, Great-great-Granddaughter of Homesteaders, 1955 — Alachua County, Florida." Homestead National Monument of America.

National Portrait Gallery. "Louis Armstrong: A Cultural Legacy." http://www.npg.si.edu/exh/armstrong/.

National Public Radio (NPR). "George Carlin Honored with Mark Twain Prize." http://www.npr.org/templates/story/story.php?storyId=96844988.

NBC Television. *Saturday Night Live* Excerpt. "The Ladies of The View Welcome Alec Baldwin." (s34: ep7) Perf. Kenan Thompson, Fred Armisen, Nasim Pedrad, Kristen Wiig. http://www.hulu.com/watch/42025/saturday-night-live-the-view.

Neale, John Mason. *Carols for Christmas-Tide*. London: J. A. Novello, 1853.

The Net. [1995]. Dir. Irwin Winkler. Perf. Sandra Bullock, Jeremy Northam, Dennis Miller. Sony Pictures, 2001. DVD.

Newman, Andrew Adam. "Marketing to a Problem That Needs a Polite Name." *New York Times* (1 Apr. 2010). http://www.nytimes.com/2010/04/02/business/media/02adco.html.

Newsweek. 19 Oct. 2009.

NNDB. "Jean Stapleton." http://www.nndb.com/people/934/000022868/.

Noel, Pamela. "Who Is Whoopi Goldberg, and What Is She Doing on Broadway?" *Ebony* (Mar. 1985): 27–28, 30, 34.

Norment, Lynn. "The Color Purple (Controversial prize-winning book becomes an equally controversial movie)." *Ebony* (Feb. 1986): 146, 148, 150, 155.

Nuns on the Run [1990]. Perf. Eric Idle, Robbie Coltrane, Camille Coduri, Janet Suzman, Doris Hare. Dir. Jonathan Lynn. Starz/Anchor Bay, 2005. DVD.

Obel, Karen. "The Story of V-Day and the College Initiative." *The Vagina Monologues: The V-Day Edition*. Foreword by Gloria Steinem. New York: Villard, 2001. 129–171.

O'Connor, John J. "'Comic Relief,' Benefit for the Homeless, on HBO." *New York Times* (31 Mar. 1986). http://www.nytimes.com/1986/03/31/arts/comic-relief-benefit-for-homeless-on-hbo.html?scp=1&sq=Comic%20Relief%20Whoopi%20Goldberg&st=cse.

———. "TV Weekend; Open Season on Husbands as Comedy Stars Return. (Weekend Desk)." *New York Times* (30 Mar. 1990). *General OneFile*. Web. 24 July 2011. Gale Document Number: A175429104. Document URL: http://find.galegroup.com/gps/infomark.do?&contentSet=IAC-Documents&type=retrieve&tabID=T004&prodId=IPS&docId=A175429104&source=gale&srcprod=ITOF&userGroupName=va0018_002&version=1.0.

Oei, Lily. "Whoopi Picks Up Pen for Kids (Pact Calls for Two Picture Books and a Chapter Book)." *Variety*. (23 Feb. 2004). http://www.variety.com/article/VR1117900604?refcatid=21.

Okuda, Michael, and Denise Okuda. *The Star Trek Encyclopedia: A Reference Guide to the Future*. New York: Pocket Books, 1999.

Osofsky, Gil. *Puttin' on Ole Massa: The Slave Narratives of Henry Bibb, William Wells Brown, and Solomon Northrup*. New York: Harper, 1969. 39–40.

Overbye, Dennis. "EXHIBITION OVERVIEW: Catch a Booming, Blazing Star." *New York Times* (2 July 2009). http://www.nytimes.com/2009/07/03/arts/design/03stars.html?adxnnl=1&ref=whoopigoldberg&adxnnlx=1328382531-gnMHL+XWogGsykhzc+J6rQ.

Palmer, Robert. *Deep Blues: A Musical and Cultural History of the Mississippi Delta*. New York: Penguin, 1982.

PBA.org. "Benilde Little." Public Broadcasting Atlanta. Between the Lines. Originally Broadcast 7 Sept. 2005, 2:10 p.m. EST. http://pba.org/post/benilde-little.

"Personal Story." *O'Reilly Factor*. 24 Nov. 2010. "The Best of the Factor." *O'Reilly Factor*. (1 Jan. 2011). *General OneFile*. Web. 19 July 2011. Gale Document Number: A245566116. Document URL: http://find.galegroup.com/gps/infomark.do?&contentSet=IAC-Documents&type=retrieve&tabID=T004&prodId=IPS&docId=A245566116&source=gale&srcprod=ITOF&userGroupName=va0018_002&version=1.0.

Pessi, Talia Bat. "Another Feminist Purim Shpiel." *Ms. Magazine Blog* (20 Mar. 2011). http://msmagazine.com/blog/blog/2011/03/20/another-feminist-purim-shpiel/.

Pienciak, Ryan. "20th ANNIVERSARY: Comic Relief." *People Weekly* (20 Nov. 2006): 143. *General OneFile*. Web. 28 Aug. 2010. Gale Document Number A155932784. Document URL: http://find.galegroup.com/gps/infomark.do?&contentSet=IAC-Documents&type=retrieve&tabID=T003&prodId=IPS&docId=A155932784&source=gale&userGroupName=va0074_remote&version=1.0.

Pitman, Todd. "Kennedy Center to open theater for families." *America's Intelligence Wire* (8 Nov. 2005). *General OneFile*. Web. 19 July 2011. Gale Document Number: A138523958. Document URL: http://find.galegroup.com/gps/infomark.do?&contentSet=IAC-Documents&type=retrieve&tabID=T004&prodId=IPS&docId=A138523958&source=gale&srcprod=ITOF&userGroupName=va0018_002&version=1.0.

The Player. [1992]. Dir. Robert Altman. Perf. Tim Robbins, Greta Scacchi, Fred Ward, Whoopi Goldberg. New Line Home Video, 1997. DVD.

PR Newswire Assoc. LLC. "Whoopi Goldberg Signs Copies of Her New Children's Book at Borders (R)." *PR Newswire* (5 Dec. 2006). *General OneFile*. Web. 23 Feb. 2012. Gale Document Number: A155479389. Document URL: http://go.galegroup.com/ps/i.do?id=GALE%7CA155479389&v=2.1&u=va0018_002&it=r&p=GPS&sw=w.

Pryor, Rain, with Cathy Crimmins. *Jokes My Father Never Taught Me: Life, Love and Loss with Richard Pryor*. New York: HarperCollins, 2006.

Puig, Claudia. "Perry Turns Poetic 'For Colored Girls' into a Soap Opera." *USA Today* (5 Nov. 2010): 5D.

"Q Who?" *Star Trek: The Next Generation*. Seas. 2, Ep. 16. Dir. Rob Bowman. Paramount Television, 8 May 1989. Amazon Instant Video. http://www.amazon.com/Q-Who/dp/B005HEU202/ref=sr_1_1?s=movies-tv&ie=UTF8&qid=1331661480&sr=1–1.

Queen Latifah. *All Hail the Queen* [1989]. Collector's Choice, 2007. CD.

QVC. "G. Beds by Whoopi Goldberg." http://www.qvc.com/cgen/render.aspx?qp=classxK974&ref=GLA&cm_ven=GOGLEPAID&cm_cat=HOMEACCENTS&cm_pla=WHOOPIGOLDBERG&cm_ite=CONTENT.

Racing Stripes [2004]. Dir. Frederik Du Chau. Perf. Bruce Greenwood, Hayden Panettiere, M. Emmet Walsh and Wendie Malick. Featuring the voices of Frankie Muniz, Mandy Moore, Michael Clarke Duncan, Jeff Foxworthy, Joshua Jackson, Joe Pantoliano, Michael Rosenbaum, Steve Harvey, David Spade, Snoop Dogg, Fred Dalton Thompson with Dustin Hoffman and Whoopi Goldberg. Racing Stripes Productions, LLC./Warner Bros. Home Video, 2005. DVD.

Randolph, Laura B. "The Whoopi Goldberg Nobody Knows (Actress Triumphs Over Drugs, Welfare, Dyslexia and Divorce." *Ebony* (Mar. 1991): 110–112, 114–116.

Reed Business Information, Ltd. (AUS) (RBI). "The Color Purple. 1985. Director: Steven Spielberg." *Australian Doctor* (12 May 2005). *General OneFile* Web. 30 Jan 2011. Gale Document Number: A132585868 Document URL: http://find.galegroup.com/gps/infomark.do?&contentSet=IAC-Documents&type=retrieve&tabID=T003&prodID=IPS&docId=A132585868&source=gale&srcprod=I.'

Reed Business Information, Inc. (US) (RBI). "Judge Orders Whoopi to Court over 'T. Rex.'" *Variety* (29 Aug. 1993). http://www.variety.com/article/VR110021?refCatId=22.

_____. "Whoopi Goldberg Has Teamed to Produce a London Incarnation of 'Sister Act.'" *Variety* 413.1 (17 Nov. 2008): 43.

_____. "Whoopi's Big Book of Manners." *Publishers Weekly* 253.39 (2 Oct. 2006): 62.

Reed Elsevier, Inc. "Whoopi Goldberg: Biography." *Variety*. Web. 10 Oct. 2009. http://www.variety.com/profiles/people/Biography/28945/Whoopi+Goldberg.html?dataSet=1.

Remembering the Magic Retrospective. Documentary included in Paramount Pictures, DVD, *Sarafina!* (2002). Dir. Darrel James Roodt. Perf. Whoopi Goldberg, Miriam Makeba, John Kani, Mbongeni Ngema. Miramax Home Entertainment/Hollywood Pictures Home Ent. DVD.

Rensin, David. "Playboy Interview: Whoopi Goldberg." *Playboy* (Jun. 1987): 51–52, 56–58, 154–157.

Richard Pryor: I Ain't Dead Yet [2003]. Dir. Billy Grundfest. Perf. Richard Pryor, Mario Cantone, Cedric the Entertainer. Comedy Central, 2004. DVD.

Richard Pryor: Live & Smokin' [1971]. Dir. Michael Blum. Perf. Richard Pryor. Genius Products, LLC, 2009. DVD.

Richard Pryor: Live on the Sunset Strip. Dir. Perf. Richard Pryor. Rastar Films/Columbia Tristar Home Video, 1982. DVD.

Richard Pryor: The Anthology, 1968–1992. Warner Bros. Records and Rhino Entertainment, 2001. CD.

Roberts, Robin, and Whoopi Goldberg. "Dishin' with Whoopi: Whoopi Goldberg Discusses Her Latest Role on Broadway." http://abcnews.go.com/?id=5517151.

Robinson, Louie. "Richard Pryor Talks ... About Love, Life, Humor, Marriage—and What Happened to His Television Show." *Ebony* (Jan. 1978): 116–118, 120, 122.

Rodrigue, George. *Blue Dog Speaks*. New York: Sterling, 2008.

———. Introd. Ginger Danto. Pref. Michael Lewis. *The Art of George Rodrigue*. New York: Harry N. Abrams, 2003.

Rodrigue: A Man and His Dog—Part 1 (1992). Dir. David DuBos. Perf. George Rodrigue (as Himself); Whoopi Goldberg (Narrator). http://www.youtube.com/user/RodrigueStudio#p/u/33/8ouHgAX5lmw.

Rodrigue: A Man and His Dog—Part 2 (1992). Dir. David DuBos. Perf. George Rodrigue (as Himself); Whoopi Goldberg (Narrator). http://www.youtube.com/user/RodrigueStudio#p/u/31/onf4noSZZ1s.

Rodrigue: A Man and His Dog—Part 3 (Solace) (1992). Dir. David DuBos. Perf. George Rodrigue (as Himself); Whoopi Goldberg (Narrator). http://www.youtube.com/user/RodrigueStudio#p/u/30/ZiXqJ7t4Y2Y.

Russell, Kathy, Midge Wilson, and Ronald Hall. *The Color Complex: The Politics of Skin Color Among African Americans*. New York: Anchor Books, a Division of Random House, 1993.

Sachs, Andrea. "Q & A Ms. Manners." *Time* (3 Dec. 2006). http://www.time.com/time/connections/article/0,9171,1565558,00.html.

"Salomé." *Easton's 1897 Bible Dictionary*. http://www.ccel.org/e/easton/ebd/ebd/T0003100.html#T0003195.

Samuels, Allison. *Off the Record: A Reporter Unveils the Celebrity Worlds of Hollywood, Hip-Hop and Sports*. New York: Amistad, 2007.

San Diego Repertory Theatre. "Board of Trustees and Board of Advisors." http://www.sdrep.org/btba.aspx.

"Satire." *Merriam-Webster's Online Dictionary*. http://www.merriam-webster.com/dictionary/satire.

Saturday Night Live: The Best of Eddie Murphy [1994]. Creat. Dir. Sharon Haskell. Exec. Prod. Lorne Michaels. Perf. Eddie Murphy. National Broadcasting Company/Lions Gate Home Entertainment, 2004. DVD.

School Daze. [1988]. Dir. Spike Lee. Perf. Laurence Fishburne, Giancarlo Esposito. Columbia Pictures, 2003. DVD.

School Without Walls (SWW). "Our History." http://www.swwhs.org/index.php?option=com_content&view=article&id=160&Itemid=17.

Searching for Debra Winger (2004). Dir. Rosanna Arquette. Flower Child Productions/Lionsgate Films. DVD.

Sendak, Maurice. *Where the Wild Things Are*. New York: HarperCollins, 1988.

Serpe, Gina "Whoopi Makes Peace with Oscar Oops." Eonline.com (27 Feb. 2008). Web. 7 Sept. 2010. http://www.eonline.com/uberblog/b57601_Whoopi_Makes_Peace_with_Oscar_Oops.html.

Shakespeare, William. *As You Like It*, ed. Samuel Thurber. The Academy of Series of English Classics. Boston: Allyn and Bacon, 1896.

———. *Romeo and Juliet*, ed. Shane Weller (Stanley Applebaum, gen. ed.). New York: Dover Thrift Editions, 1993.

———. *The Complete Works of William Shakespeare, Edited by William George Clark and William Aldis Wright, with a Copius Glossary*. New York: The American News Company, 1880.

———, *The Tragedy of Hamlet, Prince of Denmark*. Illus., H.C. Christy. New York: Dodd, Mead, 1897.

Shange, Ntozake. *For Colored Girls Who Have Considered Suicide/When the Rainbow Is Enuf: A Choreopoem* [1975]. New York: Scribner, 1997.

Sheff, David. "Playboy Interview: Whoopi Goldberg." *Playboy* (1 Jan. 1997). http://www.playboy.co.uk/the-articles/interview/130059/1/Playboy-Interview-Whoopi-Goldberg/.

Sheward, David. "The Skinny." *Back Stage West*. 47.4 (Jan. 26, 2006): 3.

Sider, Gerald M., and Gavin A. Smith, eds. *Between History and Histories: The Making of Silences and Commemorations*. Toronto: University of Toronto Press, 1997.

Silverman, Stephen M. "Fans Want Cruz Control Over Goldberg." People.com. (28 Jul. 2003). http://www.people.com/people/article/0,,626547,00.html.

———. "Whoopi Goldberg Accepts Oscar Apology." People.com (27 Feb 2008). Web. 6 Sept. 2010 http://www.people.com/people/article/0,,20180664,00.html.

Sister Act [1992]. Perf. Whoopi Goldberg, Maggie Smith, Harvey Keitel. Dir. Emile Ardolino. Buena Vista Home Ent., 2001. DVD.

Sister Act 2: Back in the Habit. [1993]. Dir. Bill Duke. Perf. Whoopi Goldberg, Kathy Najimy, James Coburn, Maggie Smith. Buena Vista Home Ent., 2000. DVD.

"'Sister Act,' B'way, Dancers. (UNION CHORUS CALLS)." *Back Stage, National* ed. (22 Jul. 2010): 25.

"'Sister Act,' B'way. (UNION MUSICALS)." *Back Stage, National* ed. (13 Jan. 2011): 40.

"'Sister Act,' B'way. (UNION MUSICALS)." *Back Stage, National* ed. (15 Jul. 2010): 25.

"'Sister Act,' B'way. (UNION MUSICALS)." *Back Stage, National* ed. (22 Jul. 2010): 25.

"'Sister Act,' B'way. (UNION MUSICALS)." *Back Stage, National* ed. (26 Aug. 2010): 24.

"'Sister Act,' B'way. (UNION MUSICALS)." *Back Stage, National ed.* (30 Dec. 2010): 32.

"'Sister Act,' Singers, B'way. (UNION CHORUS CALLS)." *Back Stage, National ed.* (29 Jul. 2010): 28.

Slade, Carole. Sisters in Arms: Catholic Nuns through Two Millennia. *The Women's Review of Books* 14.n7 (Apr. 1997): 21(2).

Smiley, Tavis. "Profile: Work of African-American Comic Pioneer Jackie 'Moms' Mabley." (9:00–10:00 a.m.) (Broadcast Transcript). 28 Mar. 2003. Washington, D.C.: National Public Radio.

Smith, Liz, and Whoopi Goldberg. "Whoopi Goldberg: 'I Was Raised to Think That Anything Was Possible in America' (Whoopi Goldberg and Liz Smith Discuss Race, Barack Obama and the American Dream)." (1 Dec. 2008). Women on the Web. http://www.wowowow.com/conversation/whoopi-goldberg-liz-smith-racism-children-barack-obama-the-view-147167?page=3%2C0.

Snoopy, Come Home! [1972]. Writ. Charles Schultz. Dir. Bill Melendez. Perf. Chad Webber, Robin Kohn, Stephen Shea, David Carey, Johanna Baer. Paramount, 2006. DVD.

Snow Buddies. Dir. Robert Vince. Perf. Jimmy Bennett, Liliana Mumy, Skyler Gisondo, Paul Rae, Richard Karn. Walt Disney Video, 2008. DVD.

Sophisticates' Black Hair: Styles and Care Guide. http://www.sophisticatesblackhairstyles.com/.

South Park Studios. "Spontaneous Combusion." Originally aired April 14, 1999. Web. 28 Aug. 2010. http://www.southparkstudios.com/episodes/103554/.

Southern, Eileen. *The Music of Black Americans: A History.* 3rd ed. New York: W.W. Norton, 1997.

Soylent Communications. "Profile: Jean Stapleton." http://www.nndb.com/people/934/000022868/.

Speech Level Singing International (SLS). "Clients of the SLS Singing Method." http://www.speechlevelsinging.com/client_list.html.

Spindle, Les. "*Sister Act, the Musical* at the Pasadena Playhouse." *Back Stage West* 13.45 (9 Nov. 1996): 23.

———. "'Sister' on Pasadena Slate." *Back Stage West* (3 Nov. 2005): 17.

Star Trek: Generations. [1994]. Dir. Perf. Patrick Stewart, Jonathan Frakes, Brent Spiner, LeVar Burton, Michael Dorn. Paramount, 1998. DVD.

Star Trek: Nemesis. [2002]. Dir. Stuart Baird. Perf. Patrick Stewart, Jonathan Frakes, Brent Spiner, LeVar Burton, Michael Dorn. Paramount, 2003. DVD.

Star Trek: The Next Generation: Full Cast and Crew. Web. 9 Aug. 2009. http://www.imdb.com/title/tt0092455/fullcredits#cast.

Stargate Atlantis: Full Cast and Crew. Web. 9 Aug. 2009. http://www.imdb.com/title/tt0374455/fullcredits.

Stearns, Marshall, and Jean Stearns. "Frontiers of Humor: American Vernacular Dance." *Mother Wit from the Laughing Barrel: Readings in the Interpretation of Afro-American Folklore.* Ed. Alan Dundes. Jackson: University Press of Mississippi, 1990. 613–620.

Steinbeck, John. *Of Mice and Men* [1937]. New York: Penguin, 1993.

Steinberg, Jacques. "Whoopi Goldberg Is Added to the Lineup of 'The View.'(The Arts/Cultural Desk)." *New York Times* (2 Aug. 2007): E1(L). *General OneFile.* Web. 28 Aug. 2010. Gale Document Number A16087652. Document URL: http://find.galegroup.com/gps/infomark.do?&contentSet=IAC-Documents&type=retrieve&tabID=T004&prodId=IPS&docId=A167087652&source=gale&userGroupName=va0074_remote&version=1.0.

Stevens, Dana. "A Zebra and His New Kentucky Home." *New York Times* (14 Jan. 2005). http://movies.nytimes.com/2005/01/14/movies/14stri.html?scp=2&sq=RACING%20ST RIPES%20MOVIE%20REVIEW&st=cse.

Stevenson, William. "Whoopi " Broadway.com (17 Nov. 2004). Web. 6 Sept. 2010. http://web.archive.org/web/20041119193425/http://www.broadway.com/gen/Buzz_Story.aspx?ci=502629.

Stir Crazy [1980]. Dir. Sidney Poitier. Perf. Gene Wilder, Richard Pryor. Image Entertainment, 2010. DVD.

Stockwell, Anne. "Whoopi's Tough Love: Has Been a Friend of Gays Since She First Hit Broadway. Now She's Back Onstage, Speaking Her Mind." *The Advocate* (18 Jan. 2005). Web. 26 Sept. 2009.

Strausbaugh, John. *Black Like You: Blackface, Whiteface, Insult & Imitation in American Popular Culture.* New York: Jeremy P. Tarcher/Penguin, 2007.

Struckmeyer, Amanda Moss. "Goldberg, Whoopi, with Deborah Underwood. Toeshoe Trouble." *School Library Journal* 55.10 (Oct. 2009): 92.

Superville, Darlene. "Malia Obama Has 13th Birthday on 4th of July." Associated Press (4 Jul. 2011). http://www.wusa9.com/news/article/157283/283/Malia-Obama-Turns-13-On-Fourth-Of-July.

Works Cited

Swarns, Rachel L. "Someone Familiar ... Stages a Homecoming." *New York Times* (9 Feb. 1997). *General Reference Center Gold.* Web. 4 Sept. 2010. Gale Document Number A150398841. Document URL: http://find.gale group.com/gtx/infomark.do?&content Set=IAC-Documents&type=retrieve&tab ID=T004&prodId=GRGM&docId=A150398841&source=gale&userGroupName=va0074_remote&version=1.0.

Swenson, John. *New Atlantis: Musicians Battle for the Survival of New Orleans.* New York: Oxford University Press, 2011.

Teachout, Terry. *Pops: A Life of Louis Armstrong.* New York: Houghton Mifflin Harcourt, 2009.

The Telephone. [1988]. Dir. Rip Torn. Perf. Whoopi Goldberg. New World Pictures and Odyssey Film Partners, 1987. VHS.

Tennyson, Alfred Tennyson. *The Works of Alfred Lord Tennyson.* London: Macmillan, 1886.

"That's That." *This Magazine* (Jan.–Feb. 2010): 44. *General OneFile.* Web. 28 Aug. 2010. Gale Document Number A217431791. Document URL: http://find.galegroup.com/gps/infomark.do?&contentSet=IAC-Documents&type=retrieve&tabID=T003&prodId=IPS&docId=A217431791&source=gale&userGroupName=va0074_remote&version=1.0.

Theodore Rex [1995]. Dir. Jonathan Betuel. Perf. Whoopi Goldberg, Armin Mueller-Stahl, Juliet Landau and Richard Roundtree. New Line Home Entertainment, 2003. DVD.

Thomas, Marlo. *Growing Up Laughing: My Story and the Story of Funny.* New York: Hyperion, 2010.

———, et al. *Thanks & Giving All Year Long.* New York: Simon & Schuster Children's Pub., 2004.

Thompson, Robert Ferris. *Flash of the Spirit.* New York: Vintage Books, 1984.

Thought Field Therapy Training (TFT). "Whoopi Goldberg Conquers Fear of Flying Courtesy of Sir Richard Branson and Thought Field Therapy." http://www.thoughtfield therapytrainings.com/Whoopi_Goldberg_Conquers_Fear_of_Flying.pdf.

"Too Hip for the Room." Bonus track in *It's Bad for Ya.* Dir. Rocco Urbisci. Perf. George Carlin. Home Box Office, 2008. DVD.

Toy Story 3. Dir. Lee Unkrich. Perf. Tom Hanks, Tim Allen. Disney/Pixar, 2010. DVD.

Toys "R" Us. About the Toys "R" Us Differently-Abled Guide. Web. 6 October 2009. http://www.toysrus.com/shop/index.jsp?category Id=3261681.

Truth, Sojourner. [Ain't I a Woman? Speech to the Women's Rights Convention, Akron, Ohio, 1851]. *The Norton Anthology of African American Literature, 2nd ed.* Eds. Henry Louis Gates, Jr., and Nellie Y. McKay. New York: W.W. Norton, 2004. 245–249.

Unchained Memories. [2002]. Dir. Ed Bell, Thomas Lennon. Perf. Whoopi Goldberg, Angela Bassett, Michael Boatman, Roscoe Lee Browne, Don Cheadle. HBO Home Video, 2003. DVD.

UNICEF. "UNICEF People — Goodwill Ambassador." Web. 10 October 2009. http://www.unicef.org/people/people_whoopi_goldberg.html.

United States Postal Service. *USA Philatelic: The Official Source for Stamp Enthusiasts.* Washington, D.C.: Stamp Services, 2011.

U.S. Senate Committee on Human Labor and Human Resources. *U.S. Senate Committee on Labor and Human Resources Hearing on the Homelessness Prevention and Community Revitalization Act of 1990.* shelfl.library.cmu.edu/cgi-bin/tiff2pdf/heinz/box00224/.../heinz.pdf.

The Vagina Monologues. (TV 2002). Dir. Eve Ensler. Perf. Eve Ensler. HBO Home Video, 2002.

Van Hise, James. *The Unauthorized Trekkers' Guide to "The Next Generation" and "Deep Space Nine."* New York: HarperPrism, 1995.

"Vashti." *Easton's 1897 Bible Dictionary.* http://www.ccel.org/e/easton/ebd/ebd/T0003700.html#T0003765.

The View. Perf. Joy Behar (herself), Elizabeth Hasselbeck (herself), Sherri Shepherd (herself), Whoopi Goldberg (herself), Barbara Walters (herself). ABCTelevision, 1997–Pres. http://www.imdb.com/title/tt0123366/.

VNU Business Media. "Mark Zoradi: Diverse Product and a Strong Local Support Team Keep BVI on Top of the World." *Hollywood Reporter* 379.6 (June 17, 2003): S-8(2).

Waldron, Clarence. "The View According to Whoopi." *Jet* (14 Apr. 2008): 57–61.

Waldron, Clarence. "The View According to Whoopi." *Jet* (14 Apr. 2008): 56–60.

Walker, Alice. *The Color Purple.* New York: Harcourt/Harvest, 1982.

Ward, Frances Marie. "Get Out of My Hair!": The Treatment of African American Hair

Warren, Marc. Whoopi Goldberg Receives the Kennedy Center's Mark Twain Prize for American Humor." (26 Oct. 2001). Web. 27 Sept. 2009. http://www.highbeam.com/doc/1P1-79135008.html.

Washington, Denzel. *A Hand to Guide Me: Leg-*

ends *And Leaders Celebrate the People Who Shaped Their Lives*. Des Moines, IA : Meredith Books, 2006.

Watkins, Mel. *On the Real Side: Laughing, Lying and Signifying: The Underground Tradition of African-American Humor That Transformed American Culture, from Slavery to Richard Pryor*. New York: Simon & Schuster, 1994.

WCBS-TV. "Original Tin Pan Alley Put Up for Sale in New York City." http://wcbstv.com/local/tin.pan.alley.2.836414.html.

West Side Story. [1961]. Dir. Jerome Robbins, Robert Wise. Perf. Natalie Wood, George Chakiris, Richard Beymer, Russ Tamblyn, Rita Moreno. MGM, 2003. DVD.

Whitaker, Charles F. "The Cultural Explosion (Freedom Cry of South African Artists and Writers Deepens the Music and Art of the World)." *Ebony* (Aug. 1994): 110–112, 114.

White, E.B., with Pictures by Garth Williams. *Charlotte's Web* [1952]. New York: HarperTrophy/HarperCollins, 1980.

Whoopi (TV 2003–2004). Dir. Terry Hughes, et. Al. Perf. Whoopi Goldberg, Wren T. Brown, Elizabeth Regen. NBC Television, 2003–2004.

Whoopi Goldberg: Back to Broadway (20th Anniversary). Dir. Marty Callner. Perf. Whoopi Goldberg. Home Box Office, 2005. DVD.

Whoopi Goldberg: Direct from Broadway [1985]. *Whoopi Goldberg: Back to Broadway (20th Anniversary Edition)*. Dir. Marty Callner, Thomas Schlamme. Perf. Whoopi Goldberg. HBO, 2005. DVD. Disk 2 of 2 (Bonus DVD).

Whoopi Goldberg: Fontaine: Why Am I Straight? [1988] Dir. Steve J. Santos. Perf. Whoopi Goldberg. HBO Video, 1999. VHS.

"Whoopi's Big Book of Manners (The Best Manners Books of 2006)." *Town & Country* (Dec. 2006): 198.

Wilkerson, Isabel. "TELEVISION; Staying Cool at Whoopi's Talk Show (Arts & Leisure Desk)." *New York Times* (29 Nov. 1992). *General OneFile*. Web. 28 Aug. 2010. Gale Document Number A174960313. Document URL: http://find.galegroup.com/gps/infomark.do?&contentSet=IAC-Documents&type=retrieve&tabID=T004&prodId=IPS&docId=A174960313&source=gale&userGroupName=va0074_remote&version=1.0.

Williams, Bina. "Plum Fantastic: Sugar Plum Ballerinas." *Booklist*. 105.9–10 (Jan. 1, 2009): 84.

Williams, Elsie. *The Humor of Jackie Moms Mabley: An African American Comedic Tradition*. New York: Garland, 1995.

Williams, John A., and Dennis A. Williams. *If I Stop, I'll Die: The Comedy and Tragedy of Richard Pryor*. New York: Thunder's Mouth Press, 2006.

The Wizard of Oz (Two-Disc 70th Anniversary Edition). Dir. Victor Fleming. Perf. Judy Garland, Frank Morgan, Ray Bolger, Jack Haley, Burt Lahr. Warner Home Video, 2010. DVD.

"Women of Color, Women of Words: Ntozake Shange." Web. 22 Aug. 2009. http://cominfo.rutgers.edu/~cybers/shange2.html.

Wonder, Stevie. *Song Review: A Greatest Hits Collection*. Motown Record Company, 1996. CD.

Work, John W. *American Negro Songs and Spirituals*. New York: Bonanza Books, 1940.

Xenon Pictures, 2002. DVD.

Yahoo! OMG! "Whoopi Goldberg Defends Christian Bale Over 'Terminator' Set Rant." http://omg.yahoo.com/news/whoopi-goldberg-defends-christian-bale-over-terminator-set-rant/18417.

Yang, Linda. "CURRENTS; A Miniature Rose by No Other Name.(Home Desk)." *New York Times* (11 Jun. 1992). *General OneFile*. Web. 28 Aug. 2010. Gale Document Number A174891796. Document URL: http://find.galegroup.com/gps/infomark.do?&contentSet=IAC-Documents&type=retrieve&tabID=T004&prodId=IPS&docId=A174891796&source=gale&userGroupName=va0074_remote&version=1.0.

"Yesterday's Enterprise." *Star Trek: The Next Generation*. Seas. 3, Ep. 15. Dir. David Carson. Paramount Television, 19 Feb. 1990. Amazon Instant Video. http://www.amazon.com/Yesterdays-Enterprise/dp/B005HEU5DG/ref=sr_1_1?s=movies-tv&ie=UTF8&qid=1331661078&sr=1-1.

You've Got Mail. [1998]. Dir. Nora Ephron. Perf. Tom Hanks, Meg Ryan, Greg Kinnear. Warner Home Video, 1999. DVD.

Zhang, Baobao. "Meet Whoopi Goldberg, Born Caryn Elaine Johnson, Academy Award-Winning Actress, Panelist on 'The View.'" *Yale Daily News* (16 Apr. 2010). http://www.yaledailynews.com/news/2010/apr/16/meet-whoopi-goldberg-born-caryn-elaine-johnson/.

Zinoman, Jason. "Whoopi Goldberg, Nothing But." *New York Times* (26 Aug. 2004). http://www.nytimes.com/2004/08/26/theater/whoopi-goldberg-nothing-but.html.

Index

abortion 12, 93, 96, 97, 175, 228–230
Absolutely Fabulous 77
Academy Awards 8, 225; *see also* Oscars
acting 2, 3, 7, 12, 14, 19, 36, 38, 43–44, 50–52, 55–56, 65, 68, 70–71, 75
"Ain't No Mountain High Enough" 184
Alabama 7, 9, 51, 145–147, 149, 167
Alice in Wonderland 122–123, 230
All in the Family 126, 170–171
Allen, Debbie 180
American Dream 3–4, 30
apartheid 162–164
Armstrong, Louis 59, 61, 83, 206–207
Armstrong, Neil 176
Arnaz, Desi 95
Around the World in 80 Days 96
Ashford & Simpson 184
The Associate 2, 77, 125, 157, 160–161, 168
Avery, Margaret 26, 63–65, 67, 69–70
Avon cosmetics 180

Bagdad Café 2, 125–130
Baldwin, Alec 77–78, 150
Ball, Lucille 95
Barrymore, Drew 187
Bassett, Angela 195, 199
Behar, Joy 4, 13, 29, 78, 93, 172–173
Belafonte, Harry 131, 231
Belushi, Jim 47–48, 185, 187
Berlin, Irving 3, 157
Beverly Hills Cop 37, 40–41
Biggums, Tyrone (fictional character) 88–90
Black Arts Movement 7
Black Power Movement 4, 142
blackface minstrelsy 68, 79 85, 91, 94, 98
Blue Dog 208–211
blues music 21, 38, 59, 65, 67–68, 139
blues philosophy 20, 58, 60–63, 80, 84
"blueswoman" 2, 26, 57–59, 61–62, 73, 75, 78, 80, 138, 141
Book (non-fiction book) 3, 4, 18, 100, 174, 176, 185

Boys on the Side 2, 185, 187, 189, 190
Brando, Marlon 160
Broadway 2–3, 11–12, 18, 27, 32–34, 40, 45, 49, 74–75, 80–81, 84, 92, 96–97, 100–102, 105, 109–111, 126, 138
Brown, James 198, 208
Brown, Oda Mae 9, 50, 52, 54, 134–138, 199, 212, 225
Burglar 26, 36, 40–41, 54, 56, 76–77, 81–82, 94, 133–135, 166, 220
Burnett, Carol 10–11
Bush, Barbara 184
Bush, George W. 98, 180, 207
Bush, Laura 98
Busia, Akosua 63–64

Caesar, Adolph 70
California Raisins 27–28
Call Me Claus 77, 169
Cara, Irene 105
Carlin, George 1, 10–11, 20–22, 29–35, 86
Cash, Rosalind 220
Catholicism 11, 20, 31–32, 75, 100, 102–103, 107–108, 113, 132, 137, 193, 199, 201, 211
Celtic Pride 17
censorship 33–34, 90, 98, 123, 213–214
Chappelle, Dave 86, 88–90
Charles, Ray 27–28
Cher 76, 218
children's literature 122–123, 210; *see also* juvenile literature
Chong, Rae Dawn 72, 237
Cinderella 217–218
civil rights 2, 19, 22, 145–149, 163, 165, 170, 214
Clara's Heart 36, 46–47, 54, 56, 125, 130–133, 148, 166, 221
Clinton, Bill 207
cocaine 86, 89–90
Colón, Willie 228
Color Purple 2, 26, 36–37, 40, 57–58, 60,

251

62–63, 65, 67–72, 74, 76, 78, 122, 133, 135, 141, 154, 166, 199, 220
Comic Relief 12, 175, 185, 204–208
Constitution, U.S. 2, 11, 30, 34, 149
Corinna, Corinna 2, 125, 138, 166, 183
Cosby, Bill 12, 86, 200, 204
Cosby Show 200
Crippled Girl (fictional character) 12, 33, 169
Crosby, Bing 184
Cruz, Célia 2, 111–15, 124, 228
Crystal, Billy 12, 86, 175, 204, 206, 208
Cusack, Joan 138
Cutty Sark 159

"Dancing in the Street" 103
Danson, Ted 14–15, 82, 92–95, 98, 182
Davis, Ossie 92
Davis, Patti 178
Davis, Sammy, Jr. 82–83, 204
The Deep End of the Ocean 192–195
Devine, Loretta 229
Diggs, Taye 197
Diller, Phyllis 11
Dior, Christian 184
Disney 2, 16–17, 100, 102–103, 107, 116, 123–124, 144, 185, 208, 216, 226
divorce 75, 120, 127, 133, 175–177, 183, 187
Dove, Rita 224
dreadlocks 2, 9, 12, 18, 38–39, 42, 96, 109, 136, 161, 168–169, 180, 196–197, 199, 213–214, 219–221, 231; *see also* hair
drug addiction 32, 87–89
dyslexia 5

Eastwood, Clint 15
Eddie 16–18, 77, 116, 124, 167–168, 182
Elise, Kimberly 229
Elliott, Sam 41
Emmy Awards 3, 8, 102, 111, 126, 181
Ensler, Eve 189, 223–224
Evers, Medgar 149
Evers, Myrlie 149–151
"Every Breath You Take" 34, 98

fashion 183–184, 218, 220
Fatal Beauty 36, 41, 56, 76, 133, 135, 166, 220
feminism 42
Fighting Temptations 110–111
Florida 7–9, 61, 107, 144, 215
Flying Nun 102, 104
Fontaine (fictional character) 36, 49, 56, 75, 84, 96–98
For Colored Girls... 226–230
Frank, Anne 33–34, 97–98
Franklin, Aretha 28, 215

Gates, Henry Louis 54, 78, 95
Gershwin, George 3

Gershwin, Ira 3
Ghost 2, 9, 36, 50–56, 95, 115, 125, 134–138
Ghosts of Mississippi 125, 145–151
ghostwriter 185
Gillespie, Dizzy 106
Girl, Interrupted 2, 125, 141–145
Girl with the Long Blonde Hair (fictional character) 12, 75, 217–218
Glover, Danny 63, 70, 154, 161, 169, 220
Goldthwait, Bobcat 40, 94
Gone with the Wind 20, 27, 37, 55, 134, 166, 188
Good Fences 169–170
"Good King Wenceslas" 138
The Good, the Bad, and the Ugly 15
Gooding, Cuba, Jr. 55
Got Milk? 180
Grammy Awards 3, 8, 75, 84, 87, 181
Grauman's Chinese Theater 231
Guinan 151–157, 208
Guinea-Bissau 8

hair 12–13, 17, 23, 45, 52–53, 55, 73, 75, 109, 122, 132, 135–136, 142, 160, 168, 176–177, 182–183, 194, 196–197, 213–225, 231
Haley, Alex 6
Harris, Neil Patrick 47, 131
Hasselbeck, Elizabeth 13, 29, 78, 172
Hawthorne, Nigel 77, 169
Hill, Lauryn 104
Holiday, Billie 228
Hollywood Squares 223
Homer and Eddie 2, 36, 47–49, 56, 185–187
homesteading 3, 7–8
Homie Spumoni 199–201
homosexuality 18, 26, 34, 77, 166, 190, 194, 197
How Stella Got Her Groove Back 2, 185, 195–199
Hughes, Cathy 171–172
humanism 5, 10, 14, 16
Hurricane Katrina 1, 176, 206–208, 211
Huston, Zora Neale 14, 60–61, 63, 116, 215

"I Will Follow Him" 103–104
India.Arie 226
Internet 2, 38, 181; *see also* World Wide Web

Jackie's Back! 108–109, 144–145, 221
Jackson, Janet 98, 229
Jackson, Samuel L. 111
Jagger, Mick 38
jazz 17, 59–60, 82–83, 107, 113, 138–139, 200, 206, 227–228
Jefferson, Thomas 4
The Jeffersons 170
Jerry Maguire 55
Jewish identity 7, 53, 71, 81, 174, 193, 199

Johnson, Caryn Elaine 5, 7, 75, 177–179, 221
Johnson, Clyde 178
Johnson, Emma 14, 80, 95, 110, 117, 119, 177–178
Jolie, Angelina 141, 143
Jolson, Al 82, 85, 92
Jones, Quincy 69, 71, 78
Joplin, Janis 187
Jumpin' Jack Flash 36–40, 52, 54, 56, 71, 76, 103, 135, 166, 220
Junkie with a Ph.D. (fictional character) 12, 28, 33, 75, 88, 90
juvenile literature 116–124, 179–180; *see also* children's literature

Kazan, Lainie 161
Khumalo, Leleti 161
Kiss Shot 36, 49–50, 56
Knowles, Beyoncé 111

LaBelle, Patti 113–114
Langella, Frank 16, 167, 174, 182
Las Vegas 104, 129–130, 186, 204, 206, 207
Lawford, Peter 204
Lee, Spike 84, 214–215, 217–218
Lewis, Jenifer 109, 139, 144
Liotta, Ray 138
Long, Nia 14
Long, Shelley 37, 76, 220
The Long Walk Home 51, 125, 145–148, 167, 221
Lumley, Joanna 77

Mabley, Jackie "Moms" 1–2, 5, 10–12, 20–29, 34–35, 74
Made in America 14–16
Majorino, Tina 138
Makeba, Miriam 162
Manhattan 3, 54, 76, 80, 112, 117, 158,-159, 170, 178, 183, 196, 216; *see also* New York
Markham, "Pigmeat" 25
marriage 62, 64, 77, 87, 131, 182–183, 190, 192
Martin, Alexandrea 75, 77, 106, 117, 177,-178, 183, 178
Martin, Dean 199, 204
Mason, Jackie 174
McMillan, Terry 195–196
menopause 223–224
menstruation 223
Miss Celie's Blues 66, 69
Mississippi 7, 86, 125, 149–151, 228
Mo'Nique 55, 170, 183
Mooney, Paul 90, 199–200
Moonlight and Valentino 185, 190–192
Moore, Demi 9, 51, 136
Morricone, Ennio 15
Morrison, Toni 60, 62, 218, 220

motherhood 14, 18, 23, 26, 177–178, 181
motherwit 23–25, 103, 177
Motown 39, 100, 101, 103–104, 108, 115, 226
Mudbone (fictional character) 11, 86–87
Muppets 213, 231, 169
Murphy, Eddie 37, 40–41, 86, 90, 109, 123, 133, 226
"My Guy" 101, 103

National Endowment for the Arts 176, 185
New York 3–5, 8–9, 11, 16–18, 28, 31–35, 37–40, 45–46, 54, 71, 75–78, 81, 85, 93–94, 101, 104–107, 110–112, 115–118, 120, 122, 126, 136–137, 148, 162, 166–168, 170–173, 176, 178, 183–184, 187, 189–190, 195, 198, 200, 204–205, 210, 214, 225, 229; *see also* Manhattan
Newton, Thandie 229
Nichols, NiChelle 151
Nobody (fictional character) 84, 90–92
nuns 49, 100–108, 115
Nuns on the Run 102

Obama, Barack 79, 115
O'Donnell, Rosie 172
Olo 179
One Ho Productions 111
Ontkean, Michael 131
Oscars 3, 9, 50–55, 69, 73, 95, 110, 122, 125, 133–134, 148, 157, 171, 181–182, 212, 221, 225; *see also* Academy Awards

Panettiere, Hayden 202
Parker, Mary-Louise 187
Performance Art 4, 84, 226
Perry, Tyler 229
Poise Pads 181
Poitier, Sidney 14, 55, 85, 108, 231
The Police (band) 34, 98
Pounder, CCH 129
poverty 10, 42, 44, 48, 60, 87, 175, 206
Premice, Josephine 96
Pryor, Richard 1, 10–12, 31, 79, 84–90, 94–95, 226

Queen Elizabeth I 225
Queen Latifah 106
Quinlan, Kathleen 131

Racing Stripes 202–204
racism 5, 25, 83, 86, 88, 149, 161, 168, 174, 182–183, 198, 220, 222
radio 16, 69, 83, 112–13, 130, 171–172, 198
Raelettes 27–28
ragtime 60
Rainey, Gertrude "Ma" 226
Ralph, Sheryl Lee 105
rap music 106, 171, 208

Rashad, Phylicia 200, 229
Redford, Robert 188
rhythm and blues 2, 100
Rice, Condoleezza 34
Roddenberry, Gene 151, 221
Rodrigue, George 185, 208–211
The Rolling Stones 38
Roots 6–7
Rose, Anika Noni 229
Ross, Diana 39, 104, 184
Ryder, Winona 145

Sägebrecht, Marianne 129
salsa music 2, 15, 111–115, 124, 228
San Diego 75
Sanford, Isabel 170
San Franscisco 12, 26–27, 40, 69, 75, 81, 84, 101, 104, 187, 196, 229
Santa Claus 23, 77, 169
Sarafina! 125, 161–165
Saturday Night Live 37, 77, 90, 109, 123
Saunders, Jennifer 77
School Daze 214
Schwarzenegger, Arnold 133
Searching for Debra Winger 12–13
Sendak, Maurice 122
Sesame Street 213, 223
sexism 5, 38, 42, 159
Shakespeare, William 19, 44, 46, 96, 109, 119, 166, 197, 213
Shange, Ntozake 226–227
Shepherd, Sherri 13, 29, 173
Shepp, Archie 228
Sinatra, Frank 204
singing 21, 34, 38, 67, 96, 98, 100–103, 108, 111–115, 120, 126, 131, 165, 183, 187, 190, 198, 201, 206–207, 224
Sister Act 2, 100–103
Sister Act 2: Back in the Habit 2, 100, 103–107
Slim-Fast 180
Smith, Bessie 59, 62, 68, 75
Smith, Will 14
Soap Dish 37, 52–53
South Africa 161–165
South Park 182
Spacek, Sissy 51, 145, 148, 167
Spielberg, Steven 40, 57, 64, 67, 69, 71, 73, 78, 122, 133
spirituals 9, 21–22, 57, 74
Stallone, Sylvester 133
Stapleton, Jean 125–126, 130
Star Trek 2, 125, 151–157, 173, 208, 221, 223; see also Guinan
Star Wars 157
Statue of Liberty 18, 168
Steinbeck, John 48, 185–186
Steinem, Gloria 193, 195

Streisand, Barbra 188
Sugar Plum Ballerinas 116–124, 179–180
Swayze, Patrick 9, 50–51, 134

Talley, André Leon 183–184
Taylor, Elizabeth 231
Telephone (major motion picture) 36, 41–46, 54, 56, 135
Texas 152
Theodore Rex 201–202
"This Little Light of Mine" (song) 140
Thompson, Kenan 77–78
Thompson, Tessa 229
Tony Awards 3, 8, 19, 81, 92, 174, 181, 225–227
Townsend, Robert 108, 144
Toys "R" Us 181–182
Truth, Sojourner 5–7, 23, 174–175
Turner, Tina 38–39, 51, 135, 199, 218
TVOne on One 171–172

UNICEF 182

Vagina Monologues 189, 223–224; see also Ensler, Eve
Vereen, Ben 92, 94
The View (TV talk show) 13, 29, 77–78, 93, 110, 172–173, 178, 211, 222–223, 225

Wake Up with Whoopi 172
Walker, Alice 2, 40, 58, 60, 67, 71, 78, 219
"Waltzing Matilda" 223
Washington, Denzel 55, 161, 177
Washington, George 168
Washington, Kerry 229
welfare 75, 176–177, 185
Wells, Mary 101, 103
Whoopi (TV sitcom) 28, 111, 170–171
Whoopi: Back to Broadway 100, 213, 217–218, 223–225
Whoopi Goldberg: Fontaine—Why Am I Straight? 36, 49, 56
Whoopi Goldberg Show (TV talk show) 171–172
Williams, Bert 1, 79, 84, 90, 92, 94, 98–99
Williams, Robin 12, 175, 204–208
Willie the Junkie (fictional character) 84
Willis, Bruce 26, 40, 77, 82, 220
Winfrey, Oprah 8–9, 34, 51, 63, 69, 72, 74, 180
Wino and Junkie (fictional characters) 87–88
Wizard of Oz 15, 144, 215
Wonder, Stevie 98, 106
Wood, James 150
Woodard, Alfre 161, 220
World Wide Web 2; see also Internet

Xanadu 211

www.ingramcontent.com/pod-product-compliance
Ingram Content Group UK Ltd.
Pitfield, Milton Keynes, MK11 3LW, UK
UKHW041935140426
5217IPUK00014B/494